T4-AIL-899

A STUDY OF ST JOHN'S GOSPEL

A STUDY OF
ST JOHN'S GOSPEL

TO WHICH ARE ADDED

I. THE JULIAN AND JEWISH CALENDARS FOR A.D. 27–29
II. A DIARY OF ALL THE EVENTS IN OUR LORD'S MINISTRY WHICH ARE MENTIONED IN THE GOSPELS
III. TABLES SHOWING HOW THE FOURTH GOSPEL DOVETAILS WITH THE THREE SYNOPTICS

BY G. H. TRENCH

AUTHOR OF
"THE CRUCIFIXION AND RESURRECTION OF JESUS CHRIST"
"THE BIRTH AND BOYHOOD OF JESUS CHRIST"

LONDON
JOHN MURRAY, ALBEMARLE STREET, W.
1918

PRINTED BY
WILLIAM CLOWES AND SONS, LIMITED,
LONDON AND BECCLES, ENGLAND.

PREFACE

In the following pages I understand the writer of the fourth gospel to be John the Apostle, son of Zebedee and Salome. Such is the tradition of the Church throughout the centuries; and the defenders of this traditional authorship have, to my mind, established and held their position impregnable against all attacks. John is second cousin of our Lord by the mothers' side; and second cousin, also by the mothers' side, of John the Baptist.

This attempt to restate the fourth gospel, whose difficulties arise from the very simplicity of its terminology, is due to the author's conviction that a recognition of this gospel involves nothing less than a recognition of the whole body of Catholic dogma on our Lord's Personality and Incarnation as set forth by Athanasius, Augustine, Leo, and the Fathers generally. They are all saying in other words what John is saying in his prologue, what he records the Baptist as saying, and what he records our Lord as saying of Himself. Dogmatic theology is not in favour in England; but there is no escape from the whole body of it, once this gospel is accepted.

If I seem to have ignored the "modernist" school, whose home is Germany, it is not from want of acquaintance with it, but from a conviction that its spirit is alien and hostile to the Faith of Christianity as originally delivered by Jesus Christ and as expanded in the consciousness of the Catholic and Roman Church to-day.

With regard to the short ministry of under two years, as against the commonly received three or three and a half years, it is supported by the explicit statement of many of the early Fathers; it is also supported implicitly by a general consensus of the Fathers, for no juggling with dates can reconcile the longer terms with (1) their practically unanimous testimony that the Crucifixion took place on March 25 of A.D. 29, and they appeal to the Roman archives, which seem to have been extant till the beginning of the fifth century; (2) Luke's notice that the fifteenth year of Tiberius was the year of John's baptizing, and that Jesus was "about thirty years old" at the time. I have examined both these points at some length in earlier books. Incidentally it is worth mentioning that between the years A.D. 18 and 35, the only year in which March 25 was a Friday is A.D. 29.

As for the Diary of events, it is put forth with some confidence, once we are rid of the interpolated verse, John vi. 4.

I am aware that the idea of a literal millennium (Rev. xx. 2–7) is not in favour among Catholics; but no one can read the Fathers of the first four or five centuries of our era without recognizing their strong and unanimous belief in it. Owing to extravagant and sensual anticipations as to the delights of that Age among a certain body of Christians known as Chiliasts or Millennarians, the whole subject of a literal millennium fell into disrepute among the main body of Catholics in the fifth century and became quietly shelved. About a hundred and fifty years ago the Spanish Jesuit Lacunza, in the guise of a converted Jew (Ben Ezra), brought the question into prominence again, and laid the foundation of a saner exegesis of the Hebrew Prophets than had prevailed during the preceding thirteen centuries. He failed, however, to distinguish the promises made to the House of Israel, to which (in Joseph) belongs the birthright, from those made to the House of Judah, to which belongs the crown. Now that we have reached the closing century of the sixth millenary (6th Day) of Adam's race and are nearing the 7th Day or Sabbatic millenary, the subject assumes a livelier practical and political significance.

G. H. T.

TYES, STAPLEFIELD, SUSSEX.
March, 1918.

CONTENTS

A DIARY OF OUR LORD'S PUBLIC MINISTRY

THE following table is based on the constant tradition of the Church that the Crucifixion took place on *a.d. viii Kal. Ap. duobus Geminis coss.*, which without question is "March 25, A.D. 29"; and it may be added that between the years A.D. 18 and A.D. 35 there is no year but A.D. 29 in which March 25 was a Friday, as may be verified by the Dominical Letter: and Friday is the week-day which alone satisfies another constant tradition of the Church as to the day of the Crucifixion.

We thus have Thursday, March 24, as the Day of the last Passover eaten by our Lord and the Twelve, which must have been, on the Jewish ecclesiastical scale, Nisan 14. From this one datum we can correlate the Julian and Jewish calendars backward day for day, taking care not to neglect any possible intercalary month.

This is not the place to explain at length the Jewish calendar in use in our Lord's time by which the Festivals were fixed, many years in advance, for the use of the pilgrims who came up to Jerusalem three times a year from the farthest limits of the Roman empire. It consisted of an 84-year cycle containing exactly 12 complete Sabbatic-year cycles: the 12 months of a common year were of 30 and 29 days alternately, with an intercalary month thrown in just before Nisan at two or three years' intervals in order to prevent Nisan 14 (Passover Day) from falling earlier than the spring equinox, and, rarely, at one and four years' intervals owing to the intervention of a Sabbatic-year.

Seeing that in A.D. 29, Nisan 14 was the equivalent of March 24, or, in other words, fell at the *earliest* permissible date (for the spring equinox of A.D. 29 fell on March 23), it is evident that there cannot have been an intercalary month in A.D. 29 nor yet in A.D. 28. Nor again can there have been one in A.D. 27, for from Oct. of A.D. 26 to Oct. A.D. 27 was a Sabbatic year, and the Rabbinists tell us that Sabbatic years were never intercalary. Therefore in the spring of A.D. 26 there must have been an intercalary month and also in the spring of A.D. 30, but none in the interval.

At the time in question the Jewish ecclesiastical months did not correspond with the moon's phases: and their "new moon" festivals (exactly like the Greek νουμηνίαι for some centuries before) celebrated no longer the new moon but the first day of the calendar month. Later, after the revolt of the nation from Rome in A.D. 66, changes seem to have been made in the Jewish calendar, and attempts to make months and moons correspond as in archaic times whilst still keeping in sight a reckoning by solar years—attempts which at length culminated about A.D. 320 in the Jewish calendar which is in use to-day.

The following table of Julian and Jewish equivalents begins in A.D. 27, with Sat., Sept. 27=Tisri 1. The call of John the Baptist can hardly have occurred before the latter half of A.D. 27, for he only reached the qualifying age of 30 in June of that year. We shall perhaps not be far out if we date his call from about Tisri 10 of A.D. 27, the great Day of Atonement, the opening day of the 30th Jubilee year, or rather the day that would have begun that Jubilee had Jubilee years been observed through and after the Babylonian Captivity. The Jubilee era like the Sabbatic-year era is Oct. of 1444 B.C. The first Jubilee year began in autumn of 1395 B.C.; the second at 50 years' interval (both terms being counted) began in autumn of 1346 B.C.; the third in autumn of 1297 B.C., and so on. The Jubilee scale did not break the Sabbatic-year scale, but was superimposed on it, so that a Jubilee year followed immediately on every seventh Sabbatic-year and fell on the first year of a fresh hebdomad or Sabbatic-year cycle. Both kinds of year—Jubilee and Sabbatic—began in autumn, as did also the civil year, though each on different days: the ecclesiastical year began in spring.

The Jubilee year in which our Lord's public ministry began—the ἐνιαυτὸν Κυρίου δεκτόν, the "welcome Lord's-year (Luke iv. 19)—was the 30th Jubilee in a straight count from 1444 B.C.: it began on Tisri 10=Mon., Oct. 6 of A.D. 27 and ran out on Elul 29=Sept. 14 of A.D. 28.

The following table covers about 19 months, from the call of John the Baptist in A.D. 27 till the day of the Descent of the Holy Spirit at Pentecost, Sunday, May 15 (Sivan 7) of A.D. 29.

"In the 15th year of the reign of Tiberius Cæsar . . . . there came a word of God to John, the son of Zacharias, in the wilderness" (Luke iii. 1, 2). The 15th year of Tiberius's reign, according to the Eastern (and Luke's) method of reckoning reigns began on Sept. 1, A.D. 27. This method is the one followed in the famous Canon of Ptolemy: it systematically antedates every reign because it reckons the first year of each king and emperor as beginning on the Thoth 1 (the New Year Day) preceding his accession, and his second year as beginning on the Thoth 1 that follows his accession.*

Therefore the Baptist's preaching and baptizing did not begin before Sept. 1 of A.D. 27: the exact beginning may have been not improbably either Tisri 1 (=Sat., Sept. 27), the New Year day of the old civil year of the Jews, or Tisri 10 (=Monday, Oct. 6), the opening day of the 30th Jubilee year

Julian month.	Jewish ecclesiastical month.	
A.D. 27.		
Sept. 1, Mon.		The New Year day of the Greeks of Syria and Antioch, of which city Luke was a Greek native or at least resident. The first day of the 15th year of the reign of Tiberius, according to Luke's method, and the universal eastern method, of reckoning regnal years.
,, 27, Sat.	Tisri 1	New Year day of the old civil year of the Jews (1st of Tisri). But for dealings with Gentiles, the Jews used the Julian months, putting, however, Jewish names to them, calling October Tisri, November Marhesvan, and so on: just as the Greeks of Asia put the Macedonian month-names to the Julian months and the Syrians put the Syrian names.
,, 30, Tues.	,, 4	
Oct. 1, Wed.	,, 5	
,, 6, Mon.	,, 10	The great Day of Atonement. The opening day of the 30th Jubilee year: all Jubilee years began on Tisri 10. Perhaps to-day John the Baptist began his public ministry: he would be 30¼ years old.
,, 26, Sun.	,, 30	
,, 27, Mon.	Marheswan 1	
Oct. 31, Fri.	Marheswan 5	These dates are given merely to show how the Jewish calendar of that year fitted to the Julian.
Nov. 1, Sat.	,, 6	
,, 24 Mon.	,, 29	
,, 25, Tues.	Kislew 1	
,, 30, Sun.	,, 6	
Dec. 1, Mon.	,, 7	
,, 24, Wed.	,, 30	
Dec. 25, Thur.	Tebeth 1	
,, 31, Wed.	,, 7	
A.D. 28.		
Jan. 1, Thur.	Tebeth 8	From this date onwards every day of the next 17 months or so is given.

* I have explained this fully in *The Birth and Boyhood of Jesus Christ;* for it is the key to the dispute of the last 16 centuries about the dates of our Lord's birth, public ministry, and death.

Julian month.	Jewish ecclesiastical month.	
A.D. 28. Jan. 1, Thurs.	Tebeth 8	
Jan. 2, Fri. „ 3, Sat. „ 4, Sun. „ 5, Mon. „ 6, Tues. „ 7, Wed. „ 8, Thurs.	Tebeth 9 „ 10 „ 11 „ 12 „ 13 „ 14 „ 15	
Jan. 9, Fri. „ 10, Sat. „ 11, Sun. „ 12, Mon. „ 13, Tues. „ 14, Wed. „ 15, Thurs.	Tebeth 16 „ 17 „ 18 „ 19 „ 20 „ 21 „ 22	
Jan. 16, Fri. „ 17, Sat. „ 18, Sun. „ 19, Mon. „ 20, Tues. „ 21, Wed. „ 22, Thur.	Tebeth 23 „ 24 „ 25 „ 26 „ 27 „ 28 „ 29	Baptism of Jesus by John, Matt. iii. 13–end : Mark i. 9–11 : Luke iii. 21–23 (pp. 27–32). John Baptist announces formally that Jesus is the Messiah, John i. 15–18 (pp. 14–19). *Jesus's public ministry begins to-day,* His age being "about 30," Luke iii. 23—accurately 30 years and 24 days.
Jan. 23, Fri. „ 24, Sat. „ 25, Sun. „ 26, Mon. „ 27, Tues. „ 28, Wed. „ 29, Thurs.	Sebet 1 „ 2 „ 3 „ 4 „ 5 „ 6 „ 7	The 40 days' fast of our Lord, Matt. iv. 1–11 : Mark i. 12, 13 : Luke iv. 2 : viz. from Jan. 18 to Feb. 26, inclusive.
Jan. 30, Fri. „ 31, Sat.	Sebet 8 „ 9	

Julian month.	Jewish ecclesiastical month.	
A.D. 28. Feb. 1, Sun.	Sebet 10	The 40 days' fast of our Lord, from Jan. 18 to Feb. 26, inclusive.
Feb. 2, Mon.	Sebet 11	
,, 3, Tues.	,, 12	
,, 4, Wed.	,, 13	
,, 5, Thurs.	,, 14	
,, 6, Fri.	,, 15	
,, 7, Sat.	,, 16	
,, 8, Sun.	,, 17	
Feb. 9, Mon.	Sebet 18	
,, 10, Tues.	,, 19	
,, 11, Wed.	,, 20	
,, 12, Thurs.	,, 21	
,, 13, Fri.	,, 22	
,, 14, Sat.	,, 23	
,, 15, Sun.	,, 24	
Feb. 16, Mon.	Sebet 25	
,, 17, Tues.	,, 26	
,, 18, Wed.	,, 27	
,, 19, Thurs.	,, 28	
,, 20, Fri.	,, 29	
,, 21, Sat.	,, 30	
,, 22, Sun.	Adar 1	
Feb. 23, Mon.	Adar 2	
,, 24, Tues.	,, 3	
,, 25, Wed.	,, 4	
,, 26, Thurs.	,, 5	Our Lord's fast ends. The Temptation, Matt. iv. 2–11 : Mark i. 12, 13 : Luke iv. 2–13. The deputation to John from Jerusalem, John i. 19–28 (pp. 21–25).
,, 27, Fri.	,, 6	"On the morrow," John i. 29–34 (pp. 25–29).
,, 28, Sat.	,, 7	"On the morrow," John i. 35–42 (pp. 32–35).
,, 29, Sun.	,, 8	"On the morrow," John i. 43*a*. Jesus went forth to Galilee. It would be a four-days' journey (Feb. 29–March 3, inclusive), from the Jordan near Jericho to Capernaum (p. 37).

Julian month.	Jewish ecclesiastical month.	
A.D. 28. Mar. 1, Mon.	Adar 9	
Mar. 2, Tues.	Adar 10	From the Jordan near Jericho to Galilee (Feb. 29 to March 3, inclusive).
„ 3, Wed.	„ 11	Arrives at His destination in Galilee (Capernaum). Call of Philip at Bethsaida his place of residence, John i. 43*b*, 44 (pp. 38, 39).
„ 4, Thurs.	„ 12	Call of Nathanael at Kana his place of residence, John i. 45–51 (pp. 39–45).
„ 5, Fri.	„ 13	"On the third day" (*i.e.* since arrival) the marriage feast at Kana, John ii. 1–11 (pp. 54–61). The day on the calendar (Adar 13) is the Feast to commemorate the death of Nicanor: see 1 Macc. vii. 49 : 2 Macc. xv. 36.
„ 6, Sat.	„ 14	
„ 7, Sun.	„ 15	
„ 8, Mon.	„ 16	
Mar. 9, Tues.	Adar 17	
„ 10, Wed.	„ 18	
„ 11, Thurs.	„ 19	
„ 12, Fri.	„ 20	
„ 13, Sat.	„ 21	
„ 14, Sun.	„ 22	
„ 15, Mon.	„ 23	
Mar. 16, Tues.	Adar 24	
„ 17, Wed.	„ 25	He removed to Capernaum; He, His mother, His brethren, and His disciples, and "abode there, not many days," John ii. 12 (pp. 62, 63), *i.e.* perhaps to the end of March, certainly not later.
„ 18, Thurs.	„ 26	
„ 19, Fri.	„ 27	
„ 20, Sat.	„ 28	
„ 21, Sun.	„ 29	
„ 22, Mon.	Nisan 1	
Mar. 23, Tues.	Nisan 2	
„ 24, Wed.	„ 3	
„ 25, Thurs.	„ 4	
„ 26, Fri.	„ 5	
„ 27, Sat.	„ 6	
„ 28, Sun.	„ 7	
„ 29, Mon.	„ 8	
Mar. 30, Tues.	Nisan 9	To-day or
„ 31, Wed.	„ 10	To-day } the pilgrim caravan would leave Capernaum for Jerusalem, John ii. 13 (p. 64).

Julian month.	Jewish ecclesiastical month.		
A.D. 28 April 1, Thurs.	Nisan 11		
April 2, Fri.	Nisan 12	To-day the pilgrim caravans would arrive at Jerusalem.	
„ 3, Sat.	„ 13		
„ 4, Sun.	„ 14	He cleanses the Temple, John ii. 14–22. The Passover killed after noon, eaten after sunset.	
„ 5, Mon.	„ 15	The Festival day, John ii. 23–end. To-night the discourse with Nicodemus, John iii. 1–21.	
„ 6, Tues.	„ 16	Jesus goes to the "country of Judea" (as opp. to the City)—probably to Bîreh—John iii. 22.	
„ 7, Wed.	„ 17		
„ 8, Thurs.	„ 18	He tarries there and baptizes, John iii. 22; John Baptist baptizes at Aenon, John iii. 23.	
April 9, Fri.	Nisan 19		
„ 10, Sat.	„ 20	The First Sabbath of the 50 days, Sabbath of *Pesah*. The Baptist's last witness, John iii. 25–end.	
„ 11, Sun.	„ 21	Jesus leaves Judea (Bîreh) for Galilee, John iv. 1–3. At Jacob's well, John iv. 4–40. John Baptist is betrayed to Herod by the Sanhedrin (p. 94).	
„ 12, Mon.	„ 22	Jesus stays at Sychar.	
„ 13, Tues.	„ 23	He leaves for Galilee, John iv. 43, 44, on hearing of John's arrest, *cf.* Matt. iv. 12–17: Mark i. 14, 15: Luke iv. 14 (pp. 113, 114).	
„ 14, Wed.	„ 24	He arrived at Kana this evening, John iv. 46 (p. 116).	
„ 15, Thurs.	„ 25	To Kana the courtier comes from Capernaum: his son is healed at 7 p.m., John iv. 46–end.	
April 16, Fri.	Nisan 26	From Kana to Capernaum: on the way, passing by the lake, He calls the four to leave their occupations, Mark i. 16–21: Matt. iv. 18–22: Luke v. 1–11 (pp. 120, 121).	
„ 17, Sat.	„ 27	At Capernaum, Mark i. 21–34. It is the "*Second First*"* Sabbath of the 50 days, Luke vi. 1–5: Mark ii. 23–end (p. 121).	
„ 18, Sun.	„ 28	He went out early to pray: He sets out for other, the nearest, cities, Mark i. 35–38: Luke iv. 43.	The leper healed {Mark i. 40–45*a*; Matt. viii. 2–4; Luke v. 12–15*a*} (p. 122).
„ 19, Mon.	„ 29		
„ 20, Tues.	„ 30		
„ 21, Wed.	Iyar 1		
„ 22, Thurs.	„ 2		
April 23, Fri.	Iyar 3		Circuit through Galilee during April and May, Mark i. 39–45*b*: Matt. iv. 23: Luke iv. 44: v. 15*b*–16.
„ 24, Sat.	„ 4	Sabbath of *Second Pereq*: it is the third Sabbath of the 50 days.	
„ 25, Sun.	„ 5		
„ 26, Mon.	„ 6		
„ 27, Tues.	„ 7		
„ 28, Wed.	„ 8		
„ 29, Thurs.	„ 9		
April 30, Fri.	Iyar 10		

* δευτεροπρώτῳ. Mac Clellan (*The New Test.* vol. i.) gives the only other known instance where this word is employed: it is there used, by a Christian writer, of "Low" Sunday—the 2nd Sunday in the 50 Pentecostal days, just as Luke has used it of the 2nd Sabbath in the Pentecostal days.

Julian month.	Jewish ecclesiastical month.	
A.D. 28. May 1, Sat.	Iyar 11	Sabbath of *Third Pereq:* it is the fourth sabbath of the 50 days. Jesus goes up the Mount at sunset and stays all night (p. 124). — Mk. iii. 1–13*a* (pp. 123, 124). Lk. vi. 12.
May 2, Sun.	Iyar 12	Appointment of the Twelve, Sermon on the Mount, return to Capernaum. {Mk. iii. 13*b*–19; Lu. vi. 13–vii. 10; Matt. v. 1–viii. 1: viii. 5–13} Afternoon. {Mk. iii. 20–iv. 35; Lu. viii. 19–21: viii. 4–18; Matt. xii. 24–xiii. 53} Sunset. {Mk. iv. 35–end; Lu. viii. 22–35; Matt. viii. 18–27} (p. 124).
" 3, Mon.	" 13	At Gerasa on E. of lake: and back to Capernaum (p. 124). {Mk. v. 1–21*a*. Lu. viii. 26–40. Matt. viii. 28–ix. 1.} The paralytic and Matthew's feast (p. 125). {Matt. ix. 1–17; Mk. ii. 1–22; Lu. v. 17–end} followed by {Matt. ix. 18–34; Mk. v. 21*b*–vi. 1*a*; Lu. viii. 41–end} (p. 126).
" 4, Tues.	" 14	
" 5, Wed.	" 15	
" 6, Thurs.	" 16	
" 7, Fri.	" 17	
" 8, Sat.	" 18	Sabbath of *Fourth Pereq:* it is the fifth sabbath of the 50 days. Jesus is at Nazareth. {Mk. vi. 2–6*a*; Matt. xiii. 54–end; Lu. iv. 16–30} (p. 126).
May 9, Sun.	Iyar 19	Round cities and villages teaching and healing. {Mk. vi. 6*b*. Matt. ix. 35–end.} Perhaps during this week occurs Lu. vii. 11–17 at Nain.
" 10, Mon.	" 20	
" 11, Tues.	" 21	
" 12, Wed.	" 22	
" 13, Thurs.	" 23	
" 14, Fri.	" 24	
" 15, Sat.	" 25	Sabbath of *Fifth Pereq:* it is the sixth sabbath of the 50 days.

Julian month.	Jewish ecclesiastical month.	
A.D. 28.		
May 16, Sun.	Iyar 26	Commission of the Twelve, who go forth (and will not rejoin Him till early June) (p. 126). Matt. x. 1–end. Mk. vi. 7–13. Lu. ix. 1–6. After they leave, He departs to their cities without them—for a week. Matt. xi. 1 (p. 126). John Baptist from prison at Machærus sends to ask (p. 126). Matt. xi. 2, 3. Lu. vii. 18–20.
„ 17, Mon.	„ 27	
„ 18, Tues.	„ 28	
„ 19, Wed.	„ 29	Jesus's answer by John Baptist's disciples, etc. Matt. xi. 4–end; Lu. vii. 1–25 (p. 126).
„ 20, Thurs.	Sivan 1	
„ 21, Fri.	„ 2	
„ 22, Sat.	„ 3	Sabbath of *Sixth Pereq*: it is the seventh and last sabbath of the 50 days.
May 23, Sun.	Sivan 4	"Jesus went up to Jerusalem," John v. 1; leaving the frontier of Galilee (Jenîn) to-day, reaching Nâblûs to-night (p. 128).
„ 24, Mon.	„ 5	This evening John Baptist is beheaded at Machærus, Matt. xiv. 1–12: Mk. vi. 14–29: Lk. ix. 7–9 (pp. 127–141).
„ 25, Tues.	„ 6	Feast of Pentecost. Jesus at Pool of Bethzetha, John v. 1–end (pp. 128–144). This evening the supper in the house of Simon the Pharisee, Luke vii. 36–end (p. 145 and pp. 441–443), at Bethany.
„ 26, Wed.	„ 7	Leaving Jerusalem this morning, Jesus would be back in Galilee on Friday, May 28.
„ 27, Thurs.	„ 8	
„ 28, Fri.	„ 9	
„ 29, Sat.	„ 10	
May 30, Sun.	Sivan 11	
„ 31, Mon.	„ 12	

Julian month.	Jewish ecclesiastical month.	
A.D. 28. June 1, Tues.	Sivan 13	
June 2, Wed.	Sivan 14	The Twelve rejoin Jesus at Capernaum, Mark vi. 30. John's disciples having buried his body come to tell Jesus, Matt. xiv. 12 (p. 146).
,, 3, Thurs.	,, 15	Jesus crosses the lake to Bethsaida-Julias on east side: feeds the 5000: sends His disciples on board to cross to the west side. (Matt. xiv. 13–24; Mark vi. 31–48; Luke ix. 10–17; John vi. 1–18) (pp. 147–153).
,, 4, Fri.	,, 16	He rejoins the ship at dawn: they land on west side: people bring their sick all day, Matt. xiv. 25–end: Mark vi. 48–end: John vi. 19–24 (pp. 154–157).
,, 5, Sat.	,, 17	Morning, His discourse in synagogue at Capernaum, John vi. 25–end (pp. 160–173). Afternoon, His talk to Pharisees and scribes from Jerusalem, Matt. xv. 1–9: Mark vii. 1–13; and to the crowds, and to the disciples, Matt. xv. 10–20: Mk. vii. 14–23 (p. 176).
,, 6, Sun.	,, 18	
,, 7, Mon.	,, 19	
,, 8, Tues.	,, 20	
June 9, Wed.	Sivan 21	
,, 10, Thurs.	,, 22	
,, 11, Fri.	,, 23	
,, 12, Sat.	,, 24	
,, 13, Sun.	,, 25	
,, 14, Mon.	,, 26	
,, 15, Tues.	,, 27	He left Capernaum (June 6) and went to the borders of Tyre, and thence through Sidon, and through the midst of Decapolis (a Gentile confederacy of towns), ending up on the lake of Galilee. (Matt. xv. 21–29; Mark vii. 24–31)
June 16, Wed.	Sivan 28	This is the circuit of Luke viii. 1–3, during which He had no headquarters.
,, 17, Thurs.	,, 29	This circuit through Gentile districts seems to occupy three months until mid-Sept.
,, 18, Fri.	,, 30	The Evangelists tell us nothing of it but its opening incident (Matt. xv. 22–28: Mark vii. 25–30) and its closing incident (Matt. xv. 29–end: Mark vii. 31–viii. 10); from which we see how He was welcomed by the Gentiles. (p. 176).
,, 19, Sat.	Tammuz 1	
,, 20, Sun.	,, 2	
,, 21, Mon.	,, 3	
,, 22, Tues.	,, 4	
June 23, Wed.	Tammuz 5	
,, 24, Thurs.	,, 6	
,, 25, Fri.	,, 7	
,, 26, Sat.	,, 8	
,, 27, Sun.	,, 9	
,, 28, Mon.	,, 10	
,, 29, Tues.	,, 11	
June 30, Wed.	Tammuz 12	

Julian month.	Jewish ecclesiastical month.	
A.D. 28. July 1, Thurs.	Tammuz 13	The circuit through the Gentile districts of Tyre, Sidon, and Decapolis continues. It lasts from June 6 to mid-Sept. These districts would be inhabited by descendants of Israelites of the Ten Tribes (cf. Matt. xv. 24), mixed with Greeks and Syrians. These Israelites though living as Gentiles are aware of their Israelite origin; see their praise of "the God of Israel" (Matt. xv. 31), a term which no pure Gentile would have used—he would have said, "the God of the Jews." That the Ten Tribes were still quite distinct from the two (Judah and Benjamin), and though living as Gentiles were not yet lost among them, appears from Josephus (*Ant.*, XI. v. 2), who says that "the Ten Tribes to this day (late 1st cent. A.D.) are beyond the Euphrates in infinite myriads impossible to be numbered": he further calls them "Israelites" as opposed to "Jews" (*ib.*). So the great mass of them had not yet begun their migration.
July 2, Fri.	Tammuz 14	
„ 3, Sat.	„ 15	
„ 4, Sun.	„ 16	
„ 5, Mon.	„ 17	
„ 6, Tues.	„ 18	
„ 7, Wed.	„ 19	
„ 8, Thurs.	„ 20	
July 9, Fri.	Tammuz 21	
„ 10, Sat.	„ 22	
„ 11, Sun.	„ 23	
„ 12, Mon.	„ 24	
„ 13, Tues.	„ 25	
„ 14, Wed.	„ 26	
„ 15, Thur.	„ 27	
July 16, Fri.	Tammuz 28	
„ 17, Sat.	„ 29	
„ 18, Sun.	Ab 1	
„ 19, Mon.	„ 2	
„ 20, Tues.	„ 3	
„ 21, Wed.	„ 4	
„ 22, Thurs.	„ 5	
July 23, Fri.	Ab 6	
„ 24, Sat.	„ 7	
„ 25, Sun.	„ 8	
„ 26, Mon.	„ 9	
„ 27, Tues.	„ 10	
„ 28, Wed.	„ 11	
„ 29, Thurs.	„ 12	
July 30, Fri.	Ab 13	
„ 31, Sat.	„ 14	

Julian month.	Jewish ecclesiastical month.	
A.D. 28. Aug. 1, Sun.	Ab 15	
Aug. 2, Mon.	Ab 16	
,, 3, Tues.	,, 17	
,, 4, Wed.	,, 18	
,, 5, Thurs.	,, 19	
,, 6, Fri.	,, 20	
,, 7, Sat.	,, 21	
,, 8, Sun.	,, 22	
Aug. 9, Mon.	Ab 23	
,, 10, Tues.	,, 24	
,, 11, Wed.	,, 25	
,, 12, Thurs.	,, 26	
,, 13, Fri.	,, 27	
,, 14, Sat.	,, 28	
,, 15, Sun.	,, 29	
Aug. 16, Mon.	Ab 30	
,, 17, Tues.	Elul 1	
,, 18, Wed.	,, 2	
,, 19, Thurs.	,, 3	
,, 20, Fri.	,, 4	
,, 21, Sat.	,, 5	
,, 22, Sun.	,, 6	
Aug. 23, Mon.	Elul 7	
,, 24, Tues.	,, 8	
,, 25, Wed.	,, 9	
,, 26, Thurs.	,, 10	
,, 27, Fri.	,, 11	
,, 28, Sat.	,, 12	
,, 29, Sun.	,, 13	
Aug. 30, Mon.	Elul 14	
,, 31, Tues.	,, 15	

The circuit through the Gentile districts of Tyre, Sidon, and Decapolis continues. It lasts from June 6 to, say, mid-Sept.

The following are the 10 cities named by Pliny (*Hist. Nat.*, v. 18), as forming the Gentile confederacy of the Decapolis :—

City	Modern name
Scythopolis	(Beisân)
Hippos	(Susieh)
Gadara	(Umm Keis)
Pella	(Fahîl)
Philadelphia	(' Ammân)
Gerasa	(Jerash)
Dion	(Adûn)
Canatha	(Kunawât)
Damascus	
Raphana	(? er Rafeh)

All, except the first, are east of the Jordan valley.

The diary of this page especially is uncertain.

Julian month.	Jewish ecclesiastical month.	
A.D. 28. Sept. 1, Wed.	Elul 16	The circuit through Decapolis continues till, say, mid-Sept.
Sept. 2, Thurs. „ 3, Fri. „ 4, Sat. „ 5, Sun. „ 6, Mon. „ 7, Tues. „ 8, Wed.	Elul 17 „ 18 „ 19 „ 20 „ 21 „ 22 „ 23	
Sept. 9, Thurs. „ 10, Fri. „ 11, Sat. „ 12, Sun. „ 13, Mon.	Elul 24 „ 25 „ 26 „ 27 „ 28	The circuit through Decapolis ends : and He returns to the Lake of Galilee ; sat on the Mount, Matt. xv. 29*b* (p. 176). The 3 days of Matt. xv. 32 : Mark viii. 2.
„ 14, Tues.	„ 29	Still on the Mount. { The crowds of infirm are healed : they are Gentiles. } Matt. xv. 29–39. { He feeds the 4000 : the loaves are of Gentile baking. } Mark viii. 1–9. He leaves by ship and comes to { Magadàn / Dalmanuthà } { Matt. xv. 39 / Mark viii. 10 } (p. 176).
„ 15, Wed.	Tisri 1	New Year day of the civil year. { A deputation of the Pharisees and Sadducees come to bargain. } Matt. xvi. 1–12. { He leaves them and crosses the lake to Bethsaidà-Julià s. } Mark viii. 11–21. At Bethsaidà-Juliàs. { Mark viii. 22–26. } (p. 177).

Julian month.	Jewish ecclesiastical month.	
A.D. 28. Sept. 16, Thurs.	Tisri 2	He came to Cæsaréa-Philippi, one day's journey north of Bethsaidà-Juliàs: Peter's confession of the Faith: Jesus "began" to teach that He should be killed, and should rise the third day. Matt. xvi. 13–21; Mark viii. 27–31; Luke ix. 18–22 (p. 177).
" 17, Fri.	" 3	He "insisted" more plainly on His death: Peter's rebuke. Jesus calls the multitudes, with His disciples, and speaks to all of His death. Matt. xvi. 22–end; Mark. viii. 32–ix. 1 (p. 177).
" 18, Sat. " 19, Sun. " 20, Mon. " 21, Tues. " 22, Wed.	" 4 " 5 " 6 " 7 " 8	On one of these days He returns to Galilee from Cæsaréa-Philíppi.
Sept. 23, Thurs.	Tisri 9	He meets His "brethren," who, with other pilgrims, are converging on Jenîn on their way to the Feast of Tabernacles, John vii. 1–9. He delays (pp. 180–183). In the evening* He goes up Mt Tabòr with Peter, James, and John: and after midnight— Matt. xvii. 1–21
" 24, Fri.	" 10	He is transfigured. This (Tisri 10) is the great Day of Atonement of the Jews' ritual. He came down from the mountain this morning and heals the demoniac boy at the foot of the mountain—tradition names Dabú-rieh as the village: it is at the north-west foot of Mt Tabòr. Mark ix. 2–29; Lu. ix. 28–43a (p. 177).
" 25, Sat. " 26, Sun.	" 11 " 12	He left, and journeyed on through Galilee to Capernaum, Mark ix. 30–33 (p. 178).
" 27, Mon.	" 13	For the last two days disciples have been gathering to Him in Galilee: to them too He talks of His death and resurrection, Matt. xvii. 22, 23: Luke ix. 43b–45. Last incidents at Capernaum before He leaves Galilee, Matt. xvii. 24–xviii. end: Mark ix. 33–end: Luke ix. 46–50. (p. 178).
" 28, Tues.	" 14	He left Capernaum with His disciples, John vii. 10: Matt. xix. 1a: Mark x. 1: Luke ix. 51. They would arrive at the Galilee frontier this evening (p. 183).
" 29, Wed.	" 15	First day of the Feast of Tabernacles. He passes through Samaria (Luke ix. 52–56) with His disciples: travelling incognito (p. 184).
Sept. 30, Thurs.	Tisri 16	He would arrive perhaps at Bîreh on His way to Jerusalem. But He has not been travelling on the Haj route, John vii. 10.

* The "six days" of Matt. xvii. 1 and of Mark ix. 2 are reckoned from the day He spoke "openly" of His death and resurrection, viz. Sat. the 18th till Thurs. the 23rd inclusive.

The "about eight days" of Luke ix. 28 are reckoned from the day He "began" to teach that He should be killed and should rise again, viz. Thurs. the 16th till Thurs. the 23rd inclusive.

Julian month.	Jewish ecclesiastical month.		
A.D. 28. Oct. 1, Fri.	Tisri	17	He arrives at Jerusalem this evening.
,, 2, Sat.	Tisri	18	"In the middle of the Feast" He entered the Temple, John vii. 14–24 (pp. 185–188).
,, 3, Sun.	,,	19	Again in the Temple, John vii. 25–31 (pp. 188–190). Perhaps to-day the "70 others" were appointed and sent, Luke x. 1–16 (p. 242).
,, 4, Mon.	,,	20	The Pharisees give orders to take Him at first opportunity, John vii. 32–35.
,, 5, Tues.	,,	21	"The last day of the Feast," John vii. 37–viii. 1 (pp. 192–197).
,, 6, Wed.	,,	22	The Feast known as *Simhat-Torah*. The adulteress: in the Temple: the blind man receives sight, John viii. 2–ix. 12 (pp. 197–226).
,, 7, Thurs.	,,	23	The sequel to the blind man's cure, John ix. 13–41 (pp. 226–234). The Sheepfold parable, John x. 1–21 (pp. 235–242).
,, 8, Fri.	,,	24	He leaves Jerusalem for Peræa (p. 243).
Oct. 9, Sat.	Tisri	25	
,, 10, Sun.	,,	26	
,, 11, Mon.	,,	27	
,, 12, Tues.	,,	28	
,, 13, Wed.	,,	29	
,, 14, Thurs.	,,	30	
,, 15, Fri.	Marheswan	1	
Oct. 16, Sat.	Marheswan	2	In Peræa. The 70 return to Him in Peræa, Luke x. 17–24. He stays in Peræa two months, till Dec. 5 (p. 243). In Matt. xix. 1 there should be a full stop after "Galilee": thus leaving an interval of 10 days for the visit to Jerusalem before "And He came to the borders of Judæa beyond Jordan," viz. Peræa. Similarly in Mark x. 1 this interval occurs between ἐκεῖθεν ἀναστάς ("arose from thence," viz. Galilee) and ἔρχεται εἰς ("and He cometh to," etc.). p. 183, note.
,, 17, Sun.	,,	3	
,, 18, Mon.	,,	4	
,, 19, Tues.	,,	5	
,, 20, Wed.	,,	6	
,, 21, Thurs.	,,	7	
,, 22, Fri.	,,	8	
Oct. 23, Sat.	Marheswan	9	
,, 24, Sun.	,,	10	
,, 25, Mon.	,,	11	
,, 26 Tues.	,,	12	
,, 27, Wed.	,,	13	
,, 28, Thurs.	,,	14	
,, 29, Fri.	,,	15	
Oct. 30, Sat.	Marheswan	16	
,, 31, Sun.	,,	17	

Julian month.	Jewish ecclesiastical month.	
A.D. 28. Nov. 1, Mon.	Marḥeswan 18	Still in Peræa, until Dec. 5.
Nov. 2, Tues.	Marḥeswan 19	
„ 3, Wed.	„ 20	
„ 4, Thurs.	„ 21	
„ 5, Fri.	„ 22	
„ 6, Sat.	„ 23	
„ 7, Sun.	„ 24	
„ 8, Mon.	„ 25	
Nov. 9, Tues.	Marheswan 26	
„ 10, Wed.	„ 27	
„ 11, Thurs.	„ 28	
„ 12, Fri.	„ 29	
„ 13, Sat.	Kislew 1	
„ 14, Sun.	„ 2	
„ 15, Mon.	„ 3	
Nov. 16, Tues.	Kislew 4	
„ 17, Wed.	„ 5	
„ 18, Thurs.	„ 6	
„ 19, Fri.	„ 7	
„ 20, Sat.	„ 8	
„ 21, Sun.	„ 9	
„ 22, Mon.	„ 10	
Nov. 23, Tues.	Kislew 11	
„ 24, Wed.	„ 12	
„ 25, Thurs.	„ 13	
„ 26, Fri.	„ 14	
„ 27, Sat.	„ 15	
„ 28, Sun.	„ 16	
„ 29, Mon.	„ 17	
Nov. 30, Tues.	Kislew 18	

Julian month.	Jewish ecclesiastical month.	
A.D. 28. Dec. 1, Wed.	Kislew 19	
Dec. 2, Thurs.	Kislew 20	
„ 3, Fri.	„ 21	Still in Peræa.
„ 4, Sat.	„ 22	
„ 5, Sun.	„ 23	Perhaps to-day He crossed the Jordan out of Peræa into Jericho.
„ 6, Mon.	„ 24	On the road from Jericho to Jerusalem (note the local touch). At Bethany in evening, supper in Martha's house, Luke x. 25–end (p. 243).
„ 7, Tues.	„ 25	First day of the Feast of Dedication: in Solomon's Porch, John x. 22–39 (pp. 244–250). Perhaps Luke xi. 1–13 (p. 243).
„ 8, Wed.	„ 26	He "went away again beyond Jordan [*i.e.* to Peræa], and there He abode: and many came to Him," John x. 40–end (p. 250).
Dec. 9, Thurs.	Kislew 27	
„ 10, Fri.	„ 28	
„ 11, Sat.	„ 29	
„ 12, Sun.	„ 30	
„ 13, Mon.	Ṭebeth 1	
„ 14, Tues.	„ 2	
„ 15, Wed.	„ 3	
Dec. 16, Thurs.	Ṭebeth 4	
„ 17, Fri.	„ 5	
„ 18, Sat.	„ 6	Again in Peræa (p. 250).
„ 19, Sun.	„ 7	This stay in Peræa lasts till March 4.
„ 20, Mon.	„ 8	Luke alone gives any details of it, xi. 14–xiii. 21. (See at February A.D. 29.)
„ 21, Tues.	„ 9	This stay in Peræa is mentioned by Matt. xix. 1*b*, and Mark x. 1*b*, where it has been lumped together with the former stay in Peræa of Oct.—those two Evangelists ignoring visits to Jerusalem in between.
„ 22, Wed.	„ 10	
Dec. 23, Thurs.	Ṭebeth 11	
„ 24, Fri.	„ 12	
„ 25, Sat.	„ 13	
„ 26, Sun.	„ 14	
„ 27, Mon.	„ 15	
„ 28, Tues.	„ 16	
„ 29, Wed.	„ 17	
Dec. 30, Thurs.	Ṭebeth 18	
„ 31, Fri.	„ 19	

Julian month.	Jewish ecclesiastical month.	
A.D. 29.		
Jan. 1, Sat.	Ṭebeth 20	
Jan. 2, Sun.	Ṭebeth 21	
„ 3, Mon.	„ 22	
„ 4, Tues.	„ 23	
„ 5, Wed.	„ 24	
„ 6, Thurs.	„ 25	
„ 7, Fri.	„ 26	
„ 8, Sat.	„ 27	
Jan. 9, Sun.	Ṭebeth 28	
„ 10, Mon.	„ 29	
„ 11, Tues.	Šebaṭ 1	
„ 12, Wed.	„ 2	
„ 13, Thurs.	„ 3	
„ 14, Fri.	„ 4	
„ 15, Sat.	„ 5	Still in Peræa. This stay in Peræa lasts till March 4. Luke alone gives any details of it, xi. 14–xiii. 21 (see at February).
Jan. 16, Sun.	Šebaṭ 6	
„ 17, Mon.	„ 7	
„ 18, Tues.	„ 8	
„ 19, Wed.	„ 9	
„ 20, Thurs.	„ 10	
„ 21, Fri.	„ 11	
„ 22, Sat.	„ 12	
Jan. 23, Sun.	Šebaṭ 13	
„ 24, Mon.	„ 14	
„ 25, Tues.	„ 15	
„ 26, Wed.	„ 16	
„ 27, Thurs.	„ 17	
„ 28, Fri.	„ 18	
„ 29, Sat.	„ 19	
Jan. 30, Sun.	Šebaṭ 20	
„ 31, Mon.	„ 21	

Julian month.	Jewish ecclesiastical month.		
A.D. 29.			
Feb. 1, Tues.	Šebaṭ 22		
Feb. 2, Wed.	Šebaṭ 23		
,, 3, Thurs.	,, 24		
,, 4, Fri.	,, 25		
,, 5, Sat.	,, 26		
,, 6, Sun.	,, 27		
,, 7, Mon.	,, 28		
,, 8, Tues.	,, 29		
Feb. 9, Wed.	Šebaṭ 30		
,, 10, Thurs.	Adar 1		
,, 11, Fri.	,, 2		
,, 12, Sat.	,, 3		
,, 13, Sun.	,, 4		
,, 14, Mon.	,, 5		
,, 15, Tues.	,, 6	Still in Peræa. This stay in Peræa lasts till March 4. Luke alone gives any details of it, xi. 14–xiii. 21 (see below).	
Feb. 16, Wed.	Adar 7		
,, 17, Thurs.	,, 8		
,, 18, Fri.	,, 9		
,, 19, Sat.	,, 10		
,, 20, Sun.	,, 11		
,, 21, Mon.	,, 12		
,, 22, Tues.	,, 13		
Feb. 23, Wed.	Adar 14	Feast of *Purim* begins, but its great day is to-morrow, *Adar* 15.	
,, 24, Thurs.	,, 15	Feast of *Purim*. He casts out a dumb demon; they ask for a sign. No sign shall be given but that of Jonah. A Pharisee asks Him to midday dinner. He denounces Pharisees and Scribes: His talk to His disciples.	Luke xi. 14–xii. end (p. 251).
,, 25, Fri.	,, 16	He is told of certain Galileans put to death by Pilate in the Temple courts, perhaps at the *Purim* sacrifices, Luke xiii. 1–9 (p. 252).	
,, 26, Sat.	,, 17	He heals a bent woman on a Sabbath, Luke xiii. 10–21.	
,, 27, Sun.	,, 18		
,, 28, Mon.	,, 19		

Julian month.	Jewish ecclesiastical month.	
A.D. 29. March 1, Tues.	Adar 20	Still in Peræa.
March 2, Wed.	Adar 21	Still in Peræa.
,, 3, Thurs.	,, 22	Still in Peræa. This morning He heard of Lazarus's illness: He stays "two days" (*i.e.* till Friday morning), John xi. 1–6 (pp. 253, 254, 256). To-day Lazarus died, and was to-day buried.
,, 4, Fri.	,, 23	Still in Peræa. Jesus left Peræa to go to Lazarus, John xi. 7–16. This is the journey which begins at Luke xiii. 22 (pp. 252–255).
,, 5, Sat.	,, 24	Jesus eats in a Pharisee's house on a Sabbath (at Jericho), Luke xiv. 1–24 (p. 254).
,, 6, Sun.	,, 25	He journeys from Jericho to Bethany, Luke xiv. 25–xvi. end. — Arriving at Bethany He finds that Lazarus died and was buried "four days" ago. He raises Lazarus this evening. — John xi. 17–46 (pp. 260–269).
,, 7, Mon. ,, 8, Tues.	,, 26 ,, 27	The Sanhedrin meet under Caiaphas. Jesus withdraws to Ephraim city, John xi. 47–54.
March 9, Wed. ,, 10, Thurs. ,, 11, Fri. ,, 12, Sat.	Adar 28 ,, 29 Nisan 1 ,, 2	Jesus stayed at Ephraim city in seclusion, John xi. 54 (p. 272).
,, 13, Sun.	,, 3	The last journey toward Jerusalem, Luke xvii. 11–xix. 28. It is from Ephraim city, north through Samaria: then east across Jordan into Peræa: then south through Peræa — 1st day. Ephraim to (?) Nâblûs (p. 273).
,, 14, Mon.	,, 4	2nd day. Nâblûs (?) to Jenîn: here the ten lepers were cleansed, Luke xvii. 12–19 (p. 273).
,, 15, Tues.	,, 5	3rd day. Jenîn to ((?) Pella in) Peræa. (?) Luke xvii. 20–xviii. 8 (p. 273).
March 16, Wed.	Nisan 6	4th day. (?) Pella to (?) Succoth. (?) Luke xviii. 9–17: Matt. xix. 3–15*a*: Mark x. 2–16 (p. 274).

„ 17, Thurs.	„ 7	to the bridge opposite Jericho and so across Jordan to Jericho:	5th day. (?) Succoth to Jericho, Luke xviii. 18–xix. 7: Matt. xix. 15*b*–xx. 28: Mark x. 17–46*a*. The Sanhedrists in Jerusalem, John xi. 55–57. (p. 274).
„ 18, Fri.	„ 8	then up to Bethphage:	6th day. Jericho to Bethphage, Luke xix. 8–28: Matt. xx. 29–34: Mark x. 46*b*–52 (p. 274).
„ 19, Sat.	„ 9	and on to Bethany.	7th day. Bethphage to Bethany: they are about ½ mile apart. Supper at Bethany, John xii. 1-8 (pp. 277-280).
„ 20, Sun.	„ 10	Palm Sunday. Bethany to Jerusalem viâ Bethphage, John xii. 10–19: Matt. xxi. 1–17: Mark xi. 1–11: Luke xix. 29–46 (pp. 281–285).	
„ 21, Mon.	„ 11	In the Temple, Matt. xxi. 18, 19: Mark xi. 12–19: Luke xix. 47–end.	
„ 22, Tues.	„ 12	In the Temple, Matt. xxi. 20–xxii. 15: Mark xi. 20–xii. 12: Luke xx. 1–19.	
March 23, Wed.	Nisan 13	In the Temple, Matt. xxii. 16–xxiii. end: Mark xii. 13–end: Luke xx. 20–xxi. 4: John xii. 20–end (pp. 286–296). Later, on the Mount of Olives, Matt. xxiv. 1–xxvi. 5: Mark xiii. 1, 2: Luke xxi. 5–xxii. 6.	
„ 24, Thurs.	„ 14	Maundy Thursday and the night after, Matt. xxvi. 17–end: Mark xiv. 12–end: Luke xxii. 7–65: John xiii. 1–xviii. 27 (pp. 297–366). The Legal Passover day.	
„ 25, Fri.	„ 15	Good Friday, sunrise to sunset: Matt. xxvii. 1–61: Mark xv. 1–end: Luke xxii. 66–xxiii. 56*a*: John xviii. 28–xix. end (pp. 367–409). The national and archetypal Passover day.	
„ 26, Sat.	„ 16	Luke xxiii. 56*b* (pp. 409, 410). The national festival-day. The Jews' Sabbath is the twenty-four hours from sunset of Friday to sunset of Saturday.	
„ 27, Sun.	„ 17	Easter Day. Matt. xxviii. 1–15: Mark xvi. 1–14: Luke xxiv. 1–48: John xx. 1–25 (pp. 411–427). The day of the '*omer* or wave-sheaf: first day of the 50 days to Pentecost.	
„ 28, Mon.	„ 18		
„ 29, Tues.	„ 19		
March 30, Wed.	Nisan 20		
„ 31, Thurs.	„ 21		

Julian month.	Jewish ecclesiastical month.	
A.D. 29. April 1, Fri.	Nisan 22	
April 2, Sat.	Nisan 23	The Sabbath of *Pesaḥ:* the first Sabbath of the 50 days to Pentecost.
„ 3, Sun.	„ 24	Our Lord appears again to the Eleven, John xx. 26–28 (pp. 427–429).
„ 4, Mon.	„ 25	
„ 5, Tues.	„ 26	
„ 6, Wed.	„ 27	
„ 7, Thurs.	„ 28	
„ 8, Fri.	„ 29	
April 9, Sat.	Nisan 30	The *Second First* Sabbath: the second Sabbath of the 50 days, and Sabbath of *First Pereq.*
„ 10, Sun.	Iyar 1	He again appears: to the seven disciples on the Sea of Tiberias, John xxi. 1–end (pp. 430–440).
„ 11, Mon.	„ 2	
„ 12, Tues.	„ 3	
„ 13, Wed.	„ 4	
„ 14, Thurs.	„ 5	
„ 15, Fri.	„ 6	
April 16, Sat.	Iyar 7	The Sabbath of *Second Pereq:* the third Sabbath of the 50 days.
„ 17, Sun.	„ 8	He again appears: to 500 on Mount Tabor, Matt. xxviii. 16, 17; 1 Cor. xv. 6 (p. 431, note).
„ 18, Mon.	„ 9	
„ 19, Tues.	„ 10	
„ 20, Wed.	„ 11	
„ 21, Thurs.	„ 12	
„ 22, Fri.	„ 13	
April 23, Sat.	Iyar 14	The Sabbath of *Third Pereq:* the fourth Sabbath of the 50 days.
„ 24, Sun.	„ 15	He again appears: to James the Little, His "brother," 1 Cor. xv. 7*a*. This James is not one of the Twelve.
„ 25, Mon.	„ 16	
„ 26, Tues.	„ 17	
„ 27, Wed.	„ 18	
„ 28, Thurs.	„ 19	
„ 29, Fri.	„ 20	
April 30, Sat.	Iyar 21	The Sabbath of *Fourth Pereq:* the fifth Sabbath of the 50 days.

Julian month.	Jewish ecclesiastical month.	
A.D. 29.		
May 1, Sun.	Iyar 22	He again appears: to "all the Apostles" (*i.e.* to the Eleven and the Seventy). 1 Cor. xv. 7*b*.
May 2, Mon.	Iyar 23	
" 3, Tues.	" 24	
" 4, Wed.	" 25	
" 5, Thurs.	" 26	Ascension day. Matt. xxviii. 18-end: Mark xvi. 15–19: Luke xxiv. 49–52: Acts i. 4–14.
" 6, Fri.	" 27	
" 7, Sat.	" 28	The Sabbath of *Fifth Pereq:* the sixth Sabbath of the 50 days.
" 8, Sun.	" 29	Matthias is added to the Eleven. Acts i. 15–26.
May 9, Mon.	Sivan 1	
" 10, Tues.	" 2	
" 11, Wed.	" 3	
" 12, Thurs.	" 4	
" 13, Fri.	" 5	
" 14, Sat.	" 6	The Sabbath of *Sixth Pereq:* the seventh Sabbath of the 50 days.
" 15, Sun.	" 7	Pentecost.* Acts ii. 1–41. The last day of the 50 days.

* The normal day for Pentecost was always Sivan 6; but the Jews having this year postponed Passover by one day, Pentecost of necessity fell late by one day. Though our Lord and the Twelve ate the Passover on Nisan 14 (the correct day), the Apostles did not therefore reckon their Pentecost to Sivan 6 (the correct day), because the archetypal Passover was the Sacrifice by our Lord of Himself on the Cross as the Paschal Lamb on Nisan 15—the day and hour when the Jews were sacrificing their paschal lambs. Thus Pentecost fell this year for Apostles and "Jews" alike on Sunday, Sivan 7, May 15.

A STUDY OF

ST JOHN'S GOSPEL

§ I

JOHN I. 1–14

The Prologue

In which John defines the Personality whom he calls The Word (viz. of God), and the Light of men.

(1) "In the beginning was the Word," *i.e.* when there was a beginning, when anything began, there already *was existing* (ἦν) the Word. "In the beginning" postulates that which is not self-existent: for that only has a beginning. God, being self-existent, cannot have a beginning. Had the Word a beginning? John says, 'No: for if we reach back to any beginning, there already was in existence the Word.' At once it is evident that to John's vision "The Word" is no other than God the self-existent.

But that is not all: he continues—

"And the Word was toward God (ἦν πρὸς τὸν Θεόν)." There is, therefore, Another who also is God: and the relation of God the Word to this Other is expressed not by the idea of existence *with*, but by the idea of existence *toward* or *facing*, for this and no other is the idea conveyed by πρὸς and the accusative. And, to cut short any timid reluctance there might be to admit that there could be more than one Person in the Godhead, he states abruptly and without reserve—

"And the Word was God." Here, then, already are plainly two Persons, of whom Each is God: and of these the One "exists toward" the Other—as though the reflection in a mirror was as real as the person reflected, and was for ever moving towards him to merge in him, and yet for ever rested unmerged in him.

Much might be said here about the tendency of the Rabbinical schools before John's time to personify "the *Name* of the Lord," "the *Presence* of the Lord," and especially "the *Word* of the Lord," in their exegesis of the Old Testament: but none of the Schools, nor even Philo who went furthest, had ventured to identify this personification with God. The mystery of the Trinity lay hidden until our Lord came to reveal it: and the Jews were, as they still are, Unitarians.

John, however, had seen the vision of Truth, had been initiated into the Mystery by the great Hierophant, and declares "The Word" to be God from eternity.

As the *Word* of God was the medium by which God communicated with His people in the Old Covenant (see the common phrase in the Prophets "the Word of the Lord came to"), so the Person by whom He manifested Himself to men under the New Covenant is called by John "The Word," viz. of God. Ideally, the word or speech of a man is that man's expression of himself to others; "The Word" is the metaphor which John in his prologue chooses by which to describe Him who is the self-expression of God to men.

Other metaphors to indicate this Revealer of God are elsewhere employed—each and all of them inadequate, because language being of its nature metaphorical is unable to represent the Absolute. Among them are *The Name* of God, for ideally the name of a person is the perfect connotation of that person: *The Glory* of God: *The Image* (*εἴκων*) of God (2 Cor. iv. 4): *The Stamp* of God's Person (*χαρακτὴρ τῆς ὑποστάσεως αὐτοῦ*) (Heb. i. 3): *The Radiance* of God's glory (*ἀπαύγασμα τῆς δοξῆς*), *ib.* Yet another that attempts to express the relationship of the First and Second Persons of the Trinity to each other is *Father* and *Son*, the eternally Begetting One and the eternally Begotten One.

Here then in the three opening sentences of John's gospel he has sought to represent to us the Life or Being of God, the eternal Flux and Reflux of the Absolute, before as yet any person or thing was created or had beginning.

(2) "This One (οὗτος) was in the beginning toward God." When first anything came into being This One (the Word) was already existing toward God. Having thus again stated the eternal existence of the Word, and the essential quality of that existence, viz. existence towards God, or the Reflux of God back to God, John continues where the book of Genesis begins—with the creation of that which is not self-existent.

(3) "All things through Him (*i.e.* the Word) came into being (ἐγένετο)." God the Word is the mediate Agent, as God the Speaking One is the originating Agent; but as neither can act without the other, Each is rightly termed Creator.

"And apart from Him not one thing came into being (ἐγένετο) which has come into being (γέγονε)." This is the charter of Christian thought which denies the eternal existence of matter as though it were, as the Pantheists hold, a mode of God—the Reflux of God into Himself. Pantheism thinks of matter with relation to God in terms which the Christian faith asserts belong only to the Word. Whereas Pantheism thinks of God and the creature as the Flux and Reflux of Deity, the Flood and the Ebb, the Outward and the Homeward, viewing the creature as the manifestation of God *to Himself*, Christianity reserves these correlations for "God" and "The Word," the "First" and the "Second" Persons of the Godhead.

Again, whilst the Creature is not self-existent, is not a mode of God, but was made by God, neither does it continue to exist apart from God the Word. For—

(4) "In Him was Life." In so far as any created thing lives it is linked to Him; for in Him Life inheres, and outside of Him there is not any Life. He did not make matter inert: He made it quick, energizing; but the quick principle issues from and inheres in Him. Were He to withdraw from matter, nothing would remain: it would, *ipso facto*, cease to exist; for there is no such thing as dead matter. We neither know what matter is,

in its ultimate analysis, nor can form any mental image of its primordial coming into being.

"And the Life was the Light of Men." In so far as man Lives, or is Man, it is in virtue of the Light which shines into his intellect from God the Word and is reflected back by his intellect into God the Word. When God is said to have breathed into Adam * the breath of *Life* (Heb. *Lives* plur., Gen. ii. 7), the Life that differentiated Adam and his descendants from all other animated creatures

* The Bible deals with none but Adam's race—the type that began about 6000 years ago: it says nothing of the types of man that preceded Adam on earth. As for the cosmogony of the first chapter of Genesis:—the construction of the Hebrew original marks a break in the narrative between verses 1 and 2: so that a wholly new section starts with the second verse. This section (Gen. i. verse 2 to Gen. ii. verse 3) seems to refer to a literal heptameron, seven days, the week of Adam's creation. It does not pretend to be an account of the original creation of the heavens and the earth and the things in them: that has been briefly stated in verse 1, and then left: that verse 1 covers the long process of evolution extending over millions of years. The new section is an account of a new inauguration following upon a cataclysm of water or of vapour, which had blotted out the face of the earth leaving it "waste and void" (*tohu va bohu*, these same words are employed in Jer. iv. 23, and are again joined together in Is. xxxiv. 11), and completely obscured for a time from the light of the sun. Nor need we suppose that the cataclysm was universal over the face of the earth, nor yet that all life in sea and on land was destroyed. None of the three verbs which the A.V. renders by "bring forth" or "bring forth abundantly," in verses 11, 12, 20, 21, 24, is ever used in the sense of a mother bringing forth progeny. Rather, owing to the cataclysm, vegetable life had been swamped and its energy suspended: and animal life had been diminished and its vigour enfeebled. With the heptameron of Gen. i. 2 to ii. 3, life on the earth and in its waters and in its atmosphere was resumed at the point where in the long process of the ages it had arrived before the cataclysm. The only new creation of this heptameron was Adam, who represented a distinct advance on the human type which had preceded him: his excellence consisting in his power to see God. Gen. i. verse 11 should be rendered "let the earth sprout (*tadše'*) grass": 12, "And the earth put forth (*tôṣe'*) grass": 20, "let the waters *creep* (*yišrṣû*) with the *creeping* living creature": 21, "every living creature that crawleth with which the waters *crept*," *i.e.* swarmed: 24, "let the earth put forth (*tôṣe'*) the living creature after its kind, cattle," etc., not as from a womb, but as from places of storage, such as caves and refuges: the temporary torpor of life gave place to vigour.

Also, in the record of the Flood, account must be taken of the word rendered *earth*, which in Hebrew is commonly used of a very limited part of earth's surface: so too of the word rendered *all* or *every*, which in Hebrew is commonly used loosely and hyperbolically—much more so in Semitic languages than with us. That record is by an eye-witness, of what he saw, not by a wireless operator. How far had Adam's descendants spread themselves over the earth?

on earth (as also, we suspect, from the pre-Adamite man) was the Divine Light which illumines his intellect, the Light whereby he apprehends and reflects God (" is made in the image of God," Gen. i. 27). Whereas God the Word, or God the Son *is* the reflection of God the Father to Himself. Adam and his descendants are *made* with the capacity to reflect back God the Word: and his Light is God the Word in him. The highest mode of Life in man is the Light which shining into him shines back toward God the Word.

In created things other than Adam and his descendants, life takes modes other than intellectual Light.

(5) Although created thus radiantly and immaculately God-reflecting, Adam by his fall obscured this radiance both in himself and in all those who sprung from him, so that ever since the sin in Eden—

" The Light shines in the darkness ": the Light which is God the Word shines ever outwards into man, but the mirror—man's intellect—is no longer luminous, no longer sensitized to catch that radiance, but dimmed it lies in the darkness:—a state which man unwittingly made for himself as the effect of sin. Sin is nothing but the *act* of turning away from God or the *state* of being averse from Him. What else is Darkness ?

" And the darkness did not apprehend it," viz. *the Light.* The dimmed mirror no longer caught the Light: Man no longer saw God aright.

Such was the state of darkness in which the human race was still blindly groping, when John brings upon the scene that man " than whom no greater man has been born of woman "—John the Baptist,* whose mission it was to be the Forerunner and Herald of the Light.

(6) " There came into being a man, sent from God, his name (7) was John. This one came for witness, in order to give witness concerning the Light ": (that Light which

* The coming of this man had been divinely announced by Gabriel, as is told by Luke in the first chapter of his gospel, where also are recorded his conception, his sanctification in his mother's womb, his birth, the divine prophecies about him, his growth and his consecrated life.

man had lost the power to apprehend and reflect, in other words, to see): "in order that all men may believe by means of him." The evangelist does not say "in order that all men may *see* by means of him," but "may believe." The power to *see* God was lost, but the power to believe remained: and belief would eventually end in sight. Many under the Old Covenant had believed in the coming Redeemer of the Race, heroes of the Faith, whose names are given in chap. xi. of the Epistle to the Hebrews, beginning with Abel the first martyr. Nor can it have been in Abraham's line alone that the Faith was handed on, *e.g.* we find it in the Gentile Magi of the East. In every religion of the world some fragments of the primeval gospel of Eden (Gen. iii. 15) have survived.

Also faith varies infinitely in intensity and in clearness: from a merely formal assent in some minds, to a burning, transmuting conviction in others. In some it is as a germ cell hardly as yet active: in others it is developed into the seeing eye and reasoned confidence.

The object of John's mission was "that all men may believe": though the Baptist's range was confined to the circuit (περίχωρος), or Valley, of the Jordan, among his disciples were the future Apostles whom he prepared for Christ to take over and perfect. From those Apostles the Faith has spread upon the world, and is destined to become universal: in this way the Baptist's witness is said to have world-wide results.

What exactly was the Baptist's "witness concerning the Light"? We shall see that later, when we come to consider chapter i. 15–36 and iii. 27–36.

(8) "That one" (ἐκεῖνος, *i.e.* John the Baptist) "was not the Light, but (he came) in order to give witness concerning the Light." At the time John the Evangelist wrote his gospel (about 100 A.D.) there were those who refused to believe that the Baptist was superseded by Jesus: even to this day the Mandœans of the Tigris river regard John the Baptist as the one and only true Prophet.

(9) "The Light, the true Light, which lightens every

man, *was coming* into the world (ἦν . . . ἐρχόμενον)." This Light is the Light which (see at verse 4), by shining into man's intellect, differentiates man from all creatures on earth. Its nature is to fully enlighten every man: give it time it will yet do its work: meanwhile, in so far as every man's intellect is not fully Light-reflecting, it is because the Light can only dimly penetrate the darkness—that inability to see—which is the result of aversion from God, inherited and confirmed by each one of us. To rekindle this light in man, to enable man again to see God, was the purpose of the Incarnation.

This Light—God the Word—"was coming into the world * (ἦν . . . ἐρχόμενον εἰς τὸν κόσμον)," *i.e.* was on the point of coming into the world, viz. at the time the Baptist was sent. This coming of the true Light into the world is the Incarnation of God the Word. This Incarnation took place (March, B.C. 4) six months after the conception (Sept., B.C. 5) of John the Baptist: the birth of the Incarnate Word took place (Dec., B.C. 4) six months after the birth of John the Baptist: and the public ministry of the God-Man began (Jan., A.D. 28) some three months after the beginning (Oct., A.D. 27) of the official ministry of John the Baptist, His forerunner and herald.

The Greek term, rendered throughout John's gospel, by "the world," is ὁ κόσμος. Its proper meaning is the created world in all its ordered beauty. But John uses it throughout to express the world considered in its microcosm—man: for man is the sum, the culmination thus far of the long process of God's evolution hitherto of the world. Owing to the sin of Adam the microcosm, the

* This appears to be almost certainly the meaning of the Greek original, taking the words "coming into the world" as referring to the nom. "the Light," and construing them with "was," rather than joining "coming into the world" with the acc. "every man." The best comment on the passage is the similar phrase in iii. 19, "the Light has come into the world," where our Lord is talking of Himself as Incarnate among men: and again xii. 46, where He says, "I am come (as) Light into the world."

The Latin Fathers, depending on the Old Latin, or on Jerome's version (venientem), refer "coming into the world" to "every man": nor could it occur to them, being unfamiliar with Greek, that any other meaning was possible, for the Latin tied them down to that. The Greek Fathers were not so hampered.

physical world (κόσμος) is regarded as alienated from God, for this physical world is bound up with man: with the fall of Adam, the recently reformed earth and all life upon it suffered a set-back; and when his redemption shall be perfected, the physical earth and all upon it will feel the uplift, beginning with Holy Land as the focus during the millennial Age.

(10) The Evangelist here passes on to the time when "The Light" no longer "*was coming* into the world," no longer was on the threshold, but was now come, was actually born into the world—moving among men as Man: "He was in the world: and the world was made through Him" (δι' αὐτοῦ, by means of Him, as he had already said in verse 3), "and the world did not recognize Him." When He came among men as Man they collectively failed to recognize Him as their Creator; for the Roman empire, acting as the at that time representative of man's highest civilization, put Him to death as a felon. And as for His own people the Jews, were they any better? No: for

(11) "He came to His own" (τὰ ἴδια, *i.e.* His own home, His own land, His own throne), "and His own people" (οἱ ἴδιοι, *i.e.* the Jews) "received Him not to themselves" (οὐ παρέλαβον). It was that very people who suggested and successfully insisted on His being put to death.

(12) "But as many as received Him," whether among His own people or among the nations, "to them He gave a right to become children of God, even to them that believe into His name" (τοῖς πιστεύουσιν εἰς τὸ ὄνομα αὐτοῦ), *i.e.* who accept Him implicitly as being all that He may assert Himself to be. Ideally, a man's name is the full expression and connotation of the man's personality. The "name" of God is the complete manifestation of God's being and action. The "name" of the God-Man is everything that is implied in His Godhead, and everything that is implied in His Manhood, *e.g.* all that is implied in His Incarnation, in His life, in His death, in His resurrection, in His Ascension, and in all that He has yet to do. None can grasp His fulness: none can make all of it

explicit to himself: we believe into all of it implicitly and thence move on to sight: some come to see more than others even in this life, make explicit to themselves something, be it more or less, of what was before implicit; but the link of one and all to Him in this life is faith.

The phrase "to believe into Him" (*πιστεύειν εἰς αὐτόν*), which we shall come upon later, has very much the same meaning as "to believe into His name."

(13) "Who were begotten, not of blood, nor of the will of the flesh, nor of the will of man, but of God." All who receive Him, or in other words "believe into His name," do so by virtue of some principle of Life implanted in them from God analogous to the principle of life implanted from a human father. And this new state of being "begotten" does not originate "from blood," *i.e.* does not depend on racial origin such as the being physically descendants of Abraham: nor yet does it originate "from the will of the flesh," *i.e.* does not depend on human affection, for neither brother nor friend can secure it for brother or friend: nor yet does it originate "from the will of man," for man cannot secure it for other men, however wide or warm his sympathies with the race may be, nor yet can he secure it for himself unaided: but it originates from God. None can believe unless God first come to aid him.*

(14) "And the Word became flesh." In these words John goes on to explain to us in what way it was that the Light "came into the world": in what form God the Word "came to His own" and was rejected by His own people. He came as Man, not as unembodied man, nor yet with a body consisting of matter peculiarly modified as the Docetæ thought: but He came among us with

* What then of the mass of the human race? We may believe that there is a vast organized Ministry working in the underworld started by our Lord Himself when "He descended into Hades" and "preached to the spirits which were in ward which sometime were disobedient what time the long-suffering of God waited in the days of Noah" (1 Pet. iii. 19, 20). Certainly the ministry in Hades was not confined to them: they are named merely as representing the highest pitch of wickedness reached by Adam's race. If the gospel was brought to them, then much more to all others.

man's material body of flesh, nerve, blood, bone: His body was of matter similarly modified as is the matter of our own bodies.

By taking to Himself that material body of flesh, He has signified that matter shall never be annihilated, however He may modify it.

In saying He "became flesh," John does not say He became *a* Man, but rather He became Man: for, in assuming human nature to Himself, He did not assume also a second Personality: His Personality is single, He is God the Word, God the Son: He never laid aside His Divine nature: He merely linked to it a human nature—the link being His Personality. As in Adam lay all his descendants, so in the New Adam they lie re-formed.

"And dwelt among us." The word rendered "dwelt" is ἐσκήνωσεν, the root idea of which seems to be *a shelter or dwelling place* (and only incidentally a tent or a booth). As such, it exactly corresponds with the Heb. *šakan* = to dwell (hence *miškan* = dwelling-place): and the radical letters are s, k, n in both Greek and Hebrew. We may be certain that John had in his mind the Heb. *miškan*, the regular word in the Old Testament for the Tabernacle, the Dwelling-place of God, consisting of wooden walls and ceiling-curtains, as distinct from the mere tent-curtains (*'ohel*) that covered these. There would seem to be no allusion in John's word ἐσκήνωσεν to the shortness or transitoriness of His sojourn among us: for though the idea of temporariness might attach to a tent, this appears to be the exact opposite of what was meant to be conveyed by the institution of the Feast of Tabernacles or *Booths* (σκηνοπηγία), viz. a promise of permanent occupation of a land of their own as against a nomad *tenting* in the wilderness.

"And we beheld His glory, a glory as of the Only-Begotten from The Father (καὶ ἐθεασάμεθα τὴν δόξαν αὐτοῦ, δόξαν ὡς Μονογενοῦς παρὰ Πατρός)." In these words John carries on the idea of the word ἐσκήνωσεν—how our Lord's human body corresponds with the *miškan*, the Tabernacle, the Dwelling-place of God under the Old

Covenant. As in the Tabernacle *miškan*, the dazzling cloud of glory showed the presence of God, so from this other *miškan* or Dwelling-place of God, viz. our Lord's human body, was seen to emanate His dazzling glory. In saying "we beheld," John refers to the night of the Transfiguration on Mt. Tabor when for once our Lord allowed His glory to shine forth: such glory as might be expected to pour forth from Him, and Him alone, who is the Only-Begotten Son, come from the presence of The Father to earth—yet ever being Begotten by, and ever present with, The Father. To that same night Peter refers in 2 Pet. i. 17, 18.

"Full of Grace and Truth." This clause, in the Greek, is probably in apposition * to the subject of "dwelt among us." As John looks back on Him in memory, or contemplates the ever-present image of Him, this is how he sums Him: "full of Beauty (χάριτος) and of Truth": Beauty (or Grace) to appeal to, and to perfect, man's ethical and æsthetical nature; Truth to appeal to, and to perfect, man's intellectual nature. Beauty and Truth: in these two ideas all is summed for Man: as Augustine felt when, regretting his wasted youth, he cried, "Too late have I known Thee, ancient Truth: too late have I loved Thee, perfect Beauty."

(*With verse* 14 *ends the Prologue.*)

* Substantially it matters nothing whether we take the word πλήρης ("full of") to be a declinable adjective, or indeclinable as recent discoveries in Hellenistic Greek seem to warrant.

§ II

JOHN I. 15–51

John the Baptist's witness. The founding of a new organization to take the place of the Sanhedrin.

(15) HERE the Evangelist begins the record of what his earliest teacher, his cousin John the Baptist, had taught about the person of Jesus:—a teaching which John the Evangelist, the pupil, has just been amplifying in his prologue. The record begins with the opening day of our Lord's ministry, the day of His baptism by John. As for the month and day of that baptism, see pp. 31, 32.

(15–18) This is the Baptist's first witness that the Evangelist quotes. It was spoken not earlier than the day of the Baptism of Jesus:—

A.D. 28.
Jan. 18 / Tebeth 25 } Sun.

(15) "John bears witness concerning Him, and he hath cried aloud" (κέκραγε, sc. officially and with no uncertain voice) "saying—*it was this man* [sc. John Baptist] *who spake*—'He who comes after me, etc.'" Such is the reading adopted by Westcott and Hort. The Evangelist thereby draws especial attention to the fact that the words which follow are those of the greatest of all the prophets, of one greater than any mere prophet, viz. the Messiah's official herald the Baptist.

The witness refers,

A. to the eternal pre-existence of Jesus Christ:—"'He who comes after me,'" sc. in point of time into the world, and in point of place as being preceded by His herald, "'has become (γέγονε) in advance of me, because He was before me (ὅτι πρῶτός μου ἦν).'" The phrase πρῶτός μου ἦν arrests attention: this pregnant use of πρῶτος with a genitive is common in Hellenistic Greek: it signifies not only "was in existence *before* me (πρὶν, or πρότερος)," but also was *the first of any* to have existence: it occurs again at verse 30: cf. also xv. 18.

B. to His Divine relationship to us:—

(16) "'Because'" (the Evangelist is still quoting* from his earliest master the Baptist) "'it was out of His fulness that we all received, and grace for grace,'" *i.e.* He gave to us all to share in His Fulness. What Fulness? The same which Paul also names as "dwelling in Jesus Christ" (Col. ii. 9), "all the Fulness of The Godhead" (πᾶν τὸ πλήρωμα τῆς Θεότητος), and again (Col. i. 19) "in Him all the Fulness (πᾶν τὸ πλήρωμα) was well-pleased to dwell, and by means of Him to change-back-again all things unto Him."

Who are "we all"? The emphatic "we" (ἡμεῖς) points to a definite body of people among whom the Baptist includes himself; and these can be no other than Christians: "all we" Christians whether Jew or Gentile. "We all received": When? When we became Christians by faith and baptism. The Baptist speaks for all Christians, Gentile and Jew, for he was well aware (as we shall see) that the Jews would reject the Lord, and be replaced, for a time, by Gentiles. He talks from the standpoint of a full, baptized, Christian: because, as S. Evodius (1st century and immediate successor to Peter as bishop of Antioch) says in his epistle τὸ φῶς, the Baptist was baptized by Christ immediately after he had baptized Christ: so also says Chrysostom, Origen, Gregory Nazianzen, and Jerome.

"'And (we received) grace upon grace (χάριν ἀντὶ χάριτος).'" When? When by faith and baptism we received of His Fulness: for we then received an automatic stream of grace from Him which was to be ever present for our daily needs—not perhaps as we see our needs, but as He sees them.

(17) "'Because whereas the Law was given by means

* Origen, and, I think, the Fathers in general extend the quotation of John the Baptist's words to the end of verse 18, for they perceive the Evangelist's motive in quoting the words of the Forerunner and Herald. The moderns are misled, both here and at iii. 31–36, by a difficulty in crediting the Baptist with so clear a vision and by an unwarranted inference as to style and terminology.

of Moses, Grace and Truth came by means of Jesus Christ.' " The Law or Old Covenant of Sinai was no doubt a great gift and privilege bestowed on Israel by God by means of Moses. Its commands kept alive ideals of virtue though it gave not power to attain: and its ceremonies were an adumbration of a reality, though the reality—means and end—was not yet manifested. But a far greater gift was to come, viz.—

" 'Grace and Truth came by means of Jesus Christ,' " *i.e.* Firstly, Jesus Christ brought to us *grace* to attain to that ideal Grace, that moral Beauty, that Virtue, to which the Law kept pointing, but to which it could not lift:—that ideal relationship between God and man, away from which we fell in Eden, but back to which all the sacrifices and ceremonies of the Law indicated a sometime return. In this ideal status human nature was manifested in the person of Jesus Christ, and through union with Him by faith and baptism all may ultimately attain to it. Secondly, Jesus Christ brought to us *truth*—power to see Truth—by rekindling His Light in our intellect.

(18) Far away greater is Jesus than any before Him: for, continues the Baptist, " 'The Godhead (Θεὸν without the article) no one (not even Moses) has ever yet seen: God Only-Begotten who is in the bosom of The Father, *He* interpreted Him.' " Moses saw but the "back" of God (Exod. xxxiii. 20–23): but Jesus Christ not only has seen Him, but *is* the Godhead-Begotten (Θεὸς μονογενὴς) Who dwells eternally in the "bosom" of the Godhead-Begetting (τοῦ Πατρός): and it is this Godhead-Begotten Who became man as Jesus Christ and interpreted to us the Godhead. Such is the Baptist's clear vision of the Person of Jesus Christ, viz. as being the Godhead-Begotten by the Godhead-Begetting: nor is any one else so, for He is the Only-Begotten, μονογενής. For though we, the adopted sons, are "begotten of God," not as He, so we. He the Essential Son, we sons by creation and by grace. Here is the Baptist's statement of that eternal Flux and Reflux of the Godhead whom we call The Father (Begetting) and The Son (Begotten).

Such was the witness borne by the Baptist on the day he baptized Jesus (Sunday, Jan. 18, A.D. 28), and was in turn baptized by Him: for this was the first day he received warrant for his official nomination of Jesus to the nation as the Christ, or Messiah, as he here calls Him (verse 17). The Baptist's announcements recorded in Matt. iii. 7, 12: Mark i. 7, 8: Luke iii. 7–14, were given before this day, and therefore do not name the Messiah, but only announce that He is coming, and that He is a greater One than His herald. The Baptist knew all along that Jesus is this Messiah—had always known it—but had been told to wait for the appointed sign before he made his official nomination.

But, it is objected, is it possible that the Baptist could have had so clear a vision of our Lord's Divinity?

If he had not this clear vision he was not competent to 'make the way straight before Him.' What sort of herald would he be who does not understand the King whom he announces? What sort of witness to the Light (John i. 8) would he be who knows not the Divine nature of that Light? The Baptist's knowledge and vision of the King was such as none other before him had had, except the Mother.* For this reason he had been sanctified in the womb by the visit to Elizabeth of Mary bearing within her God-Incarnate: at the very sound of the voice of the God-bearing Mother, the unborn six-month babe had leapt for delight (Luke i. 40–45). For thirty years in the desert had the Baptist lived in unbroken contemplation and communion with God, ever musing on the mystery of his own mission as declared in his father's prophecy, "thou, child, shalt be called the prophet of the Most High, for thou shalt go-before to prepare before Jehovah His ways" (Luke i. 76); and as declared in Malachi's prophecy (iii. 1), "behold Me, I send My messenger and he shall prepare the way before Me." 'Therefore,' mused John, 'He who sent me is the same as He for whom I am to

* It is the Catholic tradition that not only was the Mother baptized by Jesus, but Joseph also was baptized by Him: and thus these two were illumined even before John the Baptist to the perception of the Trinity.

prepare the way: therefore He whom I herald existed previously to me, as Micah seems to have seen, saying (v. 2), "His goings forth have been from of old from everlasting": indeed my father's prophecy says that He whom I herald is Jehovah Himself, as also Malachi (iii. 1) implies, and of this, Isaiah (ix. 6) seems to have had intimation when he calls Messiah "Mighty God" and "Immanuel," or God is with us.'

This mystery that Messiah was no other than the manifestation of Jehovah was for the Baptist the key to the books of Moses and the Prophets: his vision grew in clearness with the years. From his earliest infancy he had known that his little Cousin Jesus was the Messiah: therefore Jesus must be somehow God incarnate: and the amplitude of light as to how and in what sense Jehovah was incarnate in Jesus burst upon him on the day he baptized Jesus with water; for later on that day, as the Fathers have handed down, John was in turn baptized, but with a greater baptism—baptized by Him who alone baptizes with the Holy Spirit. Being thus illumined by this baptism, he would understand the words he had heard immediately before when ascending out of the river from baptizing Jesus, viz. "This is My beloved Son": and in a flash would grasp the mystery of the Trinity—how Jehovah is three Persons in one Godhead, and all Three were here present, the Godhead-Begetting (or The Father) speaking of "My Son": and the Godhead-Begotten (or The Son), viz. Jesus, "My Son"—and the Breath of the Godhead (*πνεῦμα*), viz. the Holy Spirit, under the form of a dove (Matt. iii. 16, 17: Mark i. 10, 11: Luke iii. 21, 22).

We rarely do justice in our thoughts to John the Baptist "than whom a greater hath not been born of woman": he who was "more than a prophet," for he was the Messenger to prepare the way before Messiah-Jehovah, and, as such, fully qualified by knowledge of Messiah's two natures, God and Man. Officially the Church has marked the greatness of the Baptist in that he alone with Jesus and with Mary has his birthday commemorated.

What exactly was the position immediately before

John's official nomination of Jesus as the Messiah, "who baptizeth with the Holy Spirit"? John had hitherto been universally recognized by people and Sanhedrin as Messiah's forerunner, whose mission it was to prepare the nation for Him, to identify Him officially, and to make His nature known to them:—the details of John's birth being familiar to all. Not only so, but the Boy Jesus up to the age of twelve had been recognized by the nation and Sanhedrin as being the Messiah—many details of His birth also being familiar to all (but not His being born of a Virgin). In the case of Jesus, however, there arose a strong and growing prejudice against Him, owing to His up-bringing in Galilee and in the obscurity of Nazareth, instead of in Judæa and the royal cities of Jerusalem and Bethlehem. So late as His thirteenth year He is still the hope of the Sanhedrin: see the honour with which they treated Him (Luke ii. 46, 47).

A.D. 10.

Thereafter, as He held back at Nazareth, though now no more a Child, occupying Himself as a carpenter, the resentment against Him increased. In vain, as each year He came to the festivals, did He converse with the representatives of the nation and the theologians in the temple, seeking to modify their carnal views of Messiah's reign and to raise them into the atmosphere of a Kingdom based on a moral and spiritual re-formation of mankind: a Kingdom wherein the King shall literally communicate His own excellence to all His subjects individually—beginning with His own nation in Holy Land and extending thence to the ends of the earth. His talk would be confined to the Sanhedrin, for His aim would be to win them first, seeing that otherwise the nation could not be won. To the Sanhedrin such views of Messiah's Kingdom were alien and abhorrent, for they themselves were alien to the Spirit of God. Their resentment had grown to open hostility against Him, and to a definite rejection of One who came preaching a Kingdom of God of so unattractive a form. The people had followed their lead, being no less alien to God's Spirit than were their leaders, for a nation has ever the leaders it deserves.

When John the Baptist opened the 30th Jubilee * with a national call to a baptism of "repentance unto remission of sins," it was known that he would soon officially make known the Messiah and so complete his mission: the Sanhedrin were aware that he was only waiting for the sign by which (as had been divinely told him) he should know Him. Such was the position when suddenly the Baptist announced officially to the Sanhedrin (μαρτυρεῖ καὶ κέκραγε, John i. 15) in Jan. A.D. 28, that he had seen the sign, and that the Messiah was Jesus whether they liked it or no. The announcements of Matt. iii. 7–12: Mark i. 7, 8: Luke iii. 7–14, are, as has been said, of an earlier date than that of John i. 15–18.

A.D. 27. **Oct. / Tisri**

A.D. 28. **Jan. 18 / Tebeth 25** **Sun.**

How was the intelligence received? Jesus had at once (Sun., Jan. 18) withdrawn into the desert and there for forty days (until Thurs., Feb. 26) remained in retirement:—forty days of respite given to the Sanhedrin during which to reconsider their position now that John had spoken,—John whom all

A.D. 28. **Sun., Jan. 18 to Thurs., Feb. 26.**

* The Jubilee era or starting-point was Oct. 1444 B.C., when the nation were first able to sow in peace (Joshua xi. 23). Thus the 1st Jubilee year was the year Oct. 1395 to Oct. 1394 B.C.: the 2nd was Oct. 1346 to Oct. 1345 B.C.: the 3rd was Oct. 1297 to Oct. 1296 B.C.: and so on: the 15th being Oct. 709 to Oct. 708 B.C., see Is. xxxvii. 30, where "the second year" is the Jubilee year Oct. 709 to Oct. 708 B.C., following the Sabbatical year Oct. 710 to Oct. 709 B.C. Thus the 30th Jubilee would be, in a straight count, the year Oct. A.D. 27 to Oct. A.D. 28. It was in Oct. A.D. 27 that the Baptist began his ministry, and it was in Jan. A.D. 28 that Christ began His public ministry with His Baptism. In this same Jubilee year, "a welcome *Lord's-year*" (ἐνιαυτὸν Κυρίου δεκτόν, Luke iv. 19), He was preaching in Nazareth.

True, no Jubilees were observed after the return from Babylon, but the straight run from the Jubilee era will bring the 30th Jubilee to the year Oct. A.D. 27 to Oct. A.D. 28. Jubilee years and Sabbatical years began like the civil years in the autumn, in Tisri, the "seventh" ecclesiastical month. Only the ecclesiastical year began in the spring, in Nisan (=Abib), the "first" ecclesiastical month, and that only since the Exodus (Exod. xii. 2: Deut. xvi. 1).

The Jubilee-year scale did not break the Sabbatical-year scale, but was superimposed upon it; so that a Jubilee year always followed on a Sabbatical year, and came every 50th year (both termini being counted), and coincided with the first year of a Sabbatical-year cycle. The Jubilee-year was not so much the wind-up of a past period as the inauguration of a new one with new hope.

admitted to be a prophet and sent for the very purpose of making Messiah known.

It appears that the Sanhedrin refused to modify their attitude with regard to Jesus, refused to entertain again the idea of Him as Messiah, took refuge in the quibble that Micah had prophesied He should come from Bethlehem, how then could He be from Nazareth? They purposely confound ἐκ that marks the place of nativity with ἀπὸ that marks the place of residence: again, it was a tenet of the schools that when Messiah came none would know His parentage (John vii. 27), whereas "'do we not all know Jesus to be the son of Joseph and Mary?'" Herein they ignored what during all His early years they had admitted, viz. that He was Messiah and therefore somehow of Divine origin.

On the other hand, they could hardly afford to ignore John and his testimony—such a hold had he upon the whole nation. What should be done? They would compromise with John. They would bribe him with an offer to recognize *him* as the Messiah, instead of Jesus. Would he consent?

A.D. 28.
Feb. 26 / Adar 5 } Thurs.

(19) With this object they sent an official deputation to him.

It is at this point that John the Evangelist resumes his narrative to give the second momentous testimony of the Baptist. The date is (Thurs., Feb. 26 of A.D. 28) forty days after that of the first testimony recorded in verses 15–18. It is the last day of our Lord's forty days of retirement: the day on which He had thrice repelled the temptations of Satan (Matt. iv. 1–11). John also shall to-day come forth victorious. It seems to be the afternoon: and Jesus, straight from His recent victory, is present (verse 26).

To understand the interview (19–28) that follows, we must picture the publicity in which it took place, the attendant crowds who are present to hear John's formal answer to the Sanhedrin's formal inquiry. The Sanhedrin, we may suppose, have already felt their way by hints formally conveyed to John; perhaps John has purposely let them deceive themselves as to his intentions, in order that their confusion to-day may be the more public. It is this dramatic moment to which Luke refers in iii. 15–17: at no other moment can any one (let alone the nation collectively) have awaited John's declaration of himself as Messiah. The deputation cannot overtly offer their bribe; overtly they can only suggest; but they know that John will understand.

(19) The question the deputation put to John, "Thou, who art thou?" (σὺ τίς εἶ) is an invitation from the Sanhedrin to John to announce himself as Messiah, and is also a promise that they are in that case ready to recognize him as such. This is clear from the next sentence:

(20) "And he confessed (sc. Jesus), and denied not (sc. Jesus): and his confession was in these words, 'it is not I who am the Christ (οὐκ εἰμὶ ἐγὼ ὁ Χριστός).'" That was John's first discomfiture of them.

(21) "What then? Thou art Elijah?" *i.e.* 'Say you are Elijah and expectant of a Messiah shortly to come: but you must deny that Jesus is the Messiah: and the Sanhedrin will support you.' And Elijah, perhaps, they had long thought him to be—the Elijah promised by Malachi (iv. 5, 6)—until he opened his mission by announcing himself, not as Elijah of Mal. iv. 5, but as "a Voice of one crying," etc., quoting Is. xl. 3:—a Voice not at all auspicious for them as they read on to that horror of the herald's vision in verses 6, 7, where he sees no sequel of happiness and blessedness, but the People mysteriously blighted and dying under the simoom of God's wrath.

"I am not," answered John. For John knew that Elijah was to be the forerunner of Messiah's second Coming, and would be successful in his mission to the nation (Mal. iv. 5, 6): whereas he, John, was the forerunner of the first Coming, which was to be followed by the terrible judgment on the nation foretold by Malachi (iii. 1–3). To this prophecy, as to all others that were inauspicious, the scribes or exegetists shut their eyes. This was his second blow.

"Then perhaps thou art The Prophet?" alluding to Deut. xviii. 18, 19, *i.e.* 'You have but to say so, and we promise you from the Sanhedrin their support.' This Prophet of Deut. xviii. 18 was by many understood to be the same as Messiah (see John vi. 14), and rightly so (see Acts iii. 22, etc.: vii. 37); so, too, understood by the Samaritans (John iv. 26): but by others this Prophet was distinguished from Messiah (vii. 40, 41) and variously identified as (1) a reappearance of Jeremiah (Matt. xvi. 14) whose end was wrapped in mystery, for none knew where he died; or (2) a reappearance of one of the archaic prophets (*προφητής τις τῶν ἀρχαίων*, Luke ix. 19), viz. Enoch who had not died. 'Anyway,' reasoned the Sanhedrin, 'there is doubt about the identity of the Prophet of Deut. xviii.: and if John refuses to pass as Messiah or as Elijah, let him claim to be the unknown Prophet, and we will support him: his own father's words (Luke i. 76) will not be amiss: in short, let him advance any claim for himself, provided only he withdraws his nomination of Jesus as Messiah.' Assuming John to be tempered like themselves, and liable to an appeal to ambition and self-seeking, they had hoped to silence his awkward testimony to Jesus.

Again he answered, abruptly, "No." This was their third discomfiture.

(22) "Therefore they said to him, 'Who art thou? that we may give an answer to those who sent us'": Finding John deaf to the three definite offers the Sanhedrin had commissioned them to make, the deputation suggest to him to name his own terms: what shall they report to the Sanhedrin? Then, to their confusion, they hear him say

(23) that he is that herald whose voice Isaiah spoke of, "I am a Voice of one crying in the wilderness, 'Make straight the way of Jehovah,' as said the prophet Isaiah" (Is. xl. 3): and let them remember how the glad voice of that herald was turned to dismay and horror at the vision of the People blighted by the blast of the Lord instead of being vivified: and why? (Is. xl. 6, 7.)

(24–27) The interview is continued to its close.

(24) "And there had been sent certain from among the Pharisees," *i.e.* some of the above deputation belonged, as was natural, to the sect of the Pharisees. It was these who, speaking *quâ* Pharisees, now began to save the face of the Sanhedrin by (25) questioning John's right to baptize at all. 'It was whilst you were baptizing that you saw the sign: but why are you baptizing at all? You say you are not Messiah; He we know will baptize with water and with The Spirit as Ezekiel (xxxvi. 25–27) and Joel (ii. 28) have foretold: you say you are not His forerunner Elijah, nor yet the unknown prophet; each of them no doubt will baptize us with water preparatory to the new Covenant of Messiah—it would be analogous with that sprinkling of water with which we were baptized * preparatory to the Covenant of Sinai. It was only because we understood you to be Elijah or possibly the unknown Prophet, that we came to your baptism or approved it for the people.' The Pharisees are speaking as the supervisors of rites and ceremonies without which all religions risk a degeneration to formless chaos.

(26) 'Though I am not Elijah (who is to come hereafter), nor yet your unknown Prophet, I am still Messiah's forerunner: such, as you have always known, Gabriel (Luke i. 17) and my father (Luke i. 76) announced me. For that reason I prepare you for Him, and come baptizing you with water as a seal of the fast-approaching remission of your sins by the King at His coming, if there is repentance and confession. But Messiah I am not: His baptizing, as you rightly say, will be with the Holy Spirit and with the fire that scorches sin—sin, from whose tyranny my baptizing-with-water has no power to deliver. He is the Mighty One: I am but His herald in advance. He stands there among you (μέσος ὑμῶν στήκει)'—pointing to Jesus—'the Man whom you know not (sc. whom you refuse to recognize because you cannot understand Him):

* So the Rabbis understood Exod. xix. 10. Similarly they recognized an earlier baptism of the whole of Jacob's household (Gen. xxxiv. 2) in the year of his re-entry into Holy Land west of Jordan.

the Man upon whom I saw the promised sign, and whom I named to your Sanhedrin officially six weeks ago. You invite me to come forward in His stead ; why, I am not worthy to loose His shoe : you think to set your faces against Him ; I warn you He is come to winnow the chaff from the wheat ; your time is short ; the issues of to-day's decision are momentous for you and the nation.'

Such was the purport of John's answer to-day, as we gather from a comparison of John i. 19–27 with Luke iii. 15–17. It is no new thing that the Baptist has told the deputation : they make no inquiry as to whom he means : they know he means Jesus of Nazareth, the Man whom for thirty years the Sanhedrin have had under observation, and from whom they have long since split.

(28) The interview took place at Bethany (House of the ferry-boat) on the east bank of Jordan at the spot called in Origen's time Bethabara (House of the ford)—the traditional place * of the passage of the Ark and the nation under Joshua (Joshua iii. 14–17).

Perhaps the Evangelist's reason for naming the place is a reflexion that if the deputation of to-day had been sent to welcome John's nominee, here was He standing on historic ground ready to enter the Promised Land as the promised King of the nation.

Disappointed, the embassy return to Jerusalem to report that John is intractable, and that there is no change in the situation.

(29) Meanwhile on the banks of the Jordan the drama unfolds : and the Baptist gives his third momentous testimony :—

A.D. 28.
Feb. 27 } Fri.
Adar 6 }

" On the following day (Friday, Feb. 27) John sees Jesus coming to him," coming from the grotto in the Qarantal Mountain (behind Jericho), where His forty days of fast had been passed. He comes in order that John His forerunner may bear witness to the future that awaits the King. " Behold," says John, " the Lamb of God who bears the sin of the world." At the hands of His people He will suffer death : He will give Himself as the

* The place is some five miles north of the present north end of the Dead Sea.

expiatory Sacrifice not only of the sins of His people, but of the germ of all sin in Adam's descendants, the sin of the world, the apostasy in Eden: thus wide and deep is the Baptist's vision. 'He is the Antitype of every sacrifice ordained (Gen. iii. 21, "skins": Gen. iv. 4) since Adam's sin: He is the archetypal sacrificial Lamb prefigured on the primeval Book of the Heavens—the Aries of the Zodiac, the Lamb who was slain from the foundation of the world (ἀπὸ καταβολῆς κόσμου, Rev. xiii. 8: 1 Pet. i. 20: and cf. Heb. ix. 26): He is the Lamb whom God was to provide for Himself (Gen. xxii. 8): He is the Paschal Lamb of Israel (Exod. xii. 3–14): He is the Lamb whom Isaiah (liii.) saw to be no other than the Man who was to be "despised by us," the nation, the Man upon whom "Jehovah laid the iniquity of us all," the Man who was to "bear the sin of many."' He is the Lamb whom the Baptist, with yet clearer vision, has already declared (John i. 15–18) to be not only Man, but also the eternal Son of the eternal Father: He is Jehovah who says of Himself (Zech. xii. 10) "they shall look upon Me whom they pierced."

The phrase used here by the Baptist, αἴρειν ἁμαρτίαν, "to bear sin," is exactly the Hebrew *nasa' ḥeṭ'*="*He bore the sin* of many" (Is. liii. 12); the idea of the Greek and Hebrew verbs being that of *lifting up* and so of *carrying:* the same Hebrew verb occurs again in Lev. xvi. 22, where the scapegoat is said to "*bear* upon him all their iniquities unto a land not inhabited": and again in Lev. x. 17, where the priests by eating the sin-offering are said to "*bear* the iniquity of the congregation."

"Behold, the Lamb of God who beareth the sin of the world." The words are said aloud by John for all present to hear: his announcement made six weeks ago to the Sanhedrin (the nation's appointed rulers) has been in vain: he now declares publicly, but mystically, for such as have ears to hear, the expiatory death of this Messiah God-and-Man. Only afterwards could the Evangelist, as he looked back, have caught the Baptist's full meaning.

(30) "This is He on behalf of whom I (ἐγώ, *I* whom all

know to be the appointed herald) said, 'After me cometh a Man who has become before me: because He was before me.'"* 'At first (from Oct. to Jan.), I foretold His coming without identifying Him: to-day (Feb. 27) I point Him out to all, as, six weeks ago, I pointed Him out officially to the Sanhedrin immediately after I saw the sign' (viz. on Jan. 18).

(31) "And I was not knowing Him (κἀγὼ οὐκ ᾔδειν αὐτόν)," *i.e.* officially. 'Remember, my witness to Him is not consequent on my intimate acquaintance with Him from of old. Though I personally knew Him all my life to be Messiah, as for many years our Sanhedrin also regarded Him, I made no official announcement about Him; for as yet I had no warrant to do so: my commission was definite: as you all know, I came (ἦλθον) baptizing the nation, having been divinely informed that it would be during this baptism that Messiah would be manifested to Israel.'

(32) So important does the Evangelist think it that his readers should know what the Baptist said here on this matter, that he gives an exact Greek rendering of the Aramaic words which he himself had heard spoken:—"I have beheld (τεθέαμαι) The Spirit descending as a dove out of heaven, and it abode on Him: (33) and I was not knowing Him: but He who sent me to baptize in water He said to me, 'Upon whomsoever thou shalt see The Spirit descending and abiding on Him, that is He who baptizes in the Holy Spirit.'" "That is He who baptizes in the Holy Spirit," *i.e.* incorporates into Himself

* "Was before me" (πρῶτός μου ἦν). But the Greek means much more: not only "was before me" (*i.e.* existed before I existed), but also "was the first of any to have existence." See also verse 15, and xv. 18. For this use of a superlative with a genitive cf. 2 Macc. vii. 41, ἐσχάτη τῶν υἱῶν ἡ μήτηρ ἐτελεύτησεν, "the mother died *last of all* and *later than* her sons." This pregnant use of πρῶτος seems to be the explanation of Luke ii. 2, where the idiom means "this was the *first* census ever made, and it was made *before* Quirinius was governor of Syria": the notice thus distinguishes it from the census made under Quirinius some nine years later, in A.D. 6; to which later one reference is made by Gamaliel in Acts v. 37. See Wieseler's *Synopsis*, Part I. chap. 2, where will also be found a list of many famous grammarians in support.

by baptizing in the Creative Spirit, The Spirit which proceeds from His Godhead and rests in Its entirety on His manhood. This integral descent and abiding, symbolized by the one and integral form of a dove (as against the many and distributed tongues of fire in Acts ii. 3) signified that He on whom it descended was the integral Godhead : ‘ for God gives not The Spirit by measure to Him.’

The divine communication to John was not “ that is the Messiah ” : that much John knew already : but “ that is He who baptizes in (ἐν) the Holy Spirit.” What then ? Here was a distinct invitation to John to ask Messiah to baptize him that so the Holy Spirit might illumine him yet further : and that John did so ask, and was baptized in turn by Jesus, is the tradition of the Fathers.

The words “ and *I* was not knowing Him ” (*κἀγὼ οὐκ ᾔδειν αὐτόν*) must be understood of official as against private cognizance : ‘ my private knowledge of Him as Messiah I was at this moment ignoring, waiting for the official sign of the Dove ’ : this appears from Matthew’s account of the Baptism (iii. 14, 15), from which it is plain that the Baptist had privately intimate acquaintance with Jesus, and knew Him to be the Lord (so Augustine *in Ioannem.* Tract. v. 8). The words must also be understood of imperfect knowledge as against perfect : ‘ even I, His herald, who knew Him to be Messiah, God-and-Man, did not as yet understand in what sense exactly He was Jehovah, for I knew not as yet the nature of the Three in One ’ : this is plain from the words that follow.

(34) “ And I have seen (*ἑώρακα*),” continues the Baptist, “ and have given-witness (*μεμαρτύρηκα*) that this is The Son of God.” Have seen what ? The dove descending and abiding on Him ? No : that he has already told us in verse 32 : rather, ‘ I have seen that this is The Son of God : on that day (Jan. 18) six weeks ago, I not only saw upon the Man the sign that I was told to wait for—the sign we were all awaiting, but I was to seek yet further illumination from that Man : I did so on that day and was baptized by Him in, or with, The Spirit, and was illumined as to His Person in the Trinity : with

the result that I have seen and have given my witness (verses 15–18), that He is The Son of God.'

In naming Him "The Son of God," the Baptist speaks with unclouded vision: he means nothing less than the full Christian doctrine that the Man Jesus is also the eternal Son of the eternal Father, co-equal, co-eternal. As we have seen (at verse 18) it was on the day he baptized Jesus (Sunday, Jan. 18), and *was himself baptized by Jesus*, as the Fathers * have handed down, that John received full illumination concerning the Trinity, and there and then witnessed to Jesus as being "God only-Begotten, He who is in the bosom of The Father" (verse 18), which is the full import of the term "The Son of God," as used by him to-day (Feb. 27).

In John the Baptist, the economy of the Law and the Prophets reached its acme. In John was focussed every ray of light that had vibrated in the Prophets across the mists of the times of expectation—John the last of the Prophets under the Law, the greatest of them, the sum of them. In the very womb of his mother he had recognized the God whose Incarnate presence he was later to announce. The flickering torch, that John received as the heir of all who went before, became in his hands "the lamp that burns and shines" (John v. 35): but not until after he was baptized by Messiah was he fully illumined as to what exactly was meant by the Divinity of Messiah, viz. that He is the Godhead-eternally-Begotten by the Godhead-eternally-Begetting. Not until Peter, some months later, makes his confession of Jesus as "the Christ The Son of the living God," shall we hear so clear a witness to our Lord: and even so, with Peter the vision stayed not: not till the Resurrection was his faith unalterably fixed.

As for the vision John had seen on Sunday, Jan. 18, A.D. 28, it is probable that only Jesus and he beheld it: "The heavens were opened unto him (*i.e.* to John), and he

* So Evodius (1st Century) says in his epistle, τὸ φῶς, quoted by Baronius, that the Baptist immediately after baptizing Christ was baptized by Him with the Spirit: so too the tradition is handed on by Gregory Naz., Chrysostom, Jerome. I have not been able to verify Baronius's quotation from Evodius.

saw the Spirit of God descending as a dove and coming upon Him. And lo, a Voice out of the heavens, saying, 'This is My Son the Beloved in whom I am well pleased'" (Matt. iii. 16, 17): where it is John, not Jesus, who is said to see the vision and hear the Voice, as appears from the lettering of the MSS. *επ αυτον*, on Him (not *εφ αυτον*, on Himself). The same appears from John's account (i. 32, 33). In Mark the lettering *εις αυτον* leaves it doubtful whether the *αυτον* is aspirated or not: but Mark will naturally be interpreted by the other Evangelists. It was for John's sake and not our Lord's that the vision came; as at the Transfiguration it was for the sake of the three Apostles, and not our Lord, that the vision was seen; and in the Temple (John xii. 30) it was for the sake of the Greeks, and not our Lord, that the Voice was heard.

What was the significance of the vision to John as he meditated on it? He had seen the whole Godhead *quâ* Holy Spirit descending out of heaven like a dove, and abiding on Jesus: and had heard the whole Godhead *quâ* the Father, or Godhead-Begetting, speaking, "This is My Beloved Son," sc. the Godhead-Begotten. This Jesus, then, is the Godhead Incarnate. Nearly thirty-one years ago (March 25, B.C. 4) the whole Godhead, *quâ* the Holy Spirit, had brooded over Mary and begotten of her a human embryo who is at once the Godhead-Begotten or eternal Son of God and humanity-begotten or Son of Adam. Whilst a Child He had grown and waxed strong in spirit, being filled with wisdom (*πληρούμενον σοφίας*, Luke ii. 40): *i.e.* being unceasingly and automatically filled in His human organism (body, soul, and spirit) according as that organism developed to its full strength. Again, as Boy and Man He had "advanced in wisdom and stature and grace with God and men" (Luke ii. 52), until He reached the full stature or age (*ἡλικία*) of man's capacity—the age or *ἡλικία* at which Adam had been created full-formed.

Whilst His manhood was yet embryotic in His Mother's womb Jesus was perfect God, had been so from eternity: but not till the age of thirty was He perfectly-developed man, because not till that age is the human organism perfected in its powers, the age at which service in the Tabernacle was originally allowed by Moses to begin (Num. iv. 3, 23, 30, etc.), the age at which a man could first be recognized as a teacher or Rabbi in Israel. And thus Luke, who told us of the Child being *unceasingly filled* (πληρούμενον) and of the Boy's *constant advance* (προέκοπτε), now tells us that He was " about thirty " (*i.e.* not to a day, but thirty years of age and some days over) at the time of His baptism or " beginning " of His ministry (iii. 23), and that He was *full* (πλήρης) of The Spirit when He returned from His baptism (iv. 1)—as though He were now at length fully developed man.

For all that, Jesus received nothing at His Baptism that He had not before: the Baptist merely saw that day in a visible symbol that which had actually and invisibly taken place nearly thirty-one years ago (on March 25, B.C. 4): with the difference that in B.C. 4 the descent of the Godhead had been upon an embryo or germinating cell, whereas in A.D. 28 it was upon that embryo full grown. From that earlier day the " descent and abiding " of the Godhead had been unceasing: completed in the first moment that Mary gave her consent, and yet unceasing.

Whereas the eternal Son was Begotten complete without beginning, and is unceasingly being Begotten of The Father, for to God all time is Now; the Incarnation took place at a moment in time, and the union of Godhead to Manhood in the Person of Jesus then completed is thenceforth unceasing.

The date of the Baptism cannot be accurately known. It is commemorated by all the Churches in January, and generally on Jan. 6, along with the Epiphany and the miracle of the water into wine: not that these three events are supposed to have occurred all on Jan. 6, but they each mark an inaugurating manifestation and as such are fittingly commemorated together on the anniversary of one of them. The first is known as the Epiphany or first manifestation to the Gentiles of God Incarnate: the accurate historical date of this was Jan. 6, B.C. 3.

The second is His official manifestation as the Son of God, to the nation in the person of John His forerunner: this was at His Baptism in A.D. 28. The third is the first manifestation of His power as God, in the opening miracle of His public ministry, the turning of water into wine at Kana, in March A.D. 28.

The only definite clue to the date of His Baptism is given in Dan. ix. 26, where it appears that "after the sixty-two weeks the Messiah shall be cut off." According to Hebrew usage, "after sixty-two weeks" may mean either "in the sixty-second week," or "after the sixty-second week is ended": the former is much the commoner and more idiomatic. If, then, we understand it as "in the sixty-second week," we may place the Baptism to Sunday, Jan. 18, in A.D. 28, for the sixty-second week thereafter will be the week from Sunday, March 20, to Saturday, March 26, of A.D. 29, which was the week and year in which His Passion and death occurred.

To return to the Evangelist's text:—

In verse 29 (p. 25) we were told that "on the day after" the Baptist had received and answered the Sanhedrin's deputation, "he sees Jesus coming to him." The day seems to be Friday, Feb. 27. Jesus was coming doubtless to converse with the Baptist and possibly to tell him that henceforth He opens His public ministry and begins to receive disciples: as the Sanhedrin ignore Him, He must work without them and train a society of His own to do the work those others should have done. Perhaps our Lord stayed with the Baptist this night.

A.D. 28.
Feb. 27 / Adar 6 } Fri.

(35) "The next day" (Saturday, Feb. 28) "John was standing and two of his disciples; and he looked upon Jesus walking and saith," etc. The contrast between the "standing" still and the "walking" is marked: it seems to point to the Baptist's resting on the Sabbath like every one else—1000 yards walk being the maximum distance allowed on a Sabbath; whereas Jesus as Lord of the Sabbath walked: cf. our Lord's manifest violation of the Sabbath in John

Feb. 28 / Adar 7 } Sat.

v. 8, in bidding the man carry his bed (see Jer. xvii. 21), which, as Chrysostom remarks, He there justifies (verse 17) by insisting on His own Godhead: and cf. Mark ii. 28. The contrast between John standing still and Jesus walking will also point to John's work being now finished when Jesus begins His: "He must increase, but I must decrease."

(36) It must not be supposed that the utterance "Behold, the Lamb of God" (ἴδε, ὁ ἀμνὸς τοῦ Θεοῦ) was all that John said on this occasion: these five words would hardly justify the use of λαλοῦντος, "talking," in verse 37. Rather they represent the pith of John's talk. John thus transfers over to Jesus, for initiation into deeper mysteries, such of his own disciples as were ready for the change.

(37) The first two to move (for probably all the twelve apostles were originally among John's disciples) were Andrew and John the Evangelist: for that the unnamed one was the Evangelist is asserted by the consensus of Church tradition. And they followed Jesus.

(38) And Jesus turned and saw them following, and saith to them, "What seek ye?" He knew perfectly but wished to encourage them to come and talk. They said to Him, "Rabbi, where abidest Thou?" Thereby they say they take Him as their Master, to be taught by Him; and imply they wish to go with Him for that purpose to wherever He is temporarily staying; where that is they naturally do not know, seeing that for the last six weeks He had entirely withdrawn Himself from public. Though the word Rabbi may seem inadequate after John's pronouncement about Him, it will convey their implicit acceptance here and now of all that the Baptist meant and of all that Jesus may have in store to tell them. All Faith is implicit before it can become explicit.

(39) "He saith to them, 'Come and ye shall see.' They came therefore and saw where He abides." The place was probably the grotto in the eastern face of the hill above Jericho, where all tradition says He had passed the forty days of His fast after His baptism: this grotto is some hundreds of feet above Jericho and has a noble

view over the Jordan plain with the mountains of Moab rising beyond the river and the Dead Sea. In saying "Come and ye shall see," sc. where I abide, our Lord meant more than the material grotto where He was dwelling: He meant also and mainly, 'Come and I will show you the sort of heart and disposition I require in My disciples if I am to abide in them.' And that day they learnt. As John subtly says, "they came and saw (not where He was abiding, but) where He abides (ποῦ μένει)."

"And they abode with Him that day: it was about the tenth hour," *i.e.* 10 a.m.: for John reckons the hours as we do—twelve hours from midnight to midday, and another twelve from midday to midnight—a method of notation not uncommon in the province of Asia (Ephesus) where he wrote. (See *Acts of Polycarp's Martyrdom*, VII.: Pliny, *Hist. Nat.* II. 70: Pliny, *Epist.* III. 5.) The other three instances of reckoning hours in John's gospel (iv. 6: iv. 52: xix. 14) will be considered in their places. The synoptic gospels reckon hours always as did commonly the Greeks, Romans, and Jews, viz. twelve hours from sunset to sunrise divided in three "watches," and another twelve hours from sunrise to sunset. The practice of the Roman forum, again (not infrequent to-day in South Italy and Sicily), was to reckon the hours from sunset to sunset in an unbroken count of twenty-four. The common interpretation, which assumes that John's reckoning is the same as that of the Synoptists, makes the "tenth hour" to be 4 p.m.: but, the time of year beng end of February, there will be no time for the subsequent events that occur to-day—it will be dark at 5 p.m.

(40) Our Lord, therefore, with Andrew and John the Evangelist, arrives at the grotto in Jebel Qarantal behind Jericho at 10 a.m. The two stay with Him that day to be taught by Him and no doubt shared His hospitality at the midday meal. Andrew goes to find his brother Simon, and brought him to Jesus—of course to the grotto: and it seems that later John too found his brother James and brought him—at least such is the fair inference from the words πρῶτον . . . τὸν ἴδιον.

Sat., Feb. 28.

"Andrew finds *first* of all *his own* brother Simon": which implies that afterwards the brother of the other of the two was also found and brought to the same place and on the same day. Both Simon and James were also doubtless among the Baptist's disciples, which will account for their being at this time in the neighbourhood of Jericho: it is also probable that all the twelve apostles had been first prepared by the Baptist.

(41) "We have found the Messiah," says Andrew to his brother. 'We all know how the Baptist announced officially six weeks ago that Jesus was He—the Jesus who has been brought up at Nazareth, whom we all know, whose birth was attended by those strange events, whom the Sanhedrin long recognized as Messiah till they threw Him over with contempt: but whom the Baptist, that great prophet, the forerunner, insists is He. We (John and I) are not only satisfied as you are that the Baptist is right, but we have found where the Messiah has been staying in retirement these last six weeks and where He is still. We have been with Him, listening to Him: He is about to come publicly forward; come and see Him.' Simon needed no urging: ever since John the Baptist had officially spoken, he had been ready to throw over the Sanhedrists and cast in his lot with Jesus of Nazareth, of whom in His early years it had been generally understood that He would one day come forward as the Messiah. Clearly Andrew and John and their brothers Simon and James had long been keenly interested in this matter of Jesus being the Messiah.

(42) Andrew brought Simon to Jesus. "Jesus having looked on him," as though reading his heart, which like all hearts was open to His sight, and approving him, "said 'Thou art Simon the son of John: thou shalt be called Kephas': which [the Evangelist adds for his Greek readers] is by interpretation Petros." As to this name Kephas: the Hebrew word is כֵּף (Kēph) and means rock (πέτρα), the outcropping rock, and never a stone: the Aramaic form (as our Lord spoke it) is כֵּיפָא (Kêphâ'), cf. Ki'phâ' (in the Syriac), and means a rock as in Hebrew,

though in the later Aramaic of the Targums it means also a stone. Kêphâ' becomes in Greek form Kēphas—the Greeks in such cases habitually turning a final weak guttural *aleph* (=') or *he* (=*h*) into S, *e.g.* Yehudah (Judah) becomes Ἰούδας (Judas): Manasseh becomes Manasses: Elijah becomes Elias; Jonah, Jonas, etc. Thus John, writing in Greek our Lord's Aramaic, naturally made His Kêphâ' (proper name) into Kēphas, then wishing to turn this proper name into a Greek proper name with the same meaning of *rock*, he was in difficulty, for if he rendered the Aramaic word (now Kēphas, rock) into the Greek for rock, he would have to write Πέτρα (Petra), which would be a feminine and not a masculine; this, therefore, he had to make into Πέτρος (Petros), the only possible masculine form. It was, he knew, not satisfactory, for this Greek word in the masculine happens to mean a stone, and not a rock, but the fault lay with the structural difference of the two languages.*

* Precisely the same difficulty, inherent in rendering one language into another, occurs in Matt. xvi. 18, "And I say to thee thou art Petros, and upon this *petra* I will build My church," etc. Our Lord's words, in the Aramaic He spoke, must have been (and see the Syriac version), "thou art Kêphâ' (כֵּיפָא), and upon this Kêphâ' (כֵּיפָא) I will build," etc., *i.e.* He must have used, as does the Syriac, exactly the same word in each half of the sentence: but in the turning of the words into Greek, the Greek language necessitated in the first clause ("thou art Kêphâ'"=petra=rock) the change of the feminine termination petr*a*, "rock," into the masculine termination petr*os*, to make a masculine proper name out of it, but thereby the original became obscured: obscured, however, only for a moment, for the following words prevent all misconception as to our Lord's meaning; for had He meant kêphâ' in the late Aramaic sense of a stone (πέτρος), Matthew's Greek translator (unless incompetent) must have rendered the Aramaic by ἐπὶ τούτῳ τῷ πέτρῳ = on this stone, instead of by ἐπὶ ταύτῃ τῇ πέτρᾳ = on this rock. The English language, translating straight from the Aramaic, would have given an exact equivalent, "thou art Rock (proper name Simon Rock—rock in nature and henceforth Rock in name), and on this Rock I will build," etc.: but as the English of our Lord's words is a translation of a Greek translation, we suffer for the structural difference of the Greek and Aramaic tongues. The Latin has the same abundance of inflexion as the Greek: "Tu es Petrus et super hanc petram" presents exactly the same obscurity, in place of the simplicity of the original Aramaic. Endless controversy had been spared us on this point had the Greek and Latin languages had as few inflexions as the Aramaic and English: the advocates of Peter's supremacy and see have in consequence been at a disadvantage in pressing Peter's claim, so long as their opponents could point in good faith to the difference

(43) "On the following day (Sunday, Feb. 29, A.D. 28) He willed to go-out into Galilee." This use of ἠθέλησεν ("willed") seems to be John's Greek rendering of the Hebrew הואיל, *hô'îl*, whose meaning is "to will and begin," commonly rendered by the LXX by ἤρξατο, "began," though the root means *to will emphatically* (see Gesenius's Heb. Lexicon, יָאַל, and Thesaurus). John thereby marks our Lord as deliberately making an initial move: as though this going-out (out of Judæa, the home country of the nation) into Galilee, an outlying province, noted a crisis; it is as though Judah (the Jews proper) were on this day recognized by our Lord as intractable. "He willed to go-out," and of course He went and the four disciples with Him. It would be better to punctuate this verse differently, and place a full stop after "Galilee": for what follows, viz. "And He findeth Philip, etc.," seems to have taken place on His arrival in Galilee, four days later. The words "on the third day" (ii. 1) are not to be reckoned from the date of His leaving Judæa (as is generally assumed), but from the date of His arrival in Galilee.

A.D. 28.
Feb. 29 / Adar 8 } Sun.

From Jebel Qarantal (behind Jericho), whence He started for Galilee, it is a four days' journey, whether (by way of Samaria) to Nazareth and Kana, or (by way of the Jordan valley) to Bethsaida and Capernaum. We are not told where in Galilee He went, but from the mention of His "finding" Philip, and of Philip's being "a resident of (ἀπὸ) Bethsaida," it is natural to suppose that He went to Bethsaida, and there found Philip. What He "found" He was seeking, and knew where to find, and did not come upon by accident.

Feb. 29 / Adar 8 } Sun.

Yet another reason makes it probable that our Lord went, not to Nazareth, but to Bethsaida and Capernaum, when "He willed to go-out to Galilee," viz. His wish to

between Petros (stone) and petra (rock), as though "Peter" and "this rock" had different denotation; but stoutly the Catholics stuck to what they knew was meant, even whilst the general unfamiliarity with the Semitic tongues hindered them from driving home the argument.

prepare for His approaching removal to Capernaum from Nazareth (ii. 12). Here at Capernaum He would on this occasion be the guest of Peter, His chief disciple. All tradition places Peter's house in Capernaum (and cf. Mark i. 29): and further says that it was in Peter's house that our Lord lodged whenever He was in Capernaum, for house of His own He had none.*

(43*b*) Thus it was as He was nearing Capernaum and passing through Bethsaida, that "He finds Philip," not accidentally, but having gone to get him (so, too, at ix. 35): and, as we suppose, at Bethsaida his place of residence. This Bethsaida is defined (xii. 21) as "Bethsaida of Galilee," it is the modern Khan Minieh, two miles south of Tell Hum (Capernaum), on the west coast of the lake of Galilee, and at the north end of the plain of Gennesareth. It is thus distinguished from the Bethsaida (Julias) which was at the north-east corner of the lake, and not in Galilee, but in Philip's tetrarchy east of Jordan.

March 3 / Adar 11 } Wed.

(44) It is the mention of Bethsaida and the implication of Capernaum in this verse that seem to give the clue as to the part of Galilee to which our Lord "willed to go-out." But the meaning of the verse hardly comes out in the R.V., and is totally obscured in the A.V., where no distinction is marked between the two Greek prepositions ἐκ and ἀπό. The Greek says, "And Philip was from (ἀπὸ) Bethsaida," *i.e.* Bethsaida was his place of residence: but in the same verse he is said to be "out of (ἐκ) the city of Andrew and Peter": *i.e.* he was a *native* of, or born at, the city of Andrew and Peter: which city was always known to be Capernaum. This subtle distinction between ἐκ and ἀπὸ is frequently of great importance in John's gospel, but is never made clear in the English versions. See also at xi. 1.

Philip appears to be as well acquainted with our Lord as were our Lord's cousins (second cousins on the mothers' side) James and John (the sons of Zebedee), and their

* Peter's house at Capernaum was early converted into a church, and its walls were still standing in fourth century when St Sylvia visited it.

partners in business Andrew and Peter. Like them he must have heard of the Baptist's announcement of January, and been prepared to follow as soon as Jesus reappeared from His withdrawal to "the wilderness":—though perhaps with a self-diffidence which required a direct call from our Lord personally. The "Follow Me" (43) must be understood not merely of a spiritual following, but also literally: Jesus is on the road to Capernaum, and is passing through Bethsaida: Philip of course joins those who are accompanying Him. Thus our Lord passes through Bethsaida and arrives at Capernaum on the fourth day from Jebel Qarantal, viz. on Wednesday, March 3, accompanied by five and probably by many others who had attached themselves to His train.

March 3 / Adar 11 } Wed.

(45) On the next day (Thursday, March 4), *i.e.* the second day since arrival in Galilee, occurred the call of Nathanael. Nathanael is to-day generally understood to be the same person as Bartholomew, one of the Twelve: Nathanael being the personal name, Bartholomew (son of Tolmai) the patronymic. This identification, so extremely probable in itself, seems to have been unknown to antiquity before the ninth century. Tradition makes Bartholomew of noble birth; cf. Jerome, *Epist. ad Eustachium*, "non Petro vili pescatori Bartholomaeus nobilis antiponitur": and records of Nathanael that he was learned in the Scriptures (Augustine *in Joan:* and cf. Gregory, *Mor.* xxxiii. 21).

March 4 / Adar 12 } Thurs.

"Philip findeth Nathanael." As we know from John xxi. 2, that Nathanael was "from (ἀπὸ, *i.e.* a resident of) Kana of Galilee," it is natural to suppose that Philip found him there, and there brought him to Jesus:—Jesus, with His disciples and Philip among them, arriving at Kana to-day in preparation for to-morrow's festivities, and He will be Nathanael's guest to-night. Kana, according to both Greek and Latin tradition, is the modern Kefr Kennah: it is some seventeen miles south-west of Capernaum, and nearly four north-east of Nazareth. But see note on p. 54.

Philip's words to his friend Nathanael are "Him of whom Moses in the Law wrote, and of whom the prophets wrote, we have found: Jesus, son of Joseph, who is from Nazareth." The form of the sentence suggests that he and Nathanael as well as the four others, had constantly discussed the question of Jesus being the promised Deliverer of the earliest gospel (Gen. iii. 15), and the promised Messiah of the Prophets. In childhood and boyhood He had, they knew, been generally recognized as such, at least by all who looked for the redemption of Jerusalem, by all who attached any belief to Moses and the Prophets as being inspired, and by the doctors of the Law. True the doctors had subsequently tacitly disavowed Him, as not being a Messiah to their liking: but John the Baptist, whom all knew to be a Prophet and the Forerunner whose mission was to point Messiah out officially to the nation, had seen the appointed sign on Him, and had countered the doctors. For Nathanael and his friends it was a choice between the Baptist's decided Yea and the Sanhedrin's insinuated Nay. The head and front of the Sanhedrin's objection to Him was His preference for the obscurity of Nazareth and a carpenter's trade to the splendours of the royal city and the pomp that alone embodied their idea of Messiah. They had used this citizenship of Nazareth as an argument against His claim: for, according to Micah v. 2, Messiah was to be *min* = "from" Bethlehem.

To understand the position clearly it is necessary to remember that the Hebrew (of the Prophets) and the Aramaic (the language of Palestine in our Lord's time) have but one preposition *min* to express what are two distinct meanings accurately indicated in Greek by ἐκ (place of birth), and *ἀπό* (place of residence). Jesus might therefore truly be styled *min* Bethlehem (place of birth) and *min* Nazareth (place of residence). The Sanhedrists had taken advantage of the equivocal Hebrew *min* to pretend that, as Micah (v. 2) had said that Messiah was to be *min* Bethlehem, Jesus could not be Messiah seeing that He was *min* Nazareth: but Micah meant *min* Bethlehem in the sense of ἐκ (native of) Bethlehem, and so the LXX had rendered him, and so the Sanhedrin had understood the passage thirty years ago when they had as yet no motives for dissimulation (see Matt. ii. 4–6). This did not preclude His being *min* Nazareth in the sense of (resident of) Nazareth: of this the Sanhedrists were aware, but it suited them to seize on the equivoke.

The sense comes out clear in John's Greek rendering of the Aramaic language spoken by Philip and Nathanael: Philip's words were "Jesus . . . who is *min* Nazareth": Nathanael's words were (46) "*min* Nazareth can anything good be?" Philip meant "*min* Nazareth" in the sense of resident at Nazareth, and so John has rendered him "τὸν ἀπὸ Nazareth": Nathanael meant "*min* Nazareth" in the sense of native of Nazareth, and so John has rendered him "ἐκ Nazareth." Not that Nathanael had misunderstood Philip, but he is saying, 'There is one sense in which Messiah cannot be *min* Nazareth, viz. that of ἐκ (native of) it: for Micah and tradition will not allow of it: and so there is a sense in which the Sanhedrists are right in their declaration that Jesus, being *min* Nazareth, cannot be Messiah. But (he has argued to himself) the Sanhedrists are disingenuous; for there is another sense in which Messiah might be *min* Nazareth, viz. that of ἀπὸ (resident of) it, as is Jesus, whilst still being *min* (native of) Bethlehem: "*min* Bethlehem" and "*min* Nazareth" are not incompatible as they would have us to believe.' Philip, following his line of thought that *min* Nazareth (in spite of the doctors) is no argument against Jesus, nods agreement and adds "Come and see."

(47) Had Nathanael not been sincere, he might have sheltered himself behind the quibble, as others did (vii. 41, 42, 52), and pretended that as Jesus was *min* Nazareth, He could not be Messiah, or that as Messiah must be *min* (ἐκ) Bethlehem Messiah cannot be *min* (ἀπὸ) Nazareth. It was this intellectual honesty of his that called forth our Lord's approbation, "Lo, an Israelite of the true stock, in whom guile is not":—contrasting his honesty with the disingenuousness of the scribes exemplified in their equivocation in the matter of *min* ἐκ and ἀπό. Pretending to be

impartial investigators, they seized on any excuse to justify their rejection of Him. (See again at vii. 42.)

(48) Nathanael overheard our Lord's remark, and was aware that it applied to the crisis in his life where his natural candour had had to break with the duplicity of the Sanhedrists in their search for arguments against Jesus. 'But how,' he asked, 'had Jesus so well read the processes of his mind ? and from how long back does that knowledge of him date ?' Both meanings inhere in the words πόθεν με γινώσκεις; "whence knowest thou me ?" but the latter—"from how long back hast thou knowledge of me ?"—is perhaps the principal one.

Jesus answered him, "Before Philip called thee, when thou wast under the fig tree I saw thee." *Under the fig tree :* Nathanael is arrested at this strange acquaintance with the exact circumstances of that crisis in his life : he had thought them known to himself alone : he remembered vividly that day last autumn when he was sitting under the fig tree studying the Law and the Prophets upon this very matter of the Messiah and Jesus of Nazareth, where he had formed his critical decision, viz. to break with the Sanhedrin and follow John the Baptist's lead. It is said of Rabbi Hasa in the tract Bereshith that he and his disciples were in the habit of studying under a fig tree : the old idyllic picture of sitting under one's fig tree is oddly at variance with the habits of the East to-day : by the modern Levantine the fig tree's shade is specially shunned as unwholesome. Are they too fanciful who see in this "fig tree," so strangely introduced, a second thought, a subtle reference to the Jewish polity ? On the three other occasions where the fig tree is named in the gospels (Matt. xxi. 19 : xxiv. 32 : and parallels : and Luke xiii. 6) the fig tree is the symbol of the Jewish polity : perhaps here, too, is a similar symbolism for "under the Sanhedrin's authority," *i.e.* under their disavowal of Jesus, from which Nathanael had had to free himself to follow the authority of the prophet John the Baptist who was above the Sanhedrin itself.

(49) The minute circumstantial detail connected with

that critical hour was given by our Lord to show Nathanael that all things were known to Him and all hearts open to Him: so Chrysostom. To a mind already persuaded, little is needed to produce conviction: "Rabbi" (and thereby Nathanael acknowledges Him as Master and Teacher), "Thou art The Son of God, Thou art King of Israel." In calling Him "The Son of God" Nathanael purposely adopts the title given to Him officially by the Baptist seven weeks ago (cf. verse 34): he thereby proclaims he accepts the Baptist's testimony as against the Sanhedrists, accepts it implicitly, for he by no means knows as yet all that that title means. Peter will use the same words later (Matt. xvi. 16), "Thou art the Christ, The Son of the Living God"; but, as says Chrysostom, 'Nathanael does not forestall Peter: for when Peter uses the words, he means, "The Son of God" as being *Very God*, as appears from Christ's words to him immediately after: but when Nathanael used them, he understood "The Son of God" in a limited and vague sense as being only man, though a wondrous Man.' For one moment Peter saw then what the Baptist too had seen—the eternal unceasing generation of The Son from The Father: Nathanael sees not, but accepts what the Baptist saw, and believes with his belief.

That "The Son of God" was at the time of our Lord understood by the doctors and the Sanhedrin to be a title of the Messiah ("Christ") is absolutely clear from the High Priest's questioning in Caiaphas's house (Matt. xxvi. 63), "tell us whether thou be the Christ, The Son of God," and (Mark xiv. 61), "art thou the Christ, The Son of the Blessed One?" That the Promised One of Gen. iii. 15 was to be not only the Seed of the woman but also somehow God was known from the beginning, known to Eve (see the Targum of Jonathan on Gen. iv. 1). To Mary, as she pondered on the mystery of her Son—that Son who had been announced to her (B.C. 4) by Gabriel as "Son of the Most High" (Luke i. 32), and again as "Son of God" (Luke i. 35)—the mystery had long since been made clear: how that He was the Second Person of the Holy Trinity incarnate, the Word (Memra) of Jehovah, the Shekinah: and we have seen the Boy teaching His parents this mystery in Luke ii. 49 (A.D. 10). But it was John the Baptist, the Forerunner, who had first publicly and officially applied the title to Jesus Christ, on the day he baptized our Lord (A.D. 28, Jan. 18) and was himself baptized by Him: it was he who had announced its full significance as the Evangelist declares (John i. 15–18) and had *made the title current among the people and the doctors.* From that date it became one of the recognized titles of Messiah: and, as we see in the trial in Caiaphas's house (above), the doctors refused it to Jesus *only because* they refused to see in Him Messiah. Similarly (John x. 33) they will seek to kill Him for blasphemy, for "making thyself God"—the blasphemy being not that He who claimed to be Messiah claimed to be God, for the two went together as they knew, but that He whom they refused to recognize as Messiah claimed Messiah's prerogative of being God, a claim which they rightly asserted to be blasphemy in a mere man.

How widely the title became known as denoting Messiah may be seen, not only in the use of it by the doctors (Matt. xxvi. 63: Mark xiv. 61: John x. 33), but in the use of it by Nathanael here, by "them that were in the ship" (Matt. xiv. 33), by the centurion (Matt. xxvii. 54), by Peter (John vi. 69, where he speaks from faith rather than from vision), by our Lord (John ix. 35, where He assumes the man will know whom He means), by Martha (John xi. 27).

In calling Him "King of Israel," Nathanael confesses Him as the Messiah, and gives Him the same title that the crowd from the provinces will give Him on Palm Sunday of next year (xii. 13): neither they nor Nathanael were Jews, but Israelites. The name "Judah" and "Jews" might be merged in "Israel," as it frequently is, after the return from Babylon, when Israel proper had disappeared and Benjamin represented with Judah the Covenant kingdom: but "Israel" is never merged in "Judah," nor would any Israelite have regarded "King of Judah" as an equivalent for the more glorious " King of Israel." Though the crown came from Judah, the kingdom and birthright of empire was Joseph's (1 Chron. v. 1), and therefore in the divided Nation the title " King of Israel " had been borne by the northern kingdom alone so long as it endured. This distinction is marked again in the final question which the eleven Apostles (none of them Jew) ask our Lord on the day of His ascension (Acts i. 6), " Lord, wilt Thou at this time restore the kingdom (not the Crown) to *Israel?* " *i.e.* bring Israel (the non-Jew tribes) again into favour, seeing that Judah proper had rejected Him.

(50) 'Did My power to read thine inmost heart, and My knowledge of the smallest details of thy life have such effect on crystallizing thy faith? Thou shalt see greater things than these when I begin to manifest My authority by My acts of more than human power.'

(51) And speaking to Nathanael (" He saith to him "), " Verily, verily, I say to you " (ὑμῖν, plural, *i.e.* to you disciples here present), " ye shall see Heaven opened " (ἀνεωγότα, lying permanently open): " and the angels of God ascending and descending on The Son of Man." He is the ladder of Jacob's vision (Gen. xxviii. 12) set up on earth and reaching to heaven, upon which the angels of God had been seen by Jacob passing up and down—an imperfect symbol. But it is promised to the disciples that their eyes shall be opened to understand that symbol, to see that Heaven now lies open to Earth, and that He is the archetypal Ladder, the means whereby Heaven and Earth are linked together, the living Personality in whom Godhead and Manhood are One, and in whom men may become God.

This allusion by our Lord to the vision of Jacob's ladder looks as though this vision had been the subject of Nathanael's meditation on the day referred to, when he sat last autumn under his fig tree's shade: the Baptist had at the time (Oct. A.D. 27) just begun to announce his message that the kingdom was at hand, also the King who should bring Jacob back from exile (Jer. xxx. 10, 11: and Gen. xxviii. 15, spoken from above the Ladder).

NOTE: "THE SON OF MAN"

As for the title "*The* Son of Man" (ὁ υἱὸς τοῦ ἀνθρώπου, with the initial Greek article): it occurs 83 (perhaps more correctly 80) times in the gospels and once in Acts (vii. 56), and nowhere else. Of these 83 (80) times, 32 (30) are in Matthew's gospel, 14 in Mark's, 26 (25) in Luke's, 11 in John's. In every case the title denotes our Lord alone: and in every case it is used by Him alone with the one exception of Acts vii. 56, where it is used of Him by the dying Stephen. None other ventures to call Him The Son of Man: angels and men and demons call Him the Son of God: it is He Himself who, while claiming the latter title, deigns to call Himself also The Son of Man, and insists on this lesser name. The Church, from John the Baptist onwards through Apostles and Evangelists, naturally preferred to give her Lord a higher title such as The Christ (= The Messiah), or The Son of God, or God's Son, or The Lord.

This name, "*The* Son of Man" (with the initial Greek article, ὁ υἱὸς τ. ἀνθρ.), occurs nowhere in the LXX nor yet in the apocryphal books. The Aramaic words used by our Lord, which are thus rendered in the Greek text of our gospels, were not *bar nâshâ'*, lit. "the-son-of-man" (plur. *b'nê nâshâ'*), a phrase which had come to mean in Aramaic simply "man" or "the man," or "mankind," the *bar* (son) having lost all distinctive force: but *breh d'nâshâ'*, lit. "his son, (viz.) man's," which represents an idiom very common in Aramaic and is an emphatic form in which the *bar* (son) retains its value. That this was the term used by our Lord appears from the Syriac (an Aramaic dialect) versions of the N.T.: they always preserve the phrase *breh d'nôshô'* when used by our Lord of Himself alone, and they reserve the phrase to denote Him alone: * whereas they habitually employ *barnosho'* or *bar'nosho'* (lit. the-son-of-man) when the Greek has simply ἄνθρωπος (man) or ὁ ἄνθρωπος (mankind), used generically for any and every man, *e.g.* Matt. iv. 4: xii. 12, 43: xv. 11, 18: xvi.

* It is so also even in the four places where the Greek has merely υἱὸς ἀνθρώπου (without the initial article), viz. John v. 27, "(because He is) Man's Son," υἱὸς ἀνθρώπου. Here the Greek insists on His having taken human nature to Himself, rather than on His being the one true representative of humanity: similarly God's Son (υἱὸς Θεοῦ, or υἱὸς τοῦ Θεοῦ) is sometimes used of Him instead of *The* Son of God (ὁ υἱὸς τοῦ Θεοῦ). The Syriac here (*breh d'nosho'*) is really in the nature of a gloss.

Heb. ii. 6. "(or) Man's Son" (υἱὸς ἀνθρώπου), Syr. *breh d'nosho'*. Here again the Syriac is a gloss, explaining the term as referring cryptically to our Lord; as does the writer of that epistle (verse 9).

Rev. i. 13: xiv. 14. "One like a-son-of-man" (ὅμοιον υἱὸν ἀνθρώπου). Here again the Syriac *breh d'nosho'* is a gloss. John's reference here is to Dan. vii. 13, where Daniel's Aramaic has (k)*bar' anâsh* = (One like) a son of man, *i.e.* (One like) a man: John, no less than his Syriac Version, was aware that the "One like a son of man" seen in his own and Daniel's vision was our Lord.

The omission of the initial article in all four cases calls attention to the (human) nature, rather than to the Personality, of our Lord.

26: xix. 6: Mark ii. 27: v. 8: vii. 15, 18, 20, 23: viii. 36, 37: x. 9: Luke iv. 4: ix. 25: John ii. 25*b*: iii. 27: v. 34: vii. 22, 23, 46, 51: or used for one of the genus man as against God, John i. 6: v. 34: x. 33, or as against demons, Mark v. 8: Luke viii. 29: xi. 24, 26.

Evidently the authors of our four Greek gospels had before them a peculiar Aramaic term, *breh d'nâshâ'*, never used before, and preserved for us in the Syriac versions. They therefore coined the new term ὁ υἱὸς τοῦ ἀνθρώπου in order to mark it.

We may safely assume that the authors of our Greek gospels were fully capable of dealing with Aramaic idioms seeing that Aramaic was as familiar to them as Greek. Again, the authors of the Syriac Versions of the N.T. are clearly aware that the title used by our Lord of Himself, and rendered in the Greek by ὁ υἱὸς τοῦ ἀνθρώπου, has a particular value, for, as has just been shown, they reserve for it, and for it alone, a particular phrase.

It appears indeed that this title "*The* Son of Man" as used by our Lord was a new title and *coined by Him for Himself*. Just as "Son of God," hitherto used vaguely, had been recently defined by the Baptist as meaning, when applied to Jesus Christ, *Godhead only-begotten* (μονογενὴς Θεός), expressing the eternal and unceasing generation of the Second Person of the Trinity by the First: so *bar nasha'*="the-son-of-man," hitherto used merely for "the man" or "mankind," is now modified by Jesus Christ into "*breh d'nâshâ'* "*The* Son of Man" and with a meaning applicable to Himself alone.

In what sense does He use it? He certainly does not repudiate the titles "The Son of God," "King of Israel" (in other words, Messiah), that Nathanael has just given Him: but He adds hereby another element in the connotation of Messiah, viz. that He is "*The* Son of Man." *

(1) As being the one perfect representative of the race = *The* Man:

(2) As being that Seed of the woman of the primeval gospel (Gen. iii. 15) who was to bruise the serpent's head:

(3) As asserting His incarnation: 'I, The Son of God, a stranger to the race because its Creator, am here amongst you bearing your own nature, but in its original spotlessness: and I take to-day My title therefrom.' The title Messiah had come to carry with it a false conception of the Kingdom which He was come to set up. The true conception of Messiah meant The perfect Man who, by uniting in His own person perfect human

* It is an old remark that our Lord often calls Himself The Son of Man at moments when He claims to be acting as God, *e.g.* casting out demons (Matt. xii. 28–32), forgiving sins (Matt. ix. 6: Mark ii. 10), modifying the Sabbath because He Himself had made it (Mark ii. 27, 28): or again at the moment after He has asserted Himself to be The Son of God (Matt. xxvi. 63, 64: Mark xiv. 61, 62), and again before the Sanhedrin on the following morning (Luke xxii. 69, 70): or again whilst asserting that He was in Heaven before His Incarnation and never left Heaven even whilst Incarnate (John iii. 13). For whatever can be predicated of The Son of Man can be predicated of The Son of God and conversely: because His Person is One only, though He has two natures.

nature to perfect Godhead, is not merely Himself the perfect Man, but is also the living Laboratory in which all men by sacramental union with Him are to be gradually assimilated by Him into His likeness:—a process not possible unless this living Laboratory were also God the Creator, unceasingly working to perfect this new creation. Thus the true conception of Messiah meant a King—at once God and Man—who unites all His subjects to Himself, eliminates all their imperfections by the transfusion of His own perfection, until King and subjects form one new creation The perfect Man:—that mystical Body of Paul's metaphor, where the King is the head and His subjects are the members.

NOTE: "THE MESSIAH"

It is vain to say, as do many moderns, that our Lord did not at the opening of His public Ministry admit Himself to be the Christ, the Messiah, and therefore the King of Israel. The announcement that He was so had been openly made by the angel to the shepherds on the night of His birth (Luke ii. 11) by the Magi from the East (Matt. ii. 2), by Simeon on the day of His presentation in the Temple (Luke ii. 26–32), and by Anna the prophetess (Luke ii. 38): it had never lapsed from the consciousness of the nation until in disgust with Him they threw Him over before ever He came forward, at the age of thirty, to be baptized. From that moment John the Baptist proclaims it (John i. 17) officially: the Sanhedrin, however, refuse to acknowledge Him, refuse also thereafter to accept the Baptist as a witness to Him.

A.D. 28.
Feb. 28, Sat.

In the circle of His immediate disciples He always insisted on His Messiahship: see at the very outset of His public Ministry, Andrew and John, His two earliest disciples, have been but a few hours with Him, and they come away to Simon and James saying, "we have found the Messiah"—clearly He had not repudiated but reasserted the Baptist's statement.

A.D. 28.
March 5 } Fri.
Adar 13 }

Again, when it is said of the large body of disciples who were with Him at Kana that "they believed into Him" (ἐπίστευσαν εἰς ἀυτόν, John ii. 11), it is obviously as into the Messiah, the God-Man of the Baptist's announcement (John i. 15–18), that they believed into Him: no other belief could be called "belief into Him" *: vague it was of necessity, but it was implicit; it will develop later into clear definite outline.

A.D. 28.
April 5 } Mon.
Nisan 15 }

Again, at the first visit to Jerusalem (April, A.D. 28) He clearly proclaimed Himself Messiah (or did not repudiate what all knew He claimed to be): how else could "many believe into His name" (ἐπίστευσαν εἰς τὸ ὄνομα αὐτοῦ, John ii. 23). See p. 72.

* πιστεύειν εἰς αὐτον (cf. credere in Deum), very common in John's writings, always means genuine Faith.

Wherein did the Baptism which He announced (John iii. 3–21), and which He administered by His disciples (John iii. 22–iv. 2), differ from the "baptism of John," except that the latter was only in water and the former was in water and in the Holy Spirit which *only Messiah* could dispense?

A.D. 28. April 5–10.

He proclaims Himself openly as Messiah to the Samaritan woman (John iv. 25, 26) (April, A.D. 28), and to the Samaritans (vv. 40–42).

A.D. 28. April 11–12.

When He moves on into Galilee (April, A.D. 28) to begin to preach there, saying, "Repent ye: for the Kingdom of Heaven is at hand," what else could He be understood to mean except what the Baptist meant (using the very same words), viz. that the King was come and that Jesus was He? Three months ago the Baptist had identified Jesus for the nation as being the Messiah: none could fail to understand that Jesus was carrying on what His herald had begun; that the Man whom John had identified was not repudiating John's proclamation of Him, but was here assenting to it, and awaiting a national recognition, which none the less He knew would not be given.

A.D. 28. April 13.

As Messiah the Galileans gladly welcome Him (April, A.D. 28)—the memory of the signs done by Him recently in Jerusalem fresh in their minds—and crowds come to Him from the regions north and east of Galilee and from Judæa, Peræa, and Jerusalem itself. It can be only as Messiah that He is teaching (Matt. v.–vii.): see esp. v. 11, "for My sake"; v. 17, "think not I am come to destroy the Law," etc.; v. 22, 28, 32, 34, 39, 44, where of His own authority He amplifies the Law. What else means the centurion's cry, "Lord, my servant," etc. (Matt. viii. 6), but that he implicitly recognizes Jesus to be all He claimed to be and all that was implied in the Jews' Messiah? Hence the commendation he obtains as against Israel (verses 10, 11). What else means the leper's cry, "Lord, if thou wilt," etc. (viii. 2)? or the disciple's cry, "Lord, suffer me first," etc. (verse 21)? or, "Lord, save us, we perish" (verse 25)? The cry of the blind men (ix. 27), "Son of David," can mean nothing but that they know Him to be claiming to be Messiah, and recognized Him as Messiah, and were right to do so, see His words, "according to your Faith," etc. So, too, the crowds', 'Take care, is He not, after all said against Him by the scribes, what He claims to be—The Son of David,' *i.e.* the Messiah (Matt. xii. 23)? What else can He mean (verse 28) by "If *I* by the Spirit of God cast out the demons, then *the Kingdom of God is come upon you*," than that the kingdom of Messiah is come upon you, and I am the Messiah here among you?

A.D. 28. April, May.

It is not as a chance reformer who has suddenly appeared in Jewry that He is opposed by the Scribes and Pharisees in Jerusalem and in Galilee: but as the Man who from His birth had been pointed out to the nation as Messiah, had been recognized as such by all for many years, had been gradually tacitly cast off by the nation as not being to their liking, had been again (at the age of thirty) identified for them by John the Baptist whom from his birth all had recognized as being a Prophet and the Forerunner of Messiah. This is the Man whom they are opposing: whether He choose to call Himself the Messiah, or The Son of God, or The Son of Man, or The Son of David, or whatso else, is of no moment: it is as One claiming to be the Messiah that they refuse to tolerate Him.

A.D. 28. May 25 / Sivan 6 } Tu.

Again, on His next visit to Jerusalem (at Pentecost, end of May, A.D. 29) it certainly was not as merely a reformer who habitually cured on a Sabbath that the Jews sought to kill Him (John v. 16): that charge was but a handle by which they sought to lay hold on One whom they already hated as their discarded Messiah, who still refused to withdraw, who still insisted on teaching them the Divinity of Himself even as His herald the Baptist had asserted Him, Jesus, to be "Messiah," "God only-begotten" (see under John i. 17, 18).

June 5 / Sivan 17 } Sat.

When, ten days later,* in the Synagogue at Capernaum (vi. 26–59), He is challenged to show some sign equal to those done by Moses if He wants them to believe Him, it is obvious that the speakers in comparing Him with Moses are talking to One whom they know to be claiming to be Messiah. No one but a self-styled Messiah would they have put on a parity with Moses.

A.D. 28. June.

Again, immediately afterwards, owing to the presence in Galilee of Scribes and Pharisees who have come from Jerusalem (Matt. xv. 1) to hunt Him down in accordance with their recent decision to kill Him (John v. 16), He retires for three months to the Gentile districts of Tyre and Sidon and the Decapolis (Mark vii. 24, 31): and we are told (vii. 24) that "having entered a house He would not that anyone should know." Know what? That He, Jesus, was the Jew's Messiah? No: but that He, Jesus, was present there in the house: for if it got about that He was there, it would *ipso facto* be known that "the Jews' Messiah" was there. And so it fell out. "He could not lie hid (λαθεῖν)": His presence in the house was known: at once a Gentile woman comes forth acclaiming Him as "Son of David"

* That the verse John vi. 4 is an interpolation from a marginal note and did not form part of the original text, see p. 148.

just as Galileans had addressed Him (Matt. ix. 27: xii. 23) using no other than a title of Messiah—as she knew He claimed to be.

Again, in mid-September, A.D. 28, He lands once more on the western shore of the lake of Tiberias (Matt. xv. 39). At once His old enemies the Sanhedrist party (xvi. 1) come out at Him, and He crosses back into Philip's tetrarchy. During His long absence in Gentile lands, the efforts of the Sanhedrists from Jerusalem (they of Matt. xv. 1) have been eminently successful in undermining His influence and persuading the people against Him. Fully aware of it, He calls His disciples' attention to it by the words (Matt. xvi. 13), "Whom do the folk (οἱ ἄνθρωποι) say that I The Son of Man am?"—in other words, 'Whom are the people hereabouts now saying that I the Messiah am? Not long ago they were acclaiming Me here as Messiah, and wishing to make Me King (see John vi. 15): see how little was their acclamation worth, for it was not due to spiritual insight: no longer am I to them Messiah, I am become only John the Baptist or Elijah, or one of the prophets. But whom do *you* say I am? Are you also about to fall away?' And then follows Peter's confession of Faith, 'We fall away? No. We say to-day what we have ever said since we came to you, what you have always taught us to say, "Thou art the Messiah," and by that we mean not merely The Son of Man, but also "The Son of the living God," incarnate as Man.'

A.D. 28: Sept. 15 / Tisri 1 } Wed.

Again, Matt. xvi. 20, "Then charged He His disciples that they should say to no one that He is the Christ." The date of this incident (Matt. xvi. 13–20) seems to be the day following the critical interview with the Pharisees and Sadducees (xvi. 1–4), which had caused His hurried return to the eastern side of the lake. This charge to His disciples does not mean that He ceases to assert His identity with Messiah, but it means that the disciples are not at this crisis qualified to proclaim Him as Messiah: they still retain much of the national misconception about Messiah's glory: there is serious danger that they may (without altogether meaning it) work upon the passions of the crowd, excite them to faction against the Sanhedrin, who, as all knew, had declared open war on Him, and to rebellion against the civil power. He alone is at this crisis competent to proclaim Himself to the public, for He alone knows what Messiah has first to endure; and, by insisting on His humiliations to come, He is able to restrain any popular excitement. His public insistence on His claims appears there in verses 24–28, where He is speaking not only to His disciples, but also to the crowd

A.D. 28. Sept. 16 / Tisri 2 } Thur.

(Mark viii. 34). The crowd knew perfectly that by "The Son of Man coming in the glory of His Father with His angels," He meant Himself and meant the Messiah: but, He says, not as they had pictured Messiah: there would be no facile honours for His friends, no courtly titles, no lust of the eye or pride of life; rather, the opposition that had driven Him from Jerusalem (John vi. 1), and had kept Him for the last three months out of Galilee, would prove so strong that His enemies will succeed in putting Him to death upon the gallows: this, He tells them, is the King's highway by which He will pass to His throne: but none other saw the fitness of the road. From that time forth (xvi. 21) He openly proclaims what He all along had known—that the Sanhedrin are incorrigible, that the visible Kingdom will not at this time be set up: with the brief interview of yesterday (Matt. xvi. 1–12), a crisis in the nation's history has closed.

A.D. 28.
Sept. 24 } **Fri.**
Tisri 10 }

Again, Matt. xvii. 9, "Tell the vision (of the Transfiguration) to no one until *The Son of Man* be risen from the dead." It is His synonym for Messiah, and that the three so understood is clear from their question in verse 10. This charge to the three does not mean that He Himself in any way is ceasing His claim to be Messiah, but it means that they are not to speak of the vision of His glory which they have just seen on Mt Tabor; for if the other disciples and the public hear of it, there will be roused a blind enthusiasm to make Him king—an enthusiasm that will be fanaticism because untempered by knowledge and impatient of authority. Similarly in Mark ix. 30, "He would not that anyone should know," sc. of the vision, for fear lest there should be an outburst in His favour: it would take little to rouse the Galileans now that He is back in Galilee after three and a half months' absence. But His work in Galilee is done: within a week He will have left it for good, to open His mission in Peræa after the Feast of Tabernacles. Though He keep His title of Messiah in relative abeyance, there is never any doubt, whether among "the Jews" of Jerusalem or among "the crowds" of Galilee, about His claim to be Messiah: all knew that He has come forward as Messiah no matter what the title by which He may prefer to call Himself.

A.D. 28.
Dec. 7 } **Tues.**
Kislev 25 }

Again, when the Jews of Jerusalem ask (John x. 24), "How long dost thou keep us in suspense? If thou art (not 'if thou be') the Christ tell us plainly," they are not asking for a clear *statement* as though none such had yet been made; see His answer, "I told you, and ye believe not": what they are insisting on is some startling "sign," some bit of thaumaturgy such as they have been ever seeking and have laid down as the stipulation necessary to their belief. Again, when they ask, "Who art thou ?" they are not asking Him for a statement in words, but for a convincing sign that shall be to their liking; see His answer, "What I have been telling you from the beginning."

As to the word "Messiah": it represents the Hebrew *Mašiaḥ*, meaning (The) anointed one, and is rendered by the Greek Χριστός (Christ), which means (The) anointed one. It is not without interest, when reading the N.T., to substitute the word "Messiah" wherever the word "Christ" appears: for that, neither more nor less, is the exact value of "Christ."

§ III

JOHN II. 1–12

The first return of Jesus to Galilee after His baptism. His first sign

(1) "AND on the third day there was a marriage feast in Kana * of Galilee." The "third day" does not mean the third since leaving Jebel Qarantal, for from that neighbourhood to Kana is a four days' journey (see under i. 43): but the "third day" since the arrival in Galilee that was implied in verse 43 of last chapter (see p. 37).

A.D. 28.
March 5 / Adar 13 } Fri.

The first day would be the day of arrival in Galilee

* "Kana of Galilee" (Gk. Κανά, Heb. Qanah): to distinguish it from the other Kana (Heb. Qanah, Joshua xix. 18), seven miles south-east of Tyre, which had once belonged to the tribe of Asher and to the Galilee of the Old Testament times, but was now (in the time of our Lord) outside the province of Galilee and belonged to Phenicia and the Tyrians; (see the restricted borders of the later Galilee on west and north as given by Josephus (*War*, III. iii. 1)). The Kana (Qanah) of Asher was assumed by Eusebius (early 4th century) to be the Kana (Κανὰ) of the gospel—he not observing how the old limit of Galilee had shrunk in our Lord's time. By the close of the 4th century that Kana (Qanah) of Asher had rightly been rejected as impossible, and the village of Kenna was being pointed out to pilgrims (as it is to-day) as the Kana of the gospel, the "Kana of Galilee" (Κανὰ τῆς Γαλιλαίας).

John's "Kana of Galilee" must be the same as the "village of Galilee which is called Kana (Κανὰ)," where Josephus (*Life*, 16) says he was staying on a certain occasion (A.D. 66), for there could not be two places in Galilee called Kana (Κανὰ) at that time, or John's note of distinction would be worthless. Many will be in favour of identifying "Kana of Galilee" (of John and of Josephus) with the ruins of Qanah, eight miles north of Nazareth, fifteen west of Tiberias, eighteen west by south of Capernaum: for the Greek spelling Kana exactly represents the Semitic Qanah.

Local tradition to-day, however, of both Greek and Latin Churches favours the village of Kenna, four miles north-east of Nazareth, twelve west of Tiberias, seventeen west by south-west of Capernaum. But the spelling Kenna (Κεννα) does not suit a Semitic Qanah, nor does the modern Arabic spelling Kenna suggest an original Semitic Qanah. John's "Kana of Galilee" must have been the transliteration of a Hebrew, Aramaic, and Arabic "Qanah of Galilee," since he had to distinguish from another Qanah, viz. that of Asher. By Eusebius's time the Qanah of Galilee of the gospel was probably (owing to the Jewish war) already a ruin as it is to-day.

(Wednesday, March 3): the second day would be Thursday, March 4 (see under verse 45 of last chapter): and the "third day" is Friday, March 5. In this year A.D. 28 the Day of Nicanor (Adar 13) fell on Friday, March 5. This Feast of Nicanor, on the day before the Feast of Purim, dated from B.C. 161: its formal ordainment "to be kept year by year" is given in 1 Macc. vii. 49, and see 2 Macc. xv. 36. In later times the day came to be observed, as it is still, as the Fast of Esther. The Talmud tells us that Wednesdays and Fridays were the regular days for the marriage of maidens, and Thursdays for that of widows. Marriage feasts were held always in the evening.

"And the mother of Jesus was there." At whose house was the marriage feast? There is no tradition of any value to help us. The marriage feast would be held in the house of the bridegroom, not in that of the bride.

(2) "And Jesus also was called, and His disciples, to the marriage feast." We certainly gather that the marriage was that of one who had accepted the Baptist's announcement of Jesus as being the Messiah: one in whose house our Lord's mother would be given a prominent position, and where she could take naturally a place of some authority (verses 3 and 5); one to whom our Lord was dear, for it is clear that the religious and political leaders of the people must have been already roused to a strong hostility against Jesus, more especially since the day of the Baptist's official designation of Him as the Messiah: this hostility of the Sanhedrists was not a thing to be lightly ignored: yet in the face of it we have to notice the large invitation extended to His disciples *because they were His disciples*—such would seem to be the force of the Greek (ἐκλήθη, sing.). There is again the *a priori* probability that our Lord would wish the first manifestation of His divine power to be made in the presence of His nearest relatives as having His especial care, just as after His resurrection it is to His "brethren" that His first message of assurance was sent (John xx. 17). Perhaps we shall not be amiss if we conjecture that all His near relatives were here present as guests and before He and His disciples arrived.

This is the first mention of "His disciples" as a body. Who are they? At first sight we might suppose the word means the six of John's first chapter, viz. John himself (inferred from i. 40, 41), Andrew, Simon Peter, James, Philip, Nathanael (=Bartholomew): but it appears from the failure of the wine (verse 3) that at a late moment there had arrived a *large* number of guests who had not been expected or provided for: the addition of our Lord and merely six others is not enough to account for the failure: from which we may fairly argue that there were a considerable number of followers who had already during the last two days attached themselves to the Man whom the Baptist had officially designated as the Messiah: nor is it other than probable that among this crowd of His "disciples" were all the Twelve * who were to be later chosen as Apostles, for it was to be one of the qualifications of these Twelve witnesses that they had been with Him "from the beginning" (John xv. 27): others among the crowd might be Joseph Barsabbas and Matthias, see Acts i. 21–23, where the same qualification is required and where the "beginning" must include this "beginning of the signs" by which "He manifested His glory" (John ii. 11).

(3) The mother of Jesus was not eating and drinking with the guests at table, for women did not recline at table among the men, they dined in a separate room, as is still the Oriental custom.

Hearing that the wine was run out (ὑστερήσαντος), *i.e.* that the last supply had been drawn and sent up to table, the mother of Jesus goes to Him as He reclined among the guests and says to Him privately, "They have no wine"—privately, because she wished to prevent the failure of the wine becoming known. She goes, as Hilary says, from compassion for the bridegroom, who is out of countenance at having failed to lay in a sufficiency: she goes

* The call of Matthew, for instance (Matt. ix. 9 and parallels), is certainly not the first time Matthew has accompanied our Lord: it is his final call to leave his ordinary occupation. Similarly the call of Peter and Andrew and James and John (Matt. iv. 18–22 and parallels) is not the first occasion on which they accompanied our Lord, for it is some six weeks later than the events of John i. 37–42.

to Him because it was owing to the invitation to Him and His large company of disciples that the wine had failed: she goes to Him because He has already told her that He means to inaugurate to-day His public Ministry by showing His first "sign" of more than human power, and she would not have so great a day marred: indeed she *suggests the occasion* of the "sign."

Her words "they have no wine" certainly contain an implied petition to Him to supply the need: and, if so, they contain also an expectation of a sign of His Divine power.

(4) His answer to her, "What have I and thou in common, O Woman?" has been strangely thought by some, notably by Chrysostom, to contain a reproof to His mother as to one too forward and presuming on her intimacy with Him: Christendom, whether Catholic or Orthodox, has learnt by now to know the Mother better, and is quite certain that in this Chrysostom erred. It is clear that a just apprehension of the scene must depend on the tone and the look accompanying the words, and on a just appreciation of the thirty years of intimacy between our Lord and His mother: it is also certain that John, according to his habit, has given us only salient sentences, leaving us to imagine the rest.

It will not be possible to admit that there is here even a tinge of a reproof if we at all realize what must have been the grace and tenderness ever existing between those Two; the perfect Son and the perfect Mother: He the God-Man, she made by her Creator all holy, immaculate from her conception, for it is so that we know and love her to-day. How conceive of her as moved by a touch of vanity or presumption or forwardness? Dare we impute to her so elementary and undisciplined a nature? to her who for thirty years had lived with God-incarnate in utter harmony, in tenderest intercourse, in mutual dependence day by day; to her, His mother, the highest created being He ever made? Christendom to-day, Catholic or Orthodox, will have none of it.

His answer to her, "What have I and thou in common,

O Woman ?" is to her alone; and would be at once understood by her, if, as we cannot but assume, He had already told her that He meant to-day to begin to lift the veil that had for thirty years concealed His Divinity, and to-day to inaugurate in public His Ministry.

"*What have I and thou in common, O Woman?* (τί ἐμοὶ καὶ σοί, γύναι;)." We have many instances of the phrase in the O.T., and with many various shades of meaning: *e.g.*—

(1) Reproof from a superior to an inferior (1 Sam. xvi. 10: xix. 22).

(2) Haughtiness of an equal (Judges xi. 12), resenting interference, denying the other's right. Stand off! (cf. the similar Joshua xxii. 24).

(3) The whine of an inferior, if we suppose the demons to be speaking: or the deprecation of a patient shrinking from pain, if we suppose the men to be speaking (Matt. viii. 29: Mark v. 7: Luke viii. 28).

(4) Confession of sinfulness in presence of holiness (1 Kings xvii. 18: cf. Luke v. 8).

(5) Friendly assurance that no hostility exists (2 Chron. xxxv. 21).

(6) Loving appeal to all that there is in common (John ii. 4), welcoming interference, loving to assert the other's right. See what I and thou have in common! It is as though to her humility and constant consciousness that He to whom she spoke was her God, He stooped encouraging, welcoming her intervention, putting it to her that though He was her God He was also her Son: nay, that to her alone He—God—actually owed His manhood: no man was His father, only woman was His parent. Hence the dignity of His title, "Woman" rather than the tenderness of the title "Mother." Again in that tender farewell from the Cross, He will use not the personal "Mother," but the race-wide "Woman."

'What have I and thou in common, that thou shouldst ask a petition and I should grant it?

Why, so far as I am Man, *everything:* for I have in common with thee, and thee alone, a sinless human nature: ask freely: I refuse no request of thine.' And that she so understood Him is evident from her immediate words to the attendants, "Whatso He tells you, that do ye." The words imply that she even knew what He was going to do. This He may have told her privately: for the conversation between them had been private: she having come to Him as He reclined in the place of honour, at the angle of the *triclinium.* Would He have interfered without her intervention? The implication is that He would not.

He adds, "My hour is not yet come," as saying that whilst He gladly grants her petition, the exact moment for His action has not yet quite come. It will not be come until the wine is finished, as Augustine says, lest any might think He had merely mixed wine with water to increase its bulk rather than changed water into wine. Or the words may rather mean that, instead of creating a supply upon the moment, He intends to act under such conditions as shall exclude all suspicion of collusion, furnish many and credible witnesses, and also point to the *symbolism* of His act which shall distinguish it from an empty thaumaturgy.

(5) His mother knows that her petition is granted, and from her words to the servants it would seem she is also aware that it will be made by Him the occasion for the first manifestation of His Divinity. Christendom, Catholic or Orthodox, has long seen in this His first miracle the value our Lord attaches to His mother's supplications and the pleasure He has in granting them. The circumlocution "His mother" or "the mother of Jesus" which John uses many times in his gospel (never giving her simply her name) seems due to a wish to emphasize the dignity of her position—the "blessed among women." We may suppose she sent the servants to our Lord where He reclined at table, telling them to get His instructions

and to carry them out however strange they might seem.

(6) The six stone water-jars "containing two or three firkins apiece" seem to have been of different sizes and contained each from 18 to 27 gallons, say an average of 22 or 23 gallons, and a total of 135 gallons. Earthenware jars of similar size and often very much larger are commonly used to-day in Italy for holding water for household purposes. These of the gospel were necessary for the constant ablutions customary with the Jews, whether of hands or of cups and pots, etc. (Mark vii. 3, 4). In this mention of "the Jews' manner of *purifying* (καθαρισμός)," John is implying a comparison with the Christians' manner of purifying, viz. Baptism, of which καθαρισμὸς is one of the technical Christian terms. And herein lay the symbolism of this the first "sign": the water of Jewish cleansing became the wine of Christian Baptism, the one a ritual cleansing of the body, the other a sacramental inebriating of the soul.

The word "there" (ἐκεῖ) need not be pressed to mean in the guest chamber, for the ruler of the feast seems to have known nothing of the doings of the servants: it may mean no more than in the courtyard of the house, used loosely as in Matt. xxvii. 55, "and there were *there* (ἐκεῖ) many women beholding *from afar off* (ἀπὸ μακρόθεν)."

(7) "Jesus saith to them, 'Fill,'" etc. The orders are given to the servants in a low tone secretly, as we gather from the ignorance of the ruler of the feast (verse 9). This order to "Fill the water-jars with water," and the notice that "they filled them up to the brim," were meant to preclude any suspicion that wine was secretly poured in.

(8) The servants having carried out His orders come to Him for further instructions, and receive them: "Draw out now and bear unto the ruler-of-the-feast." They were of course to draw out from the water-jars which they had filled with water. The *now* (νῦν) seems to contrast with His former words, "My hour is not yet come," viz. for supplying wine, but *now* the conditions He wanted have been observed. The ruler-of-the-feast (ἀρχιτρίκλινος)

would be one of the bridegroom's near friends and a guest, as is argued from the merry familiarity with which he calls to him (verse 10).

(9) No one in the guest chamber seems to have been aware of what had been going on, beyond that they may have noticed the servants coming to and from Jesus, though this might easily have passed unmarked in the general noise and hilarity. The miracle is done in the nick of time. When the new supply was brought first to the ruler of the feast for him to taste, he and all the guests would at first attribute the slight delay (if any) in bringing it to some care in unsealing a special vintage : after tasting it he calls to the bridegroom by name (φωνεῖ) and congratulates him on this his excellent wine.

(10) The truth would at once be out amid the surprise and thanks of the bridegroom for so splendid a wedding gift,* the bewilderment of the many, and the enthusiasm of the disciples at this first sign (11) of Messiah's power. The result of the "sign" was that "His disciples believed into Him" (ἐπίστευσαν εἰς αὐτόν)†: not that they had not believed "into" Him before from the moment they attached themselves to Him, but Faith has many degrees from simple assent to certitude. The miracle would merely arrest the attention of non-believers, whereas it was certain to deepen the faith of disciples. It was the "beginning of His signs," the first act of our Lord *quâ* God, God the Son, Θεὸς μονογενής, as the Baptist, realizing the mystery of the Trinity, had called Him : and, as the Evangelist says, it was a "manifestation of His glory" (ii. 11), viz. the "glory of Him *quâ* Only-Begotten come from The Father" to earth (τὴν δόξαν αὐτοῦ δόξαν ὡς μονογενοῦς παρὰ Πατρός) (John i. 14).

* We may remember that there had been no vintage last year, for from Oct. A.D. 26 to Sept. A.D. 27 was a Sabbatic year : the gift would have a special value in the spring and summer of a year following a Sabbatic.

† "Believed into Him." This phrase πιστεύειν εἰς αὐτόν, or again πιστεύειν εἰς τὸ ὄνομα αὐτοῦ, "believe into His name," always represents genuine belief : it means so to believe as to *merge into*, and is perfectly rendered by the Latin *credere in Deum* of our Creeds. It is not at all the same thing as πιστεύειν αὐτῷ. See under viii. 31.

It appears that some of the details given by John were given to him by the Blessed Virgin.

(12) "After this He went down to Capernaum, He and His mother, and His brethren and His disciples." The Greek μετὰ τοῦτο "after this," expresses not a mere sequence in time, such as would be the meaning if μετὰ ταῦτα had been used, but also an ethical sequence, *i.e.* that this going down to Capernaum was in part due to this "beginning of His signs," this His first public act by which He began to show who He was, and by which He began to train a body of disciples to replace the Sanhedrin who had failed Him. The busy Capernaum was a city better suited than Nazareth to be His headquarters in His new scheme. We infer that they went straight from Kana to Capernaum, that all named had been present at the wedding, and that they all went down from it together: say on Sunday, March 7, for the Saturday, March 6, would be a day of obligatory rest.

A.D. 28. Sun., March 7, at the earliest.

The Greek text by the form of the sentence and its use of κατέβη (sing.) implies that this removal was owing to our Lord, and that the others named went because He went. It marks a definite and final break-up from Nazareth, explained by the engrained prejudice of the Nazarenes against accepting their carpenter as the Messiah: and it marks a removal to Capernaum as to their future residence. The house which our Lord made use of at Capernaum was according to all tradition that of Simon Peter (see p. 38), who had been already indicated as the chief of the disciples (i. 42 compared with the later Matt. xvi. 18). It is improbable that His mother lived in the same house: she with her modesty would wish to remain as much as possible in the background, and He would wish her to be shielded from the publicity which must inevitably henceforth centre round any house in which He lived: she may likely enough have lived here with her "sister," *i.e.* first cousin and nearest relative, Salome, the mother of the Apostles James and John, and wife of Zebedee.

The "disciples" who accompanied Him to Capernaum were probably for the most part residents of Capernaum and its neighbourhood: they had set out with Him (so we have supposed) from Capernaum to Kana and now return with Him: they have none, as yet, received the final call to abandon their ordinary occupations.

But who are these who are called "His brethren"? It is a question that has for many centuries vexed the Church and has been answered varyingly at various times. The general outcome seems to be that by the term "brethren" are meant His nearest relatives, in agreement with the common Hebrew use of the word, of which many instances occur in the O.T. They are the sons of Clopas (also known as Cleopas), the half-brother of Joseph by the father's side, and are therefore our Lord's first cousins and nearest relatives. They are certainly not sons of the Blessed Virgin: nor are they sons of Joseph by a former marriage: Joseph was virgin as was Mary his wife. Had they been sons of Joseph by a former marriage, the heir to David's throne would have been the eldest of them (viz. James the Little), and not our Lord, for our Lord's legal claim to the throne lay through Joseph, who in the eye of the Law was His father. The whole royal stock of David, so far as was known, had died out with the exception of Joseph (and he was heir only by the law of Levirate) and Mary: this latter was the only known blood descendant left, being the only child of Joachim, the last male blood descendant.

Capernaum is beyond doubt to be identified with the modern Tell Hum on the north-west shore of the lake of Tiberias. The distance from Kana to Capernaum is eighteen miles, about a day's journey: leaving Kana on Sunday, March 7, they would arrive at Capernaum in the evening

Till about end of March, A.D. 28.

"And they continued there not many days." Evidently they all not only went down there together, but also all left it at about the same time together: and the reason for their leaving appears in the next verse, viz. the approach of "the Jews' Passover," to which festival the people of Galilee naturally went up.

§ IV

JOHN II. 13–END

Passover at Jerusalem. Jesus and the Sanhedrin

(ii. 13) "AND the Passover of the Jews was near, and Jesus went up to Jerusalem." It is the Passover of A.D. 28. The 14th of Nisan (the day the Passover was killed) was, this year, Sunday, April 4. The bulk of Galilean pilgrims to the Feast would arrive at Jerusalem on Friday, April 2,* leaving Capernaum or other centres toward the end of March: thus the "not many days" of verse 12 will cover at the most three weeks.

A.D. 28.
April 4 / Nisan 14 } Sun.

"The Jews' Passover." The words arrest. Why "the *Jews'* Passover"? John uses the term "the Jews" throughout his gospel to signify the hostile party, the nation *quâ* represented by the Sanhedrin. It would thus seem that he means to imply that though Jesus "went up to Jerusalem" at that date, He did not do so in order to keep the Passover. The nation had already rejected Him, and the Baptist's testimony to Him: their national Passover had thenceforth no virtue that He should keep it this year with them (see Origen *in Johann.*). The same inference will be drawn at v. 1 (Pentecost of this year): † and again at vii. 2, 8 (Tabernacles of this year). In xii. 1 and xiii. 1, John is speaking of the last Passover eaten by our Lord and the Twelve (twenty-four hours before the nation ate it), and therefore he does not add "of the Jews":

* Others, requiring special Levitical purification of seven days, such as Nazirites who had touched a dead body (Num. vi. 9, cf. Acts xxi. 23–27: also cf. John xi. 55 and Josephus, *War*, VI. v. 3) would arrive in Jerusalem as early as Friday, March 26.

† John vi. 4 is spurious—this verse being a marginal note by a commentator which has found its way into the text (see pp. 148, 149).

in xix. 14, " the Preparation of the Passover," see the true meaning of the phrase as given there, pp. 379, 380. In xviii. 28 the context shows of course that " the Passover " in question is that which " they " (the Jewish nation) meant to eat that evening, and therefore the qualifying words " of the Jews " were not needed.

Arrived at Jerusalem, our Lord entered the Temple area. If the date of the following scene is the morning of Sunday, April 4, this cleansing of the Temple would coincide with the symbolic cleansing of every house which was obligatory this morning (Nisan 14)—consisting in the removal of all leaven.

(14) " And He found ": not as coming upon incidentally, but as having found what He went to find and knew He should find. It was an abuse which He must have noticed every year He had come up to the festivals—an abuse which only now He undertakes to correct, now that He has reached the age of thirty, the age of a qualified Rabbi. The part of the Temple (ἱερῷ) in which " He found " the sacrificial animals and their sellers would be the Court of the Gentiles, the large outer court where a year later He again found them (Mark xi. 17, where the words " for all the nations " point to this particular court). The day may be the morning of Sunday, April 4, which in this year was Passover day, Nisan 14: or it may be some days earlier.

April 4 } Sun.
Nisan 14 }

The " changers of money " (κερματιστάς) seem to be those who supplied small change for the shekel. Any one, for instance, buying doves for " purification " or for " sin-offering " would be required to put the exact value of the doves according to the day's market scale of prices into the particular treasury-chest appointed for that purpose: it was the priests' business to convert the money in this chest at the end of the day into doves and sacrifice them. (See Edersheim's *Life and Times of the Messiah*, I. 368–370.)

(15) The scourge made of " twisted rushes " (σχοινίων) was not to cause pain, but was merely a symbol of authority.

The animals were driven out, and the sellers would, of course, go with them, by a gate which seems to have opened at the south-east corner on to the ramp which ran along the outside of the east wall of the Temple enclosure: it would be the only gate by which animals for sacrifice could be driven into the court.

"Poured out the small-money (κέρματα) of the exchangers (κολλυβιστῶν)." The κολλυβισταὶ were those who changed foreign money into shekels: for no coin bearing a king's or emperor's head or symbolic animal was accepted in the Temple treasury. The κέρματα (small coins) of these κολλυβισταὶ would represent the percentage deducted by them: it was these κέρματα that alone were "poured out" and the tables of the κολλυβισταὶ alone that were upset—as though to protest against the percentage or making of profit in the Temple area.

(16) The doves which were ordered to be taken up would be lying tied together in bundles, and would be taken away on poles on the sellers' shoulders.

"Make not My Father's house," etc. He does not identify Himself with the nation: He speaks to them of My Father (as He will again frequently later on), using the words in a sense peculiar to Himself, as previously in Luke ii. 49. He is publicly asserting His Divine Sonship as Messiah. The Jews' leaders and Sanhedrists who quickly arrived on the scene are aware of His meaning: they know He is claiming to be Messiah: they have always known His claims, ever since His birth, but they have long since put Him aside as rejected, nor have they been induced to reconsider their position by the recent testimony of the Baptist whom they had always known to be Messiah's herald. It is the first occasion on which He shows Himself to them as One having authority, for it is the first time He has been in Jerusalem since He became thirty, the age at which His Ministry began.

The object of the Court of the Gentiles, which He thus clears, was to serve as a symbol that the Gentiles had a right and a status in the House of God though they came not in on the same terms as Israel. He asserts their rights, whilst He objects to their Court being turned into a warehouse (οἶκον ἐμπορίου) for the sacrificial animals which were meant for the Mosaic ritual: a ritual that was not to be imposed upon the Gentile.

It may be that in this act of cleansing the Temple He was exercising a more than human power, letting His Divinity emanate from Him so that no resistance was possible to His will: one and all fell back passive in that Presence (cf. xviii. 6). Here is no impetuosity of a fiery zealot, it is the calm of irresistible authority. The pilgrims from the provinces would watch the expulsion with some enjoyment: they had no sympathy with the scandals and extortions of the Temple-market, of which the profits went in great measure to the chief priests and other prominent Temple officials. His disciples would watch it with a deeper interest, as the first overt act of Messiah face to face with the leaders of the nation whom they knew to have already disavowed Him: it woke in them no foreboding of trouble to come: the idea of possible failure had not occurred to them.

(17) They called to mind the words, "Zeal for Thy house shall devour (καταφάγεται) Me," and they remembered how all the Prophets, each in his turn, had found himself in similar opposition to the formalism of the hierarchy and of the civil authority of his day.

(18) The court being cleared, the Sanhedrists come to Him indignant that this Man should find fault with the system they had sanctioned, ignoring their authority: this Man of whom they had had a life-long cognizance, whom in His youth they had made much of as the long-promised King, but whose views of Kingship were so alien from their own that they had cast Him off. For thirty years He had made no move, living in obscurity in Galilee: impatiently had they watched Him: vainly had they urged Him to come forth and do some sign worthy of the nation and the King that were to dominate Rome and the world. Has He at last begun to act? Will He at last consent to do some startling "sign" worthy of Messiah? Some sign such as Moses worked when he brought out the

nation from the Egyptian bondage. 'What sign * do you show us to justify this act? Without some supernatural sign of your power, some startling physical phenomenon brought about by you and approved by us, we shall not recognize you, and without us you cannot win the nation. Long ago we gave you to understand our terms: you went your own way. Even if you are the appointed Messiah, we refuse you unless you comply with our conceptions of what Messiah should be and do. Is it, then, peace or war?'

(19) Jesus answered them, knowing them better than they knew themselves, seeing the inevitable outcome of the thoughts that were working in them—the death that awaited Him at their hands, though they themselves had hardly as yet formulated the ultimate issue.

He would give no such sign as they required: He had ever refused it. Any such sign, far from helping them, would blind them more. As years ago He told them, He had not come to work the vanities of thaumaturgy: He had come to make a holy people: and not till He had a holy people would He set up the visible Kingdom here in Jerusalem. He knows that the issue between them and Him is one of life and death: and He accepts. They cannot have the sign they want, but they shall have a greater. Listen, "Destroy this Temple (ναόν), and in three days I will raise it up." He spoke to be understood: He was speaking to learned theologians, to students of the Law and the Prophets, familiar with every theory of Messiah's personality, familiar with strange details of His own birth, familiar with His life-long claims to be

* The recorded occasions of a formal request for "a sign" are five in number:—

(1) At Jerusalem, at this Passover of A.D. 28, by "the Jews"; John ii. 18.

(2) At Capernaum, about May of A.D. 28, by "Scribes and Pharisees"; Matt. xii. 38.

(3) In Capernaum synagogue, on June 5 of A.D. 28, by "They"; John vi. 30.

(4) At Dalmanutha, about mid-Sept., of A.D. 28, by "Pharisees and Sadducees": Matt. xvi. 1: Mark viii. 11.

(5) In Peræa, on Feast of Purim, Feb. 24 of A.D. 29, by "some of them"; Luke xi. 16.

Messiah, familiar with the recent testimony of John the Baptist—Prophet and herald of the King—who had announced Him as "God only-Begotten" and "Man" (John i. 18, 30): and they understood His meaning: knew that by "this Temple" He meant His Body,* the true Temple (*ναός*, lit. dwelling-place) of the Incarnate God. That the Sanhedrists knew also that He was referring to raising His Body from the dead † seems to follow from their words to Pilate a year later (Matt. xxvii. 63), "we remember that that deceiver said while he was yet alive, 'After three days I will arise.'" It is more probable that they have in mind this interview in the Temple than either of those recorded by Matthew (xii. 39, 40 : xvi. 4).

(20) As, however, they had long decided not to recognize Him as Messiah, it suited them to ignore His meaning; and with some insolence they wrested His words to the stone sanctuary of that Temple in which they were standing. The Jews, therefore, said to Him, "In forty-six years was this Temple (*ναός*) built, and wilt thou in three days raise it up!" mocking Him. The rebuilding by Herod was begun in his eighteenth year (Josephus, *Ant.* XV. xi. 1): his eighteenth year, according to Jewish reckoning, began on 1st of Nisan (about April) of B.C. 20: if the Temple was begun in the autumn of that year, it would have been 46½ years a-building ‡ in April of A.D. 28. This reckoning by *completed* years, instead of by *current*, is also employed in the "seven years" of the building of the first Temple (1 Kings vi. 38, where "seven years" means 7½ years completed, as is clear). So also here, the

* That they knew His words had a subtler meaning appears from the report of this His saying given a year later at His trial in Caiaphas's house before the Sanhedrin. There one of the "two false witnesses" describes our Lord as having said that He would "build another Temple *not-made-with-hands*" (*ἀχειροποίητον*, Mark xiv. 58). This word shows it was common knowledge that He had not been talking of rebuilding the stone Temple.

† The resurrection of the body was a thesis familiar to both the Schools of which the Sanhedrin consisted: the Pharisees maintaining it, the Sadducees denying it (see Acts xxiii. 6–8).

‡ For this use of the aorist (*ᾠκοδομήθη*) see the Greek of Ezra v. 16, *ἀπὸ τότε ἕως τοῦ νῦν ᾠκοδομήθη καὶ οὐκ ἐτελέσθη*, "from that time until now it has been building and is not finished."

"forty-six years" are=$46\frac{1}{2}$ years completed. They were not aware of the irony in their words: for the autumn of B.C. 20 seems to have been the very date of the Blessed Virgin's birth, and with her birth began in a sense the building up of that human Body which He took from her immaculate body. Thus both the Temple of which they were speaking and the Temple of which He was speaking had been "forty-six years" in building at this April of A.D. 28. Mary was fifteen at the Annunciation, March 25 of B.C. 4.

(21) John adds, lest his readers might miss that which the Sanhedrists knew, "But He was speaking concerning the Temple (*ναοῦ*) of His body," *i.e.* the Temple which was His body.

(22) Not till He was risen from the dead, a year later, did His disciples understand what He meant by 'being killed, and rising again in three days': how predicate *death* of Messiah? But when He was risen they "remembered that He used to say (ἔλεγεν) this." In this "used to say" John has in his mind two other occasions at least where our Lord refers to the sign of the prophet Jonas and the three days and nights in the grave, see Matt. xii. 39, 40, spoken to "scribes and Pharisees": and Matt. xvi. 4, spoken to "His disciples."

"And they believed [*i.e.* after His resurrection] the scripture and the word which Jesus had said," *i.e.* they received an increase of faith and intuition: that crisis in John's own case is recorded in xx. 8. Both here (ii. 22) and in xx. 8, "the scripture" is the prophecy contained in Ps. xvi. 10, which seems to have been so commonly interpreted of Messiah that both Peter (Acts ii. 31) and Paul (Acts xiii. 35) assumed that their application of it to Messiah would be at once admitted by their hearers.

It is obvious that this interview between Jesus and the Sanhedrists presupposes a long mutual acquaintance: nothing but a long-standing hostility on their part, an obduracy that has been proof against many appeals in the past, would account for the abruptness with which He attacks their systematic Temple abuses, refuses to confer with them, and foretells the issue of the war between them and Him. It is the encounter of old-time opponents. There is no new breach here.

(23) "When He was in Jerusalem at the Passover *on the festival-day*" (ἐν τῇ ἑορτῇ, and so Jerome *die festo*), *i.e.* Nisan 15, which in A.D. 28 was Monday, April 5. The term ἡ ἑορτή, when connected with the Passover, seems to mean (and so Jerome always renders it) the *one* day, Nisan 15: which in common speech meant the twelve daylight hours of that Day, just as with us. John reckons all Days from midnight to midnight, as did the Romans, and not from sunset to sunset; his one exception is, and necessarily, the Jewish Sabbath. Thus ἐν τῇ ἑορτῇ here is not tautological with ἐν τῷ Πάσχα, "at the Passover, during the feast" (R.V.), which hardly is sense: but "at the Passover, on the festival-day" (as A.V., following Jerome): John thereby specifying the exact day of the octave of the feast, viz. Nisan 15.

A.D. 28.
April 5 / Nisan 15 } Mon.

For John's habitual use of τὸ Πάσχα to signify the whole octave of Unleavened Bread, Nisan 14–Nisan 21 inclusive, see at xix. 14.

It was, therefore, on Monday, April 5, Nisan 15, that He did the many "signs" of His Divine nature which induced "many" to "believe into His name" *when they beheld them* (θεωροῦντες, the word implies seeing with some intelligence).

"Believed into His name": believed with genuine faith (ἐπίστευσαν εἰς, see p. 61) into His name, *i.e.* into Him as being what He called Himself, and what He had been called by Divine announcement, *e.g.* by the Angel of His nativity, "a Saviour, Messiah the Lord" (Luke ii. 12): by the prophet Zecharias 'the world's long-promised Deliverer,' "'Ανατολὴ (צמח Ṣemah) * from on high" (Luke i. 68–79): by the prophet Simeon, "the

* The exact meaning of this remarkable title I have shown in my *Birth and Boyhood of Jesus Christ* to be the star *Ṣemah*, *i.e.* the Child in the arms of *Virgo* (the Virgin) of the primæval zodiac.

Lord's Christ," *i.e.* Jehovah's Messiah (Luke ii. 26–32): by John the Baptist, "Jesus Christ," *i.e.* Jesus the Messiah, "God only-Begotten," "The Baptizer with the Holy Spirit," "The Son of God" (John i. 17, 18, 33, 34): and by the Father's Voice, "My Son, the Beloved" (Matt. iii. 17, and parallels). All these attestations to Him were known to the nation *; some had been known ever since His Infancy.

The phrase "believe into His name" is used only four times in the N.T. John i. 12 : ii. 23 : iii. 18 : 1 John v. 13. None can ever grasp the whole of what is connoted by "Jesus Christ, The Son of God": some will see deeper than others, but the link of one and all to Him is faith; and all true faith is implicit, whether it be a cold assent or a burning certitude.

These "many" who "believed into His name" were doubtless not only from the provinces of Galilee and Peræa and yet further afield, but also from Jerusalem: still they were in the main Benjamites, Levites, and members of the ten tribes: the Jew proper (of Judah) did not accept Him.

(24) But, in spite of these "many," Jesus "did not trust Himself to them": not as though their faith was no faith, for as we have seen it was genuine of its kind (πίστις εἰς) although timid †: but "because He of Himself knew all men" and therefore knew that these who believed into Him, being but a tiny fraction of the nation, would not be able to withstand the pressure put upon them by His enemies, for the nation and its representatives were obdurately hostile to Him: and (25) "because He had no need that anyone should bear witness concerning man," *i.e.* He knew men without any possibility

* The message given by Gabriel to Mary would not be common knowledge, in which He is called "Jesus," *i.e.* Salvation of Jehovah: "Son of the Highest": "King for ever": "God's Son" (Luke i. 31–35). Nor yet would the message by Gabriel to Joseph (Matt. i. 20–23) be common knowledge, in which He is called "conceived of (ἐκ) the Holy Spirit": "the Saviour of His people from their sins": "The Virgin's Son," the "Immanuel" of Is. vii. 14.

† We shall find again the same faith, genuine of its kind, but as yet timid and weak, in "many even of the rulers" (*i.e.* members of the Sanhedrin), a year later just before the Passover of A.D. 29. See xii. 42.

of error—His knowledge of each individual not depending on outside sources: "for of Himself He knew what was in man," *i.e.* in each individual case He read man as God reads him, and before the man himself was aware of the issues to which he was moving.

§ V

JOHN III. 1—END

The New Birth. John the Baptist's Self-effacement.

A.D. 28.
April 5 Nisan 15 { Mon., after sunset.

THE date of the following interview with Nicodemus is probably the night after the festival-day on which the "signs" (ii. 23) had been done: *i.e.* the night following Nisan 15, the night following Monday, April 5. The scene is not improbably that Garden of Gethsemane on the foot of the Mount of Olives where our Lord so frequently passed the nights later in this year (John viii. 1); and again in the following spring, Luke xxi. 37: xxii. 39: Matt. xxvi. 30, 36: Mark xiv. 26, 32: John xviii. 2; where still is shown to-day the large natural grotto which tradition marks as the frequent night-shelter of Him and His disciples.

(1) Nicodemus was not only "a ruler (ἄρχων) of the Jews," he was also one of the Sanhedrin (vii. 50), and a Pharisee. He has been thought by many to be the Nicodemus spoken of in the Talmud as one of the richest and most distinguished citizens of Jerusalem—Nicodemus being his Greek name, his Hebrew name being Bunai son of Gorion; and there is a Bunai mentioned in the Talmud among the disciples of Jesus. (See Edersheim's *Life and Times of Jesus*, III. 6: and Lightfoot's *Hor. Heb.* on this passage in John's gospel.) He was doubtless one of the "many" mentioned in ii. 23, who "believed into His name as they beheld the signs which He did": believed, that is, that He was what they knew He had been declared to be at His birth, and what the Baptist had pronounced Him to be to the Sanhedrin's delegates six weeks ago (i. 19–27): and of these delegates Nicodemus had, not

improbably, been one—one of those "from among the Pharisees," verse 24.

(2) He came because his faith was as yet nebulous, vague, wanting outline: and he came as to a Divine Teacher who he knew could teach him. He came by night not because he was pusillanimous and afraid of consequences to himself if he were seen: want of courage, as we shall see later, is not at all a note of his character: but because in the tumult and excitement that must have filled Jerusalem to-day there had been no possibility of having any conversation with our Lord, nor was there any better prospect for to-morrow: he sought to secure quiet and leisure for the interview which he knew would be for him decisive. Again, he came by night out of a generous prudence: since the purging of the Temple he feared that the feud between this Man and the Sanhedrin might end in death: he was aware how hostile was the feeling of the Sanhedrin: had not the Christ but yesterday foretold and accepted His doom "though ye destroy this Temple (His body), in three days I will raise it up." He —Nicodemus—was quite clear about his own decision to abide by Jesus, but there was no public object to be gained by his declaring as yet openly for Him: could he not better aid the cause by concealing his attitude from the rest of the Sanhedrin, so being in a better position to deflect the torrent of their mischief by his counsels (cf. vii. 50, 51)? The same course, according to tradition, was adopted by Gamaliel (Acts v. 34–39), he being at the time secretly a Christian.

So Nicodemus is come for light. He calls Him only Rabbi, though he believed Him to be Messiah and therefore somehow Divine, just as we have heard Andrew and John the Evangelist calling Him simply Rabbi (i. 38), though they also at the time believed Him to be Messiah. As they there, so Nicodemus here, implies that he takes Him implicitly for his Teacher and that he is come to have his faith made explicit. From his word "we know," some have inferred he did not come alone; anyway he is speaking for certain others also whom he knows to be in similar case with himself, and who have applied to him "the teacher of Israel" for advice: they, like him, reflecting on (θεωροῦντες, ii. 23) the "signs" they had seen to-day, have seen in them the quality which removes them from a senseless thaumaturgy and marks them as stamped with the beneficent activity associated by the Prophets with Messiah.*

(3) "Jesus answered him." In the following account given by the Evangelist, he has preserved, as is his invariable custom in recording our Lord's discourses, only certain salient sentences spoken by Him, from which he leaves it to his readers to fill in the context. John does not venture to recast our Lord's discourses in a diction of his own: he merely abridges by preserving what he saw to be the critical headings. Undoubtedly the interview was one of considerable length: and John may well have been present at it.

(3) "Jesus answered him": No doubt Nicodemus had gone on to put his difficulties into words—not that his words were necessary to our Lord, seeing that of Himself He knew exactly what was in each man (ii. 25). As His "answer" was the answer to what was uppermost in the thoughts of Nicodemus, from that "answer" we may formulate them somewhat as follows: that whilst believing Him to be the Messiah and to be all that the Baptist His forerunner had announced, he cannot reconcile that inglorious life at Nazareth with what was expected of Messiah and His Kingdom: also he wishes to learn *what is that "Baptism of The Holy Spirit"* upon which the Baptist had laid such stress in connection with Him.

And the answer is to the effect that the Kingdom of God is not what they all understood it to be: if it were, it would be a thing disastrous both for them and for the world: what would it profit them to have their heel upon Rome? what would it profit the world to merely change the Roman for the Jew? The Kingdom of God was something other: and to belong to it a radical change

* It was to this quality in His "signs" that our Lord appealed when seeking to convince John's disciples that He was indeed Messiah (Matt. xi. 4, 5). See note to x. 25.

was needed in man's spiritual vision, a change such that only the grace of God could confer, a change so vast that it was literally a birth into a new life: without which new birth a man "cannot see the Kingdom of God." *

(4) Nicodemus: 'If the change be so great as to be literally a new birth, where is the power that can compass it? The world has grown old, and all its systems have disappointed: I too am grown old in Judaism, nor have I found any vivifying power inherent there. Is so unheard-of a change possible to us? How can it result from the simple rite of that baptism which you bring, and of which indeed John the Baptist spoke so high?'

(5) Our Lord abates not one jot. Nicodemus had understood Him to be speaking literally of a new birth, and He insists He means no less. They themselves talked of the water-baptism of proselytes as a new birth, but Nicodemus was rightly aware how little that availed to holiness; it was but a metaphor: rightly too might he complain of the national baptism by John the Baptist, how little it had availed. But John's baptism was only in water, and was only preparatory: it was a formal sign, promise, assurance, that if repentance were present all sins were about to be remitted at the advent of the King who was already at the door: it did not pretend to quicken to a new life.† Had not Nicodemus heard John announce that He the Messiah was to baptize not only with water, but also with the creative *Spirit?* There, in The Spirit, lay the vital principle of the new Birth. John the Baptist himself had asked to be baptized with this Baptism

* "Cannot *see* the Kingdom of God," ἰδεῖν τὴν βασιλείαν τοῦ Θεοῦ. A common Hebraism for cannot *enter into* it, *enjoy* it, *belong* to it, as again in Luke ix. 27. The same idiom occurs in "to see death," ἰδεῖν θάνατον, *i.e.* to die (Luke ii. 26: Heb. xi. 5): "to see corruption," ἰδεῖν διαφθοράν, *i.e.* to suffer decay (Acts ii. 27, 31: xiii. 35): "to see good days," ἰδεῖν ἡμέρας ἀγαθάς (1 Pet. iii. 10): "to see grief," πένθος ἰδεῖν (Rev. xviii. 7), etc.

† John's baptism in water was a baptism "unto repentance," εἰς μετανοίαν (Matt. iii. 11), and "unto remission of sins," εἰς ἄφεσιν ἁμαρτιῶν (Mark i. 4), and "of repentance unto remission of sins," μετανοίας εἰς ἄφεσιν ἁμαρτιῶν (Luke iii. 3). It was a preparation for, and a formal assurance of, an approaching enduring repentance and remission of sins: but it could confer neither the one nor the other. Both the one and the other are the work of the Holy Spirit.

(Matt. iii. 14): it was necessary to all who were to be members of the Kingdom of God—the new creation: without it a man "cannot enter into the Kingdom of God." Again our Lord insists with His emphatic ἀμὴν, ἀμὴν, on the necessity of Christian Baptism,* and on its nature as being a new Birth. The rite of Christian Baptism takes effect though the effect is not necessarily apparent in or to the child or man. It is an actual grafting into the spiritual body (the σῶμα πνευματικόν) of Christ, so that there, as in a Living Laboratory, the new Sap of His Godhead and sinless Manhood may circulate, and, as it were, work a chemical change. The rite is effective on all on the spiritual plane, and the seal will be visible to us all after death. To the consciousness of the recipient it may not begin to be effective till after death.

(6) That a new creative act is necessary to raise the human race Nicodemus must himself allow. "That which has been born of the flesh is flesh": man, since his Fall, can reproduce but his own likeness, fallen man, a nature at conscious war with itself, ever proclaiming to itself its own discord, seeing the better way but unable to follow it. On the other hand, "that which has been born of The Spirit is Spirit": the creative Spirit of God reproduces the likeness of Itself: if the creative Spirit work in the man It will make him into a new creation: but without this new vitalizing power man must remain without help or hope. Therefore (7) "Marvel not that I said to thee, 'Ye (ὑμᾶς) must be born anew'": ye Jews no less than Gentiles, for he (Nicodemus) must allow that the ones no less than the others were bound by their chains, enslaved by the inherent taint.

(8) But let no one think that this new Birth, this Creative act, must take effect with sudden objective manifestation or subjective consciousness: not with observation does it come: "The Spirit breathes where It wills and Its

* The laws of God are made for man, not man for the laws. None will venture to bind Him within the limit of His norm. The law of the Sabbath was His, but we shall hear Him proclaiming Himself Lord of the Sabbath, and therefore not immutably bound by it.

voice thou hearest, but thou knowest not whence It comes and where It goes": at one moment It is heard insistent, at the next It is become imperceptible—so it is with the Spirit Birth and the stirrings of the Spirit Life in the baptized. None can observe its beginning, or can define the law of its action.*

(9) Nicodemus asks, "How can these things happen?" He is not incredulous: he is amazed. He believes this Divine Teacher implicitly, but he wants more light. His is not the cry of a man who refuses to consider mysteries he cannot understand: he would not so have found light: he accepts the teaching though it is beyond him, because he has accepted the Teacher as divine: he asks to understand how a baptism, apparently consisting in nothing but the application of water accompanied by a formula of words administered by Jesus or His disciples, can operate the new Birth he has just heard of. The whole thought is new to him, if it means a literal new Birth, and the Divine Teacher insists on no less.

* At first sight it seems to us strange to have in this discourse of our Lord Christian Baptism presented in its full doctrinal bearing, at this the beginning of the public Ministry. But the Baptist's momentous announcement must have fired all imaginations—that announcement to the whole nation that the baptism he was himself administering was as nothing to that Baptism of The Spirit which was to be given by Him whom he heralded. Again, there was the Baptist's proclamation to the Sanhedrin's delegates that the Man, the Messiah, who was to operate this Baptism of the Spirit of God was Jesus and none other, whether they liked it or no: it must have set all the theologians (Nicodemus among them) and doctors of the Law agog to inquire into the significance of this Baptism of The Spirit foretold by Ezekiel (xxxvi. 25–27) and Joel (ii. 28). Again, we may fairly suppose that our Lord had recently begun His Baptizing by means of His disciples, for immediately after this interview with Nicodemus we read of His removal into the country (γῆν) of Judæa, as opposed to the city of Jerusalem, and of His Baptizing there—with nothing to make us suppose that it was a new beginning on His part that day. Nicodemus therefore came inquiring into the objective efficacy of this new Christian Baptism: could it really operate without visible result? was it more than a symbolic rite? His question has been often repeated down the centuries. The answer he received may be a hard saying, but it is plain: we can take it or leave it: we shall come to a similar parting of the ways in chap. vi. pp. 168–170.

Let us say it boldly, the Sacramental system is a system of "magic," insisting on definite rites and formulæ of words, accompanied by intention on the part of the hierophant and a state of assent on that of the postulant or his legitimate proxy. The sole real Hierophant is Jesus Christ, the agents here are but His proxies. The Christian Sacraments are not mere symbolic rites.

(10) The answer: "Thou art the teacher of Israel and recognizest not these things?" *The* teacher (ὁ διδάσκαλος), as though Nicodemus was allowed by the Sanhedrists to be the wisest among them. This remark of our Lord implies that the doctrine of a re-birth of water and Spirit (ἐξ ὕδατος καὶ πνεύματος) as being due when Messiah came was not unfamiliar to the patriarchs, prophets, and seers of the Old Testament, and should not have been strange to Nicodemus as one of the teachers of Israel—at least now that he had heard it recalled: it was familiar to John the Baptist.

(11) The subject is widened: "Verily, verily, I say to thee: what We know, of that We talk: and what We have seen, of that We bear witness: and Our witness ye receive not." The "we" cannot refer to His disciples, nor even to the Baptist, for their knowledge was not first hand, and in verse 13 as also in v. 34–37, He puts aside all merely human witness as being inadequate: the "we" can mean no other than the Triune Godhead, of whose three Persons only two are expressly named in viii. 16–18, viz. the Father and I,—the Two adequate witnesses of viii. 16–18, whose witness, however, was not received either there or here. As constantly when talking with the theologians afterwards, so here to Nicodemus, He is speaking of the mysteries of the Godhead, for to make known the nature of the Three in One He "was sent" and "came."

In "ye receive not Our witness," the reproach is not addressed to Nicodemus, or to those for whom he was spokesman, but to the Sanhedrin collectively as being the nation's representatives: also His allusion is not to any recent break with them, but to their long-standing hostility of many years.

(12) "If I told you the earthly things and ye believe not." Here again the allusion can hardly be, as is generally assumed, to the conversation just held with Nicodemus: the words are not, "if I told thee—and thou believest not," but, "if I told you—and ye believe not": it is the Sanhedrin whom He has in view. Nicodemus was not one who believed not, but one who believed. It is also hard to

see how "the earthly things" (τὰ ἐπίγεια) can possibly mean the hidden mysteries of the Sacrament of Baptism, which would naturally come under the head of "the Heavenly things" (τὰ ἐπουράνια). Rather is the allusion here to talks held by Him with the doctors ranging over long years, ever since He began them at the age of twelve (Luke ii. 42–47), talks about the true nature of the Kingdom of God *upon earth*, the purpose of Him the King now that He is come *upon earth*, and the attitude towards Him to be taken by the nation if the Kingdom of Righteousness is now to be set up *upon earth:* little to the liking of the doctors were His views: long ago they had virtually rejected Him: of the same mind are they now, now that He has publicly come forward as Messiah. And He is fully conscious of His doom.

"How shall ye believe if I tell you of the Heavenly things?" Again the reproach is not to Nicodemus, but to the collective Sanhedrin whose ears are closed to the whole message concerning the Heavenly things, the Sacramental mysteries, the nature of the Three in One, the Incarnation of God, and the nature of the union of mankind to Him which means for them Life: mysteries not suited to the simple understanding of the peasants of Galilee, and therefore never mentioned in the synoptic gospels. But John's gospel shows that our Lord spoke often of them to the theologians of Jerusalem, who ought to have been competent to receive them.

(13) "And no one hath ascended into Heaven," etc. And none but He could be the Hierophant of these mysteries: for here is not one who has gone up into Heaven from earth and come back again; none has done so, and none could do so: but here is One whose home is Heaven—even God, One who has come down thence to earth in becoming Incarnate as Man, though still remaining in Heaven as God. And why became He Incarnate? That to Him the whole sinful race of man may be united by a Sacramental union: and He thus being incorporate with all the sins of the world may purge them in that Living Laboratory, His body, by the alchemy of the Holy Spirit.

(14) "As Moses lifted up the serpent in the wilderness, even so shall The Son of Man be lifted up." What sort of a reception was the God-Man to be given? He here foretells not merely His death at the hands of the nation which He had already declared in ii. 19, but a death upon the Cross which He will again announce in viii. 28, and again in xii. 32. There is no doubt at all in His hearer's mind as to His meaning: for Nicodemus being the great teacher of the Law, knew that the serpent lifted up by Moses (Num. xxi. 8, 9) was "a symbol of salvation . . . for he who turned to it was saved not because of that which he gazed upon, but because of Thee the Saviour of all," *i.e.* Thee whom it symbolized (Wisdom xvi. 6, 7): and see Just. Mart. *Apol.* I. 60: *Dial.* 94. Also Rabbinical tradition has it that the pole of the brazen serpent set up by Moses was in the form of a cross.* (See Buxtorf's *Rab. Lex.* and Buxtorf's Comm. on Deut.)

The death of Christ was due to the presence of sin in the world, for had it not been for sin—alienation from the sanctity of the God-Man—neither Jew nor Gentile would have crucified Him. In the desert all who were bitten of the serpents' poison were bidden to look on the uplifted serpent, type of Him who was "made sin," and in whom sin was killed; and all who did so were healed. So should The Son of Man be lifted up, (15) "that every one who believes in Him should have eternal Life." It is belief in Him, the God-Man, that confers union with Him, but belief must be complemented with the rite of Christian Baptism: His words are quite plain, "born of water and Spirit" (verse 5): and he who is so united to Him has in him the germ of eternal Life.

* There is a remarkable notice by Ibn Ezra (1150 A.D.) the Jew, a famous astronomer and commentator on the O.T., who speaks of a south polar constellation which according to ancient tradition was in the shape of a Cross, like the pole on which the brazen serpent was lifted up. From this ancient tradition we may assert that the Southern Cross was one of the forty-eight original constellations: but being the most southern, it had passed partly or wholly out of sight to Mediterranean latitudes before Eudoxus of Cnidus (B.C. 370: lat. 36° 40′) wrote his *Phœnomena*, or at least before Hipparchus of Rhodes (B.C. 150: lat. 36° 30′) made out his list of the stars of the separate constellations.

(16) It is our Lord, not John, who speaks on to the close of verse 21. Were The Son of Man merely man, there would be no life-giving power in him: but this Son of Man is also the eternal God: *quâ* Man He was crucified and died, *quâ* God He is not susceptible of death but is Himself the Author of all life: for He is not an adopted Son of God; He is co-eternal with The Father, being eternally generated. Without union with this Author of life, the world (ὁ κόσμος, *i.e.* man, as being the microcosm) has no life: for by his Fall he has alienated himself from God, an alienation that every man inherits and bequeaths, and that alienation is the real Death.

(17) "God sent not The Son to the world to judge the world, but so that the world may be saved by means of Him." It is not because the world rejected the Incarnate God that sentence lies against the world; the world was already alienated and lay, wittingly or no, self-condemned. The Father sent The Son in order to win back the world to Life by means of Him.

(18) "He who believes into Him (ὁ πιστεύων εἰς αὐτὸν) does not come into judgment (οὐ κρίνεται)," is not in process of being judged: "but he that believes not has been already judged," *i.e.* shows *ipso facto* that the sentence lies against him, "in that he has not believed into the name of the Only-Begotten Son of God." But for the sin in him, the alienation he has for God, he would have leapt to the Author of Life as iron leaps to a magnet: that he is not so drawn is itself the verdict.

(19) "And this is the judgment, viz. that the Light has come into the world, and mankind loved the darkness rather than the Light; for their works were evil." He, the Light of the world, He who is for the intellect Truth and for the moral perception perfect Beauty, He became Incarnate and lived among men; and what happened? Did they crowd to Him to draw and absorb Light and Truth and Beauty? They cast Him from them; they did away with Him: there was no room, they said, for them and Him. He is aware the Sanhedrin have years ago rejected Him: He knows how the end will be.

(20) "For every one whose actions are ill (ὁ φαῦλα πράσσων) hates the Light, and comes not toward the Light; so that his works may not be reproved.

(21) "But he who does the Truth comes toward the Light, so that his works may be manifested as having been wrought in God." *Does the Truth*, "right action is true thought realized," as Westcott comments.

Here ends the account of the interview with Nicodemus: but there will be little doubt that before he left, he asked for and received Christian Baptism. He had come to our Lord acknowledging Him to be a Divine Teacher (verse 2): he had been instructed this night in the mysteries of the Spirit birth, and solemnly (ἀμὴν, ἀμὴν) informed of its necessity. Christian Baptism was already being administered by Christ's disciples (see iv. 1). Assuredly Nicodemus did not leave without first submitting himself, and obtaining so great a privilege.

Many moderns maintain that verses 16–21 are the Evangelist's words and not our Lord's, on the ground that "nowhere does St. John attribute to our Lord the key words of his own terminology." The truth, rather, is that the terminology used by John is the exact Greek rendering of the Aramaic terminology used by our Lord. John has steeped his thought in our Lord's terminology and has made it his own. John has borrowed from Him, and not sought to improve upon Him. Much the same had happened to John's earlier teacher, John the Baptist (see verses 31–36). For the simple terminology and metaphors of our Lord's talks as recorded by John's gospel, whether to Jewish theologians accustomed to abstract thought, or to the Twelve whom He is initiating into the mysteries of Theology, see notes on viii. 16, 42, 54; xvii. 6: and at close of chap. xvii.

(22) "After these things Jesus and His disciples came into the country of Judæa" (εἰς τὴν Ἰουδαίαν γῆν), *i.e.*

A.D. 28.
April 6 } Tues.
Nisan 16 }

into the *country* part of Judæa as opposed to the *city* of Jerusalem: a similar distinction occurs again in Mark i. 5, "all the country of Judæa and all the Jerusalemites" (πᾶσα ἡ Ἰουδαία χώρα καὶ οἱ Ἱεροσολυμεῖται πάντες), and again in Acts xxvi. 20, "at Jerusalem and in all the country of Judæa" (Ἱεροσολύμοις εἰς πᾶσάν τε τὴν χώραν τῆς Ἰουδαίας). A misunderstanding of this γῆν accounts for the spurious Ἰουδαίας in Luke iv. 44.

"His disciples": we have already had notice of them in ii. 2, and have inferred that they form a not inconsiderable number, and include, along with others, the Twelve who were later selected out.

"And there He tarried with them and baptized." The particular part of Judæa where He tarried or delayed (διέτριβε) was probably Bîreh (Beeroth of the O.T.). It was the regular halting-place of the first day on the route from Jerusalem to Galilee: to its abundance of water was due its name. It was here that Joseph and Mary, eighteen years before, discovered that the Boy was not in their company. Here at Bîreh He would be on the route of the pilgrims returning to Galilee from the Passover which was just over: no other place would be so suitable to catch them: many of them had been drawn to believe into Him by the "signs" which He had done in the City on the festival-day (ii. 23 and iv. 45), and had doubtless heard Him teach there. As for the Jews proper of Judæa they were never drawn to Him: His one object in coming to Bîreh, and there delaying, was to intercept the Galileans, and to baptize those who believed into Him. Such as were admitted to Baptism would naturally linger at Bîreh with Jesus and His other disciples.

A.D. 28.
April 6–10
Nisan 16–20

As for the time of year of this delay at Bîreh, it seems to have been from Tuesday, April 6, to Saturday, April 10, as will gradually appear. Passover (Nisan 14) in this year A.D. 28 was on Sunday, April 4: the "festival-day" would therefore be Monday, April 5. The Galileans and other provincials were required to stop at Jerusalem only the two first days of the eight-day festival, from midday of Nisan 14, on which day the Paschal lambs were killed and eaten, till sunset of Nisan 15, or perhaps (for this is not clear) till the morning of Nisan 16, when the *'omer* or first sheaf of the new barley harvest was "waved." Thus the Galileans would begin their return on Nisan 16 (this year, Tuesday, April 6); halt that night at Bîreh; move on the following day to Nâblûs (Shechem); and reach Jenîn on the border of Samaria and Galilee on Thursday evening, April 8. On the evening of "the festival-day" (Nisan 15, Monday, April 5), as we have seen, was held the interview with Nicodemus: on the following day (Tuesday, April 6, Nisan 16) it seems our Lord and His disciples left the City early for Bîreh, there to await the pilgrims who would pour in on that evening. We have already seen (ii. 13) reason to suppose that during this the year of His public Ministry He kept none of the national feasts with the nation, though He went up to Jerusalem for them: all were voided for this year by the national apostasy, but became valid again in the following year when His new Church (as yet purely Hebrew) was instituted on the day of Pentecost. He and His disciples would not be bound by any Rabbinical requirement to stay over the morning of Nisan 16 before leaving the City.

(22) As to the nature of this baptism by Christ: the weight of patristic authority is almost entirely in favour of the view that this baptism administered by Christ or rather by His disciples (iv. 2) was no other than Christian Baptism—that "Birth *of* (ἐκ) water and Spirit" which has been already so recently and so urgently insisted on by our Lord in His talk with Nicodemus.* The phrase "to be baptized in the name of Jesus" (Acts ii. 38: viii. 16, etc.) would mean to be baptized into all that that name connoted, and into all that He claimed to be or to teach. Explicit definite knowledge was not necessary to Faith then, nor is it now. This Baptism by Christ, or rather by His disciples (iv. 2), was never repeated on its recipients, nor was ever substituted by or complemented by a later one. Those who had received it were recognized after the resurrection of Christ as requiring no other: whereas

* Tertullian is the chief objector, maintaining that this early baptism administered by the disciples of our Lord before His resurrection and the day of Pentecost was no more than the baptism administered by John the Baptist. He has support from Chrysostom, but is opposed by the Fathers generally.

those that had received the baptism of John had subsequently to receive Christian Baptism (Acts xix. 3–5). This Baptism by Christ or by His disciples (John iv. 2) was the same in quality as Christ's own Baptism in which The Spirit had "bodily" descended on Him and *remained* there (i. 32): Christ transmitted this Baptism by baptizing: but "He Himself baptized Peter only: after which, Peter baptized Andrew and the sons of Zebedee: these, again, baptized the rest of the Apostles" (so Evodius, τὸ φῶς, as quoted by Baronius, *Annales*, xxxi. 40. Evodius succeeded Peter as bishop of Antioch). The same statement is made by Clement Alex. We cannot say that the efficacy of this Baptism remained latent till after Pentecost: the seal was once for all and indelible. It is not probable that this Baptism of regeneration was bestowed on many in these early days at Bîreh, and certainly not with that facility with which John's "baptism of repentance" was given: but it would have certainly included the Twelve who were later selected out of the body of disciples. The report brought to the Baptist (iii. 26) that "all are coming to Him" (Jesus) was purposely an exaggeration, as was also that brought to the Pharisees (iv. 1) that "Jesus is making and baptizing more disciples than is John."

(23) Meanwhile the Baptist had moved from the east bank of Jordan (Bethany i. 28), where being in Herod's kingdom he had been secure from the Sanhedrin, and going north was now on the west bank: and "was baptizing at Aenon near to Salim, because there were many waters there." This Salim (Σαλεὶμ) is identified by Eusebius, and by the best opinion to-day, with a place he calls Salumias, six or eight miles south of Scythopolis (Bethshan), and on the borders of Samaria and Galilee: it would be the modern Tell Rid'ah where there are copious springs; it is in the Jordan valley, near where the road from Scythopolis to Shechem (Nâblûs) left the valley. Salim (Σαλεὶμ) must not be confounded with Salem (Σαλήμ), an ancient name of Jerusalem (Gen. xiv. 18: Heb. vii. 1, 2: Josephus, *Ant.* I. x. 2: and *War*, VI. x.), nor yet with the Salem which was near Shechem

(Nâblûs), in the heart of Samaria. At this latter place John would have been far outside the jurisdiction of Herod, who was also tetrarch of Galilee, whereas Herod evidently seizes him at Aenon (on the borders) immediately after the interview of iii. 26–36. The warmth of the Jordan valley would be necessary to John's baptism.

The "many waters" (ὕδατα πολλὰ) points to a copious volume of stream or else to water spread over a large surface as in a lake or in flood, or in large reservoir: the notice implies that John required abundance of water in that his baptism was by immersion, whereas that of Christ's disciples was by aspersion or affusion.

John at Aenon would be on the high road from Nâblûs (Shechem) to Gaulonitis and Damascus, and would thus intercept the pilgrims from the east, as they were returning from the Passover.

"And they came to him (παρεγίνοντο) and were baptized": these are the pilgrims from the east, not the natives of Palestine; for the latter had been coming to John for baptism all the last six months. These of the text are clearly postulants who had had no earlier opportunity. This large body would arrive here on the evening of Thursday, April 8—Aenon being about twenty miles, or one day's journey, north-east from Nâblûs; whilst Jenîn was one day's journey due north from Nâblûs. Nâblûs was thus the point of divergence for the two pilgrim streams returning (1) northwards via Jenîn to Galilee and Cæle Syria, and (2) north-eastwards via Aenon to the Haurân and Damascus. These latter, arriving at Aenon on Thursday evening, would be baptized on the following days, Friday and Saturday, April 9, 10: the Saturday being a day of obligatory rest.

A.D. 28. April 10, Sat.

(24) "For John was not yet cast into prison." We have here a note of the last day of John's freedom. We have reached Saturday, April 10, and it was perhaps on Sunday evening, April 11, that he was seized by Herod as we shall see. (See under iv. 43.)

(25) "There arose, therefore, a questioning on the part of John's disciples with a Jew about purifying." The

"therefore" has, of course, reference to the two different baptisms that were being concurrently administered, the one by Christ's disciples, the other by John. The "questioning" concerns the relative merits of the two, and carries a protest against what seemed to be a competition with John. The two baptisms were clearly not the same: that of Jesus was meant to supersede John's, as surely as Jesus the Messiah meant to supersede John His herald. We must bear in mind that the disciples of Jesus had previously been disciples of John, but that only a few of the vast numbers baptized by John had gone on to declare for Jesus in spite of John's urgency, for all the efforts of the Sanhedrin and the doctors were put forth to hold them back.

A.D. 28.
April 10 } Sat.
Nisan 20 }

This "questioning" (ζήτησις) arose among, was started by (ἐκ), John's disciples, who were supported and backed up by (μετὰ) a certain Jew unnamed: for this is the meaning of the μετὰ Ἰουδαίου, "along with," "aided by," "in common with, a Jew." Had the meaning been that the dispute was between John's disciples on one side against a Jew on the other (as is the common view), the phrase would probably have been πρὸς Ἰουδαῖον. Cf. Mark ix. 14, συζητοῦντας πρὸς αὐτούς = disputing with, *i.e.* against them: Acts ix. 29, συνεζήτει πρὸς τοὺς Ἑλληνιστάς = disputed with, *i.e.* against the Hellenists: xv. 2, ζητήσεως πρὸς αὐτούς = a questioning with, *i.e.* against them: xxv. 19, ζητήματα εἶχον . . . πρὸς αὐτόν, they had questions with, *i.e.* against him.

In view of John's habitual use of the word "Jews" throughout his gospel we cannot but understand "Jew" in this passage in the same sense: he must be a typical Jew, hostile to Jesus, an adherent of the Sanhedrin, and almost certainly a representative and delegate of the Sanhedrin. What, then, is he doing here? We shall not be far off the mark if we conjecture that he is voicing the thoughts of John's disciples, and that he has been sent down from Jerusalem by the Sanhedrin on an embassy to John to make a last attempt to come to terms with him.

Thinking John will prove as venal and self-seeking as they were themselves, the Sanhedrin have sent this plenipotentiary to work upon John's self-esteem, (26) to join with his disciples in indignant protest that Jesus is supplanting him, to point out how "all" men (the exaggeration is intentional) are falling away to his rival; 'how fatal has been that witness you gave to Jesus three months ago (Jan. 18), and again six weeks ago (Feb. 26), when the Sanhedrin's deputation came urging you to repudiate him: even now it may not be too late to undo the mischief: the Sanhedrin would support you: why not work with them? They need your authority, but also you need their protection against Herod, who is being urged by your enemy Herodias to put you to death. Again they put it to you, why not come out as Messiah yourself? they and you working together could put it through.'

(27) John's answer: Why come with such futile guile? "A man cannot take anything unless it has been given to him of Heaven." How should I feign to be what I am not? Each man has his own work laid out for him by God: beyond it none may or can go.

(28) "You yourselves," and in this very appeal, "bear me witness that I said, 'it is not I who am the Messiah,' but 'I have been sent before Him.'" John here recalls his answer to the delegates of the Sanhedrin (i. 20), and his unvarying declaration to the nation that he was Messiah's herald, not more nor less.

(29) 'Yonder is the Messiah The Son of God who, as Jehovah, promised through the prophets that He would wed the nation, as a bridegroom * a bride: and the seal of this His new union is not the merely external rite of the old covenant with Abraham, but the infusion of His Spirit into man's spirit—that very rite of the Baptism which He is administering, and of which you come complaining. I am but the Bridegroom's friend and right-hand man,

* See Is. lxii. 5, "A Bridegroom rejoicing over His bride, thy God shall rejoice over thee." Cf. Hos. ii. 19: also our Lord's assertion that He was the Bridegroom (Matt. ix. 15), an assertion made to these very "disciples of John" three weeks later in Galilee.

whose duty it was to make all preparations for the wedding, that there might be no delay when the Bridegroom came to claim the nation as His bride. My work is done: henceforth I "stand" and wait: for He has come: I have heard His voice and delight to hear it. This is the end to which I worked and waited. It is the fulness of my joy.'

(30) "It must be that He increases, but that I decrease": 'Henceforth, gladly I stand aside and pass into oblivion, while He moves down the ages on from strength to strength.'

(31) * "He who comes from above," as does He, "is above all": the "comes" signifies His coming into the world in His Incarnation.

"He who is of (ἐκ, native of) the earth is of (ἐκ) the earth, and talks of (ἐκ) the earth." 'Such is the position of every son of Adam: all of us belong to this earth and are subject to the limitations of this sphere of being: not one can talk at first-hand of things of Heaven, he can only know and talk of them in so far as has been revealed to him.'

"He who comes of (ἐκ, native of) Heaven," as does He, "is above all": is above all men and all created things.

(32) "And it is of what He has seen and heard that He bears witness." 'In telling us of Heavenly things He tells us of what He knows at first-hand, for Heaven is His home: as, for instance, when He tells us of the nature of the Godhead and of the Sacramental mysteries.'

"And His witness no one receives." 'And yet no one credits His report.' Not, of course, absolutely "no one," but relatively; in that the nation officially by its representatives the Sanhedrin, and collectively as being misled by them, did not receive Him: of this the Baptist was aware all along ever since the critical announcement on Jan. 18.

* It is the Baptist who is still speaking and to the end of the chapter, as Chrysostom and others have clearly seen. It is foreign to the Evangelist's mind to recast or to amplify the discourses of our Lord or of the Baptist in words of his own. Those two had been his teachers, and their words were too precious to him to permit of his placing his own on a parity. The Baptist's peculiar mission lent moment to the exact words of his witness to Jesus.

(33) But "he who receives His witness seals the statement that 'God is true.'" The aorists ὁ λαβὼν and ἐσφράγισεν, seem to be gnomic aorists, and as such are idiomatically to be rendered by the present rather than by the past 'received,' 'sealed.' The Baptist is making a formal dogmatic pronouncement:—whoso receives as true the witness that Jesus bears is *ipso facto* affirming that God is true, that God is to be trusted: for whoso trusts Jesus is trusting God, for Jesus is God (see i. 18).

(34) "For He whom God sent * talks the things of God" (ῥήματα = things *quâ* described or narrated). Jesus is sent as The Father's Representative, and is the only adequate Representative. He cannot but give the true account of The Father, and of the whole Godhead.

"For not by measure does He (viz. God) give The Spirit" to this His Representative. The Baptist here utters the mystery of that which he saw in the vision on Jan. 18, when he saw The Spirit descending integrally as a living dove and abiding on Him (see i. 33), signifying that upon this Man the whole Godhead abides. To other men The Spirit is doled out by measure according as they can contain: Jesus the God-Man contains the whole: and seeing that He has The Spirit in all fulness, He manifests God adequately.

(35) "The Father loves The Son," this God-Man who is the eternal Son; "and all things has He given into His hand": for by means of The Son He formed the world of created things and beings, and by means of The Son He will re-form creation.

(36) "He who believes into The Son has life eternal": for it is belief into the God-Man, accompanied by the Baptismal rite, that confers union with the God-Man, the Author of Life, whose divine Sap thenceforward flows in, and transforms, those who are united to Him.

* Jesus was "sent" if we regard the Incarnation from the standpoint of The Father's share in it. He "came" if we regard it from that of The Son. Or again, we may talk of the whole Godhead sending and of the whole Godhead coming, for the whole Godhead is in The Father and the whole Godhead is in The Son.

"But he who disobeys The Son shall not see Life." The word ἀπειθῶν (rendered "disobeys") means to be "refractory to," to "refuse to be persuaded by": it is the Heb. *sôrēr* (סוֹרֵר) in Is. lxv. 2, "unto a *refractory* People," where the LXX render ἀπειθοῦντα. "Shall not see Life," *i.e.* shall not enter into Life (see note on iii. 3), whilst they remain refractory to The Son: for there is no other Door to Life.

"But the wrath of God abides upon him" as being by sin in Adam already alienated from God, and as not having laid hold of the only means whereby may be effected (1) his adoption as a son, (2) the transformation of his nature, (3) his union with the Godhead.

So ends the last recorded witness * of the Baptist: the utterance of one who has his vision fixed on the mystery of the Incarnation of God in the Person of Jesus, and on the mystery of the Holy Trinity. It is the vision of absolute Truth. Already (in i. 18) we have seen him intimately and divinely illumined as perhaps no other man, so as to be capable and adequate to "bear witness concerning the Light"—the φῶς, the Divine Λόγός. That was his commission.

Where all language is inadequate, the very simplest metaphors of "coming," "sending," "seeing," "hearing," "Son," "Father," are preferred. Wherever, in this gospel, our Lord speaks to trained theologians or to the Twelve whom He is training, or the Baptist speaks to theologians, the diction is the same whenever attempt is made to render into words the vision of abstract Truth: also John the evangelist, in his epistles, is found using the phraseology of our Lord and of the Baptist; those Two had been his teachers. The two Johns, who seem to have surpassed all men in keenness of vision, drew ultimately from one and the same fount. The Synoptists, who write for popular use, preserving the words of our Lord, and of the Baptist as they were spoken to popular audiences,

* He will yet make from prison a last effort (Matt. xi. 2, 3: Luke vii. 19) to transfer his own disciples to Jesus: for this is the true meaning of that incident which has been misrepresented by the later commentators.

make no attempt to record the teaching addressed to trained theologians.

The interview (26–36) took place (so we have suggested) on Saturday, April 10. John's answer has been so decisive and final that, as we conjecture, "the Jew" holding the Sanhedrin's warrant (cf. the warrants issued to Saul, Acts ix. 2) hands him straightway over to Herod the tetrarch who at once imprisons him, Sunday, April 11. Herod had not ventured to arrest him before, being afraid of the national veneration for John: but now that the Sanhedrin are with him he can act. Thus was John "betrayed" (παρεδόθη, Matt. iv. 12: Mark i. 14) by the Jews to Herod and "imprisoned" by him (John iii. 24: Luke iii. 20), as we suppose on Sunday, April 11.

A.D. 28. April 11 / Nisan 21 Sun.

NOTE ON JOHN THE BAPTIST

As to our Lord's commendation of John (Matt. xi. 11), "Among them that are born of women there has not arisen a greater than John the Baptist, but he that is less in the kingdom of Heaven is greater than he": the meaning is probably to be got from Matt. xviii. 1–4, "Who is greatest in the kingdom of Heaven?" . . . "Whoever shall humble himself as this little child, he is the greatest in the kingdom of Heaven." We should therefore understand, "but he that is less (*i.e.* humbler than John, if there be such a one) is in the kingdom of Heaven greater than John," *i.e.* humility is the great virtue in the kingdom of Heaven, and none is greater than John, because none is humbler. Our Lord is not contrasting John with the members of the kingdom; for John, having been baptized by Christ (as the Fathers have handed down), was a member of the kingdom of Heaven: and in the *Nobis quoque* of the Mass he is named at the head of the martyrs, before Stephen.

§ VI

JOHN IV. 1–42

Samaria and the Samaritan Woman

(1) To return to our Lord. We left Him (p. 85) at Bîreh on Tuesday, April 6, baptizing among the returning pilgrims, the bulk of whom would pass on from Bîreh to Nâblûs on the following day, Wednesday, April 7. Our Lord did not pass on with them but delayed (διάτριβε, iii. 22) at Bîreh or in the neighbourhood (say from April 6–11) until He learnt that exaggerated reports of His activity among the pilgrims had reached the Pharisees at Jerusalem—reports purposely exaggerated by the indignation of John's disciples and by the malice of the hostile Jews.

"When therefore the Lord knew that the Pharisees heard 'Jesus is making and baptizing more disciples than is John,' * He left Judæa and departed again into Galilee." The reports would be carried to the Pharisees of Jerusalem on Thursday, April 8, and intelligence of the effect caused would be brought back to our Lord on Friday, April 9.

A.D. 28. April 11 Nisan 21 Sun.

(3) Aware of their malice He anticipated action against Him by leaving Judæa on Sunday, April 11 (immediately after the Sabbath) to go into Galilee.

* Verse 2 has the parenthetical notice that "Jesus Himself was not baptizing, but His disciples were," *i.e.* His disciples were with His authority baptizing with that same Baptism "in water and The Spirit" that He had already operated on them (see the remarks on iii. 22, p. 86). Thus this notice iv. 2, is reconciled with the statement of iii. 22. The place and the time are the same in both notices. It is of course not John the Baptist's symbolic baptism that our Lord's disciples are administering, but that efficacious Baptism which had been the theme of His discourse with Nicodemus on the night of April 5 (pp. 76–81), as given in the first half of last chapter, and had called forth John the Baptist's answer (iii. 25–36) at the dispute on the two baptisms (pp. 88–93).

(4) "And He had to go through Samaria." The haj (or pilgrim) route between Judæa and Galilee lay through Samaria: the regular first day's halt was at Jacob's well, close to Sychàr and Nâblûs (Shechem): the distance from Bîreh is a full day's journey of twenty-three miles: He would therefore arrive here with His disciples in the evening of Sunday, April 11, at sunset ("the sixth hour," John iv. 6).

(5) "Therefore cometh He to a city of Samaria which is called Sychàr": the force of the "therefore" is that this city of Sychàr and its territory was the natural halting-place. There is scarcely a doubt that Sychàr is the modern village 'Askar: the Bordeaux Pilgrim (333 A.D.), our earliest post-Apostolic authority, distinguishes Sychàr from Neapolis (=Nâblûs on the col between mounts Ebal and Gerizim), and from "Sichem" (=Shechem of O.T., which the LXX render by Sychem, Συχέμ, as does Stephen in Acts vii. 16): which latter he says lay at the foot of the hill and in the plain: Eusebius also distinguishes the three: and they are constantly mentioned as distinct down to the 12th century. Neapolis (Nâblûs) was built by Vespasian in the latter half of the 1st century A.D. to replace Shechem (Sychem) which had been probably destroyed in his recent war though it survived as a village to the 12th century. Neapolis was built close to, and to the west of, Shechem: it did not exist in our Lord's time, though Shechem and Sychàr did. To-day Shechem no longer exists: but is commonly merged in Nâblûs. Sychàr (modern 'Askar) lies about 1½ miles east of Nâblûs, and some 650 yards north of Joseph's tomb, and about half a mile north of Jacob's well. The five sites of Nâblûs, Shechem, Sychàr, Joseph's tomb, and Jacob's well, all lie in an isosceles triangle of which the two sides measure 1½ miles each; with a base of half a mile occupied by Sychàr, the tomb, and the well; the apex being Nâblûs, on the west.

"Near to the field (χωρίον) which Jacob gave to his son Joseph." From a comparison of Gen. xii. 6: xxxiii. 18, 19: xlviii. 22: Joshua xxiv. 32: and Acts vii. 16

("which Abraham bought . . . in Shechem," R.V.), it would seem that Abraham originally bought the field at Shechem where he first pitched his tent in Palestine, and where the Lord appeared to him for the first time since he entered the land, and where he built his first altar to the Lord: that he bought it for a sum of silver, as he afterwards bought Machpelah in Hebron: and that he bought this Shechem field from the sons of Emmor: that to this very spot came Jacob 180 years later, on his return from Mesopotamia with great wealth and retinue, following in Abraham's track; came, knowing that this piece of land was his by right of inheritance from his grandfather who had bought it: found that by lapse of so long a time his claim was disputed: had to fight for it, and won it by his bow and spear (Gen. xlviii. 22) "from the Amorite": and, having established thus his claim to it, yet thought it prudent to go through a formal act of purchase for a merely nominal price, "100 lambs" (£10 or so): thus conciliating his neighbours who owned the surrounding land, and precluding any subsequent dispute of his claim. Anyway, tradition seems to have it that the "field" where Abram first pitched his tent and built an altar (Gen. xii. 6, 7) was the same field that Jacob won with his bow and spear and bequeathed to Joseph (xlviii. 22) and also bought for "100 lambs" (xxxiii. 19): in it was Jacob's well, sunk by him, to which Christ came (John iv. 4): in it was Joseph's tomb (Joshua xxiv. 32)—the tomb and the well are 180 yards apart: in it was the famous oak by Shechem where the teraphim or "strange gods" were buried by Jacob (Gen. xxxv. 4): and under the same oak Joshua set up the great stone (Joshua xxiv. 21) "by the sanctuary of the Lord," *i.e.* by the holy place where Abram had set up his first altar.

(6) "And Jacob's spring (πηγὴ) was there." This "spring" of Jacob is beyond doubt that known to-day by Samaritan, Jew, Christian, and Moslem as the "spring" ('ain), or "well" (bîr), "of Jacob." Its present depth is no more than 75 feet owing to accumulation of stones and rubbish at the bottom (so Anderson, who went down it in

1866): Maundrell (end of 17th century) found it to be 105 feet deep: whilst Arculf, in 7th century, who drank from it, says "the well that I saw has a depth of twice twenty orgyiæ," and he gives an orgyia correctly as about six feet; he therefore gives the depth as about 240 feet in his time. Maundrell found fifteen feet of water in it as late as May. It is not to-day a spring (πηγὴ) properly so called, where water gushes up from below, but a very deep cistern (φρέαρ) into which water percolates from above: and it is dry all the summer. Doubtless Jacob sank it in drought till he struck the gushing spring, as did Isaac further south (Gen. xxvi. 19), till he reached the "living waters" or spring. But that Jacob should go to the vast labour of sinking this well in a neighbourhood of abundant rivers and surface springs may be explained by his being a stranger with many flocks in a country already strongly occupied, exactly as the O.T. describes his position: cf. Isaac's similar position (Gen. xxvi. 14–22).

"Jesus, therefore, being wearied from the journey, was sitting thus at the spring," *i.e.* at what was still known as Jacob's *spring*, though it was now no more than a cistern (φρέαρ, verses 11, 12). The "therefore" implies that this well was the usual halting-place of pilgrims traversing Samaria. "Was sitting thus," *i.e.* as one tired, as one simply resting, as though without any other immediate purpose.

"And it was about the sixth hour." As to the hour, we have already seen (at i. 39, p. 34) that this Evangelist reckons the hours differently from the three Synoptists. Whereas they reckon twelve hours from sunset to sunrise and another twelve from sunrise to sunset, so that the "sixth" hour is with them midday, John reckons them as we do, viz. twelve hours from midnight to midday, and another twelve from midday to midnight, so that the "sixth" hour with him is sunset (and sunrise). This passage (iv. 6) is the second that proves it. The common interpretation, which assumes John's reckoning to be the same as that of the Synoptists, makes the "sixth hour" to be midday:

April 11, Sun., sunset.

but this halt at Jacob's spring is clearly paralleled by the regular halt here for the night by all Galilean pilgrims to and from Jerusalem: it is the midway point between Judæa and Galilee—the only place at which pilgrims passed a night on Samaritan territory: they had to break the journey somewhere, and probably here alone did the Samaritans allow their unwelcome rest. Again, He would not be "wearied by the journey" at midday, though He might easily be so by sunset. Again, midday is not the hour at which women draw water for the house, but sunset is. Again, at midday the men (ἄνθρωποι) would not have been in the city (verses 28, 30), but in the fields at work: whereas after sunset they would naturally be in the city and near the evening meal.

(7) "There cometh a woman of Samaria to draw water." "Of Samaria" (ἐκ τῆς Σαμαρείας), *i.e.* a native of the country called Samaria. It is not necessary to suppose that she lived within the walls of the city of Sychàr, half a mile off: her house was probably nearer Jacob's well than was the city of Sychàr, but Sychàr was her nearest city (see verse 28). The people who lived within the walls do not seem to have used this well, it being too far off, and there being an abundance of good water within shorter distance.

It is obvious that the Samaritans, ever since the Baptist came preaching six months ago, must have been moved by his announcement of the Messiah's approach, and at the news that he had marked out the Man: they must also have heard and been startled by rumours from Jerusalem telling how the Jews' Messiah had come publicly forward, doing "signs" last week in the City at the Passover. It was but three days ago that northern pilgrims returning along this road had been discussing with animation what they had seen and heard. The bitterness between Samaritan and Jew would probably be more than commonly keen just now: for it is usual that when one sect is stirred by special religious exaltation, its neighbour feels a corresponding fervour, and the sense of differences between them is intensified.

The woman suspecting nothing comes to the well. She sees a solitary Jew, seemingly one of the pilgrims, returning from Jerusalem, sitting on the well-head as though wearied with the day's journey. Without a second glance she lets down her pitcher, draws it up full, and is about to return, when suddenly the stranger begs her for a drink.

"Jesus says to her, 'Give Me to drink.'" What! a Jew making a kindly advance to her, placing himself under an obligation to her, showing his friendly feeling to her so that she may talk freely with him (see a similar opening in Gen. xxiv. 17). Had He not been alone but been accompanied by His disciples, the woman would certainly not have ventured to come near and talk: hence John's remark that—

(8) "His disciples had gone away to the city (*i.e.* Sychàr) to buy food." No doubt she gives Him the pitcher to drink from, and He, having drunk, returns it to her.

(9) "Therefore the Samaritan woman says to Him, 'How is it that thou being a Jew askest drink from me being a Samaritan woman? for Jews do not have intercourse with Samaritans:'" She implies, of course, that the intolerance lies with the Jews. Yet, to her surprise, here was a Jew taking the initiative in friendliness, going even so far as to ask for a drink from her pitcher, which other Jews would have held to be unclean.

(10) Jesus replies with a tender but compelling tone, which must have arrested her, that if she knew what gift God was in these days giving, and Who the speaker was that was asking her for a drink, their mutual positions would have been reversed: she would have asked of Him, and His gift to her would have been Living water; for that was what God was now giving.

(11) The woman answers, "Sir" (κύριε): she had not so addressed Him at first: she has now recognized in Him something above the common: already the beginnings are stirring that will end in Faith: already the miracle of His grace is working in her: He has sensitized her soul.

A similar case occurs in iv. 49, where again the use of the word κύριε marks an access of spiritual insight. "Thou hast nothing to draw with, and the cistern (φρέαρ) is deep": she is slowly realizing that He is not speaking of literal physical water, for He has no means of reaching it and has even begged for it. Also the cistern (φρέαρ) did not contain 'living water,' for it was no longer a πηγή, a gushing spring. "Whence therefore hast thou the Living water?" 'By this "Living water" (so she argues), He must have some bigger meaning, He must imply a claim to be a greater than the patriarch Jacob, for the best the patriarch could do for us was to give us this (spring which is now but a) cistern, and this water which is no longer living or gushing.'

(12) "Can it be thou art greater than," etc. (μὴ σὺ μείζων εἶ . . .). The phrase does not mark incredulity, but marks a dawning belief that startles: precisely as in verse 29, μήτι οὗτός ἐστιν ὁ Χριστός; means "can it be that this is the Messiah!" So here, 'I half believe thou *art* greater than, etc., and that thou art dealing with a Spring and Water greater than Jacob's well.'

(13) His answer is in effect that she is right in her surmise: for "Everyone who drinks of this water shall thirst again, but whoso drinks (14) of the Water that I (emphatic ἐγὼ) shall give him shall never thirst." This Living Water He will give is the "water and Spirit" of iii. 5, which originates the new Birth.

Here one might ask, 'What then? shall the baptized not thirst? rather "blessed are they that hunger and thirst after righteousness," and who should so hunger and thirst but the baptized? Therefore the promise that he "shall never thirst" refers not to this life, but to the Resurrection life when the work begun here in the new Birth shall have been perfected by the complete sloughing off of the old and by the complete putting on of the new Man.

"The Water which I shall give him shall become in him a Spring (πηγὴ) of Water leaping-up into eternal Life." This "Water leaps-up into eternal Life" because it is animate with the Spirit of God, the Divinity of our

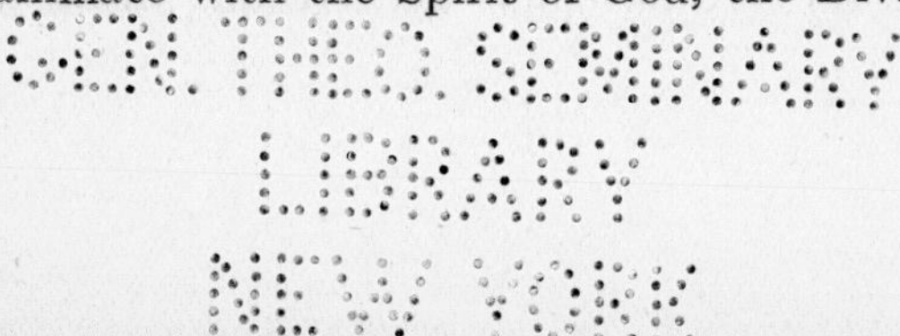

Lord: and rising like sap in His mystical Body makes all His members live the eternal Life. Weak though the Spring be to-day because of the obstructions it meets with, there is promise of a more copious flow.

(15) The woman is now quite aware that His meaning lies not on the physical but on the spiritual plane: and that He is talking in metaphor. She was no ignorant peasant, nor was He talking 'over her head.' Though no one ever grasped the whole of what He meant, He never spoke above the dawning intelligence of a *bonâ fide* listener: to do so would have been to belie the principle of the Incarnation—the coming down to be within reach of a hand. In her answer, "Sir, give me this Water, that I thirst not nor come all this way (διέρχωμαι) hither to draw," the woman is not making a silly jest: she is boldly and intelligently carrying on the metaphor which He had begun. Her meaning is that she may neither herself thirst nor yet (he whom she loves, viz.) her man, for whom she comes here drawing water: she asks for the draught of Life both for herself and that she may pass it on to her "husband."

(16) Jesus reading her desire, which He Himself has wakened, to possess and to spread the spiritual Life, falls in with her desire, but out-tops her hopes, bidding her to go and call this her "husband," to bring him she loves along with her here to the fountain-head to the Giver of Life. He speaks of her "husband" purposely, though knowing the man is not so: by showing a generous confidence in her, He means to compel her to a generous confidence in Himself, which will result in her making a full and generous avowal of her position.

(17) She answers, "I have not a husband": the words are her confession of her irregular life. She has reflected 'will this Man of God be so kindly to me when he knows the whole truth about me? but at all costs I will tell it out to Him.' She was of those who are won by trust, not by rebuke.

(18) "Jesus says to her, well saidst thou, 'Husband I have not,' for five husbands hadst thou, and he," etc.

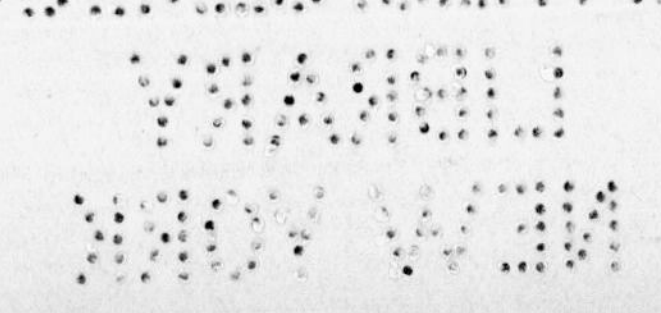

His answer came that, though all her life lay open before Him, she had done well to confess her position, viz. that she was living with one who was not her husband: and as a proof of His knowledge of her past He tells her that she had had five husbands (of whom at any rate four, and possibly all five, were either dead or legally separated from her) and that he whom she now had was not her husband. Also that in her confession she had shown a love of truth in that she had made no attempt to screen herself.

(19) This proof of His knowledge of her past takes her aback: she was certain that her past was unknown to her neighbours: she had probably not always lived here. The effect in her case is similar to that in the case of Nathanael (see under i. 48, 49): a fresh light breaks upon her with regard to this Stranger: the knowledge He has shown argues that He can be no less than a Prophet, for to the Prophets many secret things lay open: but she has no idea that He is more: "Sir, I perceive that thou art a Prophet."

Although a Jew, He being a Prophet may be trusted to solve that question which was at the root of the hostility between Samaritan and Jew—the question whether Jerusalem was or was not the one religious centre for all Palestine, a question that must have become urgent with many Samaritans in view of the Baptist's activity during the last six months.

(20) Samaritans had long had their religious centre in Samaria, in their temple on Gerizim, built 4th (or 5th) century B.C. as a rival to that at Jerusalem. Jews, on the other hand, maintained that no Temple was permissible in Palestine except the one at Jerusalem, though there was no restriction as to the number of synagogues that might be built. Men might worship at the latter by prayer and by listening to the reading of the Law and the Prophets: but at the Temple alone was plenary, sacrificial, worship allowed; and to the Temple the nation had to journey three times a year to the great festivals. The Jews had succeeded in destroying the Samaritan temple about B.C. 130, and had hitherto prevented their rebuilding

it. Samaritans were willing to recognize both Temples, one at Gerizim for themselves, one at Jerusalem for Jews: what they objected to was the exclusiveness of Jerusalem's claim—the claim to be the only place where a full worship was possible. The woman wants to know how the truth stands.

(21) The reply is to the effect that an "hour" is coming when neither the worship at Gerizim nor the worship at Jerusalem would be the acceptable worship of The Father.

(22) *Gerizim is ruled out* because "*you* (Samaritans) worship that which you know not," viz. a God whose character, and whose purposes toward the human race, as revealed through the Prophets, were unknown; inasmuch as Samaritans recognized no revelation later than Moses: whereas "*we* * (Jews) worship that which we know," *i.e.* Jews are acquainted with the character and purposes of the Being they worship, having before them the further revelation made through all the Prophets from Samuel till John the Baptist? "For (the promised and expected) Salvation comes forth from (ἐκ) the Jews," as Samaritans themselves must admit from Jacob's prophecy (Gen. xlix. 8–12). The woman might therefore think that He was, in His answer, pronouncing in favour of Jerusalem. But no:

(23) *Jerusalem too is ruled out:* for "an hour is coming, indeed now is, when the true worshippers shall worship The Father in spirit and truth: for indeed The Father seeks that those who worship Him should be such:

(24) "God is Spirit: and they who worship Him must worship in spirit and truth." In "spirit and truth" instead of in a mere formalism which had lost touch with the Truth; of which its sacrifices were types, but only types.

His words did not dissolve the obligation of the Jew to worship at the centre of unity, Jerusalem; nor did the

* He here identifies Himself, not so much with the Jews as with the *Prophets* of His nation, among whom the woman ranked Him, as she had just expressed in verse 19. So Chrysostom.

Apostles so understand, as may be seen from the practice of the Hebrew Christian Church: for so long as the Temple was standing, the Hebrew Christians of Palestine took part in all the Temple ritual and worship, as did also Hebrew Christian pilgrims from abroad, as is clear from the book of Acts of the Apostles. But the time was fast coming when the Temple and its ritual was to end, because the nation failed to recognize the Antitype or Truth, of whom all their ritual was but a figure. Had the Jews, alongside of ritual and symbolism, worshipped in spirit and truth, as all their Prophets were ever trying to secure, they would not have come short in their day of trial, nor would their Temple and nation have been destroyed: and the obligation to worship at Jerusalem would still *for them* have stood. We may suppose that when the conversion of Judah comes about toward the end of this Age, and the reunion of the ten tribes with Judah is effected, and the Temple rebuilt, as Ezekiel saw in vision, Jerusalem will again be the centre of religious unity rather than Gentile Rome: the change being accompanied by that vast effusion of The Spirit of which Joel speaks, and of which only the pledge or earnest has as yet been given.

(25) The woman is arrested by our Lord's words about the necessity of worshipping in spirit *and truth*, and by His promise that the time of such worship was not merely coming but at hand. She says, yes, " I know that Messiah " (who is called Christ) * " is coming." John the Baptist's

* *ὁ λεγόμενος Χριστός*, "Who is called Christos," *i.e.* Anointed. The words are not the woman's but the writer's, as in every other case in the N.T. They are not merely or mainly his Greek rendering of the Hebraic word Messias, but are rather a statement of the name that was more familiar to his readers. This is made more certain by instances where the second name has not the same meaning as the first, *e.g.* Matt. i. 16 (and often), *Ἰησοῦς ὁ λεγόμενος Χριστός*, "Jesus who is called Christos": Matt. iv. 18 (and x. 2), *Σίμωνα τὸν λεγόμενον Πέτρον*, "Simon who is called Petros," where Petros is the name by which this Simon was better known to the Greeks for whom the Greek version of Matthew was made: Col. iv. 11, *Ἰησοῦς ὁ λεγόμενος Ἰοῦστος*, "Jesus who is called Justus," where Justus is the Latin name by which this Jesus was better known to the Colossians. It is the same in John xi. 16: xx. 24: and xxi. 2, *Θωμᾶς ὁ λεγόμενος Δίδυμος*, "Thomas who is called Didymus," where "Didymus" (Twin) is only incidentally the Greek rendering of the Hebrew "Thomas."

mission must have roused the whole of Palestine—Samaria * as well as Judæa and Galilee—to the expectation of Messiah's imminent advent. "When *He* (emphatic ἐκεῖνος, He at last, He for whom all have waited) "comes, He will announce to us all things"—will reveal to them all Truth. So only would they know Him whom they worshipped: so only would they give Him proper worship. She would readily admit that Messiah was to come from the Jews: she would also recollect that many said He had appeared last week in Jerusalem and had done "signs." It probably even flashed upon her suddenly 'what if this Man were He?' and, with the flash, came His words—

(26) "I that am talking to thee am He."

(27) "Hereupon came His disciples," who were probably a considerable number, including among others all who were later selected as the Twelve (see under ii. 2): "and they were wondering that He was talking with a woman": it being against Rabbinical etiquette that a Rabbi should talk with a woman in a public place. "However no one said, 'What seekest Thou?' or 'What talkest Thou with her?'" Great as was their surprise, they felt it was not a matter for their intrusion, unless, or until, He chose to speak to them of it.

(28) At the coming of all these people, "the woman left her pitcher" there—showing she meant quickly to return—"and went off to the city" of Sychàr: "and she says to the men" (or "the folk," τοῖς ἀνθρώποις) (29) "'Come! see a Man who told me all things that (ever) I did! Can this be the Christ?'" "Can this be" (μήτι οὗτος ἐστιν), exactly as in verse 12, 'it almost seems to me that He

* There is remarkable evidence of the veneration in which the Baptist was held by the Samaritans. After the Jews had betrayed him to Herod, Herod had him carried to Machærus in Peræa (Jos., *Ant.*, 18, v. 2), there imprisoned him, beheaded him, and handed over his head to Herodias's daughter: the body was taken by John's disciples and buried. Where? According to all tradition, at *the city of Samaria* (Rufin., xi. 28: Jerome *ad Marcellam*: Theodoret., iii. 3). With the Samaritans his body was safe, for Samaria was independent of the Sanhedrin and of Herod. Here, in a rock tomb alongside that of the Prophet Elisha, his bones lay, until in the reign of Julian (A.D. 361–363) they were scattered. The cenotaph of the Baptist is held in veneration to-day by Christian and Moslem alike.

must be.' 'Come and talk to Him, hear Him, feel His personality; and you will agree with me. This must be the Man of whom John the Baptist spoke as being the Christ or Messiah: this must be the Man we hear of as having come publicly forward in Jerusalem as Messiah.'

Neither she nor the Samaritans as a body associated with the Messiah (the Christ or the Anointed One) any very definite idea: at any rate He would be a very wonderful Prophet (Deut. xviii. 15, 18), about whom there was much mystery and great expectation: and He would prove to be the long-promised "Saviour of the world" (see at verse 42).

(30) "They went-forth out of the city" of Sychàr—no doubt her "husband" among them—"and they were on their way to Him." The distance between city and well being half a mile.

(31) "In the meanwhile the disciples were asking Him 'Rabbi, eat'"; as they produced the food they had brought back with them. They call Him *Rabbi* (see under i. 38): that He was really God dwelling among them, the disciples had not yet learnt to realize, though they believed all that the Baptist had said of Him. How many of us too repeat *bonâ fide* the Creeds without at all realizing all that the words import.

(32) To their anxious care for Him He replied, "I (ἐγὼ, emphatic) have a food for eating which *you* do not know"—a food which to you is not food. And thereby He drew a distinction between Himself and them, whilst not denying that their physical hunger was shared by Him.

(33) "The disciples therefore," not understanding Him, "said one to another, 'Can it be that some one brought Him food to eat?'" *i.e.* in their absence.

(34) Jesus, knowing what they were whispering, says to them that He was not talking of their sort of food, but "*My* food," viz. that of which I spoke just now as being not known to *you* as food, "is to do the will of Him that sent Me and finish His work." The aorists ποιήσω, "do," and τελειώσω, "finish," show that He has here in mind, not so much the constant aim of His life as that aim

exemplified on this particular occasion, where He has made so rapid a finish in the conversion of the Samaritan woman. In the following verses He lays the stress on the idea of finishing, on the rapidity with which He finishes, on the power He shows in bringing a work to a finish almost as soon as He sets His hand to begin it. And in that again He differs from them.

(35) " Do not *you* (emphatic ὑμεῖς) say," *i.e.* is it not a common proverb among men at sowing-time, " ' Yet a four-month * and the harvest comes ' ? " *i.e.* among men seed-time and harvest are far apart, a long and tedious wait is needed for all growth before its end is reached, so that the man who sows is often not the man who reaps. But see the difference here where I have been the husbandman : " Look, I say to you, lift up your eyes and behold the fields, how that they are white unto harvest." His metaphor is taken from barley fields : barley whitens to harvest, wheat reddens. But His appeal is to the human harvest, viz. the Samaritans from the city of Sychàr who are seen hurrying to Him.

(36) " *Already* " (emphatic) " the Harvester " (meaning Himself) " is receiving wages, and is gathering fruit into Life eternal, with the result that the Sower " (viz. Himself) " is rejoicing along with the Harvester," *i.e.* it is not an hour ago that I began to sow, and already I am reaping the harvest : it is not as when men sow and they have to wait long for the harvest to mature.

(37) ' Not with Me has the proverb held good that the sower is one and the reaper another ; but that saying is true in your case, in this that (ἐν τούτῳ) (38) I sent you to harvest what *you* (ὑμεῖς, emphatic) never laboured to grow : the work of tilling and dressing and sowing the ground in

* ἔτι τετράμηνός ἐστιν = " yet a four-month." Seed-time in Palestine was from middle of Tisri (October) to middle of Kislev (December) : see Wieseler's *Synopsis*, Sect. 2, chap. 2, for Rabbinical statement. From end of seed-time (mid-Dec.) to beginning of harvest gives thus an interval of four months, for the barley harvest begins mid-April in the Jordan valley and on the lake of Tiberias. The date at which our Lord is speaking in the text seems to be accurately, Sunday, April 11, of A.D. 28. Barley harvest begins at Nâblûs in May.

Israel and Judah was done by other hands—the hands of Moses and of the Prophets: *you* (ὑμεῖς) enter into the benefit of their labour.'

What exactly is the bearing of this whole episode? or at least what is the instruction conveyed in it by our Lord to the disciples? He seems to use it as a means of heartening them up to the work before them. His public active Ministry has but recently begun: it is but a week since His first overt appearance as Messiah in Jerusalem: the Sanhedrin and the doctors of the Law have shown their open hostility to Him: His disciples may well have been despondent at the prospect, doubting the possibility of overcoming the difficulties ahead. He will do a sign to encourage them. In the space of half an hour, during which they were absent buying food, He has converted to a belief in Himself as Messiah one of that most stubborn Samaritan race—a race that for five centuries had been more bitter against the Jew than any other race upon earth: and not only so, but so vivid is the Faith He has by His divine power breathed into her that she has hurried to the town, a-flame to make public her discovery, and so strangely has the grace of God co-operated with her, touching the hearts of her hearers, that she is now hastening back to Him with all that town behind her. If He can do this in so short a time, with such perverse material as Samaritans, how simple should prove the task He has given His disciples, viz. that of converting their own people who for centuries had been instructed as to Messiah by the Prophets with an ever-increasing clearness of definition.

On the spiritual plane, this work of His was analogous with that first miracle at Kana on the physical plane. In one case, His instantaneous change of water into wine as against His ordinary lengthy process by which He causes the vine to elaborate water into wine: and in this other case, His instantaneous conversion of the Samaritan sinner as against that secular process of education by means of the Prophets which He used with Israel and Judah.

(39) "And of that city many of the Samaritans believed

into Him, because of the word of the woman bearing witness 'He told me all things that (ever) I did.'" Such is John's comment on the marvel of that day as he looks back on it and ticks off the details one by one:—

1. It was but *one* city, and a small one: but 2, it produced *many* believers: and 3, they were *genuine* believers (ἐπίστ. εἰς αὐτόν): and 4, of that difficult material *Samaritans:* and 5, the effect was done by *one simple* argument: and that 6, uttered by a *woman:* and 7, she was *the* notoriously lax woman: and 8, her witness *could not be corroborated*, for it dealt with secrets known only to her.

(40) After making this pregnant reflection, the Evangelist continues the narrative. "When, therefore, the Samaritans were come to Him, they asked Him to abide with them" (παρ' αὐτοῖς, at their city). As, in any case, our Lord and His disciples would have passed the night here (it is the night between Sunday and Monday), the Samaritans by this request meant that He should not leave them on the following morning as did all other pilgrims, but that He would prolong His stay: which He did. For—

"He abode there two days": * which means that He stayed there the remainder of that day (Sunday) and the next day, Monday, April 12. Greeks, Romans, and Jews, in numbering days, habitually reckoned both terms (*a quo* and *ad quem*). So He must have left the city *Monday* evening.

Whilst He Himself stayed at Sychàr "two days" He seems to have sent on His disciples ahead to Galilee. An invitation by the people of Sychàr to Him to be their guest cannot be supposed to cover all His followers. A friendship for Him personally would not efface the ingrained

* Although John reckons the civil Day (twenty-four hours) as we do, and as the Romans did, from midnight to midnight (see at iv. 53: xx. 19), he like everyone, whether Hebrew, Greek, Roman, or modern European, reckons the natural day (as opposed to night) from sunrise to sunset. In all these languages one word has to serve for these two different meanings. It is only the context that can determine whether the Heb. *yom*, the Gk. ἡμέρα, the Latin *dies*, the English *day*, etc., means the twenty-four hours or only the hours of daylight. John is here using ἡμέρα (day) in the sense of the civil Day.

prejudice between Samaritans and His co-nationals. The custom would still be binding, as regards His disciples, that they should pass on as quickly as possible out of Samaritan territory, viz. on the morning of the morrow, Monday, April 12. Further, as we shall see later, He seems to have given an intimation to at any rate some of them to make arrangements for finally leaving their several occupations, so as to be able to join Him more continuously when He arrives in Galilee after them. And again, they would be told to spread the news in advance of Him that He was coming almost at once.

(41) "And" during His stay at Sychàr "many more believed because of His word." In the Greek there is no contrast between the effect of His word and that of the woman's word: the A.V. wrongly inserts "own." John's meaning is simply that during the stay His reasoning and discoursing added greatly to the number of the believers and supplemented the woman's work.

(42) "And to the woman they said (imp. ἔλεγον), 'No longer is it because of thy talk that we believe: for we ourselves have heard and know that this One is indeed The Saviour of the world.'" They are not ungenerously disparaging her work, but they are saying that the impression they all received from hearing Him was precisely the same as was hers: all alike in His presence became aware that their inmost thoughts and all their past were bare to His vision: in that blaze of light which revealed to each his own true self, each recognized how this Man knew and responded to all his needs.

In calling Him "The Saviour of the world" (ὁ Σωτὴρ τοῦ κόσμου) they not only confess Him to be The Saviour of the race first promised in Eden (Gen. iii. 15), but they see in Him *The Saviour of the world* of whom their own patriarch Joseph was the type: for the title conferred on Joseph at the time of the famine by Pharaoh (Gen. xli. 45) of (*Ṣapnath Pa'aneaḥ*, or as the Coptic is better preserved by the LXX). Ψονθομφανὴχ meant *The Saviour of the world* according to modern Egyptologists and Gesenius, thus agreeing with Jerome who rendered it *Salvator mundi.*

No more is heard of these converts: for Acts viii. 5 deals not with Samaria the province, but with Samaria the capital town (ἡ πόλις), which was some seven miles distant to the west of Sychàr. The readiness with which the district (verse 25) received the gospel may have been due to this beginning at Sychàr.

The name of the Samaritan woman of John's account is given in the Greek hagiology as St. Photinia.

NOTE.

The notice (verse 40) "He stayed there two days," coupled with that in verse 43, "after the two days He went out thence," makes it certain that He did not prolong His stay in the city beyond the Monday evening, for had He stayed on to Tuesday morning, John must have said, "He stayed there *three* days" and "after the *three* days He went out"—according to the constant usage of Hebrew, Greek, and Latin: *e.g.* Mark's "after three days" (μετὰ τρεῖς ἡμέρας), viii. 31: ix. 31: x. 34 = Matthew's "on the third day" (τῇ τρίτῃ ἡμέρᾳ), xvi. 21: xvii. 23: xx. 19. Also see Matt. xxvi. 2 and Mark xiv. 1, where "after two days" = to-morrow. And again, John xi. 6, pp. 254, 258.

We may infer, perhaps, that leaving the city on Monday evening He passed that night alone in prayer in the open, as He did at other crises in the Faith of His disciples. The crisis here would be due to yesterday's betrayal by the Sanhedrin to Herod of His herald John the Baptist.

§ VII

JOHN IV. 43–54

The second return of Jesus to Galilee. The courtier's son healed.

(43) "And after the two days He went out thence." Leaving the city on Monday evening, He presumably left the district on Tuesday, April 13. Apart from the request of the Samaritans, there was probably a secondary reason that determined this "two days" stay at Sychàr. At iv. 1–3 we have seen reason to name Sunday evening, April 11, as the date of the arrival at Jacob's well: at iii. 23, 24, we saw reason to name Sunday, April 11, as the date of John's betrayal to Herod at Aenon on the north-east border of Galilee and Samaria.

April 13 } Tues.
Nisan 23 }

Now, it seems that Herod had but recently returned from Rome (the voyage mentioned by Josephus, *Ant.* XVIII. v. 1) to his tetrarchy of Galilee and Peræa, and yet more recently married Herodias in spite of John's protest. It seems also that almost immediately after this return from Rome to Tiberias, his capital, he was forced to move to Machærus his southernmost fortress ninety miles off on the frontier of Peræa and Arabia: it had recently been transferred to him from Aretas (probably as a result of Herod's late interview at Rome with the emperor), and here his presence was for some months required as a check upon that powerful sheikh. Hither he took with him his new wife, his court and army, and his prisoner John. Herod's long residence here accounts for his never having seen Jesus before the Passover of the following year (Luke xxiii. 8).

We may conjecture that one object of our Lord's

waiting the two days at Sychàr was to give time for Herod's removal to Peræa before He Himself ventured to return to Galilee.

The news of the Baptist's "betrayal" or "delivery over" to Herod would reach Sychàr (eighteen miles from Aenon) on the following day, viz. Monday, April 12. On Tuesday, April 13 (Herod now being well on his way to Machærus), our Lord was free to return into Galilee. Thus the data given by the Evangelist John tally exactly with the account of Matthew (iv. 12) who says that "Jesus on hearing that John had been betrayed" (or "delivered over," παρεδόθη), "withdrew into Galilee": and with Mark (i. 14), "after John had been betrayed (παραδοθῆναι) Jesus came into Galilee": and with Luke (iv. 14), "Jesus returned in the power of The Spirit into Galilee." The three Synoptists leave a complete blank between the Temptation of our Lord and His return to Galilee—a space of seven weeks from February 26 to April 13, which John has filled in.

April 13, Tues.

Leaving Sychàr district early on Tuesday, April 13, He would reach Jenîn (Engannim of O.T.) —the regular next stage—on that evening: it is on the border of Samaria and Galilee and about twenty miles from Sychàr.

(44) Why, it might be asked, did He go into Galilee instead of preaching in Judæa? for Judæa was His native country, and Jerusalem the national centre. Because, says John, "Jesus Himself bore witness that 'A prophet in his own country has no honour':" *i.e.* in His own life Jesus was a remarkable instance of the truth of the proverb that, etc. "In his own country" applies in this case to our Lord's natal Judæa, He having been born at Bethlehem. The proverb is again quoted in Matt. xiii. 57 = Luke iv. 24, where the application is to Nazareth (in Galilee), His home of thirty years.

(45) "When therefore He was come to Galilee, the Galileans welcomed Him, having seen all that He had done in Jerusalem on the festival-day (see p. 71), for they too went for the festival-day": the term ἡ ἑορτὴ (the festival),

when used in connection with the Passover,* means the one day (Jerome's *dies festus*), Nisan 15 (the *ḥag*, ἑορτὴ, festival-day of Num. xxviii. 16, 17). This (according to the popular usage of reckoning days whether of Jew, Greek, Roman, or ourselves) was reckoned from sunrise to sunset (the twelve hours of daylight). According to the Jewish ritual usage, stringently observed by all Jews in the case of their weekly Sabbath, the Day (twenty-four hours) began twelve hours earlier at sunset just as the ecclesiastical Day does in the Latin and Greek Churches still. According to the civil usage throughout the Roman empire, the Day (twenty-four hours) began at midnight, six hours later than the ecclesiastical Day and six hours earlier than the daylight day, just as it does throughout Christendom to-day.

It may be added here that the interval between sunrise and sunset was divided into twelve cairic "hours," so that an hour of daylight was necessarily longer in summer than in winter and only corresponded with our hour at the equinoxes. The interval between sunset and sunrise was divided into four equal "watches" of three cairic hours each, an hour of night being shorter in summer.

In the present passage (verse 45) the term ἡ ἑορτὴ (the festival-day) means the one day Nisan 15, whether we reckon it by popular, or by civil, reckoning: nor had our Lord, as it seems, stayed in Jerusalem beyond Nisan 15 (April 5), though the Galileans as a body might remain there till after the morning of Nisan 16, April 6 (see at iii. 22).

The disciples who had left Sychàr on Monday morning, April 12 (see at verse 40) would have arrived that same evening at Jenîn: they had a day's start of Him, and would, of course, have spread the news as they crossed into Galilee that He was following on the next day: the chief of them, Peter, Andrew, James, John, would reach home at Capernaum on Tuesday evening, April 13. Thus, when our Lord crossed the Galilee frontier at Jenîn, He would be met

* When, however, this term ἡ ἑορτὴ is used in connection with the Azyms (Feast of Unleavened Bread), or with the Feast of Tabernacles, it is applied to the whole eight or seven days over which each of these two festivals extended.

and welcomed by many Galileans who were waiting for Him.

(46) "He came therefore again to Kana of Galilee, where He made the water wine": He is without His disciples, and seems to have gone from Jenîn straight to Kana, where five weeks ago He had made the water wine.

April 14 / Nisan 24 } Wed. He would thus arrive there on the evening of Wednesday, April 14. The distance from Jenîn to Kana is twenty or twenty-six miles, according as we take Kana to be the modern Kefr Kenna or Qanah (see p. 54).

At first glance Luke (iv. 16–30) appears to imply that He went first straight to Nazareth. Further consideration, however, will show that Luke has not pretended here to use chronological order, for it is clear from his verse 23 that our Lord must have done signs and wonders in Capernaum before this visit to Nazareth: whereas from John (iv. 54) it is also clear that the "sign" described by him in verses 46–53 must have preceded any signs and wonders done in Capernaum. A close examination of Luke's gospel will show that the section from iv. 16–ix. 15 consists of documents whose arrangement has been purposely based by him on an order other than chronological.

Our Lord did not go at this time to Nazareth: for so strong was the prejudice there against accepting the carpenter as the Messiah that a month ago, immediately after His first miracle at Kana, He had removed definitely from Nazareth to Capernaum, which became henceforth His headquarters (see at ii. 12).

In revisiting Kana the intention may have been to revisit those two at whose marriage feast He had been a guest five weeks ago—a household which were probably all believers in Him.*

"And there was a certain nobleman whose son was ill

* Many of the early Fathers are of opinion that that marriage was never consummated: that His presence transformed it, evoking a rarer conception of sexual values: and that both bridegroom and bride, becoming His disciples, followed the counsel of perfect chastity.

at Capernaum." This nobleman (βασιλικὸς, a man belonging to Herod's court) had possibly been detained by his son's illness at Capernaum and therefore had not accompanied Herod when the latter set out for Machærus two or three days ago. It has been conjectured that he was the same as Chuza, Herod's "steward" or "deputy" (ἐπίτροπος) of Luke viii. 3, the husband of Joanna. The word ἐπίτροπος ranges from a viceroy to a farm bailiff.

(47) "This man having heard 'Jesus is come out of Judæa into Galilee,' went-off to Him," on behalf of his son. The news as to our Lord's arrival in Galilee would easily reach him on Wednesday evening, April 14: he would learn through those disciples who had arrived home at Capernaum yesterday evening (Tuesday, April 13: see at verse 45), that Jesus was to be at Kana to-night (Wednesday), and that He would be coming on to Capernaum on Friday. On Thursday, however, when a turn for the worse caused his boy's life to be despaired of, he could not afford to wait till Friday, but hurried off at once to Kana where he would arrive in the evening (April 15, Thursday). He is already acquainted with Jesus and His claims.

"And he asked Him to come down and heal his son, for he was at the point of death." It is improbable that this man would have requested and expected Jesus to come away twenty miles off unless he knew that He was expected anyhow at Capernaum to-morrow.

April 15, Thurs. evening.

(48) "Jesus, therefore" (*i.e.* as reading his heart) "said to him, 'Unless ye see signs and wonders, ye will not believe,'" *i.e.* believe Me to be what I claim to be. It would seem as though this courtier had said to himself, 'If Jesus succeeds in healing my son, I will believe His claims, for the boy is past all human help.' Hence our Lord's reproof: and it was accepted aright as being deserved.

(49) "The nobleman saith unto Him, 'Sir, come down before my child dies.'" The point lies in the word "Sir" (κύριε). Precisely as in verse 11, where the same word marked an access of spiritual insight, so here: the magnetism of our Lord's presence has stirred beginnings

that will grow into Faith. It would seem that the father is no longer making conditions or mental reservations.

(50) "Jesus saith to him, 'Go thy way: thy son liveth.'" The state of mind that our Lord desired in him has been effected: the healing of the boy now will serve to help on the father to a fuller faith: and where the father leads, the son and the household will follow (verse 53*b*). "The man believed (aorist) the word that Jesus said to him," viz. that his son is past the crisis and will live.

"And he went his way" (imperfect). There should be a full-stop before this clause: for it is clear from what follows that the father's return did not take place till the following day (viz. Friday, April 16): for—

April 16 / Nisan 26 } Fri.

(51) "Whilst he was on the journey down to Capernaum his servants met him with the message that his boy is living": and

(52) To his inquiry as to the hour at which he began to mend, they replied, "*yesterday* during the seventh hour the fever left him."

(53) "Therefore the father recognized that it was at that hour in which Jesus said to him, 'Thy son liveth.'"

The "seventh" hour is 7 p.m. according to John's mode of reckoning hours, which has been explained at i. 39 (p. 34) and iv. 6 (p. 98). This is the third passage that proves John's method. The common reckoning, used by the Synoptists, would make the "seventh" hour to be 1 p.m.: but that will require us to believe that the father stayed on at Kana all that afternoon; and we ask, why, when having been told to go his way, did he not hasten back to that son whose life he had secured. Whereas, if the hour was 7 p.m., he would naturally not return till the morrow, as the crisis was past: but with the early morning he would start for home, and the account then reads straightforward and natural.

We further find from this χθὲς ("yesterday") that John reckons Days as we do, and as the Romans did, viz. from midnight to midnight. See also xx. 19. The words "yesterday at the *seventh* hour," etc., should not be taken as the actual words used by the servants, else we should have to suppose that they too used John's 'Asiatic' notation of hours. John has not quoted them word for word—why should he ? but he has given the gist of their words *in terms that would be plain* for his readers of Ephesus. Also in verse 51 he has not quoted their very words, for the true reading is " met him, saying that his son lives " (λέγοντες ὅτι ὁ παῖς αὐτοῦ ζῇ), not as A.V., " met him, saying, ' thy son lives.' "

" And he himself believed and his house " : he would bring up his boy and other children in his own Faith ; and the rest of the household would, not uncommonly in those days, follow the master's lead.

(54) " This again as a second sign did Jesus, having come out of Judæa into Galilee." The " again " refers back to the similar peculiarity that had accompanied the first sign (ii. 11) He did : viz. that it was done on a return from Judæa into Galilee (i. 43). John does not mean that this was the second sign Jesus ever did, for he has already at ii. 23 told us of signs done at Jerusalem in the intervening time ; but he means that this was the second sign He did having the same peculiarity of being done *on a return from Judæa to Galilee.* This was therefore the first sign He did in Galilee after this return.

With the close of this fourth chapter in John's gospel, there follows an interval of five or six weeks from Friday, April 16, to Tuesday, May 25, which is occupied by the first Galilean mission between Passover and Pentecost of A.D. 28. Details of this interval are given by the Synoptists who begin their account of the Ministry with this return of our Lord into Galilee immediately after the imprisonment of the Baptist, which is the point to which John has brought us.

Our Lord went straight from Kana to Capernaum, as we suppose, on Friday, April 16. On arrival there, it is His intention to begin at once an active propaganda in Galilee, recognizing that the authorities in Jerusalem were intractable. His work will have to be done not by means of them,

April 16 / Nisan 26 } Fri.

nor yet merely independently of them, but in the face of their opposition. John, His faithful herald, has been betrayed to Herod and thrown into prison. Henceforth He Himself will take open action.

His preaching is in identical terms with what the Baptist's had been, "The Kingdom of God is at hand: Repent: and Believe the good news," viz. that Messiah is here and ready to set up the Kingdom of God upon earth, if they are ready to receive Him on His own terms. And in this adoption of the Baptist's language, He identifies Himself with the work of His forerunner, and sets to it the seal of His approval. The Baptist had pointed out Jesus as the Messiah, and had said the Kingdom was at hand: now that the Baptist is in prison Jesus comes with the same message, that He Himself is the Messiah and that the Kingdom is at hand.

As the Sanhedrin have failed Him, the next step will be to train a body of men who shall take their place.

On this Friday, April 16, on His way to Capernaum, occurs the call of Peter and others, *e.g.* Mark i. 16, Matt. iv. 18, Luke v. 2: it is their second call, the call to surrender henceforth their ordinary occupations. They had received a first call to discipleship some six or seven weeks ago (John i. 37–42), and they will receive yet a third call (viz. to the Apostolate) a month hence (May 2, Sunday).

To the interval between the close of chap. iv. of John's gospel and the opening of chap. v. belong—

Matt. iv. 18–end of xiii. Mark i. 16–vi. 13. Luke iv. 15–ix. 6.	=	The Galilean ministry between Passover of A.D. 28 and Pentecost of same year.

The interval extends from Friday, April 16, of A.D. 28 to Tuesday, May 25, of the same year, and falls in what would have been the 30th Jubilee year (October, A.D. 27 to October, A.D. 28) had Jubilee years been still observed after the return from Babylon.

NOTE ON THE GALILEAN MINISTRY (APRIL AND MAY OF A.D. 28) AS BLOCKED IN FROM THE SYNOPTISTS

The diary of this interval seems to be as follows. Mark gives the chronological sequence more nearly than does either of the other two Synoptists: but none of the three attached importance to the mere time-sequence of the incidents related. It is an interesting study to trace the reasons that have governed the order in which those incidents are placed by the three severally.

In the following brief outline I have dealt with Mark's scheme as being the simplest. It is easy to fill in on this framework the further details given by Matthew down to the end of his chap. xiii., and those given by Luke down to his chap. ix. 6.

A.D. 28.	Mark	
April 16, Fri.	i. 16–20.	The definite call of Simon and Andrew, James and John, to leave their former occupations.
„ 17, Sat.	„ 21–28.	In the Capernaum synagogue, lasting till late afternoon. The fame of Jesus at once spread to all the region adjacent to Galilee.
„ „	[ii. 23–28.]	On this afternoon falls the incident ii. 23–28, rubbing the ears of wheat: their hunger must have been great to justify a breach of the Sabbath regulations: it would be due to the long session in the synagogue lasting far beyond the hour of the mid-day meal. In the Jordan depression, in which lie the lake of Tiberias and Capernaum, wheat harvest begins toward end of April. For the exact day of this incident see the footnote,* viz. the Saturday which fell this year on April 17, Nisan 27.

* This incident of rubbing the ears of corn is fixed to this Saturday by Luke's ἐν σαββάτῳ δευτεροπρώτῳ, a phrase which needs explanation and has been satisfactorily explained by the authors of *l'Art de Vérifier les dates* (vol. ii. of 2nd series), and, so far as I know, by them alone. Of the seven Sabbaths or Saturdays that necessarily fall in the fifty days between Nisan 16 (the day of the wave-sheaf, Lev. xxiii. 11, 15) and Sivan 6 (Pentecost, Lev. xxiii. 15, 16), the first is called *Sabbath of Pesaḥ*, the second is called *First Pereq*, the third is *Second Pereq*, and so on, and the seventh is *Sixth Pereq*. The word *Pereq* means chapter: and these six Sabbaths are so called because on each of them is read one of the six chapters of the book of *Aboth*, which is in the Talmud. This explains Luke's δευτεροπρώτῳ, "on *Second-First* Sabbath," viz. the Sabbath that was the *second* Sabbath in the fifty days, and was also called *First Pereq*, the Sabbath on which the first of the six homilies was delivered whose gist now forms the book of *Aboth*.

A.D. 28.	Mark	
April 17, Sat.	i. 29–31.	In Peter's house in afternoon: the cure of his mother-in-law, who at once provides them with food.
" "	" 32–34.	Cures done at door of the house immediately sunset closed the Sabbath.
" 18, Sun.	" 35–38.	Next morning our Lord goes with His disciples to the neighbouring towns: a circuit begins of nearly a fortnight; Chorazin (Kerazeh) and Bethsaida (Khan Minieh) are among the towns visited.
	" 39.	Summary of the whole Galilean ministry: the summary is followed by specified instances.
April 18 / Nisan 28 } Sun.	" 40–44.	Cure of the leper at the very beginning of the circuit of verse 38.
	" 45.	Results of that cure: they culminate after a fortnight in the incident of ii. 1–12. This accounts for chap. ii. being out of place chronologically in regard to chap. iii. and the following block down to v. 21*a*. For its beginning (ii. 1–12) is intimately connected with the cure of the leper just recorded in the last verses of chap. i. Mark's intention is to follow up the ethical consequences of that cure of the leper. The leper had been told on April 18, Sunday, to go and show himself to the priest. This, of course, necessitated his going to Jerusalem: give him three days for his journey, and a week in Jerusalem to fulfil the requirements of the Law (Lev. xiv. 10). There the Scribes and Pharisees are greatly stirred by the amazing cure which has just been verified by the priest (April 27, Tuesday). They hurry up to Capernaum to counteract our Lord's influence in the province of Galilee, and are already in Capernaum when Jesus re-enters the city "after some days" (Mark ii. 1), viz. a fortnight since He cured the leper.

This return of His to Capernaum is the same as the return mentioned again in v. 21*a*, on May 3, Monday, early.

Mark ii. 1–12, May 3, Monday (the paralytic cured and his sins forgiven). The presence of these "Pharisees and doctors-of-the-Law" "out of Galilee and Judæa and Jerusalem" (Luke v. 17 describing this scene), is no doubt due to the verification at Jerusalem of the

A.D. 28.	Mark.	
		leper's cure: so that that verification has had the effect Jesus intended (εἰς μαρτύριον αὐτοῖς, Mark i. 44), viz. of bringing the doctors of the Law up to Him in Galilee that they might reconsider their position. This scene of Mark ii. 1–12 as described by Luke where "Pharisees and doctors-of-the-Law out of every township . . . were seated," certainly suggests a formal session of inquiry, before which Jesus has been summoned.
		The reason having thus been shown why the section Mark ii. 1–12 holds the position it does, the next incident (ii. 13–22) comes naturally: for not only did it happen on the same day (as appears from Matt. ix. 9, "passed-by *from there*," viz. the house), but just as vv. 1–12 showed the hostility of the hierarchy because He claimed power to forgive sins, so did this next incident (vv. 13–22) show their hostility because "He ate with publicans and sinners," and did not keep the fasts of the Pharisees, viz. Mondays and Thursdays.
		This leads Mark to recall a third and earlier occasion for their hostility, viz. His authorizing His disciples "to break the Sabbath" under stress of great hunger (ii. 23 to end of chapter). That day, as we learn from Luke vi. 1, was Saturday, April 17: see footnote, p. 121.
		That, again, leads Mark to mention yet a fourth occasion (iii. 1–6) for their hostility, viz. His "healing on the Sabbath." But with this fourth incident of iii. 1–6 (healing the withered hand) Mark resumes the chronological order which he had abandoned at ii. 1, and he does not again break it.
		[The above block of incidents (Mark i. 40 to iii. 6), viz. 1, the leper's cure; then, after an interval, 2, the cure of the paralytic and forgiveness of his sins; 3, the eating with publicans and sinners; 4, the charge against His disciples of Sabbath breaking; 5, the healing of the withered hand; 6, the consequent decision of Pharisees and Herodians to kill Him,—occurs entire in Luke also (v. 12 to vi. 11).]
May 1, Sat.	iii. 1–6.	Healing of the withered hand in the synagogue—of Capernaum no doubt.

A.D. 28.	Mark	
May 1, Sat.	iii. 7-12.	He withdrew to the shore of the lake, followed by the great multitude: healed them: charged them not to make Him conspicuous (φανερὸν), *e.g.* by causing riots out of enthusiasm for Him (Matt. xii. 9–23).
,, ,,	iii. 13*a*.	Went up the Mount of Beatitudes in the evening after sunset, and passed the night in prayer there (Luke vi. 12).
May 2 / Iyar 12 } Sun.	,, 13*b*-19*a*.	Next morning on the mount the appointment of the Twelve to the Apostolate. Same day the Sermon on the Mount (Luke vi. 13 to end: Matt. v–viii. 1).
,, ,,	,, 19*b*.	He returns home (εἰς οἶκον) to Capernaum: healing the centurion's servant on His way (Luke vii. 1–10: Matt. viii. 5–13).
,, ,,	,, 20, 21.	The crowd so throng Him that it was impossible to eat the mid-day meal, so that His friends come to rescue Him, saying He is beside Himself (for want of food).
,, afternoon.	,, 22-end.	His discourse to the Pharisees and Scribes from Jerusalem, who accused Him of working by Beelzebul (Matt. xii. 24 to end). They are specially referring to the cure of the demoniac yesterday (Matt. xii. 22, 23. Between vv. 23 and 24 of Matt. xii. come the Sermon on the Mount of this morning). His mother and His brethren come.
,, ,,	iv. 1-34.	On this same day (Matt. xiii. 1) He went forth to the shore of the lake and taught the crowd from Peter's ship (the ship to which the "boat" of yesterday, Mark iii. 9, belonged) in parables: explaining the parables afterwards to His disciples in the evening in the house (Matt. xiii. 1–52).
,, after sunset.	,, 35.	He gives orders to cross the lake.
,, ,,	,, 36-end.	They cross the lake in a tempest, to Gerasa on the east side (Matt. viii. 18–28).
May 3, Mon.	v. 1-20.	At Gerasa: the demoniacs and the swine (Matt. viii. 28 to end).
,, ,,	,, 21*a*.	Recrosses the lake to Capernaum (Matt. ix. 1) where a great crowd gathered to Him. For they were all waiting for Him (Luke viii. 40). This is the return to Capernaum of Mark ii. 1: its place chronologically is here, as appears from Matt. ix. 1.
,, ,,	(ii. 1-12.	Cure of the paralytic and forgiveness of his sins (Matt. ix. 2–8. See pp. 122, 123).

A.D. 28.	Mark	
May 3, Mon.	ii. 13.	He went forth (from the house) again, by the lake side: the crowds: He taught them.
" "	" 14.	"And as He passed-by" (Matt. ix. 9 has "as He passed-by from there," *i.e.* from the cure of the paralytic), He bids Matthew (*i.q.* Levi) to follow Him (Matt. ix. 9). This is not Matthew's first call any more than was the call of Peter and Andrew, James and John on the lake, April 16, a first call for them (see p. 56). It is probable that all the Twelve had been with our Lord and had recognized themselves as His disciples (among a number of others) ever since He came to Galilee early in March, two months ago: for they were all probably present at the opening miracle at Kana of Galilee on March 5, see p. 56. All the Twelve had been appointed to the Apostolate yesterday morning on the Mount of Beatitudes. Matthew with the rest of the Twelve had no doubt crossed with Him to Gerasa last night. We may suppose that this morning Matthew has been making his arrangements at the custom house for a final withdrawal. Neither public nor private business could be abandoned suddenly without notice and due formalities.
" "	" 15.	The feast in Matthew's house. This great reception-feast (δοχὴ μεγάλη) made by Matthew seems to have been a mid-day dinner. Not improbably it was given to celebrate the appointment yesterday of the Twelve to the Apostolate. It would have been arranged for overnight: and the rumour about it would account for all the people having been expecting His return this morning (Luke viii. 40).
" "	" 16, 17.	The Pharisees and Scribes murmur at this feasting with publicans and sinners (Matt. ix. 11–13).
" "	" 18–20.	Also the Pharisees and John Baptist's disciples (John himself is in prison) murmur at any feasting at all on this particular day (Matt. ix. 14, 15), it being a Monday: Mondays and Thursdays were fast days with Pharisees.
" "	" 21–22.	His answer to them (Matt. ix. 16, 17). The scene of this interview between the Pharisees, etc., and our Lord was the shore of the lake,

A.D. 28.	Mark	
May 3, Mon.	ii. 21–22.]	cf. Matt. ix. 18 with Mark v. 21*b*: so after the feast in Matthew's house He went out to the shore. It is Matthew (ix. 18) who shows that the section Mark ii. 1–22 comes chronologically immediately before Mark v. 21*b*.
„ „	v. 21*b*.	And He was by the sea: *i.e.* Sea of Galilee=Lake of Tiberias.
„ „	„ 22–end.	Jairus's daughter is raised to life (Matt. ix. 18–26). This is followed by the cure of two blind men and a dumb demoniac (Matt. ix. 27–34).
	vi. 1*a*.	He leaves Capernaum and comes to Nazareth.
May 8, Sat.	„ 1*b*-6*a*.	At Nazareth with His disciples. (Matt. xiii. 54–end; Luke iv. 16–30, a section which is chronologically out of order as is evident from verse 23.)
May 9–15.	„ 6*b*.	A circuit of about a week. (Matt. ix. 35 to end of chapter. The "harvest plenteous, labourers few," is a metaphor taken from the busy wheat-harvest going on around, at mid-May.) Here falls the incident of the widow of Nain's son raised to life (Luke vii. 11–17).
May 16 } Iyar 26 } Sun.	„ 7–11.	The commission of the Twelve, who went out by twos (Matt. x. 1 to end of chapter).
	„ 12–13.	The doings of the Twelve during the following two or three weeks, until they meet our Lord again at Capernaum at beginning of June, after His return from Jerusalem, at Mark vi. 30.
May 16–20.		Meanwhile, "after ending His charge" to the Twelve, "He removed to teach and preach in their cities," *i.e.* without the Twelve (Matt. xi. 1): the cities being chiefly Chorazin, Bethsaida, and Capernaum—a group at the north-west part of the lake. Here follow the incidents of Matt. xi. 2 to end of chapter * and Luke vii. 19–35, viz.—
May 16, Sun.		John Baptist from his prison at Machærus (some ninety-five miles to the south), sends two of his disciples to Jesus.
about May 20 } Sivan 1 } Thurs.		Jesus's answer to them and John: His praise of John Baptist (Matt. xi. 4–19). He upbraids the cities Chorazin, Bethsaida, and Capernaum, where most of His acts of power had been done. This marks the close of His Galilean ministry (Matt. xi. 20 to end of chapter).*

* The section Matt. xii. 1 to end of xiii. is a block that is not in chronological order with what precedes.

A.D. 28. May 21, Fri.	During Mark vi. 12–13.	"There was a feast of the Jews, and Jesus went up to Jerusalem" (John v. 1): it is the Feast of Pentecost (Tuesday, May 25). Leaving Galilee, May 21, Friday, He might arrive at
„ 24, Mon.		Jerusalem, May 24, Monday evening.
„ 24, Mon.		John Baptist is beheaded this evening at Machærus.
„ 25, Tues.		The Feast of Pentecost. Our Lord at Jerusalem (John v. 1 to end of chapter). The Twelve are not with Him—having been sent forth on their mission on Sunday, May 16.
„ 25, Tues. evg.		On this evening the supper (at Bethany, see p. 441) given by Simon the Pharisee (Luke vii. 36 to end of chapter). [Luke viii. 1–3 is the journey through Tyre and Sidon and Decapolis (June 6 to Sept.), when He had no headquarters: it began after the return from this visit to Jerusalem at Pentecost, and thus is naturally mentioned here after the supper—the connection of thought being "Mary the Magdalene" of viii. 2, who was the same as the "woman who was in the city, a sinner," of vii. 37.*]

* The section Luke viii. 4 to end of chapter is another block not in chronological order with what precedes. It is interesting to trace the reasons why the chronological sequence is departed from. Obviously, many reasons might induce a writer to neglect it in his details.

§ VIII

JOHN V. 1–47

Pentecost at Jerusalem: the paralytic healed

(1) OMITTING all details of the first, the Galilean, ministry, which he thought had been sufficiently described in the three earlier gospels, John proceeds to block in a second gap which had been left by the Synoptists, viz. the visit to Jerusalem at the time of the Feast of Pentecost of this same year A.D. 28.

The Twelve are not with our Lord on this visit. They had been sent out on their commission on May 16 (p. 126), and will not rejoin Him till early June after His return to Capernaum from Jerusalem (p. 146).

"After these things there was a feast of the Jews: and Jesus went up to Jerusalem." Μετὰ ταῦτα ("After these things"), unlike μετὰ τοῦτο ("after this") of ii. 12, implies no dependence on, or ethical connection with, what precedes, but expresses merely a temporal sequence. He would leave the Galilean frontier on Friday, May 21, and be at Jerusalem on May 24.

This "feast" was the Feast of Pentecost, as the early Fathers held, *e.g.* Tertullian, Origen, Cyril, Chrysostom, Theophylact: the chief exception being Irenæus, who thought it was a Passover, but he was induced to that opinion by his faulty premiss that the Ministry lasted three years and a half, so that in his contention with the Gnostics he was driven to eke out the gospel details as he best could so as to cover that length of time.

A.D. 28.
May 25 / Sivan 6 } Tues.

The calendar shows that Pentecost (Sivan 6) fell this year on Tuesday, May 25.

"Feast of the Jews." From John's peculiar use of

the term "the Jews" throughout his gospel, he implies here (as we have also seen at ii. 13, and shall see again at vii. 8) that our Lord did not keep this feast with the nation, nor any of the feasts in this the year of His Ministry. His rejection by the nation had voided their festivals of all virtue and significance. But He will go up to Jerusalem at their several seasons to meet the concourse of the people.

(2) "And there is at Jerusalem by the Sheep (Gate) a pool, which is called in Hebrew Bethzetha, having five porticos." The "is" (ἔστι) clearly asserts that when John wrote (101 A.D.) the pool was still extant and had not been destroyed at the overthrow of Jerusalem by Titus in A.D. 70. The "Sheep (Gate)" is no doubt the same as the "Sheep Gate" mentioned by Nehemiah (iii. 1, 32: xii. 39), which stood at the north-east corner of the old city walls, considerably to the north of the Temple.

As to the pool that stood by this Gate, it is in all probability to be identified with the twin pool * re-discovered during excavations in A.D. 1888, thirty yards to the west of the church of St Anne, on the hill which Josephus (*War*, V. iv. 2) calls Bezetha. The pool was extant and well known for some centuries after the war of A.D. 70; but after the ruin caused by the Persians in A.D. 616, and by the Saracens in 636 A.D., it was lost under piles of rubbish: thereafter a tradition gradually grew by which

* This, the true pool of Bethzetha, is some three or four hundred feet north of the Birket Israel: it is a twin pool, for it consists of two communicating pools side by side excavated out of the solid rock: they were found vaulted over with wagon vaults of heavy masonry, the crown of the vaulting being flush with the original surface of the ground, which was many yards below the present. The five porticos were not porticos around and between two oblong open pools, but round and between the two vaultings over the pools; and access was got to the water by steps down through the vaulting. In these five porticos lay the sick folk, and on the site of one of them have been found the ruins of the church that was built toward the close of the 4th century, to commemorate this miracle. No church had yet been built here as late as 370 A.D., and the five porticos had been in ruins from, probably, the date of the destruction by Titus. Peter of Sebaste 371 A.D. is the earliest writer to mention the church. The pool and church and market-place here were known as the προβατική (*i.e.* belonging to the *Sheep* Gate) until the 7th century. The pool was known in Eusebius's time (4th century) indifferently as the προβατικὴ κολυμβήθρα (Sheep pool) and the λίμναι δίδυμοι (Twin ponds).

K

the name was transferred to the great *Birket Israel*, which was in reality the enormous fosse which alongside the Castle of Antonia defended the north of the Temple area.

(3) " In these (porticos) were lying a multitude of the infirm, blind, halt, withered; waiting for the moving of the water." For the last clause of this verse see under verse 4.

(4) " For an angel of the Lord at a certain season used to go down in the pool and trouble the water: he therefore who was first to go in after the troubling of the water used to be made whole of whatsoever disease he had " (lit. " no matter what disease he was held by ").

From MSS. evidence, this verse and the last clause of verse 3 seem not to be by John, but to be a very early insertion (at least as early as Tertullian, 2nd century) from oral tradition, to explain the position which verse 7 had left obscure. " An angel of the Lord ": Ambrose, Augustine, Chrysostom, etc., agree that the angel was one of the invisible host, and not a human official; and, as Ambrose says, " the water was visibly moved in order to show that the angel had descended," and that the water was now endowed with healing property: for the angel came and went unseen.

" At a certain season ": *i.e.* as Tertullian and Cyril say, ' once a year, viz. at Pentecost.' The crowd of infirm folk were not lying here all the year, but they came or were carried here just before the day of Pentecost (Sivan 6) each year: for how many years past the pool had had this particular property on this one day of the year does not appear, but evidently for a considerable number, as the phenomenon was well established.

This angel who quickened the water so that it healed was a type of the Holy Spirit who quickens the water of Christian Baptism so that it washes of all sin, as many of the Fathers comment. Chrysostom here observes, ' When God wished to instruct us in the belief of Baptism now nigh at hand, He drove out by means of water not merely pollutions (external, such as water might naturally reach), but diseases (internal, for which water could not naturally avail).' And He healed the man beside the pool, but without his touching the pool, to show that He could heal without the water—typical, we might say, of *Baptism of intention.*

"Of whatsoever disease he had": a clear indication that the healing power of the water was not natural but miraculous, *i.e.* supranormal: though it was a power effective against every disease, it was bestowed only at a certain season and available only to the first comer; and in these limitations it contrasted with the boundless powers inhering in the water of Baptism.

(5) "And there was a certain man there who had been thirty-eight years in his infirmity."

(6) Jesus seeing this man lying thus and knowing of his long infirmity says to him, "Wilt thou be made whole?"—not as though there were doubt about it, else why was he here? but as rousing him from apathy or despair to hope: He wishes the man's will to co-operate with Him. It is at this moment, so it seems, that the water was troubled, and the man, pointing to the turmoil, the shouting, the pushing of the crowd to secure the first dip, explains to the Stranger his (7) difficulty, how that he has no man to help him into the pool before another forestalls him in going down the steps. The man is touched by the sympathy and dignity of this Stranger who, at a moment when every one else is absorbed in watching the efforts to reach the pool, turns with keen and kind interest to his distress.

(8) It is during this confusion all around them that Jesus says to him, "Rise, take up thy bed * and walk." The command, though threefold, is one and indivisible: the man was not to stop at the "Rise" and think himself cured: the terms on which he was cured were that he should go on to taking up his bed on his shoulder and then walking with it.

(9) "And immediately the man became whole and took up his bed and began to walk" (περιεπάτει, imp.).

* κράβαττον, this "bed" is a light wooden frame on four short legs, the corded sacking supports a thin mattress clear of the ground. They are still seen in Egypt.

"And there was a Sabbath on that day." This last clause does not mean that the day was a Saturday: the peculiar phraseology, ἦν δε σάββατον ἐν ἐκείνῃ τῇ ἡμέρᾳ, shows the meaning to be that "on that day (it being a Feast day, viz. Day of Pentecost) there was *a solemn-rest* (σάββατον)." Similarly by σάββατον the Greek translators of the O.T. render the Hebrew word *Šabbaṭôn* ("solemn-rest") in Exod. xvi. 23, and again the Hebrew word *Šabbaṭ* in Lev. xxiii. 32*b*, where it is used of the Day of Atonement as being a day of "solemn-rest": and in Lev. xxv. 2, where it is used of the Sabbatical year as being a year of "solemn-rest": and in Lev. xxiii. 15*a*, where, according to Rabbinical use and exegesis, the word means, not the Saturday, but the festival-day of the Passover. The Day of Pentecost was another of these days of *rest* from servile work (Lev. xxiii. 21). Thus the "solemn-rest" or Sabbath was not confined to Saturdays, it extended to the great festivals of the year, which fell in different years on different week-days: exactly in the same way as our "day of obligation" is not confined to Sundays.

May 25 / Sivan 6 } Tues.

The calendar shows that Sivan 6 (Feast of Pentecost), the day with which we are dealing, fell this year A.D. 28 on Tuesday, May 25.

(10) The man had walked but a few steps carrying his bed, before "the Jews," *i.e.* the Sanhedrists, the party of the hierarchy, caught sight of him and stopped him, saying, "It is a Sabbath" (*i.e.* a day of solemn-rest), "it is not lawful for thee to take up (and carry) thy bed." They were perfectly right, from their point of view, in stopping the man from violating the Sabbath (see Jer. xvii. 21): no doubt they forcibly stopped him there and then: no doubt, too, our Lord knew he would be stopped, and for that reason had not told him to go home or to carry his bed to his house, as He had told the paralytic in Mark ii. 11, where the day was not a Sabbath. It seems that the man had gone but a few steps before he was stopped: for when, after being stopped, he tried to point out our Lord, he is still in the same place thronged by the crowd at the pool, though our Lord had edged away.

(11) The man justified his action, saying, "He who made me whole, it was He who said to me, 'Take up thy bed and walk.'" It is as though the man said, 'I am aware it is a day of rest, and that carrying any burden to-day is technically unlawful, but look at me, you all know me, the helpless cripple of thirty-eight years: not five minutes are gone since I was suddenly cured, not by being dipped in the pool, but by a man who simply told me to rise, take up my bed and walk: those I understand to be the conditions of my cure: if men may carry me into the pool to be cured and not break the law of "rest" in doing so, cannot I carry my bed to secure my cure and not break the law of "rest" in doing so?'

(12) "They asked him, 'Who is the man that said to thee, "Take up (thy bed) and walk"?'" The Greek idiom is not so much asking for the name as wanting the person identified by being pointed out.

(13) But he that was healed neither knew His name, nor was able to point Him out: "for Jesus had withdrawn: a crowd being in the place," viz. in the porticos over the pool. The reason of the crowd being here was to see the cure which they knew was due to be done in the pool to-day: their attention was evidently occupied in watching the water and the cure that was being effected in it: hence no one had been aware of our Lord's healing of the paralytic done behind their backs, nor yet noticed His withdrawal from the place.

(14) "After these things," and probably on this same day, "Jesus finds him in the Temple (ἱερῷ), and said to him, 'Behold, thou art become whole: sin no more, lest a worse thing come to thee.'" The words recognize that in some cases, without prejudice to any particular case (ix. 3), physical infirmities are the natural consequences of sin.

May 25, Tues.

(15) "The man went away and told the Jews, 'It is Jesus' who made him whole." A needless difficulty has been made as to the man's motive in telling the Jews who it was that healed him. Our Lord, probably on the day of the cure, went to the Temple, where, of course, He knew

the man was, to find him: and there had further talk with him (of which we have only a fragment given in verse 14), for it was His habit to heal the whole man and not only the body: and as the result, the man thenceforth was won. In his zeal for the new-found Messiah he goes to "the Jews," *i.e.* the Sanhedrists, and tells them that 'the Man who worked that cure on me was no other than Jesus, the Man of whom we have all heard both here and throughout Galilee as the healer and Messiah, the Man to whom John the Baptist witnessed when you yourselves sent your deputation to ask him, the Man you have all obstinately set yourselves against: look to it: I at any rate take my stand with Him: make what you like of it.' The man's position is closely similar to that of the blind man of ix. 30–33 in his impatience of what seemed to be the culpable blindness of the hierarchy.

(16) "And for this cause were the Jews persecuting Jesus, viz. that He was doing these things on a Sabbath" or day of solemn-rest. "Doing these things," *i.e.* violating the Sabbath by causing a man to carry a burden on a Sabbath. The imperfects "were persecuting," "was doing," show that this was not the beginning: but that our Lord, when in presence of the Sanhedrists, had already violated the law of the Sabbath as given for man, and had justified His action on the ground that He, as being the God-Man and Author of the Sabbath, was not tied by the Sabbath as were they, for the Sabbath had been appointed for those who were only men.

He had already in Galilee frequently healed on the weekly Sabbath (Saturdays), and the defence of His action that He made on these occasions seems to have permanently silenced His objectors, for thereafter He was not again accused of breaking the Sabbath by merely healing on a Sabbath. As Augustine observes: "On this occasion" (at the pool of Bethzetha) "the Jews did not blame the Lord for healing on the Sabbath, lest He should answer them" (as He had already done in Capernaum) "that if any of them had a beast fallen into a well he would pull it out on a Sabbath day: but they objected to His telling the man to carry his bed" on a Sabbath. This carrying of his bed, as Chrysostom here observes, 'was a manifest violation of the Sabbath,* and was in no way necessary to the miracle: but this order given to the paralytic Christ justified to the objecting Jews by insisting on His own Godhead (verse 17), and on His right to deal with His own laws.'

A previous rather similar instance occurs in Mark ii. 28 (=Matt. xii. 8: Luke vi. 5) at the very beginning of His Galilean ministry, where He argues that the Sabbath was made for the sake of man and not man for the sake of the Sabbath; and He gives a case where man's necessity overrode the ritual law (Mark), and another case where even the ritual law overrode the Sabbath law (Matt. verse 5)—much more shall He The Son of Man, the Messiah, the God-Man, be Lord of the Sabbath, for He was Author of the Sabbath, Maker of the ritual law, and Creator of man for whose sake all divine laws were made.

(17) "My Father works until now; I too work." 'The cure was My Father's and Mine.' Here is the justification our Lord gave of His order to the paralytic to take up and carry his bed. The object in so ordering the paralytic had been to attract the attention of "the Jews," to have a handle as it were to His discourse (of which only the pith is given) in verse 17, to the effect that just as The Father continues to work on the Sabbath by maintaining the course of Nature and interfering as it were constantly in His own laws in order to counteract the otherwise disastrous effects of man's errors, or as here at the pool by requiring that under given conditions burdens (viz. sick men) shall be carried on a Sabbath, so did He The Son. The Jews had seen clearly the issues: 'yes, God may modify His own laws for man's emergencies, but no man has authority to modify them: who is the *man* (ἄνθρωπος) that dared to bid thee take up thy bed? (verse 12).' And our Lord answers them here in verse 17. 'If I were indeed but man you would be in the right to withstand

* See Jer. xvii. 21, "Thus saith the Lord, 'Take heed to yourselves and bear no burden on the Sabbath day . . . as I commanded your fathers.'"

me, but I am also God, God The Son, and as such I have the same authority to act as has God The Father, for the One cannot act without the Other.' The discourse is given exceedingly concisely by John, as usual,—just the pith of it. But he shows (verse 18) that "the Jews" (the Sanhedrin and the high priests) understood our Lord quite correctly, as meaning that His Father was God, and that He too was God and co-equal: His relation as Son to The Father was peculiar and was not shared by any other man.

(18) And understanding Him so, "the Jews sought the more to kill Him for this cause, viz. that He not only was loosing the Sabbath," *i.e.* violating the Sabbath regulations as in commanding the paralytic to carry his bed, "but also was saying that God was His own (ἴδιον) Father, making Himself equal with God." The Jews were in no sort of doubt as to His meaning, viz. that He claimed absolute equality with God, nor has the Christian Church any doubt about it. The Jews, not understanding how it was possible, refused to believe Him: the Christian Church, believing Him, moves on to understanding.

(19) "Therefore," *i.e.* because they understood not, "Jesus answered and said to them, Verily, verily, I say to you, The Son"—whether as God or as Man—"cannot do anything of Himself unless He see The Father doing it: for whatever things He (The Father) does, these The Son also," whether as God or as Man, "likewise does." He is teaching the mysteries of the Holy Trinity, explaining the relation of The Father and The Son in the Godhead: how The Son cannot act without The Father originating action, and how The Father cannot act without The Son's executive. Hence The Son, the God-Man, is omnipotent as The Father. He is explaining also, by inference, the mystery of the Incarnation—that God The Son in becoming Man ceased not to be God, and that the Personality of Jesus is the Personality of God The Son. He is talking to Jewish theologians, to members of the Sanhedrin, to doctors of the Law who might follow His meaning: He is initiating them into the deepest

May 25, Tues.

mysteries of the Christian Faith: He therefore uses language very different from what He used when talking in Galilee to disciples in their novitiate or to the multitudes for whom such teaching would not have been suitable.

(20) "For The Father loves The Son and shows Him all things that He Himself does": hence the God-Man is omniscient as The Father.*

"And greater works than these," viz. such miracles as they had already seen worked by Him whether in Galilee or here at the pool "will He (The Father) show Him," and, by implication, will The Son, the God-Man, do, "so that ye may wonder." The Hellenistic ἵνα with subjunctive "so that," expresses result quite as often as purpose: it is the Hebrew ל with infinitive. Every Greek and Hebrew student is aware of the influence the Aramaic language had upon the classic Greek between the age of Alexander's conquest of the east and the second century of our era. Mixed colonies of Greek and Jew spread from Persia to the western Mediterranean; almost monopolizing, with the Syrians, the trade of the inland Sea.

The effect upon the Jews of the "greater works" yet to be done by our Lord would be wonder: He hardly promises that the wonder will pass into Faith. The "greater works" here named will be the raising of Lazarus from corruption to life again on this physical plane—the great miracle of nine months hence, specially meant for the Jews: also His own Resurrection to life on the physico-spiritual plane—the crowning miracle of all: also the raising to life on the same physico-spiritual plane of "many bodies of the saints who had slept" (Matt. xxvii. 52).

(21) 'You Pharisees admit that The Father raises from the dead and quickens. My message to you from The Father is that it is The Son's act every whit as much as The Father's.' The resurrection of the dead was

* Mark xiii. 32 is explained by the theologians thus:—Nescience of the day and hour of the judgment is predicated of The Son not *absolutely* but κατ' οἰκονομίαν, *i.e.* though absolutely and in Himself He knows it (for He knows all that The Father knows); yet officially, and *quâ* our Teacher and Revealer of God's purposes to us, He knows it not; for to reveal it to us would not be expedient for us.

already a tenet among the Pharisees, though the Sadducees denied it.

(22) Let them not wonder at this : for The Son has a yet more awful prerogative, viz. that of the final judgment. " It is not The Father who will pass judgment on any one, but He has given all the judgment to The Son," to the God-Man who as being Man will judge all men :

(23) " So that all should honour The Son even as they honour The Father. Whoso honours not The Son honours not The Father who sent Him." The Incarnation is every whit as much The Father's act as it is The Son's : The Father " sent," The Son " came."

(24) " Verily, verily " (words always preparatory to a mystery lying beneath the surface-meaning), " I say to you, he who hears My word and believes Him who sent Me," as having sent Me and as speaking through Me, *i.e.* believes implicitly all that I am teaching about the God-head of The Son and all that is involved in the Incarnation of The Son, " has Life eternal," for by his faith into the Man-God he partakes of His life, " and he does not come into judgment," for he is already reconciled to The Father, " but he has passed-over out of Death into Life."

(25) " Verily, verily, I say to you an Hour is coming, and now is, when the dead shall hear the voice of The Son of God, and they that hear shall live." The reference is not to all the dead (see verse 28), but only to those who belong to the " first resurrection " (Rev. xx. 4, 5*b*), which immediately precedes the Millennium. [An " Hour " (*ὧρα*) on the great dial of the equinoctial precession is a space of some 2000 years more or less, varying with the constellations—in this case ***Pisces***.]

(26) " For as The Father has Life in Himself, so also to The Son He gave to have Life in Himself " which He imparts to those who are united to Him.

(27) " Also He gave Him authority to execute judgment, because He is Man's Son," * and, He being Man, all men

* This is the only instance in the gospels where the term " Man's Son " (*υἱὸς ἀνθρώπου*, without the article) is applied to our Lord. In every other instance, and there are some eighty, the title is " The Son of Man " (*ὁ υἱὸς τοῦ ἀνθρώπου*) : see at i. 51 (p. 46).

have guarantee that fullest sympathy and understanding will accompany His judgment in each individual case, whilst His being God is guarantee against error. The Greek υἱὸς ἀνθρώπου, "Man's Son," lays stress on His true Human nature rather than on His Personality: the Syriac (which renders by *breh d'nôshô'*, as though the Greek had the article ὁ υἱὸς τοῦ ἀνθρ., "The Son of Man") is really a gloss laying stress on His Personality by using one of His titles.

(28) "Wonder not at this," viz. what He says of executing judgment, for there is to be a judgment of all soon or late, "for an Hour is coming in which *all* that are in the graves shall hear His voice:

(29) "And they shall come-forth (of the graves): they that wrought good, unto a resurrection of Life; they that acted evil, unto a resurrection of judgment." The "Hour" of the general resurrection (verse 28) is not the same as the Hour of the first resurrection, of verse 25: for, whereas the first resurrection precedes the Millennium (Rev. xx. 4, 5*b*), the second or general resurrection follows after the Millennium (Rev. xx. 5*a*, 12-15)—we may suppose during the Hour of *Aquarius* which follows on that of *Pisces.**

(30) As for the justice of His judgment, "I am not able, I (ἐγὼ), to do anything of Myself: even as I hear, I judge." So intimate and indissoluble is His union with The Father that He cannot act apart from The Father: as nothing is hidden from God The Father, so is nothing unknown to God The Son. 'Here is the guarantee against

* Those who hold with Origen that all will in the long, long run be saved, so that the works of the devil shall be destroyed (1 John iii. 8) will hold that for those who are still found reprobate at the second or general resurrection, there waits a further term or terms of probation in "The Lake of The Fire" (Rev. xx. 14). Phrases such as εἰς τὸν αἰῶνα, "for the Age," or "for ever," and εἰς τοὺς αἰῶνας τῶν αἰώνων, "for the Ages of the Ages," or "for ever and ever," are essentially dissimilar from the phrase of the Creed "without end," which is predicated of His Kingdom. The idea of infinity does not inhere in the words "everlasting" or "eternal" which derive from *ævum*, αἰών (Age). It is urged that eternal Life is unending because it is God's Life: but that eternal punishment must end when its aim (reform) is attained, and God's aims do not fail. To infinite Love would not the final loss of one soul be failure.

error, that I the Judge am not only Man, but also The Son who "hears" and voices The Father.'

"Also My judgment is just"—beyond all possibility of error—from yet another aspect, viz. "because I seek not My own will but the will of Him who sent Me." 'My human will is in perfect harmony with My Divine Will, and the will of the Sent with that of the "Sender."'

(31) "If I (ἐγὼ) bear witness about Myself, My witness is not true," *i.e.* 'If I stand alone (such is the force of the ἐγὼ) in bearing witness about Myself, etc.' Our Lord not so much disavows all self-interest, self-seeking *quâ* His Manhood: as asserts that another Personality, viz. God the Father, affirms all that He Himself asserts. He is not *arguing* with the doctors: He is *teaching* them truths about His own human nature and about the relationship of The Father and The Son in the Godhead (see under viii. 17).

(32) "There is Another (ἄλλος) Who bears witness about Me." This Other is certainly not John the Baptist, but seems to be God the Holy Spirit: and ἄλλος (one of three or more) is used in preference to ἕτερος (one of only two), as implying that besides The Father "Who sent Me," there is yet a Third in the Godhead, viz. the Holy Spirit, Who witnesses to Him in men's hearts.

"And I know that the witness which He witnesses about Me is true," *i.e.* 'I as perfect sinless Man know how the Holy Spirit witnesses in men's hearts in proportion as they are knit to God.' (This truth is further expressed in verses 37 and following.)

(33) Though the witness of the Holy Spirit in men's hearts is witness enough where hearts are clean, He had provided for their weakness an outside witness even John, whose birth had been supernaturally foretold to them by an angel in the Temple: John, whom as boy and man, they had ever regarded, and rightly regarded, as Messiah's forerunner. "*You* have sent unto John," and rightly, to ask who was the Messiah, "and John has borne witness to the truth." 'But did you accept his witness? the witness of him whom you had for thirty years known to

be Messiah's forerunner. And why did you not?' The allusion is to the Sanhedrin's embassy to the Baptist (i. 19: in Feb.), and again to their later and final attempt (iii. 25, 26: in April), to suborn him.

(34) "But I (ἐγώ) accept not My testimony from man. But these things I say in order that you may be saved," *i.e.* 'Though you refused this emergency-witness, viz. John, whom in view of the dulness of your spiritual perception I had provided for you, his is not the essential testimony to which I appeal: I remind you of John's witness to Me only because you once looked upon him and rightly looked upon him as the Prophet specially appointed to guide you to Messiah.'

Lest John's disciples should say that John had appointed the Messiah and had given authority and status to Jesus as Messiah, John's last act had been to send two of his disciples to Jesus to ask Him if He was the Messiah—not as though John were in doubt, but as showing his disciples that his own warrant lay ultimately in Jesus God-and-Man: and that apart from Jesus there was no witness on earth worth anything (Matt. xi. 2: Luke vii. 19).

(35) "He (ἐκεῖνος) was * the lamp that burns and shines," *i.e.* The failure of John's work was no fault of John's: so far as he was concerned (such is the force of the emphatic ἐκεῖνος) he did all that could have been done: he gave no uncertain flicker but a steady flare, lighting the way toward Me as Messiah.

"And so far as *you* were concerned (ὑμεῖς), you were

* The "*was*" (ἦν) seems to imply that John was at this time dead—a fact known to our Lord. It was not yet generally known at Jerusalem, for Machærus, where John was beheaded, was forty miles distant. We may hypothetically place John's death to the late evening of yesterday, Monday, May 24.

The notice Matt. xiv. 13 (Thursday, June 3) does not imply that our Lord did not know of the fact before June 3, though John's disciples thought that was the first He knew of it, just as it was the first the public knew of it. His withdrawal by ship into Philip's tetrarchy was in order to remove His own disciples from the excitement caused by the news: the moment was critical: the populace wanted to force His hand and make Him king: His enemies and Herod Antipas had, perhaps, resolved to arrest Him that night (p. 159). "The Jews," as we have seen at John v. 18, were already resolved on His death.

willing to exult for an hour in his light," *i.e.* 'You had eagerly awaited John's pronouncement as to Messiah's identity and Personality—for a time: but the instant John pointed to *Me* as the Messiah, you turned your back upon him as well as upon Me.'

(36) "However, as for Me (ἐγὼ δὲ) I have as My testimony a greater testimony than John's: for the works which The Father has given Me to accomplish—the very works which I do—it is these that witness concerning Me that The Father sent Me," *i.e.* The essential testimony to His incarnation as Messiah is not human testimony, not even that of John the forerunner, but the testimony given by His works: they are the very works foretold of Messiah by the Holy Spirit. The "works" to which He refers embrace His whole life and conduct, His magnetism that draws this and repels that, showing what He values and what He contemns, in short all that declares His thought and Personality, including those supernormal works done since the public ministry began. It was but last week that up in Galilee He had, quoting Isaiah, appealed to these last-named works when seeking to convince John's disciples (Matt. xi. 5). But without the Spirit of God in the hearts of men to interpret those works aright, they will miss their effect, for the testimony to Jesus is the Spirit of God: and for this reason His mighty-works (δυνάμεις) were not done where there was no incipient faith (Mark vi. 5): they were not done as thaumaturgy, to excite an unreasoning wonder.

(37) "Also The Father who sent Me *He* has borne witness concerning Me," *i.e.* Not only do His works witness to Him inasmuch as they correspond with the works foretold of Messiah, but The Father also He has borne witness to Him, esoterically in the hearts of all who are drawn to Him or shall be drawn to Him, and exoterically at His Baptism (Matt. iii. 17: Mark: Luke). But "you have never yet heard His voice," whether within or without, "any more than you have ever seen His shape." This latter indeed was not possible. But why was His voice not apprehensible by their ear? Because—

(38) "You have not His word abiding in you: for Him whom *He* sent *you* believe not," *i.e.* If His word were abiding within them and not only carried in their phylacteries, they would have been sensitized to receive the impress of God Incarnate: whereas, as it is, they cannot recognize Him, so alien are they to Him.

(39) "You search the scriptures because you think that in them you have eternal Life": and you are right, "those very scriptures are what witness concerning Me." And yet see how alien are you to their Spirit (such is the force of the contrast, ὑμεῖς . . . ἐκεῖναι); for when I, of whom they witness, come, (40) "you are not willing to come unto Me in order to have Life"—that eternal Life which they declare to be in Me alone.

(41) "It is not glory from men that I accept," *i.e.* I make no call on that vain show which you so desire in your Messiah—the desire which makes your search of the scriptures vain.

(42) I appeal to "the love of God" in men's hearts: had you the love of God in your hearts, you would have accepted Me: Love of God would respond to God.

(43) "*I* am come in My Father's name," as the representative and manifestation of My Father, for The Son is the manifestation of The Father: "and you do not accept Me, because you have not the love of The Father in you: but if another * come in his own name," *i.e.* seeking his own glory, "him you will accept," because his spirit of self-seeking will be akin to your own.

(44) "How can you believe? you who accept glory from one another, and seek not the glory which comes from the Only One, God." The spirit of self-seeking, of wanting recognition and glory from men, is deadly to Faith.

(45) "But" do not think that *I* will accuse you before The Father" for not recognizing Me: "there is one that accuses you, viz. Moses, in whom you have set your hopes."

* This other who was to come in his own name and be accepted by the Jews as their Messiah is that false Messiah Bar Cochab, whose rebellion (A.D. 131–135) under Hadrian led to the ruin of the nation and their exile from Jerusalem.

(46) "For had you believed Moses, you would have believed Me: for of Me *he* wrote":—*he* (ἐκεῖνος, emphatic), though you who read him are not aware.

(47) "But as you believe not his writings" because your spirit is opposed to his who sought not his own glory, but the glory of God, "how shall you believe My sayings?" for his spirit and his writings were informed by My spirit.

Note to Verse 5

This man, cured after thirty-eight years of sickness, has always been held to be a type of the Jews: the thirty-eight years have been regarded as pointing to the $38\frac{2}{3}$ years' wandering in the desert between the pronouncement of the doom in Num. xiv. 23 on the 10th day of Ab according to their tradition, in 1490 B.C., and the entry into Canaan on the 14th day of Nisan in 1451 B.C.: also the "five porticos" in which the sick lay have been compared with the five books of the Mosaic Law.

But we seem to require that the cure of this man after his thirty-eight years of sickness (*i.e.* in his thirty-ninth year of sickness) should be a prophetic type of a yet future healing of the Jews, for they certainly have not yet been healed. What then will the thirty-eight years signify in such a prophetic type? It has been suggested that each of these thirty-eight years represents a Jubilee-year: reckoning from the 30th Jubilee which was beyond question the year from Oct. A.D. 27 to Oct. A.D. 28 (the year in which the events of chapter v. took place), thirty-eight more Jubilee years would run out in Oct. 1889–1890 A.D., and the 39th will not be finished till 1939 A.D., which will be the 69th since the cycle began in Oct. 1444 B.C. Elsewhere also the seventy "weeks" or hebdomads of Dan. ix. 24, have been viewed as seventy hebdomads of Sabbatical years (=70 Jubilee-year periods), and the 70th "week" or hebdomad would begin with 1939 A.D., and would run out with the 70th Jubilee year, which begins in Oct. 1987 A.D.

The interval between chapters v. and vi. of John's gospel may be filled in thus :—

A.D. 28. May 25 } Tues. Sivan 6 }		On this evening (Feast of Pentecost), immediately after the events of chapter v., occurs the supper in the house of Simon the Pharisee (Luke vii. 36–end. See p. 127 and pp. 441, 442). The interval between chapters v. and vi. of John's gospel is very short : see at vi. 4.
May 26, Wed. „ 28, Fri.		Leaving Jerusalem on Wednesday, May 26, immediately after the Feast of Pentecost, our Lord might be back in Galilee by May 28, Friday evening.
about } June 3, Thurs. }	Matt. xiv. 12.	The disciples of John the Baptist having taken away his dead body from Machærus and buried it (tradition says at the town of Samaria, where it would be secure from both Herod and the Sanhedrin), came and told Jesus : about June 3.
June 3, Thurs.	Mk. vi. 30.	The Apostles re-assemble at Capernaum, joining Jesus there, and report to Him on what they had done and taught since He had sent them forth about a fortnight or three weeks ago : see at p. 126.

§ IX

JOHN VI. 1–21

(Cf. Matt. xiv. 13–34 : Mark vi. 31–53 : Luke ix. 10*b*–17)

The third return of Jesus to Galilee. The feeding of 5000 *men*

THIS chapter seems to follow on chapter v. at an interval of nine days. Between chapters v. and vi. come chronologically Matt. xiv. 12 : Mark vi. 29–31 : Luke ix. 10*a*.

(1) " After these things Jesus went away across the sea of Galilee, which is that of Tiberias." This verse corresponds with Matt. xiv. 13 : Mark vi. 32 : Luke ix. 10*b* : and for the feeding of the five thousand, about to be described by John, we have all four gospels to draw from. The day seems to be Thursday, June 3, A.D. 28.

A.D. 28. June 3 / Sivan 15 } Thur.

Jesus has returned from Jerusalem to Galilee and Capernaum where He has been joined by the Twelve (Mark vi. 30), no doubt by a previous appointment. The Twelve had been to Israelites beyond Galilee (where He shortly will follow) since their Commission on May 16, and had not been with Him at Jerusalem for the Feast of Pentecost. News of John the Baptist's death has been brought to Him to-day by John's disciples (Matt. xiv. 12), who have taken the body and buried it : and this is probably the first authentic information the public have of that crime of Herod's. Mark (vi. 31) tells of the excitement that was seething at the time (in Capernaum) : on the one side, the populace always favourable to our Lord would be urging Him (cf. John vi. 15) to take decisive action and at last to show His hand : on the other, " the Jews " or Sanhedrist party have decided to put Him to death (John v. 18), and have hurried up from Jerusalem (Mark vii. 1) to Capernaum in order to counteract Him in Galilee ;

and we may conjecture that Herod Antipas the king means to arrest Him this evening (cf. Luke ix. 9).

(1) To avoid the fanatical zeal of His friends and the danger from His enemies, He " went-away across " the lake of Tiberias with the Twelve, in Peter's ship, from Capernaum (Tell Hum) to the north-east corner of the lake, to the thinly-inhabited district there (ἔρημος τόπος = desert place, Matt., Mark) belonging to the city of Bethsaida-Julias (Luke). The site of this city is to-day marked by the ruins of et Tell, about 1½ miles from the north-east shore. The point they made for seems to be determined by " the mountain " (John vi. 3, 15), which juts out into the lake at the Wady Shukeiyif, for there is no other hill in this neighbourhood near the lake: it is four miles south of Bethsaida-Julias. The site of the miracle is further identified by the " much grass in the place " (10), and by Mark's (39) " green grass " (see below at verse 10). The miracle that follows is the only one of our Lord's Ministry of which all four Evangelists have left an account.

June 3, Thurs.

(2) The crowd fanatically enthusiastic for Jesus, and many of them may have come in to Capernaum with the Twelve, seeing Him embark and make for the opposite (east) shore, ran round by the north shore of the lake and reached the east side before the ship (Mark). The distance straight across by ship from Capernaum to the site of the miracle is five miles, that by road is seven miles.

When He stepped out of the boat (ἐξελθὼν, Mark), " He saw a great crowd and was moved to pity for them," in that the Sanhedrin and Herod (their appointed leaders) were misleading them:

(3) " And He went up into the mountain " (which here juts into the lake, at Wady Shukeiyif) " and there sat with His disciples ": *sat*, says John, *i.e.* teaching His disciples and the crowd, sitting being the formal attitude for a teacher among the Jews. Luke adds that " He received them and talked to them about the Kingdom of God, and healed those that had need of healing." His

talk about the Kingdom of God would be a corrective of their expectation that His temporal reign was now about to begin.

(4) "And the Passover, the feast of the Jews, was nigh." This verse is an interpolation from a false marginal gloss. Whilst there is no patristic authority in its favour earlier than Constantine's time, there is the very strong authority of Irenæus and Origen (West and East, 2nd and 3rd centuries) against its genuineness. See pp. 241–243 of *The Birth and Boyhood of Jesus Christ.*

Briefly, the argument in favour of the verse is that all the MSS. extant and all the versions have it. On the other hand, none of the MSS. is earlier than B (Vaticanus), about A.D. 340. But against the verse we have much earlier evidence extant in the writings of two of the earliest Fathers of West and East, viz. Irenæus (died c. A.D. 202), Bishop of Vienne in France, and Origen of Alexandria (died c. A.D. 253). These two happen to be the only Fathers before Diocletian's persecution who throw any light as to this verse: their evidence is decisive that it did not exist in any MS. they knew of: and Origen was the greatest collator of MSS. of the gospels as well as the greatest expert on the N.T. text that the Church had before modern times, also he had the famous library of Alexandria to his hand.

1. Irenæus, contending against a Gnostic theory of a one-year Ministry, brings forward, three passovers from John's gospel, viz. the first, "after Kana"; the second, when our Lord "cured the paralytic"; the third, at the Crucifixion. It is impossible that he could have omitted vi. 4 (which would have proved his case to the hilt), had it existed in his MSS., rather than strain at v. 1, which did not prove his case. (See his *Hær.*, II., xxii., 3.)

2. Origen (on John iv. 35) arguing against the Gnostic Heracleon's theory that the harvest was a "four-month" ahead and that the time, therefore, must be winter, prefers the view that the seed-time was a "four-month" back, and that the actual time of John iv. 35 is barley-*harvest* (April), because, says he, mark the sequence of events in

the succeeding chapters : how chapter iv. is closely followed by the "feast" of v. 1, and that again by the "feast of Tabernacles" (vii. 2). The argument obviously requires the absence of any intervening Passover at vi. 4 : it proves that verse vi. 4 was not in Origen's MSS. Clearly neither orthodox nor heretic had ever heard of this verse before Diocletian's persecution, when for ten years (A.D. 303–313) the resources of the empire were employed in the attempt to destroy every MS. of the New Testament canon.

This verse, at first a marginal chronological conjecture, crept into the text early 4th century, when owing to the dearth of old MSS. and to the multiplication of copies from Eusebius's faulty MS. the interpolation became perpetuated and universal.

It is this interpolation that has been the main cause of the difficulties in determining the dates of our Lord's birth and death. Until we are again rid of it those difficulties remain insoluble in spite of all juggling with fact: and until we are again rid of it, it is impossible to reconcile Luke's date of the Baptism "in the fifteenth year of the reign of Tiberius Cæsar" (iii. 1, cf. his use of "Cæsar" in ii. 1, "Cæsar Augustus") with the unanimous testimony of the Fathers that the date of the Crucifixion was Friday, March 25, A.D. 29—a date they could always verify in the archives of Pilate's governorship, archives to which the early apologists refer the sceptics. This latter date falls in the fifteenth year of Tiberius's reign according to the Western and official reckoning of reigns, viz. from the day of accession : whilst Luke has followed the Eastern reckoning of reigns, viz. from the day of New Year preceding accession. I have explained this at some length in *The Birth and Boyhood of Jesus Christ*, pp. 74–80.

(5) The day wore on (Mark, 35), and the crowd kept gathering in ever-increasing numbers throughout the afternoon. The disciples suggest sending them away that they may get themselves food in the neighbouring villages and hamlets (Luke and Mark). Jesus, however, means to entertain them as host : 'No : give *ye* (emphatic ὑμεῖς) them to eat (Mark) : they shall be our guests for

this evening': and He asks Philip, "Where can we buy loaves to feed them?" not asking as for information, but (6) as testing Philip's faith in His resource.

(7) Philip is in despair: "Two hundred pennyworth * of loaves is not sufficient for them that each of them may take a little."

(8) Andrew, however, Simon Peter's (elder) brother, says to Him in effect:—

(9) 'There is *our own food* here, which was meant for this evening's meal—five loaves of coarse barley bread and two fishes: gladly will we be the hosts: but that is all there is.' Is Andrew half venturing to suggest? he might call to mind that scene of three months ago, where water was made into wine. The two fishes were evidently already cooked and ready for our Lord and the Twelve. The word "small" in A.V. is certainly wrong: the Greek word (ὀψάριον), though in form a diminutive, had lost its sense of diminutiveness: and to-day the modern Greek (ψάρι) for a fish, however large, is the same word as that used here by John, and again in xxi. 9, 13.

(10) Jesus said, "Make the men (ἀνθρώπους = men, women, and children) sit down." Mark adds, "by companies on the green grass."

John continues, "And there was much grass in the place." This notice marks, not the time of year, but a peculiarity of *the place*. The place is the well-irrigated plain of Buteiḥa, where the never-failing streams would supply a succession of mowings down to end of May. This plain is some three or four miles long north to south: on the north it immediately adjoins the city of Bethsaida-Julias, and is closed on the south by "the mountain" (verses 3, 15) at the Wady Shukeiyif, where is the cove off which the "ships" from Tiberias (23) arrived on the following morning.†

June 3, Thurs.

* Two hundred "pennies" (δηνάρια): if we reckon one "penny" (δηνάριον) as the amount of a labourer's daily wage (see Matt. xx. 2), say 3*s.* [pre War rate], the sum would figure out to a value of £30 of our money.

† The traditional site of this miracle (as early as end of 4th century. See St Jerome and St Sylvia) is on the *west* side of the lake and in the little bay of et Tabigah, just north of the other Bethsaida—the "Bethsaida of Galilee"

"Therefore they sat down, the *men* (ἄνδρες = men only) in number about five thousand," *i.e.* not counting the women and children who sat with them, and who must have raised the figures considerably. To secure order, method, decency, promptitude, they were arranged in groups, each group consisting of fifty *men* besides the contingent of women and children belonging to each. Fifty into five thousand gives one hundred groups, which Mark (40) has noted, "and they sat down in companies reckoned by (κατὰ) a hundred and reckoned by (κατὰ) fifty," *i.e.* a hundred clumps of fifty men each, agreeing with Luke's "in clumps of about fifty *each*" (ἄνα).

(11) "Jesus therefore took the loaves and gave thanks and distributed to those that were reclining, and likewise of the fishes, as much as they would": or, as Luke writes, rather more fully (agreeing with Matthew and Mark), "having taken the five loaves and the two fishes He looked up to heaven (= John's "gave thanks") and blessed them, and He brake them, and He gave (imp. = kept giving) to the disciples to put before the crowd." In blessing the loaves and fishes He qualified them to serve His beneficent purpose. It was not the integral loaves or integral fishes that were multiplied, but the broken portions of them, to signify a closer unity than separate loaves would have indicated.

(xii. 21), the modern Khan Miniyeh. But it is not possible to reconcile this site with the data of the Evangelists. Tradition was probably led astray by 1. The gradual obliteration of the name of the eastern "Bethsaida" after its change to "Julias" (see Josephus, *Ant.*, XVIII. ii. 1): 2. The fact that the bay of et Tabigah (corrupted from the Greek ἑπτάπηγον)—the little bay just north of the western Bethsaida, and separated from it by the hill promontory of Tell Oreimeh, which juts into the lake—was the traditional and true site of the miracle of John xxi. where one loaf and one fish fed seven disciples: this latter meal of our Lord's providing was known as the *Mensa Christi* (Christ's Table), and the great stone at which He and the seven sat on that occasion was long pointed out here under that name. The name *Mensa Christi* came not unnaturally to be applied to that other Christ's Table—Table of our Lord's providing—where five loaves and two fishes were multiplied to feed five thousand men: 3. The faulty reading of a few MSS. such as the Codex Sinaiticus, which describes the scene of the miracle of the five loaves and two fishes as being near to Tiberias. This same MS. has been also responsible for much confusion as to the site of the Emmaus of Luke xxiv. 13: for instead of "60" furlongs it reads "160."

(12) And when all (including of course the Twelve) had eaten and were filled, He said to His disciples, "Gather together the *fragments* (κλάσμάτα) that remain over, so that nothing be lost." The *fragments* are not the half-eaten morsels and crumbs which might well be left for birds and beasts, but the broken portions which He had handed for distribution.

(13) So the disciples gathered together twelve baskets * —full of the fragments (κλασμάτων) of the loaves, and of the fishes.

(14) "Therefore the men (ἄνθρωποι), having seen the sign which he did, said (ἔλεγον=kept saying), 'This one is of a truth The Prophet who comes into the world'": *i.e.* The Prophet promised at Deut. xviii. 15, 18.

"He who comes into (or to) the world (ὁ ἐρχόμενος εἰς τὸν κόσμον)," is a title of the Expected One: so also in xi. 27. Cf. "I have come into (or to) the world (ἐλήλυθα εἰς τὸν κόσμον)," xii. 46: xvi. 28: xviii. 37. The shorter title, "The Coming One" (ὁ ἐρχόμενος) has the same meaning.

(15) "Jesus, therefore, perceiving that they were about to come and take Him by force to make Him king, withdrew again into the mountain Himself alone," *i.e.* the mountain where He had been sitting before (3).

We learn from Matthew and Mark that "immediately" after the miracle "He compelled His disciples to embark on board the ship and to go before Him across † the lake while He dismissed the crowds." But it is from John that

* The word for basket used in connection with this miracle by all four Evangelists is κόφινος, a sort of basket especially used by Jews (cf. Juvenal iii. 14: vi. 542) such as this crowd would be called. But in connection with the similar miracle of the feeding of the four thousand, where the crowd was mainly Gentile, the word used for their baskets is σπύριδες: see Matthew (xv. 37: xvi. 10) and Mark (viii. 8, 20), who alone record or refer to it.

† προάγειν αὐτὸν εἰς τὸ πέραν (Matthew), which is quite plain, viz. to the far side of the lake, *i.e.* the west side. Προάγειν εἰς τὸ πέραν πρὸς Βηθσαϊδάν (Mark) = to the far side of the lake (*i.e.* west side) *facing* (πρὸς) Bethsaida (Julias). Had Mark meant *toward* Bethsaida (viz. the Bethsaida of Galilee, the modern Khan Minieh south of Capernaum) he would have said εἰς (and not πρὸς) as is the constant usage of the N.T. writers when speaking of cities or countries. Matthew and Mark, therefore, both agree with John, who says (verse 17) that they were going "across the sea to (εἰς) Capernaum."

we gather the reason for His sending away the disciples, viz. that He saw the crowds were in great excitement and were meaning to come and violently carry Him off and declare Him their king and Messiah in opposition to the civil power ; perhaps already He saw His disciples beginning to be caught in that wild enthusiasm. It was not for them to choose His times : when His time for Kingship is come, as King He will come. So, having first sent off His disciples into the ship, He dismissed the crowds and went away up the mountain alone " to pray " (Matthew, Mark).

Meanwhile what of the Twelve ?

(16) John (omitting to say that they had been ordered to do so) tells how " when evening (ὀψία) was come, His disciples went-down to the sea.

(17*a*) " And went on board ship : and they were going (ἤρχοντο) across the sea to Capernaum."

From Mark (vi. 47) we learn that it was still " evening " (ὀψία) when they were halfway across (ἐν μέσῳ τῆς θαλάσσης), *i.e.* when they had gone some 2½ miles. " Evening " (ὀψία) is from sunset onwards : say, in that latitude and in beginning of June, from our 7 p.m. till, at latest, the end of the first watch. For the two meanings of ὀψία see note on xx. 19.

(17*b*) " And it had already become dark " (σκοτία), " and Jesus had not yet come to them." Not that He had promised to join them on board, for there was no other boat for Him (32), and they did not expect Him to walk the sea, as is clear from their fright when He did : but John looking back afterwards on that night's events, wishes to bring out the fact that, although through that night they were in so sore a plight, and although as the event proved it would have been so easy for Him to come and set all smooth, He chose to let them fight it out alone and endure. It was because of His absence that they were in difficulty : but His absence was only temporary. His coming at the close of that night brought for Peter's barque calm upon the waters : His second Coming at the close of this Age will bring for His Church calm on the world's strife.

(18) "And the sea was rising high (διηγείρετο) by reason of a great wind blowing." Verses 17*b*, 18, cover a dark night * of storm and toil lasting from 8 p.m. till 4 or 5 a.m. Similarly, between verses 47 and 48 of Mark vi. there is the interval of the long night till Jesus sees them in the dawn still struggling and distressed (βασανιζομένους) at the oar, "for the wind was contrary," *i.e.* a head or west wind (Mark).

(19) "When therefore they had rowed about twenty-five or thirty *stades*, they behold (θεωροῦσι expresses their concentrated gaze) Jesus walking on the sea and drawing nigh unto the ship." Now, as they had got halfway across (Mark, 47), or some twenty-three stades, whilst it was yet "evening," and as when He came to them in the early dawn they had gone only some twenty-five or thirty stades (John), they had made but about half a mile through the night, or little more than held their own. A "stade" is roughly a furlong. Mark (48) says He came toward them "about the fourth watch of the night," *i.e.* towards its close and in the early dawn, say about 4.30 to 5 a.m. of Friday, June 4, the latitude being about 33°. And he adds the remarkable detail that Jesus "meant to pass-by them" (ἤθελεν παρελθεῖν), *i.e.* overtaking, as though He had wished that the mere vision of Himself should prove sufficient support and assurance to them. It was their fright whilst not yet recognising Him that caused Him to modify His action.

(19) The "therefore" of the verse belongs to the word "rowed," which in the Greek is the emphatic word and begins the sentence: Ἐληλακότες οὖν, When they had therefore *rowed*, etc. Its meaning is that owing to the violence of the head wind it had been impossible to use the sail and that all hands had been at the oars to keep the ship head on: in this position, as rowers facing rearwards, they saw Jesus coming up their wake.

That night of storm and effort symbolized the close of this Age of Peter's captaincy till our Lord comes visibly

* The moon was entering her last quarter to-day, and would not be rising till late.

again: just as does that other night of toil and little profit (John xxi. 5). The one occasion marks the perils that will assail the Church in the days of Antichrist; the other marks the small results she will then be showing till He joins her. On both occasions Peter steps forth as captain of the ship eager to lay down his charge.

"And they were afraid." From Mark and Matthew we learn that they thought "it is an apparition," and they cried out for fear: for all saw Him and were troubled. Clearly none recognized Him until He spoke.

(20) "But He saith to them, 'It is I, be not afraid.'"

Here Matthew adds Peter's venture, "Lord, since it is Thou (εἰ σὺ εἶ), bid me come unto Thee upon the waters." And He said, "Come" (singular). "And Peter went down from the ship and walked upon the waters *and came* toward Jesus." [Such seems to be the correct reading, καὶ ἦλθεν.] "But seeing that the wind was strong, he was afraid, and beginning to sink he cried out, saying, 'Lord, save me.' And straightway Jesus stretched out His hand and laid hold of him: and He says to him, 'O-thou-of-little-faith, why didst thou doubt?' And when they (Jesus and Peter) were come up into the ship, the wind ceased."

(21) John, omitting this incident of Peter, as being already adequately recorded by the earliest Evangelist, continues, "Therefore they were willing to receive Him into the ship. And straightway the ship became (ἐγένετο) at the land to which they were going." From this detail given by John it is inferred that the ship seemed to move automatically, without sail or oar, in obedience to His will: so that without effort of the disciples or crew it quickly passed over the remaining distance (two miles or so) and came to shore.

Matthew, having said that on the entry of Jesus and Peter into the ship the wind ceased, adds, "and they who were in the ship worshipped Him, saying, 'Verily God's Son art Thou.'" The words "and they who were in the ship" seem to distinguish the other eleven apostles, who had not left the ship, from Peter who had made the venture just described; as though the writer were pointing how it was Peter who first of them had had the eye to see Him and the ear to hear Him and the heart to recognize Him, whilst as yet the rest were scared. If on this occasion it was Peter who first identified Him, on a later one (John xxi. 7) it was John.

Mark tells how "they (*i.e.* the disciples) were greatly amazed," evidently at our Lord's command over the forces of Nature, wind and wave: and adds the reflection that they had not adequately understood, or were not properly intelligent about, the matter of "the five loaves," where His complete command over the phenomena of matter had been already demonstrated.

The question arises, where exactly did they come to land on this early morning? John says the ship arrived "at the land to which they were going" (ἐπὶ τῆς γῆς εἰς ἣν ὑπῆγον), which from verse 17 seems to have been Capernaum, *i.e.* the rural district belonging to that city. Mark (45) says they had been ordered to go "to the other side over-against Bethsaida" (εἰς τὸ πέραν πρὸς Βηθσαιδάν), *i.e.* to the west side of the lake opposite the territory of Bethsaida-Julias, and in verse 53 he defines this landing-place as "Gennesaret," *i.e.* the fertile plain called Gennesaret, which is on the west shore and extends about three miles north and south, reaching from Magdala on the south to Tell Oreimeh on the north, 1½ miles from the city of Capernaum (Tell Hum). Matthew (xiv. 22) agrees with Mark that they had been ordered to go to the other side (εἰς τὸ πέραν), *i.e.* to the west side, and says (34) that having crossed over (διαπεράσαντες) "they came to land at Gennesaret" (ἦλθαν ἐπὶ τὴν γῆν εἰς Γεννησαρέτ). Perhaps the northern end of this plain belonged to the district of Capernaum, this being the chief town of the neighbourhood.

June 4 / Sivan 16 — Fri.

It was already day when they came to land—say about sunrise, our 5 a.m.; for Mark (54) says that when they disembarked, "straightway" the folk recognized them and ran about that whole region and began to carry about on their beds those that were sick where they heard that

He was; and wheresoever He entered, into villages or into cities, or into open country (ἄγρους), they laid the sick in the market-places and besought Him that they might touch but the hem of His cloak, and as many as touched it were made whole." With this account Matthew's closely agrees. These are the details that filled up the busy day of Friday, June 4, as He travelled about that thickly populated district. Both Matthew (xiv. 34, 35) and Mark (vi. 53, 54), after naming Gennesaret, are careful to limit the activity that follows to "all *that* neighbourhood" or region (ὅλην τὴν περίχωρον ἐκείνην and ὅλην τὴν χώραν ἐκείνην), *i.e.* of Gennesaret. The mention of "villages, cities, hamlets," does not argue a tour of several days: this whole region of Gennesaret and Capernaum was densely populated, cf. the notice at Mark vi. 33, where at brief warning, crowds run together afoot "*from all the cities*" and outran the ship as it crossed the lake from Capernaum to Bethsaida-Julias: see again Mark vi. 36, where even in a place which is called "desert," there is mention of the surrounding "hamlets and villages" as being in reach of thousands of folk for the purchase of food within the last hours of an evening.

We must remember that a crisis has been reached in the relation of our Lord to the Sanhedrin and to Herod. News has just been made public of the death of John the Baptist at Herod's hands: our Lord has but just returned from Jerusalem where the Sanhedrists have resolved upon His death (John v. 18). The Sanhedrists have hurried up from Jerusalem (Matt. xv. 1: Mark vii. 1) in order to counteract His influence in Capernaum and to drive Him out of Galilee. It is His last day of activity here, for to-morrow (Saturday, June 5) will take place His last two disputes with the Pharisees and Scribes in Capernaum synagogue, viz.—

A. John vi. 25–59, followed by His talk to His disciples (vi. 60–end).

B. Matt. xv. 1–9: Mark vii. 1–13: followed by His farewell caution to the crowd (Matt. xv. 10–11: Mark vii. 13–16):

and His subsequent talk to the disciples (Matt. xv. 12–20: Mark vii. 17–23) in the house that evening.

On the following morning (Sunday, June 6) He will leave Galilee for three months, to be passed in the borders of Tyre, in Sidon, and along the midst of the borders of Decapolis. The names of the ten cities that formed this Greek confederacy are given on p. xx.

§ X

JOHN VI. 22–71

In Capernaum. The new Manna

(22) BUT to return to the scene of the miracle of Thursday. It is the next day, Friday, June 4: and the crowd who had passed the night there are looking about for Jesus. They had seen the disciples put off in the ship's boat (πλοιάριον) yesterday evening and join the ship (πλοῖον) and start for the opposite shore: they had also seen that there was no boat there by which the ship could be reached except the ship's boat in which the disciples had pushed off: they had also seen that Jesus had not subsequently joined the ship and the disciples by that boat, but that the disciples had gone off in the ship without Him. And yet He is not here. Where, then, is He?

June 4 } Fri.
Sivan 16 }

(23) Although at nightfall there had been no other boat or ship here, there had arrived near to the scene of the miracle, during the night, ships (πλοῖα) from Tiberias (Herod's capital on the west side of the lake, seven or eight miles south of Capernaum): these ships may have been caught by the storm and driven before it, and their owners might now be glad to make a profit by transporting the crowd across to Capernaum by means of the ships' boats (πλοιάρια, verse 24).

It has, however, been not inaptly conjectured that Herod Antipas, foiled in his desire to arrest Him yesterday and hearing that He escaped across the lake, sent these ships from Tiberias (his capital) in the night with troops on board, with orders to capture Him if He returned in Peter's ship. They came "*nigh* to the place where," etc., for the troops could not land, as this east side of the lake was not Antipas's territory, but belonged to his brother Philip Herod. Other soldiers also would naturally have been sent to prevent escape round the head of the lake at the bridge. It was these preparations to arrest Him that, becoming known to the crowd next day (Friday), caused them to ask Him, 'when did He get to Capernaum, for were not both the ways of passage barred ?'

(24) To Capernaum and its neighbouring cities the crowd belonged: to Capernaum they decide to return, expecting that Jesus will soon rejoin His disciples there: and they take advantage of the "boats" (πλοιάρια) and the calm after the storm. These "boats" are, of course, the boats belonging to the ships (πλοῖα) from Tiberias; each ship towed her own boat: cf. Acts xxvii. 16, 17.

By sunset of this day, Friday, our Lord would be back in the town of Capernaum for the Sabbath which then began: and here until the Sabbath was ended He would be safe from Herod and His enemies.

(25) On Saturday morning the people, who had crossed yesterday from the east side of the lake, finding Him in Capernaum, ask Him in the synagogue there (as appears from verse 59), "Rabbi, when didst thou get here ?" implying that they had been vainly searching for Him on the other side, and that they were surprised to find Him here.

June 5 / Sivan 17 } Sat.

The crowd are no longer in the wild enthusiasm for Him that moved them on Thursday evening when they wanted to seize Him and make Him king. What has happened ? Since their arrival at Capernaum yesterday, Friday, they have again come under the influence of the Scribes from Jerusalem who have come up (Matt. xv. 1: Mark vii. 1) to Capernaum to counteract Him and drive Him away. And so successful are these His enemies that to-morrow (Sunday, June 6) He will leave Galilee for Gentile districts.

(26) "Verily, verily, I say to you, ye seek Me not because ye saw signs, but because ye ate of the loaves and were filled," *i.e.* not because they saw in Him and in that miracle what they ought to have seen, viz. the sign that He their Messiah, who in His care for their bodily needs

had created bread for them and dispensed it to them, was willing and able to feed them with Bread for their spiritual needs: but they sought Him because they had seen a bit of thaumaturgy which, while incidentally satisfying their bodily hunger, appealed to their craving for a vain show of power. They had thought yesterday that they believed in Him as their Messiah, but that belief had not been genuine or adequate: it was not based on Faith—a God-given grace. Augustine's remark comes to mind: 'It is not because we believe the miracles that we believe in Thy Divinity, but because we believe in Thy Divinity we believe the miracles.'

(27) Let them work not for such bread as He had given them on Thursday evening, which was in itself dead, and of which the effect was but temporary: but let them work for the Food whose effect is eternal Life: Food which He, The Son of Man, would give them. "For Him (τοῦτον, this One, pointing to Himself) The Father, *i.e.* God, sealed." Sealed, marked with His own seal as His own, set apart consecrated to this purpose, viz. of giving Food which shall issue in eternal Life. There is, no doubt, an allusion to the visible seal, or sign, by which Jesus had been, as all had heard, marked out to the Baptist, viz. the Holy Spirit descending in a bodily form in the likeness of a dove and abiding on Him at His baptism. Hence the term *to seal* became a common ecclesiastical synonym for *to baptize.*

(28) 'And how,' say they, 'are we to act so as to work for the spiritual food you speak of, and work the works of God?' *i.e.* collaborate with God.

(29) 'This is collaboration with God: viz. believing into Him whom He sent as having indeed been sent by Him.' Our Lord has, of course, in mind all that is implied and contained in that statement: therein contained is the whole Christian verity which by long contemplation the Church has slowly evolved and expressed in her dogmas: and as with the Church, so with the individual; the indefinite becomes definite as he ponders on a truth; and the individual and the mass (the Church) see alike when their Teacher is One and the Same.

His hearers, of course, only get tiny glimpses of His meaning : and John has given us only a very brief abstract of the discourse.

(30) They reply, 'Belief in you ? but give us an overwhelming sign. (31) The miracle of the loaves and fishes by which you fed us on Thursday was wonderful : but you can do much more than that, if, as we think, you are the Messiah : that miracle, great as it was, is not comparable to Moses' achievement ; for he gave us bread out of the skies, and not common bread, but manna, and his gift was on a vaster scale, viz. to the whole nation, and repeated daily for near forty years : do us some sign as much greater than his, as Messiah is greater than Moses.'

(32) "Verily, verily, I say to you, Moses," etc. The mystery words, "Verily, verily," make it probable that the English should be, "Moses gave you not *The* Bread out of (ἐκ) Heaven," *i.e.* ideal Bread.

(32–33) The contrast was not what they made it, viz. Moses and the manna, as against Jesus and the multiplication of the loaves and fishes. The real contrast was *Moses and the manna* as against '*My Father*' *and* '*Me who am The Bread.*' The contrast in our Lord's mind is threefold : 1. Moses gave the one ; but My Father gives the Other : 2. The manna was only from the air (as we talk of the birds of heaven) ; but this other Bread is out of the Bosom of God The Father, for It is the eternal Son : 3. The manna fed only the body and for a time ; this other Bread is the ideal Bread, for it feeds body and soul, and generates in them Life eternal.

(33) "For the Bread of God's giving is that (Bread) which cometh down out of (ἐκ) Heaven." The Greek can equally well be rendered, "*He who* cometh down out of Heaven," *i.e.* from the Presence of The Father, *i.e.* He who became Incarnate ; and this is the meaning present to His mind though not, of course, to theirs : "and giveth Life," not merely bodily sustenance : and "to the world," not merely to one nation.

(34) They caught on only to the idea of bread, but understood that the kind spoken of resembled the manna

of Moses in coming down from the skies and so being supernormal: they perceived also that it surpassed the manna of Moses in that it was to give Life instead of mere sustenance; and in being not for one nation only, but for the whole world, which argued a world-wide empire. They therefore said to Him, 'Lord, give us this bread and give it us *always* (as Moses did his) and that sign will be good enough for us.'

(35) "Jesus said to them, '*I* am (ἐγώ εἰμι) the Bread of Life'": in other words, He replies that He is giving It: inasmuch as He is that very Bread He spoke of, which gives Life: that whoso comes to Him to be fed shall never hunger unsatisfied: and whoso believes into Him shall never thirst unsatisfied.

(36) 'But as I said to you, you have seen Me living among you doing signs among you, but you do not believe into Me': they had indeed wanted to make Him King two days ago, but it was a king made to their own fancy that they had acclaimed: they thought they had in Him the king they were looking for: they thought they believed in Him: He was not the sort of king they had in their mind: it was not in Him that they were believing: they were wanting Him to realize their ideal—in other words, to *come to them:* whereas it was they who must come to Him.

(37) "All, which The Father gives to Me, shall get home to Me (πρὸς ἐμέ ἥξει)." The totality (πᾶν) of the race is given and shall reach Him its goal: it is The Father's gift to Him: "and no individual that is on the way (τὸν ἐρχόμενον) to Me will I cast out." No argument can be found here against the Universalists—their position being that while the whole human race has been given by The Father to The Son, the individuals get home to Him at long intervals reaching over various Ages.

(38) 'For I have come down from Heaven' (become Incarnate, though His hearers knew not how) 'to do the will of Him who sent Me as His representative, and not to act apart from Him.'

(39) 'And this is His will as regards all that collective

body of individuals, that totality (πᾶν) which He has given to Me, viz. that I lose no fraction of it: but that I raise it up whole at the last day.'

(40) And as to the scheme by which that end shall be gained—

"This is the will of My Father, that every one who gazes on (θεωρῶν) The Son, and believes into Him, should have eternal Life: and that I should raise him up at the last day." In this "gazes on" The Son there is certainly a reference to the bronze serpent that was lifted up by Moses in the wilderness upon a pole (shaped like a cross, as Rabbinical tradition says), and every one who looked on it was healed. The simple act of looking on that bronze serpent is now replaced by the act of believing into Him whom it typified, viz. God The Son, who in that Living Laboratory, His crucified body, eliminates the sin of all who by faith are grafted into Him, and transfuses into them His own Life. The process is slow: begun here, it is continued in the underworld, and is consummated at "the last day." There is no necessity to suppose that "the last day" here is one only day for all individuals alike: for to each Age there would be its own "last day."

41–46

The Jews, the hostile party, members and adherents of the Sanhedrin, here interrupt. They are the Pharisees and Scribes who are mentioned here by Matt. xv. 1, as being "from Jerusalem," for the discourse of Matt. xv. 1–20 belongs to the evening of this same Saturday. They for many years past had rejected Him in spite of knowing He was the One whose birth was heralded and accompanied by such wonders: they had never lost sight of Him, and had through His Childhood and Boyhood centred their hopes upon Him: with advancing years they had rejected Him, for we must suppose that each year as He came to Jerusalem to the festivals He had continued the practice of teaching the doctors which He had begun the year He became legally adult (Luke ii. 42–47): and unless the

June 5, Sat.

doctors accepted Him, the Nation would not. The doctors had rejected Him for no other reason than that He would not fall in with their views: in other words, would not *come to them.* Having rejected Him, they had to deny that He was anything more than an ordinary man.

(41) "Therefore the Jews murmured concerning Him because that He said, '*I* am the Bread which came down out of Heaven.'" They quite see He is claiming to be God.

(42) "And they said," *i.e.* aloud to the public in the synagogue where the talk is taking place, see verse 59, "'Is not this Jesus, the son of Joseph, whose father and mother *we* know?'" The emphatic "we" (ἡμεῖς) means primarily the Jewish doctors who are speaking: it means 'we whose business it is to see that you are not led astray, we who have gone into the matter of this man's claims. Do not you all know we have decided that he has no right to them and is no more than a mere man, the son of Joseph and Mary? How can he be saying *now*, after all these years of obscurity among you, "Out of Heaven I have come down"?'

(43) "Jesus answered and said to them," viz. to "the Jews," *i.e.* to the doctors and Sanhedrists, "'Murmur not among yourselves':" *i.e.* as though this were some new claim of His: they, the doctors, had long ago and often heard it: they had long ago rejected it. Their rejection neither dismayed nor surprised Him, for—

(44) 'No one can come to Me in the right spirit unless The Father who sent Me works in him to draw him: and what The Father begins in him *I* (ἐγὼ) will complete in him by raising him to full Life at the last day when the long process is complete: for neither The Father, nor I The Son, can work independently of each other: what the One wills, that the Other wills.

(45) 'As the prophets say, "they (the sons of the true City) shall all be taught of God": all, therefore, that "come" to Me are taught by God, The Father: and the fact that one "comes" to me is proof that it is The Father that opened his ears and understanding: for by no other way can any one come to Me.'

(46) 'Not that any one has direct or immediate communication with The Father except the eternal Son: for The Father communicates with all through The Son, and all communicate with The Father through The Son.' That is the law of Life: the Son of God, the God-Man, is the medium of union between God and man. Even when The Father draws, He draws through The Son: the whole Godhead works together: but it draws through and to the Godhead-Incarnate: and it is the Godhead-Incarnate that is the link between God and man to lift the human race.

He is teaching the theologians about the Godhead, how that the Unity of God is not the final word of revelation concerning the one God. So long as it is thought that there is but one Person in the Godhead, the Incarnation and the whole scheme of Redemption cannot possibly be understood.

47–51

June 5, Sat.

After the foregoing diversion, of verses 41–46, caused by "the Jews," He resumes His discourse to the Galileans at the point where He had been at verse 40.

(47) "Verily, verily, I say to you, He that believes has eternal Life" already in him. "He that believes" is a shortened form for "he that believes into Me" or "into The Son": for there is no other genuine Faith. And "he has eternal Life" already, because in virtue of that faith the germ of eternal Life is already in him, the new manhood begotten of God has already begun to be formed in him.

(48) He here returns to the subject of the manna and the Bread of Life, last mentioned at verse 35.

"*I* (ἐγώ) am the Bread of Life": *i.e.* the Bread that gives Life.

(49) The manna which their fathers ate in the wilderness had no germ of Life in it: they ate it and died.

(50) "This," pointing to Himself, "is the Bread which comes down out of Heaven," not merely out of the sky,

as did the manna, "in order that a man (τις, indefinite) may eat of It and not Die." And lest any should think He was speaking merely metaphorically, and also in order to call special attention to His words, He repeats—

(51) "*I* (ἐγὼ) am the Living Bread, that came down out of Heaven." *Came down, i.e.* in being conceived and born of Mary: "came down *out of Heaven*," but at the same time never left Heaven, for He never ceased to be God.

"If a man (τις) eat of this Bread," pointing to Himself, "he shall Live for ever." The manna sustained life on the physical plane, and for a time: and they that ate it assimilated it to themselves, and died. But the Living Bread originates a new Life on the spiritual plane, and for eternity: and It assimilates the eaters to Itself, so that they Live for ever

"And the Bread which *I* will give is My Flesh, on behalf of the world's Life." By "*My Flesh*" is meant *My human nature, i.e.* body, soul, spirit: as in the phrase, "The Word became *Flesh*," which means God the Word assumed to Himself *human nature.* It is only because that human nature continues linked to His divine Personality, that it can give eternal Life to those who are united to it. And He gives His Flesh so that the world may Live—"the world" (ὁ κόσμος) being mankind, the microcosm in whom this earth is summed.

52–53

(52) Again the hostile party ("the Jews") cause a diversion. "The Jews therefore wrangled (ἐμάχοντο) with each other, saying, 'How (πῶς, in what way) can this one give us his flesh to eat?'"

June 5, Sat.

(53) "Jesus therefore said to them, 'Verily, verily, I say to you, Unless ye eat the Flesh of The Son of Man and drink His blood ye have not Life in yourselves.'" He does not answer their wrangling question, "How?" They were in no mood to learn. The how is not essential: it is enough to accept implicitly our Lord's meaning: but reverence itself will urge us to try to understand.

At any rate, to "the Jews," the hostile party, He made no attempt to explain away His startling words as though they were but metaphor. But He gave them a further statement which they, doctors of the Law well versed in the theory of Sacrifices, would not fail to understand. The "eating of the flesh and drinking of the blood" was a plain allusion to the *Sacrificial* idea. It had already been suggested in verse 51, "the Bread which I will give is My Flesh, on behalf of the world's Life." Where animals were sacrificed, they were so killed that all the blood was drained out from the body and offered apart. Similarly in the ritual of the Mass, the Sacrifice is symbolized by the separateness of the two species bread and wine, each of which is severally consecrated to symbolize that the Victim has been *sacrificed*, inasmuch as the Blood is separate from the Body. In the same ritual, later, the Resurrection is symbolized by the dropping of a fragment of the Wafer into the Wine, signifying that the union of the Body and Blood has again taken place, and that Life has returned as at the Resurrection. Again, in every religion he who eats of the sacrifice is incorporated into the sacrifice.

(54) "He that eateth My Flesh and drinketh My Blood": *i.e.* whoso is sacramentally united to Him, the world's Sacrifice, has the germ of eternal Life already in him: and by virtue of this sacramental union, "*I* will raise him up at the last day." "*I*" because our Lord is the germ of Life which the Sacraments plant and foster in us. "At the last day" because the process of sanctification is a slow one, and is not consummated until the resurrection of the body: not that growth ceases then, rather the conditions are then at last favourable to growth.

(55) "For My Flesh is true Food, and My Blood is true Drink." What we eat and drink to sustain physical life is but a dim figure of the spiritual Food and Drink which originates that spiritual Life which alone is true Life.

(56) "He that eateth My Flesh and drinketh My Blood abides in Me and I in him." The eating and drinking of this Sacrificed Victim is a continual process (τρώγων . . .

καὶ πίνων, pres.), and not an act done once and done with (aorist). He who eats of this Victim is *ipso facto* united with that Victim. The act of union once effected, the slow assimilation to that Living Victim begins.

(57) Jesus was sent as the representative of the Living Father—The Father who is self-existent. Jesus is also the eternal Son, Living because of The Father (διὰ τὸν π.); for there is no Son without The Father, and no Father without The Son. Whoso eats the Flesh of Jesus and so is one with Him, shall Live because of Him (δι' ἐμέ): for whoso eats of that Flesh is also participant in the self-existent Godhead, inasmuch as in Him the God-Man Humanity and Godhead are united.

(58) "This," pointing to Himself, "is the Bread which," etc. Once again He sums up the contrast between the dead manna from the skies and the Living Bread from Heaven which gives eternal Life.

(59) "These things He spoke in synagogue, teaching in Capernaum," and no doubt *on a Sabbath*, as several MSS. add. The notice seems to cover the whole discourse from verse 26. The day, from a comparison of the four gospels, seems to be Saturday, June 5, of A.D. 28.

June 5, Sat.

The scene here shifts from the synagogue to the house (Peter's house), which was our Lord's habitation when in Capernaum. The day is still the Saturday.

(60) "Many therefore from among His disciples, having heard it said, 'Hard is this saying: who can hear it?'" It seems probable from verse 67 that these murmurers did not include any of the Twelve. The murmurers had understood Him literally when He spoke of "eating My Flesh and drinking My Blood," and He had meant it literally: but the literal meaning needed to be understood correctly.

(61) "Jesus, aware within Himself that His disciples are murmuring about it, said to them, 'Is this a stumbling-block to you?'" He does not unsay anything: He does not tell them He has been speaking allegorically or that there is nothing that may not be explained away.

He had been speaking the literal truth when He talked of "eating My Flesh": but He helps them over one misconception.

(62) Did it seem impossible to them to believe that He meant a literal eating of His Flesh? Let them not think of His Flesh *as they see It now.* "If therefore ye behold The Son of Man going up to where He was before" —that should help them. Suppose they were to see this very Flesh of His not merely risen from the dead but ascending to Heaven, they would find it easier to understand, for they would then realize that this Flesh of His exists not only *as they see It now*, viz. in Its phenomenal or physical mode, but that It exists also in a spiritual mode. And it is in Its spiritual mode that He gives It as Food: but *under either mode* It is one and the same Flesh: for matter has many modes, and the Sacraments energize mainly on the spiritual plane of matter.

(63) "It is the Spirit that quickens: the flesh profiteth nothing": it is when eaten in Its spiritual mode that His Flesh quickens: if eaten in Its "physical," sensuous mode (like the flesh of sacrificed sheep or cattle) It would profit nothing, for spiritual Life does not belong to that plane: and "the things (64) (ῥήματα = things spoken about) which I have spoken to you are Spirit and Life," *i.e.* belong to that spiritual plane of matter with which alone life that is Life has to do.

"But there are from among you certain who do not believe": *i.e.* do not believe into Him: and therefore cannot feed on Him. And He knew exactly the state of mind of each individual there present. He does not say they will not hereafter believe. "For," explains John, "Jesus knew from the beginning who they are that do not believe and who he is that shall betray Him"—knew before the persons themselves knew.

(65) "And He said, 'This is why (διὰ τοῦτο) I have said to you (viz. at verse 44) that no one can come unto Me unless it have been given to him of The Father.'" Many there who called themselves His disciples were about to leave him: He knew it: He knew which they

were: had known all along. Had The Father drawn them, The Son could not but know; neither could The Son fail to know that The Father had not drawn them as yet: for The Father does all things through The Son.*

(66) "From this time many from among His disciples went away back and no longer walked with Him." Had He been talking allegorically or symbolically, He would not have let these go off and away under a misconception that He was talking literally. He made them certain He was not talking symbolically, but literally; and thus it seemed to them impossible nonsense: but the nonsense lay, perhaps, in their misconception of matter.

It is the crisis of the first great apostasy in His Ministry. His enemies, "the Jews," have to all appearances carried the day. His greatest Prophet, John the Baptist, had been put to death some ten days ago: He had Himself been driven from Jerusalem by attempts to kill Him some ten days ago (v. 18): it is probable that Herod Antipas, induced by the Sanhedrists, had planned a sudden attempt to seize Him yesterday in Galilee which He frustrated by crossing for a few hours to the east side of the lake beyond Herod's jurisdiction: His enemies, Scribes and Pharisees from Jerusalem, have arrived in Capernaum (Matt. xv. 1: Mark vii. 1) hot foot, to oppose Him in Galilee, to silence Him by orders from headquarters at Jerusalem, to stifle the growing movement here at its source, to hunt Him from Galilee as they had already hunted Him from Judæa, and they will be successful. After the dispute that will take place in the synagogue this afternoon (Matt. xv. 1–11: Mark vii. 1–13), followed by the instruction given in the house to His disciples (Matt. xv. 12–20: Mark vii. 14–23), He will leave Galilee to-morrow for, as it seems, some

* If none can "come" unless The Father draw him, is he then for blame who does not "come"? If The Father has not drawn him, there is some reason that makes it either "impossible" (in view of free will and circumstances), or inopportune (in view of the large scheme of the Universe) that he should be drawn as yet: but the "as yet" of this life covers but a tiny fraction of the individual's existence. Did He not wait till mankind, at its central focus, was ripe for His first Coming? Is He not waiting, and there, again?

three months' absence in the pagan districts of Phœnicia and Decapolis (Matt. xv. 21 : Mark vii. 24), where large numbers of Israelites dwelt as Gentiles, among Gentiles.

(67) "Jesus therefore," as though abandoned by all others, "said to the Twelve, 'Will *ye* also go?'" It is the first mention of "the Twelve" by this Evangelist: and the reason is simple. In chapters i.–iv. no mention is made of them, for the Twelve had not yet been chosen: they were chosen in the interval between the events recorded in chapter iv. and those recorded in chapter v. They are not mentioned in chapter v. because they were not with Him in Jerusalem for Pentecost (the Festival of chapter v.), He having sent them on a mission to Israelites in the regions beyond Galilee (Matt. x. : Mark vi. 7–11).*

(68) Simon Peter as spokesman for the Twelve answered, "Lord, unto whom shall we go away? It is matters of Life eternal that Thou hast (*ῥήματα ζωῆς αἰωνίου ἔχεις*)." To whom should they go? To the Scribes, the doctors of the Law? No: they stayed with Him, to learn of Life, fuller Life, ever-expanding Life.

(69) "And *we* (viz. we the Twelve) have believed and have come to know (*ἐγνώκαμεν*) that *Thou* art The Holy One of God." They had believed it when they first came to Him last February at the bidding of John the Baptist the greatest of the Prophets:—John whom the Sanhedrin themselves for thirty years recognized as having been sent in order to prepare them for Messiah and to "officially nominate Messiah unto Israel" (cf. *ἀναδείξεως αὐτοῦ* [John's] *πρὸς τὸν Ἰσραήλ*, Luke i. 80): John whom they only this year disowned because the Messiah whom he nominated was not to their liking.

Since then, the Twelve, by constant converse with Him, had found their assenting faith developing toward

* The section Matt. xii., xiii., is not in chronological order in reference to what precedes it. None of the Synoptists has attempted to follow a chronological order in the account of the Galilean ministry from mid-April to early June. John alone has accurately preserved the time sequence throughout his Gospel, a sequence which has unfortunately been obscured for us by a conjectural and misleading copyist's note (viz. vi. 4) having become incorporated into the text early in the 4th century.

conviction ("we have come to know") that He was The Holy One of God. The Holy One (ὁ ἅγιος) means the consecrated One, The One specially set apart by God and for God's purposes. The phrase is like that in verse 27, "This One the Father *sealed*."

(70) Peter's declaration on behalf of the Church is approved by our Lord: but He adds a caution that there will always be disingenuous ones and traitors in even high places in the Church: for even in the inner circle of the Twelve is one, and one whom He had Himself deliberately placed among the Twelve—not from having mistaken the man, but in order to teach them that very lesson. "Was it not I myself who chose out you the Twelve? and from among you one is a devil." The etymological meaning of the word, διαβολος, from which is formed our word *devil*, is one who *throws*, or is thrown, *into confusion* (δια βαλλειν), one who disorders what was in order; there is not necessarily inherent in the word intentional malice—that will depend upon the personality of him who confuses, and on his motives of action.

(71) "He was speaking of Judas, son of Simon Iscariot: for it was this one who was to betray Him, one from among the Twelve." Not only was Judas's father from Karioth, but Judas himself was from Karioth, as we learn from all four gospels. For all call him Iscariot, which means "a man of Karioth," or in its Hebrew form Qeriyoth: see Joshua xv. 25, where it is named in a list of the southern cities of the tribe of Judah. This Judas was the only Jew (accurately so called as meaning of the tribe of Judah) among the Twelve: the other eleven being from Galilee (Acts i. 11) and belonging to the tribe of Levi and possibly other tribes.

The miraculous extension of modes of matter, displayed in the feeding of the five thousand, was meant by our Lord to be an aid to the understanding, preparatory to the discourse on "eating His Flesh" that followed it in the synagogue of Capernaum, as recorded by John: and mainly as such has John repeated an account of this miracle which had already been described by all three Synoptists.

It is the only point at which they and John are in contact until Passion week.

The difficulty felt by the disciples who (verse 66) fell away was due to a misconception of matter. It is doubtless *de fide* that matter was called into being by God as certainly as the so-called immaterial spirits were called into being by Him. Matter is indestructible by any process at the command of man. Though no single mode of matter is essential to it, it cannot subsist apart from mode. Although bread is matter under one modification, and water is matter under another, and flesh is matter under another, matter exists apart from all the accidents or modes that appeal to our present senses: *e.g.* it exists as ether, and ether is our so-far ultimate analysis of matter: or rather, as it hitherto defies detection by any physical sense, ether is a postulate of science, necessary to account for certain phenomena, a postulated mode of matter pervading all denser modes, and in which all denser modes swim.

Matter, it seems, exists at one and the same moment in a "physical" mode and in a "spiritual" mode, on a "physical" plane and on a "spiritual" plane. There is, as Paul says, a physical (φυσικὸν) body, and there is a spiritual (πνευματικὸν) body, but the one no less than the other must be regarded as matter. Our Lord's "flesh" or physical body that was born of Mary and that hung upon the cross is the very same material Body which He gives and which we receive in the Holy Sacrament—only the modes of Its matter differ.

To Christ during His life on earth, matter had no limitations. Only dependently on His will, and not absolutely, can the matter of His earthly body be said to have been subject to the limitations of matter as we know matter. This is so whether before His resurrection or after it: whether when Incarnate on earth or since His Ascension: for He was always Lord of matter, seeing that He never ceased to be God.

Thus, water He made into wine, wine He made into His Blood: bread He made into His Body: loaves and fishes He extended indefinitely: He walked on water, making His body probably imponderable: He instantly transferred the ship from one point to a point some two miles distant. Not only did His risen body pass through solid rock, but He similarly caused His earthly body at His birth to pass through the closed womb of His mother.

That same earthly body He showed (to the three on Tabor) modified in a state of transcendent glory, as the Shekinah or Indwelling Presence of the Godhead shone out of it. That same earthly body He showed after His resurrection, again modified.

His divine will was not confronted by any limitations in His relation to matter: His human will was aware of them: but they vanished if or when He summoned His divine will.

Not being self-existent, matter might conceivably be annihilated by Him who called it into being. We are perfectly certain it never will be so annihilated, for in the Incarnation God has assumed it to the Godhead, when He assumed the whole human race to the Godhead—that race to whom matter is indissolubly bound.

For the mind that has grasped the truth that to the all-seeing Eye there is no Before no After, no Then no There, no Time no Space, but all is Here and all is Now, and that the primordial cell is no older than is the tree or the man we look upon, the Universe is but the caravanserai of all created things, as the eastern sage expressed it. The self-existent He alone abides: but as He has assumed human nature (body as well as spirit) to Himself, He thenceforth invested man, as well as matter (in one mode or another), with an existence without end.

THE INTERVAL BETWEEN JOHN VI. END AND VII. 1.

The interval between chapters vi. and vii. of John's gospel may be filled thus :—

A.D. 28. June 5, Sat.

On the afternoon of this day on which our Lord delivered His discourse of chapter vi. in the synagogue of Capernaum occurred His interview with "Pharisees and Scribes who had come from Jerusalem" (see at p. 157): His words to the crowd on the same subject: and His words to the disciples in the house on the same subject (Matt. xv. 1–20: Mark vii. 1–23).

June 6, Sivan 18, Sun.

From there (Capernaum) He arose and "withdrew to the districts of Tyre and Sidon," and "through Sidon to the Sea of Galilee through the midst of the borders of Decapolis" (Matt. xv. 21–28: Mark vii. 24–31). This is the circuit of Luke viii. 1–3, during which "the Twelve were with Him, and certain women," viz. "Mary who is called the Magdalene" (see pp. 441–445) "and many others." The Twelve, as we saw at p. 145, had recently rejoined Him at Capernaum, about June 3: and Mary Magdalene had been recently cured at Jerusalem (pp. 441, 442): these "women" are named by Luke to show how the wants of our Lord and His companions were supplied during this long circuit outside of Galilee, during which they no longer had a headquarters in Peter's house in Capernaum.

Sept.

Returns "to the Sea of Galilee," from the borders of Tyre, Sidon, and Decapolis—all of them Gentile districts.

Sept. 12, Elul 27, Sun.

"He went up on to the mountain and sat there" (Matt. xv. 29). Neither the text nor tradition seems to help us toward the identification of this mountain on the lake: we neither know whether it belonged to the Decapolis confederacy or not, nor on which side of the lake it was. For though He took ship from it to reach Magadan, nothing is said of His crossing the lake.

Sept. 12–14.

The "three days" of Mark viii. 2. Great crowds came to Him there, bringing their sick, and He healed them all. These are Gentile Israelites, as appears from their phrase, "the God of Israel" (Matt. xv. 29, 31: Mark vii. 31–end).

Sept. 14, Elul 29, Tues.

The miracle of the seven loaves (Matt. xv. 32–end: Mark viii. 1–10). These seven loaves are of Gentile baking and the baskets are Gentile baskets (σφυρῖδες): hence their distinction in Mark viii. 20 from the loaves of Jewish baking and the Jewish baskets (κόφινοι) of viii. 19.

Tentatively the date Sept. 14 is suggested, as being this year = Elul 29, the last day of the Jubilee year, to which an allusion seems to lie in Matt. xv. 31. Much depends on the date of the Transfiguration. On this same day He and the Twelve came by the ship to Magadan or Magdala or Dalmanutha, on the west side of the lake.

A.D. 28. Sept. 15 / Tisri 1 Wed.

The Pharisees and Sadducees come out to Him for a sign. The day here suggested was Tisri 1, the first day of their civil year. This is probably a formal, and is also a hostile, deputation of Sanhedrists after His long absence from Galilee. The terms they require are the old ones, "a sign from heaven."

He crosses to the other side of the lake (to the north-east corner) (Matt. xvi. 1–12: Mark viii. 11–21). They come to the district of Bethsaida-Julias (at the north-east corner of the lake), where He heals a blind man (Mark viii. 22–26).

Sept. 16, Thurs.

He comes to the district of Cæsarea-Philippi: the town is a day's journey from Bethsaida-Julias. "On the way Peter's confession of the Faith, and the promise to Peter. Our Lord "began" to point out to His disciples that He must be rejected by the Sanhedrin and be killed in Jerusalem and rise again "*on the third day*," alluding to the "sign of Jonah" which He yesterday told the Sanhedrists they should have (Matt. xvi. 13–21: Mark viii. 27–31: Luke ix. 18–22).

Sept. 18, Sat.

He was talking *openly* (παρρησίᾳ) about this His rejection and death, so that Peter rebukes Him privately, and is rebuked: He calls the crowd to Him and even to them speaks plainly of His death by crucifixion (Matt. xvi. 22–end: Mark viii. 32–ix. 1: Luke ix. 23–27).

Sept. 23, Thurs. evg.

"After six days" (Matt. xvii. 1: Mark ix. 2), "About eight days after these words (λόγους)" (Luke ix. 28), He goes up Mt Tabor in Galilee. Matthew and Mark date their "six" days from the close of this new teaching about His death (Saturday), whereas Luke dates his "eight" days from the beginning of it (Thursday). The "began" of Matt. xvi. 21 and Mark viii. 31 implies a continuation on subsequent days.

Sept. 24 / Tisri 10 Fri.

This night after midnight of Thursday–Friday He was transfigured before the three disciples on Tabor (Matt. xvii. 2–8: Mark ix. 2–8: Luke ix. 29–36). The day is Tisri 10, the great Day of Atonement, when the high priest clothed in shining white *byssus* entered the Holy of Holies. At the Transfiguration Jesus was doubtless seen standing between Elijah and Moses: is it merely a coincidence that this night of Tisri 10 stands exactly midway between Iyar 11 (May 1), the day on which is commemorated the Assumption of Elijah, and Adar 7 (Feb. 16), the day of the death of Moses? This Tisri 10 is also the day on which Moses received the Tablets of the Law the second time and came down with face shining (Exod. xxxiv. 29), and a similar glory seems to have still radiated from the face of our Lord many hours after His transfiguration (see ἐξεθαμβήθησαν, Mark ix. 15). The day is also the Julian autumnal equinox (Sept. 24): as other cardinal points are marked by the Annunciation, the Birth, the Passion.

A.D. 28. Sept. 24, Fri.

In the morning He came down from the Mount; and at the foot of it healed the *lunatic* demoniac (Matt. xvii. 9–21: Mark ix. 9–29: Luke ix. 37–43*a*): the traditional site of the miracle is the village of Dabúriyeh at the north-west foot of Mt Tabor. The moon had been full on Wednesday, Sept. 22.

Sept. 24–28.

For these days "He abode in Galilee," John vii. 9. Mark (ix. 30–32) has "they went on their way through Galilee," *i.e.* from Mt Tabor, and He taught His death and resurrection to His disciples, *i.e.* the disciples of Galilee whom He had not seen for three months. Matthew (xvii. 22, 23) has "whilst they were gathering together (συστρεφομένων) in Galilee," *i.e.* the little band of His genuine disciples who were rallying together to accompany Him and the Twelve to Jerusalem—the pilgrim caravan having started before (John vii. 9, 10).

Sept. 27, Mon.

At Capernaum: the collectors of the half-shekel for the Temple. According to Rabbinical authorities this half-shekel might in different localities be paid at any of the three great festivals (Greswell, *Dissertations*, ii. 378): *e.g.* on this occasion, just before the Feast of Tabernacles. The collectors would assume that He was not going up to Jerusalem, as the other pilgrims had already started, and so they collect it at Capernaum (Matt. xvii. 24–end). "In that hour" came the disciples: the dispute as to who is the greatest, etc. His answer and His subsequent discourse (Matt. xviii. 1–end: Mark ix. 33–end: Luke ix. 46–50).

Now we shall see how John takes up and carries on from Sept. 23.

§ XI

JOHN VII. 1–36

From Galilee to Jerusalem. Feast of Tabernacles

(1) JOHN resumes the story in late September, after an interval of over $3\frac{1}{2}$ months (viz. from early June to late September)—an interval only slightly touched upon by Matthew (xv. 21–xviii. 35), by Mark (vii. 24–ix. 50), by Luke (ix. 18–50). During this interval our Lord has been absent in the Gentile districts of Tyre, Sidon, and Decapolis, has landed (mid-Sept.) for a few hours at Dalmanutha (Magdala), has withdrawn for a few days to the neighbourhood of Cæsarea Philippi, and has just returned to Galilee (Mt Tabor, Sept. 23, 24). It is at this point that chapter vii. begins.

A.D. 28. Late Sept.

(2) The Feast of Tabernacles (Tisri 15–Tisri 21) preceded His death by six months, and fell in this year A.D. 28 on the seven days from Wednesday, September 29, when it began, to Tuesday, October 5, when it ended. The eighth day, Tisri 22 (Wednesday, Oct. 6), was a separate Feast (p. 198).

As both Friday and Saturday (Sept. 24, 25) were, this year, days of obligatory rest, for Friday was Tisri 10, the great Day of Atonement, the Galilean pilgrims would collect at Jenîn (on the border of Galilee and Samaria) on Thursday, Sept. 23: stay here for the two days of obligatory rest (Sept. 24, 25): leave Jenîn on Sunday, Sept. 26, reaching Nâblûs that evening: leave Nâblûs on Monday, Sept. 27, and arrive at Bîreh (on the frontier of Judæa) in the evening: leave Bîreh on Tuesday, Sept. 28, and reach Jerusalem at noon.

Thus on Thursday, Sept. 23, the various pilgrim bands would be collecting and converging on Jenîn, and to-day in the neighbourhood of Mt Tabor He would intercept His brethren and other pilgrims (Tabor lies just halfway between Capernaum and Jenîn): and to-day He had the conversation with His brethren (John vii. 3–9), who might see that He and His disciples were not going up to Jerusalem. To-night, after midnight of Thursday–Friday, and therefore on Friday, Sept. 24, He will be seen "transfigured" on Mt Tabor, by Peter, James, and John (p. 177).

Sept. 23 / Tisri 9 — Thurs.

Sept. 24 / Tisri 10 — Fri.

(3) His "brethren" are His first cousins; who, as being His nearest of kin, are technically termed "brethren": this terminology is seen again and again in the Old Testament. They are the sons of Clopas (same as Cleopas), the half-brother of Joseph—Joseph and Cleopas having the same father, Jacob of the tribe of Levi: but Joseph was in the eye of the Law the son of Eli of the tribe of Judah: for Jacob "raised him up" as seed to the dead Eli, in accordance with the Levirate law. Thus Clopas and his sons are of Levi's tribe, whilst Joseph is of Judah's. These "brethren" of the text are James the Little, Joses, Simeon, Jude, none of whom was of the Twelve.

Sept. 23 / Tisri 9 — Thurs.

They urge Him, "Remove from here and go to Judæa, that so Thy disciples also (*ἵνα καὶ οἱ μαθηταί σου*) shall clearly see" (*θεωρήσουσιν*, which always means to observe with careful attention, or else to see with the intellect) "Thy works that Thou doest," *i.e.* they too shall see as clearly as we already do (such is the force of the *καὶ*) the result to which your action is leading: it must end in your being put to death by the hierarchy, and that will be the end of the movement.

(4) 'You claim to be the nation's Messiah: come out then into the open and face the authorities instead of living here in a remote province, or hiding in Phœnicia and Decapolis: come up to the metropolis, where the whole nation is gathering for the great Festival of the year.

If you do these great works we all hear of, and we do not deny it' (for such is the force of εἰ . . . ποιεῖς, indic.), 'show yourself to the world, win the world's admiration, so that it will follow you: for unless you win the world's approval, you will effect nothing. But obviously you have no chance against the hierarchy.'

(5) "For not even His brethren believed into Him" (ἐπίστευον, imp., *i.e. were as yet believing*, afterwards they did believe). His brethren were thinking that His success depended on the world's attitude to Him: in other words, they believed in the world rather than in Him. They are often confused with the Apostles James son of Alphæus, Judas (= Lebbæus = Thaddæus) son of James, and Simon the zealot. After the Resurrection they were famous in the Church: three of them, viz. James the Little, Simeon, and Jude, being the three first bishops of Jerusalem.

(6) "My time is not yet at hand." Far from seeking the world's approval as His brethren wished, He was aware that the world in self-defence would first compass His death. The time in the world's history had not yet arrived for the setting up of the visible Kingdom or for His open and universal triumph.

"*Your* time is always ready." From *their* point of view the time was all ready for Him to come forward as the world's king, was always ready, nothing needed changing, He had but to fall in with the times and declare Himself as the embodiment of the national ambition.

(7) "The world cannot hate you, but Me it hates, because I testify of it that its works are evil." *They* were in entire harmony with the prevailing temper of the world, and with the carnal outlook of the nation, which merely wanted a king who should wrest the world's empire from Rome and perpetuate and fulfil the world's vain self-complacency. Whereas He, He was in utter antagonism to it; for the spirit of the world's self-sufficiency is restive under the very thought of God, and seeks to set Him on one side and forget Him.

A universal empire indeed awaits the reunited Twelve-tribed Nation, as had been promised them; but they must first be ripe for it.

(8) "You, go *you* up to the Feast." *They* were in harmony with the spirit in which it was kept: *they* approved of the prevailing temper, outlook, and ideal.

"*I* do not yet go up to this Feast," *i.e.* to keep it: "for My time is not yet fulfilled." This Feast of Tabernacles He would not keep until He keeps it at a later Coming that will usher in a better Age: not till then would His time for it be fulfilled. It is probable that the reason why He did not go up with the pilgrims was that He was aware of a plot among the Jews to seize Him on the road or immediately on arrival in Jerusalem. For their set determination see verses 1, 11, 19, 25, 30.

From the beginning of His public Ministry our Lord was out of harmony with the nation at all their festivals: none of them did He keep with the nation; though He went up to Jerusalem, as their dates came round, in order to have the vast crowds for His audience and witness. The Jews' rejection of Him already had made all their festivals meaningless, for He was the fulfilment and the only meaning of them all. This appears from John's marked phraseology throughout: *e.g.* ii. 13, "*The Jews'* passover was at hand, and Jesus went up to Jerusalem": v. 1, "There was a feast of *the Jews* (*i.e.* Pentecost), and Jesus went up to Jerusalem": vii. 2, "*The Jews'* Feast of Tabernacles was at hand . . . I go not yet up unto this Feast . . . but when His brethren were gone up *to the Feast*, then went He also up." These words, "to the Feast," in verse 10 are most unfortunately misplaced in the A.V. and in the commonly received Greek text, and the whole passage is thus obscured. He did not go up *to the Feast*, *i.e.* to keep the Feast, He only *went up*, *i.e.* to Jerusalem. He did not keep the Feast in Jerusalem; for *the* day of obligation was the *first* day. By John's peculiar use of "the Jews" throughout His gospel to represent the hostile and anti-Christian party of the day, he shows that these

End of Sept.

feasts as kept by them had no longer any vitality. So Origen, on ii. 13, remarks that the words "the passover of the Jews" point to the emptiness of the ceremonial.

He has transformed the Feast of the Passover in sacrificing Himself as the Paschal Lamb (and we should note the "with you" of Luke xxii. 15: and the "with My disciples" of Luke xxii. 11, meaning *not with the nation*). He has transformed the Feast of Pentecost: He has yet to transform the Feast of Tabernacles.

(9) He and His disciples did not go up with the pilgrims, but "abode still in Galilee" (vii. 9), evidently for a very few days, as He still arrived in the Temple when the Feast was only half through (*i.e.* on Saturday, Oct. 2).

We have placed the Transfiguration to the night of Sept. 23–24. After this talk with His brethren (p. 180) He then travelled back from Mt Tabor through Galilee (Mark ix. 30) to Capernaum (Mark ix. 33): there at Capernaum occurred the incidents of Matt. xvii. 24–xviii. end, Mark ix. 33–end, Luke ix. 46–50. The collector of the half-shekel (Matthew) naturally came to collect it when our Lord arrived at Capernaum: for he would assume that Jesus and His disciples were not going to Jerusalem for the Feast, seeing that all other pilgrims had left, and so would argue that He would pay the money here at Capernaum if at all.

Sept. 27 / Tisri 13 } Mon.

(10) "But when His brethren had gone up to the Feast, then He too went up." This is the correct reading: and see the R.V. as against the A.V.

This His departure from Galilee (end of Sept.) is that named in Matt. xix. 1,* Mark x. 1,† Luke ix. 51. On Tuesday, Sept. 28, He and His

Sept. 28, Tues.

* There should be a full stop at the word "Galilee" in Matt. xix. 1: for He did not go to Peræa straight from Galilee, but was at Jerusalem during the latter part of the Feast of Tabernacles: thence He moved "to the frontiers of Judæa beyond Jordan" (εἰς τὰ ὅρια τῆς Ἰουδαίας πέραν τοῦ Ἰορδάνου), *i.e.* went to Peræa, which was east of Jordan.

† Mark, like Matthew, takes no notice of the short visit to Jerusalem, but merely mentions that He removed from Galilee, changing the scene of His Ministry "to the frontiers of Judæa, even (*i.e.* viz.) beyond Jordan" (εἰς τὰ ὅρια τῆς Ἰουδαίας, καὶ πέραν τοῦ Ἰορδάνου); Peræa being on the frontier of Judæa, whereas Galilee was not, for Samaria divided Galilee from Judæa.

disciples would leave Capernaum: and be at the frontier of Samaria in the evening.

On Wednesday, Sept. 29, He would arrive at the hostile village in Samaritan territory indicated in Luke ix. 52, and at the friendly one of verse 56. That He sent messengers in advance to make preparations (Luke ix. 52) would be because all the pilgrim caravans to the Feast had passed some days ago, and thus His arrival would not be expected: also there were many travelling with Him to be provided for. On Thursday, Sept. 30, they would arrive at Bîreh, the last halting-place on the route. On Friday, Oct. 1, they would reach Jerusalem, and so be in the city before the Sabbath began at sunset of Friday. Thus He would naturally appear in the Temple on Saturday, Oct. 2, on the middle day of the seven days' Feast (verse 14).

Sept. 29 / Tisri 15 — Wed.

Sept. 30 / Tisri 16 — Thurs.

Oct. 1, Fri.

Oct. 2 / Tisri 18 — Sat.

(10) John remarks on this journey that He went up "not openly, but as it were covertly," *i.e.* not in company with the pilgrim caravans, *nor yet by the pilgrim route:* also not as Jesus, but *incognito.* Hence the strange opposition shown by the Samaritans on this occasion (Luke ix. 53). On the great pilgrim route from Galilee to Jerusalem (viz. *viâ* Jenîn, Nâblûs, Bîreh), the Samaritans would be by usage of centuries, and probably by written treaty, tolerant of the pilgrims' passage: but off the main route (the Ḥaj route as Moslems would say to-day) their hostility to the pilgrims would be always keen.

(11) Meanwhile, at Jerusalem, His delay was causing much agitation. "Therefore"—seeing that He was late, and not among the pilgrim caravans—"the Jews (the hostile, hierarchical, national party) were seeking for Him at the Feast and saying, 'Where is *he*?'" (emphatic *he*, ἐκεῖνος, the one man we want): for they meant to kill Him at the first good opportunity that offered (vii. 1, 19: v. 18).

End of Sept.

(12) "And there was much muttering concerning Him among the crowds" who were from the provinces: some—

the more independent temperaments—venturing to say, 'He is a good man: there's no harm in him': others objecting, "Nay: but he is causing the crowd to go astray"—away from the doctors. These latter are the more conservative party who might rather be afraid that His influence was likely to snap the principle of authority, although as to Him personally they were in His favour; if only the authorities could see their way to recognize Him.

(13) "However, no one was for talking (ἐλάλει) openly about Him, for fear of the Jews." Though the crowds were as a whole favourably inclined to Him, no one spoke out boldly in His support, because they knew the hierarchy were against Him and the movement.

(14) "When it was already the middle of the Feast, Jesus went up to the Temple and He taught." The Feast lasted seven days; viz. in A.D. 28, from Wednesday, Sept. 29, to Tuesday, Oct. 5: so He appeared on the fourth day, viz. Saturday, Oct. 2, in the Temple, and began teaching. His teaching, one may suppose, would be adapted to the vast crowds as was His Sermon on the Mount, and would not be the theological discourses which He addressed to a more learned audience: *e.g.* to Nicodemus (chapter iii.), to the woman of Samaria (chapter iv.), to "the Jews" (chapter v.), to the spokesmen of the Galilean crowd in the synagogue (chapter vi.), varied with "the Jews" in same chapter, to "the Jews" and "the Pharisees" (chapters vii., viii.)—in short, all the discourses preserved by John. John is not concerned to give his readers the elementary teaching of Christ given to the crowds, as recorded by the Synoptic gospels, but wishes to select from our Lord's teaching stronger food adapted to other needs.

Oct. 2 }
Tisri 18 } Sat.

As to the part of the Temple in which He taught: A few days later (viii. 20) He was teaching in "the Treasury," *i.e.* in the porticos surrounding and giving on to the "Court of the Women," which was the main court of those reserved to the nation. On the other hand, two months later (x. 23) the "Portico of Solomon" is named as the place selected: that was on the extreme east of the Temple area and bordered the largest court of all, viz. the "Court of the Gentiles"—open to every one of all nationalities: this "Portico of Solomon" was the part the Apostles chose later to frequent (Acts iii. 11, and especially v. 12) as though our Lord had habitually chosen it.

(15) "The Jews" (the hostile and hierarchical party) listened on to the end of His address: and then, as the great audience broke up, began expressing to each other their astonishment at His learning. "Learning," to a Jew, meant exclusively learning in the Law and Theology and the sacred books. 'Where did He get it? we know He never learnt in the Schools, for we have never lost sight of Him since His birth: it has been a matter for wonder to us ever since He began teaching here in the Temple at twelve years of age.' It is clear the Jews had no definite fault to find with the teaching they had just heard: their question implies it could not be said to be unorthodox. It had been based on Moses and the Prophets: it threw light on them and explained them: it was not opposed to traditional exegesis, but it was ampler. It seemed indeed to bring the sacred books and the best Rabbinical exegesis into one large consistent whole: but it went beyond in its freshness and clearness of vision.

(16) "My doctrine is not mine, but His who sent Me." True He had never learnt in the Schools: for all that, His doctrine was not the invention of a new teacher. It was the teaching of God who sent Him to represent Him, just as in earlier days He appointed Moses to take their training in hand. His doctrine was the fulfilment, development, of the principles inherent in the Law of Moses when that Law is rightly understood.

(17) Nor could any of them, if his will was set to God, be in doubt about the source or the truth of the teaching they had just heard. For it was the willing to *do* God's will, as revealed hitherto in the principles of the Law, that gave the power to recognize the voice of God when heard. Like responds to like. (18) If a man teaches a new system of his own he seeks praise for himself; and his teaching, being but his own, is worthless: but if a man's teaching

seeks praise for God who sent him (for if he seeks praise for God, he is sent by God), his teaching will be true.

(19) Did not Moses give them the Law? they admitted it was the expression of the will of God: and yet "not one of you *does* the Law." Talk about it there was in plenty: but will to *do* was the best interpreter of it. From not willing to do it, they failed to know its spirit: from not knowing its spirit, they thought He was breaking it. But was He? Let them formulate their charge. "*Why* go ye about to kill Me?" The Jews, or official party, to whom He is speaking, gave no answer to His question, remaining silent, not willing to admit openly that such was their purpose.

(20) But the crowd from the provinces, who were unaware of this extreme measure determined by the hierarchy, gave as their own answer, 'Nay, nay. no one seeks to kill you: we heard rumours indeed in Galilee that you expected some such end: but it is a delusion you are under.' They are speaking *bonâ fide*, and are friendly.

(21) Jesus, ignoring this remark of the crowd, and still addressing the still silent Jews, gave the real answer to His own question, "Why do you seek to kill Me?" viz. Because He seemed to them to break the Law against bearing burdens on a Sabbath: as on the occasion of that cure He did on a Sabbath the last time He was here: which had offended them then (pp. 134–136) and was still a matter of astonishment to them all (πάντες θαυμάζετε).

(22) "Look at it this way," He says, or "Reason it out thus (Διὰ τοῦτο·)": "Moses has given you circumcision—not that it dates from Moses, but from the Fathers [long before Moses]—and on a Sabbath you circumcise" without scruple as on any other day: for instance, if the eighth day since a boy's birth be a Sabbath, he must be circumcised on that day in spite of Sabbath laws (Lev. xii. 3).

(23) But if one member may be as it were made sound on a Sabbath, why be angry because He had made the whole of a man sound on a Sabbath? The former case they justified in that the beneficent patriarchal (and

Mosaic) law, which required circumcision to take place on the eighth day after birth, was older than and took precedence of the Mosaic Sabbath laws. The latter case He justifies by God's yet older and wider laws of Humanity which also take precedence of the Mosaic, purely national, Sabbath law, which forbade a man carrying a burden on the Sabbath (v. 16).

There is nothing here to warrant the idea that the institution of the seventh-day rest dates from Moses, but quite the opposite. It dates from the Adamic cosmogony: but at the time of the Exodus, Moses added more stringent laws as to the Sabbath day, which were never meant for any nation but Israel.

(24) 'Judge not superficially: but judge in accordance with the underlying principles of justice.' Here this day's teaching seems to end.

(25) We may suppose that on the following day, Sunday, Oct. 3, He is again in the Temple teaching openly and without hindrance, which causes surprise among certain of those who lived at Jerusalem. This group are not the hierarchical party, nor yet do they belong to the crowds from the provinces: they are "Jerusalemites," residents at Jerusalem, who were familiar with the official objections raised against Him, and aware of the Sanhedrin's intention with regard to Him. They remark, "Is not this He whom they seek to kill?"

Oct. 3, Sun.

(26) 'And yet here He is in the very Temple boldly confronting the rulers, and they are silent. Can it be that, in spite of all they say, they are in truth aware that this one is the Messiah?' (27) 'And yet, how can this one be the Messiah? for we know (οἴδαμεν) all about this man and his family: we remember the events connected with his birth; we have watched him grow from child to man: but when Messiah comes, no one discerns (γινώσκει, ask as he may), whence He is.' They have in mind Malachi's "He will *suddenly* come to His Temple": where Malachi means 'without their being prepared to recognize Him,' for Malachi is there (iii. 1) talking of His first Coming.

They, however, took it to mean 'in full manhood suddenly'—as against one who had grown up under their eyes, and whose birth and parentage was known to them. This is remarkable: thirty years ago, at the time of His birth, the Sanhedrin had formulated no such teaching: for, when asked by Herod where Messiah was to be *born*, they said "at Bethlehem" (Matt. ii. 4, 5): therefore in those days they expected Messiah to be born of a mother like any other man, and no doubt expected to know of His birth and watch Him grow to maturity. And this had continued to be their opinion all the years of His Childhood and Boyhood, so that we find Him at the age of twelve welcomed by "the doctors" (Luke ii. 46, 47) as the nation's Pride, their Hope, their Glory. It was not till years later, when they gradually fell foul of His ideals and tacitly disavowed Him, that they began to orientate their outlook afresh and sought to recast their exegesis of the Prophets in such a way as to exclude all possibility of Jesus being the Messiah. Amongst other prophecies they found this one of Malachi to their purpose, so explaining it to the people that all might know that none whose parentage and birth were known (as was the case with Jesus) could possibly be Messiah: they would support their teaching by that other dark prophecy (Isa. liii. 8), "Who shall declare His generation?" and as we have seen (at i. 46), they had twisted Micah's "from Bethlehem" to exclude Jesus as being "from Nazareth."

(28) He is aware of their surprise at His boldness, and also of their intellectual difficulty. He emphasizes for them His boldness by raising His voice as one speaking with the weight of authority, there, in the very Temple: teaching not this time the crowds, but those learned objectors who had just expressed rabbinical and theological difficulties.

'It was true they knew Him, and they knew whence He was, for His human parentage was known to them. And yet, along with that, they did not know whence He was: and in this, their expectation about the Messiah was being realized: for He was come from One whom they did not know, Him who alone has authority to send the Messiah, Him who is the God of Truth: but what Truth was there in them that they should recognize the Sender or the Sent?'

(29) "*I* know Him, for from Him I am (*παρ' αὐτοῦ εἰμί*)," *i.e.* from Him I have My being, by eternal generation, "and He it is who sent Me," *i.e.* from Him I have also My mission: but under both of these headings that saying they quoted was true of them all, "when the Messiah comes, no one knows whence He is."

(30) An unofficial attempt was here made by His opponents to arrest Him: but, when it came to laying a hand on Him, none was bold enough; for a power went forth from Him that stayed them. He could not be taken till the hour of destiny came, when He and The Father should allow His arrest. This emanant power was again felt (xviii. 6) on the night of His arrest.

Our Lord's discourse is over: He perhaps here leaves the Temple, crossing the great court, from the Portico of Solomon toward the gate of exit.

(31) As a result of His discourse, "Many of the crowd" from the provinces "believed into Him" as the Messiah; saying among themselves in under-tones: 'This must be Messiah; anyway when Messiah comes will He do more signs by which we may know Him than this One did?'

(32) It was, perhaps, on the next day, Monday, Oct. 4, that the Pharisees moving about the crowded courts heard these muttered remarks still echoing; and, recognizing their dangerous tendency, they and the chief priests sent certain of the Temple police (who were Hebrews of the tribe of Levi) to take Him before He left the Temple area to-day, or, failing that, to take Him at the first opportunity when He entered the Temple again—so we gather from verse 45, where the time is fixed by verse 37 to Tuesday, Oct. 5.

Oct. 4, Mon.

(33) Jesus, being aware of what they had done (for to Him all things were known) said to this the national party who refused Him: "For a little while yet I am with you" (viz. another six months): "and" (thereafter)—

(34) "I withdraw to Him who sent Me." The day

would come that they should seek their Messiah who was no other than Himself, and they should not find their Messiah, because they sought their Messiah elsewhere than in Him. His special reference seems to be to their vivid expectation, forty-two years later, of a sudden deliverance (see Josephus, *War*, VI. v. 2) by Messiah, which alone supported them to resist Titus with such obstinate courage, ending in the national ruin. "And where *I* am, *ye* cannot come." Not until all their ideas about Him personally, and about Messiah, were changed, could the gulf between Him and them be bridged.

And with those words He passes out of the Temple area. The gate of exit for the public lay in the north half of the west wall: and that of ingress in the south half of the same west wall. The gates in the north, south, and east walls were not open to the general public.

(35) Therefore "the Jews" said among themselves, 'Whither is this one about to go that we the privileged People shall not find him? if he is Messiah, as he claims, he cannot sever himself from us: for Messiah without us is not thinkable.

'It cannot be that he is going to those of us who are dispersed among the Greeks, and so teach the Greeks also?'—a premonition of what actually did happen under the Apostles, some thirteen years later.

The speakers might perhaps have had in mind the fact that some three weeks ago, on returning through Decapolis (which was a Greek confederacy) He had fed a crowd of four thousand who were Gentiles, and probably Gentile Israelites (Mark vii. 31–viii. 9). In any case the terms τὰ ἔθνη ("Gentiles") and Ἕλληνες (Greeks) were at this time frequently used synonymously by the Jews.

(36) And "What can he mean by that 'ye shall seek Me and shall not find Me: and where I am ye cannot come'?" They will hear the same words again on Wednesday (viii. 21) and be equally perplexed.

Note.—The foregoing, from verse 14 to verse 36 inclusive, which has here been taken as covering the three days Saturday, Sunday, Monday, may equally well be taken as confined to the one day Saturday (of verse 14). In either case verse 37 opens with the following Tuesday, Oct. 5, Tisri 21.

§ XII

JOHN VII. 37–52

The last and great day of the Feast

(37) "On the last day, the great day, of the Feast."

A.D. 28. Oct. 5 / Tisri 21 } Tues.

The time is three days later than verse 14: it is "the last" and seventh day of the Feast, viz. Tuesday, Oct. 5, A.D. 28.

The Feast of Tabernacles lasted seven days: of which the seventh and last was "the great day" and marked by extra ceremonies. The "eighth day" was a different Feast altogether, as Edersheim shows from Rabbinical authorities: and the peculiar rites of the seven days of Tabernacles were not observed on that day.

So, He is again in the Temple: "He was standing" in some conspicuous place, for He meant to be seen of all: "and He cried aloud," as with authority, "saying," etc.

(38) It is evident that our Lord here delivered a discourse, of which John has given us only the salient sentences: a discourse in which He claimed to be the dispenser of the Holy Spirit, of which the outpouring had been figured by the ritual just performed. If they would but understand, the whole ritual of the Feast prefigured, and centred in, Him. His reference is to that pouring out of water at the great altar, which was made on each of the seven days of Tabernacles. On this, the seventh day of the Feast, the procession round the altar was repeated seven times: this seventh and last day was known as "the Great Hosanna." The water-pouring was held by the Rabbis to be significative of the pouring out of the Holy Spirit in "the latter days," the days of the Messiah, when the general harvest of the nations should be gathered in. This outpouring of the Spirit prophesied by Joel yet awaits

its perfect fulfilment, ushering in the millennial Age, when the conversion of the Jews will be as " life from the dead " (Rom. xi. 15) to the Gentiles : for the Pentecost of A.D. 29 (Acts ii.) was but the firstfruits of The Spirit, and is but firstfruits still.

The Feast of Weeks or Pentecost was the Feast of First-fruits, or the beginning of wheat harvest; whereas the Feast of Tabernacles was the Feast of the general harvest or ingatherings.

(38) " He that believeth into Me, as said the Scripture, rivers out of his belly shall flow of living water." " As said the Scripture." The nearest approach in the O.T. as we have it is Isa. lviii. 11, " thou shalt be like a spring of waters, whose waters fail not." See the very similar figure in iv. 14, " The water that I shall give him shall be in him a spring of leaping water, (leaping) unto Life eternal."

(39) " This He spake of The Spirit which they who believed into Him were about to receive," viz. at Pentecost to start with ; and, as we may believe, at a fuller outpouring yet to come.

" For the Holy Ghost was not yet given, because Jesus was not yet glorified," *i.e.* not yet given visibly, copiously, and with such manifestations as it was at Pentecost after our Lord was glorified. Why was the Spirit not given visibly and abundantly before His Ascension ? " In order," says Leo, " that this gift and pouring forth of the Holy Spirit might be acknowledged to be the fruit of His Passion, Ascension, and Triumph : just as kings give largesses on occasions of great joy, triumph," etc. The sending of The Spirit was the *sign* of the glorification of Christ.

(40) " Some of the crowd hearing these discourses " or " words " (John, as has been said, has given only salient sentences, or headings of the address), " said ' This one is of a truth The Prophet.' "

" The Prophet " is the " Prophet " of Deut. xviii. 18, whom Peter (Acts iii. 22) identifies with our Lord. See also John i. 45, " Him of whom Moses in the Law . . . wrote " : also under i. 21.

(41) " Others said," boldly and definitely, " ' This one is the Messiah.' "

" Others said, ' How so ? for can it be that Messiah comes out of (ἐκ) Galilee ? ' " The preposition rendered " out of " (ἐκ) refers to birth and origin, not to residence. (42) " ' Said not the Scriptures that Messiah cometh out of (ἐκ) the seed of David and from (ἀπὸ) Bethlehem, the village where David was ? ' " They were right that Messiah was not to come out of (ἐκ, *i.e.* not to be native of) Galilee, for He was to be out of (ἐκ, *i.e.* native of) Bethlehem. They were wrong, however, in thinking He was to be a resident of (ἀπὸ) Bethlehem and in that sense to be from Bethlehem. The reference, of course, is to Micah v. 2. " Out of thee, Bethlehem," etc. The Hebrew and Aramaic preposition *min* has the meaning of both the Greek prepositions ἐκ and ἀπὸ, and may be rendered by either. John's discriminating use here of ἐκ and ἀπὸ shows us exactly how the objectors were here understanding or misunderstanding the Hebrew *min*. See also under i. 45, 46. The LXX had rightly rendered it in Micah v. 2 by ἐκ, and the Sanhedrin had so understood it (Matt. ii. 5) before they became, many years later, disingenuous. His opponents knew that He had been born at Bethlehem, and therefore was ἐκ Bethlehem and not ἐκ Galilee : but in view of the equivocal meaning of the Hebrew preposition, they now disingenuously founded on it an objection to Him for not being ἀπὸ Bethlehem, *i.e.* resident of Bethlehem. Nathanael (John i. 45–47) had seen through the equivocation and their disingenuous mistake : hence our Lord's commendation of him as being " without guile " : but the subtlety of that passage and of this one has been missed by the A.V., and is obscured even in the R.V. in chapter i. by rendering ἀπὸ sometimes by " of " and sometimes by " from."

(43) Thus there arose a cleavage in the crowd, because of Him and their difference of opinion about Him : (44) and some of them wished to go so far as to seize Him. But this second unofficial attempt to take Him was frustrated (as the former one of verse 30), perhaps by a power

that went out from Him. And at this point He leaves the Temple area.

(45) The Temple police (Levites), who had been told off yesterday (verse 32) to take Him at the first opportunity on His reappearance in the Temple, came to the chief priests and Pharisees to explain why they had not done so to-day. The attempt made had not been made by them: and the reason for their inaction was that they had been so impressed by His words that they preferred to have nothing to do with His arrest.

(47) "The Pharisees answered them." The Pharisees take the lead as being the more religious, and more zealous than the Sadducean chief priests. 'Can it be,' they ask, 'that you also, you Levites, have been led astray? (48) Has any one of the rulers (*i.e.* the Sanhedrin), or of us Pharisees who know, believed into Him? (49) Only this ignorant crowd from the provinces have done so: and they having no knowledge of Law or of theology, are, as such, accursed and easily led astray.'

(50) Nicodemus, himself one of the Sanhedrin, and a secret disciple of Jesus ever since he went to Him (iii. 2), speaks up in the only way that could possibly be of service to Him—using tact and judgment, (51) 'Are we not condemning Him unheard? that is, against the Law.' As one of the Sanhedrin, and speaking to rigid observers of legal forms, he insists on the legal formalities being observed: anxious for a formal hearing not only for our Lord's sake, but also for the sake of the Sanhedrin, and of the nation whose fate hung on the Sanhedrin's action.

(52) They reply with some impatience: "Can it be that thou also art out of (ἐκ, native of) Galilee?"—the same as were the ignorant crowd who were favourable to our Lord. 'Now search and thou shalt find that out of (ἐκ, native of) Galilee a prophet has not arisen in all our history' (lit. "does not arise").

Westcott (on this passage) objects that "Jonah, Hosea, Nahum, and perhaps Elijah, Elisha, and Amos, were of Galilee," and implies that the Pharisees were, therefore, here talking inaccurately. But he has failed to notice the force of the ἐκ. They did not mean that the Prophets had not been residents of (ἀπὸ) Galilee, but that they had not been natives of (ἐκ) Galilee. And they were right, for though the six named above had lived and prophesied in Galilee like our Lord, yet, like Him again, they were not natives of Galilee. For—

Hosea * (according to Christian tradition *v.* Ephrem Syrus: and there is nothing opposed to it) was of Issachar, a native of Belemon, thought to be near Dothan: and not in Galilee. A Jewish tradition makes him a native of Gilead: and not in Galilee.

Nahum,* a native of Elkosh. Though some put this Elkosh in Galilee, others, with greater probability, and see the *Vitæ Prophetarum* of 4th century, place it south of Beit Jibrîn, in Judæa, and make him to be a Simeonite.

Elijah * was a native of Thisbe in Gilead (east of Jordan): see Josephus, *Ant.* viii. 13, 2 (ἐκ πόλεως Θεσβώνης τῆς Γαλααδίτιδος χώρας).

Elisha * was a native of Abel-Meholah, in the Jordan Valley, twelve miles south of Bethshan and therefore in Samaria and not Galilee.

Amos * was a native of Tekoa in Judæa (ἐκ Θεκουέ, as the LXX render Amos i. 1).

Jonah alone seems to have been a native of Galilee: Gath-Hepher, his native town (2 Kings xiv. 25, τοῦ ἐκ Γεθχοφέρ) being the same as Gittah-Hepher in Zabulon (Joshua xix. 13). The Pharisees might, however, ignore him in that his mission lay mainly to Nineveh and not to Israel.

* See also Hasting's "Dictionary of the Bible."

§ XIII

JOHN VII. 53–VIII. 59

The eighth day. The adulteress. Jesus and the Sanhedrists

EXTERNAL evidence is perhaps against the twelve verses (vii. 53–viii. 11) having formed part of John's original text. If not John's, it was a very early interpolation: it may possibly have had the sanction of Simeon or Jude (early 2nd century), the second and third bishops of Jerusalem, "brethren" of our Lord, the last survivors of the Apostolic age. These two seem to have been connected with the editing of this gospel, for they are probably the "we" of xxi. 24, and the two unnamed disciples of xxi. 2.

But the last word has by no means been said on the text of the N.T. The Western text may yet be found to have been unduly slighted.

(vii. 53) "And they went each one to his own house: and Jesus went to the Mount of Olives" (viii. 1). The chief priests and Pharisees went from the Temple "each one to his own house" in the evening: the particular spot on the Mount of Olives to which Jesus went was probably the garden of Gethsemane, at the foot of the Mount, and the natural grotto in it, which tradition marks as the scene of His final betrayal, "the place to which Jesus often resorted with His disciples" (xviii. 2).

A.D. 28.
Oct. 5 / Tisri 21 — Tues.

(viii. 1, 2) These two verses closely resemble Luke xxi. 37, 38 (a passage belonging to the week of the Passion five months later).

(2–11) Doubtless this incident is historical even if it formed no part of John's text: and it probably belongs chronologically to the place it occupies in our text, viz. to the "morning" (verse 2) after "the last day, the great day, of the

Oct. 6 / Tisri 22 — Wed.

Feast" of Tabernacles (vii. 37). That is, it belongs to the day after the seven days' Feast of Tabernacles was ended: that is, it belongs to the eighth day since the Feast of Tabernacles began: it is the day called "the eighth day" in Lev. xxiii. 36, 39; Num. xxix. 35; 1 Kings viii. 66; 2 Chron. vii. 9; Neh. viii. 18: a Festival by itself, as Edersheim has shown from Rabbinical sources in his *Life and Times of Jesus*, etc., vol. 2, pp. 156, 176, a Festival known in the Jewish calendar as the *Simḥat-Torah*, "Joy of the Law." On this day (Tisri 22nd), for those in Palestine the last portion of the Law was read in the synagogues; the year's cycle of lessons beginning again on the following Sabbath with the 1st chapter of Genesis.

(2) "And early in the morning He came again to the Temple, and all the People kept coming (ἤρχετο) to Him." "All the People" (πᾶς ὁ λαός). The phrase is often, but by no means always, used as here of the bulk of the covenant People—the commonalty—as against their leaders the Sanhedrists (*e.g.* Luke iii. 21: vii. 29: xviii. 43: xix. 48: xx. 6, 45: xxi. 38).

Oct. 6 / Tisri 22 } Wed.

"He sat down and He taught them." Whether He taught them on this occasion in the Court of the Women (where the Treasury was), or in the Portico of Solomon, it is evident that the teaching was over and the audience dispersed before the incident of verse 3 occurred: for throughout that incident (3–11) the only persons present seem to be Jesus, "the Scribes and the Pharisees," *i.e.* members of the Sanhedrin, and the woman.

(3) In contrast to the eagerness of the commonalty to be taught by Him, the narrative describes the position of the Sanhedrists who come to set a trap for Him. The scene has changed to the Court of Justice in the Temple enclosure.* "The Scribes and the Pharisees bring a woman taken in adultery, and having stood her (στήσαντες

* This Court-house, which was in the north-east of the Temple enclosure, is not to be confounded with the Council Hall of the Sanhedrin, which ran alongside the Court of the Women.

αὐτὴν) in the midst," *i.e.* of themselves sitting as her judges, (4) "they say to Him" whom they have invited to enter as one claiming to understand and to fulfil the Law, "'Master (διδάσκαλε), this woman has been taken in adultery, in the very act: (5) and in the Law Moses commanded us to stone such (women): thou, therefore, what sayest thou?'" This was not a formal sitting of the Court, for the day was a Feast day: the object was to get a damaging pronouncement from Him.

The passage in the Law that they refer to is probably not Lev. xx. 10, nor Deut. xxii. 22 (for in these cases Talmudic tradition says the mode of death was strangulation, and not stoning), but Deut. xxii. 23, 24: from which it is to be inferred that this woman was betrothed but not yet married, and that the man was not he to whom she was betrothed. The Law of Moses was quite plain, but the sense of the community was in our Lord's time averse from so severe a punishment. Were they, then, to obey Moses? or, if not, how did He justify this non-fulfilment of the Law?

(6) They knew He would not on this point advise a strict conformity with the Mosaic Law, for the public conscience of the day was against enforcing the penalty in all its rigour, and custom had long ignored it. It was, however, one thing to tacitly ignore a command and another to say formally that it was not binding. Here was a difficulty with which the Scribes and the Pharisees had long been faced, nor had any satisfactory defence yet been found for their habitual practice.

"But Jesus stooped down and with His finger He wrote" (imp. κατέγραφεν, implying a prolonged action) "on the ground." The gloss, "as though He heard them not," gives correctly His purpose in so writing, viz. to seem to have not heard their question, and to be pursuing a train of thought remote from His immediate surroundings. He declines to act as judge here as again some months later (Luke xii. 14).

(7) "But when they continued asking Him, He lifted Himself up and said to them, 'He of you that is sinless,

let him be the first to cast a stone at her.' " By this answer He tacitly approved their non-exaction of the extreme penalty of the Law on the ground that the public conscience of the day could not approve the penalty, because the public morals of the day were too loose. The nation were forced in practice to shut their eyes to this provision of the Mosaic Law, because, and as long as, the national conscience was callous to the sinfulness of adultery. The fault lay not with the Mosaic Law, but with the nation: the Mosaic Law was not too severe for the sin, but the nation's conscience was too blunt to the sin. He would not abate one tittle of the Law, but it must lie in abeyance until the coming in of a better Age.*

(8) Having thus implicitly asked them why it is that they do not carry out the Mosaic penalty, He leaves their conscience to give them the answer; and an answer that

* We may suppose that when Holy Land is reoccupied by the Representatives of the reunited nation of Israel and Judah in the millennial Age, the Mosaic Law will there (and, of course, there only) be observed in a perfection and with a loving devotion such as it never yet received. We may suppose that in the rebuilt Temple (see Ezek. xl.–xlviii.) the Mosaic ritual will be observed as a type no longer obscure but fully comprehended; whilst in the same Temple the Christian ritual of the Mass will be celebrated; and in both cases by a Christian Hebrew priesthood. Outside of Holy Land, the Christian ritual of the Mass will alone be observed. We must suppose (unless the O.T. prophets are to be classed as fanatical neurotic visionaries) that in the millennial Age the Tribes of Israel reunited to Judah will be a Christian nation under their national king acting as Christ's viceroy: that they will by their Representatives reinhabit Holy Land—Palestine physically regenerated: that Jerusalem, rebuilt on a remodelled ground-surface, will be the centre of the world: that to that reunited nation will have been adjudged (Matt. xxv. 31–46, which is the judgment of the nations *quâ* nations) the kingdom of the whole earth—an earth all Christian, whose focus of sanctity and social progress will be Holy Land. This judgment of nations immediately precedes the millennium.

It would further seem that after the great advance marked by the millennial Age, and after the great judgment of individuals which follows it (Rev. xx. 11–15), there will succeed an Age as much better than the millennial as the millennial will be better than is this of ours to-day. To that post-millennial Age belong the last two chapters of *Revelation:* in it our Lord reigns as visible Monarch of the world, and the New Jerusalem takes the place of the millennial Jerusalem: even then the " nations " still need to be " healed " by " the leaves of the Tree of Life," although death shall be no more among them. Not even in that post-millennial Age are we at the goal: for beyond that far vista of the progress of the race, there is due an Age when our Lord " shall hand-over the Kingdom to God, even to The Father " (1 Cor. xv. 24).

will incidentally solve the difficulty that underlay their question of verse 5.

"And again He stooped down, and He wrote (imp.) on the ground," as being no longer interested in the matter, thus giving them opportunity to walk out without meeting those all-seeing eyes that shamed them.

(9) "And they, having heard, went out" (the imp. ἐξήρχοντο, marks the gradual action) "one by one, beginning with the elder ones." The gloss, "being convicted by their conscience," gives the correct reason of their exit—the sense that not only they themselves, but the whole nation for whom they acted, came too far short of that ethical standard which the Law presupposed. It would be injustice and hypocrisy to carry out the penalty in one or two sporadic cases, taken at random out of a multitude left unpunished.

"And He was left alone, and the woman being in the midst": in the midst, that is, of the Court-house where she had been placed (3). There is no one else present.

(10) "And Jesus, having lifted Himself up, said to her, 'Woman, where are they? Did no one condemn thee?'" Was there none found to pass judgment and pronounce that the penalty be carried out?

(11) "And she said, 'No one, Lord.' And Jesus said, 'Neither do *I* condemn thee.'" The others had been unable to condemn her to death, because conscious of the laxity of morals prevalent among themselves and the whole society of the day: Jesus was unwilling to condemn her to death, because, though sinless Himself, He knew the state of society was such that to enforce the rigour of the Law would be to make justice unjust. But, lest she or others should think that lenient to the sinner He was careless of her sin, He dismissed her, "Go": but cautioned her and encouraged her, "henceforth sin no more." *

* In the forbearance shown to the adulteress (type of Israel and Judah) on this festival of *Simḥat-Torah*, "Joy of the Law," some have seen a guerdon of the yet future forgiveness to be pronounced upon the reunited nation toward the end of this Age, previous to their return to Holy Land, when the nation's charter comes again into force.

(12) "Again therefore talked Jesus to them, saying," etc. This "again" does not refer to the incident (vii. 53–viii. 11) here preceding (unless that formed part of John's original text), but refers to chapter vii. 37–52, and implies that the discourse viii. 12–59 took place on the day following. We are thus, as explained at verse 2, at the morning of Wednesday, Oct. 6, Tisri 22, and, of course, in the year A.D. 28.

Oct. 6 } Wed.
Tisri 22 }

The following discourse (viii. 12–19) took place in "the Treasury" (τῷ γαζοφυλακίῳ, verse 20), the western one of the four porticos that surrounded and gave on to the Court of the Women, near the Council Hall of the Sanhedrin.

(12) "*I* am the Light of the world." He may be contrasting Himself with the lights from the great candelabra which had illumined the Temple during the last seven days, and which were to-day standing unlit in the Court of the Women. He is certainly claiming to be Messiah, the world's King, whom the Rabbis figured as the Enlightener: whom in His infancy Simeon had announced to be "Light" for the nations, and the Covenant-People's "Glory" (Luke ii. 32): Him whom the Evangelist calls the source of "Life" and "the Light" that illumines the intellect of every human being (John i. 4).

"He that follows Me shall not walk in the darkness"; the darkness which owing to man's inherited sin battles with the Light in him. "But he shall have the Light of Life," Light that is Life and that shall eventually disperse the darkness.

John, as is his custom, has only given us salient sentences of this discourse: and to understand it, we must remember that the Pharisees were never in doubt as to what Jesus claimed, nor as to what had been claimed for Him by John the Prophet and Forerunner, nor as to what had been proclaimed of Him at His infancy. As Child and Boy He had been recognized by the nation as the promised Messiah: but long before His public ministry began He had been gradually disowned and definitely set aside. It is because we do not correctly estimate the historical relation of Jesus to the Sanhedrin in those long years before His public ministry began, that we find it difficult to-day to visualize the gospel history; and more particularly that part of it preserved by John, viz. our Lord's theological discourses to the Jewish doctors or to that inner circle of disciples whom He was training to take their place.

(13) "Therefore, said the Pharisees to Him," etc. The Pharisees quite understood His Messianic meaning: but they will not have Him. 'You make statements about yourself, but why should we believe you? they are corroborated by no evidence that satisfies us. We want what we have wanted from years back—some unmistakable "sign" of your mission.'

(14) He admits He is bearing witness about Himself: He accepts for the moment their objection: but let them recollect, the sole object of all laws about witness is to ensure the getting at the truth: and it belongs to the very nature of this particular case here that He *must* give witness about Himself: no one else is qualified to give witness about His nature and about His essential work. He alone can do that, for He alone knows who He is, or what He means to do, or how He means to do it. None of them, nor of the race of man, can bear witness at first hand about His Being.

"As to My particular case,"—such is the force of the emphatic ἐγὼ, the first "I" of this verse: He says that although He is bearing witness about Himself, His witness is true in its facts (ἀληθής), for He has absolute and perfect knowledge of His own nature (and that nature is the point He is giving witness about): seeing that He knows (A) whence He came; knows, that is, that He is the eternal Son, the second Person of the Godhead, who came to them by becoming incarnate as the God-Man: and (B) whither He withdraws; knows, that is, that He withdraws unto God whence He came, withdraws incarnate henceforth for ever bearing with Him the whole human race: for He will withdraw (at His ascension). But they know neither The Father from whom He came and to whom He returns, nor yet the work that He came to begin and withdraws to finish.

(15) "You (ὑμεῖς, emph.) judge according to the flesh." Their judgment about Him was vitiated by their limitations: even in their courts of justice they have to judge in a rough-and-ready fashion, according to the best evidence they can get: and their judgments are necessarily imperfect, for they have to depend on evidence which is human, and, as such, at best but approximately adequate: —probable only, not certain, for man cannot have absolute knowledge. "I (ἐγὼ, emph.) judge no one": He has not come (at this His first coming) to judge any one, acquit, approve or condemn.

(16) "But, in My case (ἐγὼ), even if I do judge, My judgment is true" (ἀληθινὴ), ideally true, and not only in accord with the forms of law: "because I am not alone, but (there are) I and He who sent Me," *i.e.* His judgment is true because He has absolute knowledge and omniscience, seeing that He has always the Godhead with Him: He is not merely man and, so, alone: there are always The Father and Himself inseparable.

(17) And, again, in that matter of bearing witness about Himself (referring back to verse 14): It is written even in their Law (Deut. xvii. 6)—imperfect as all human systems must be—that the witness of two men (ἀνθρώπων, not even the more worthy ἀνδρῶν) is to be accepted as true, (ἀληθής), even though being human they are liable to err.

(18) 'But in this very case, where He is speaking about Himself, there *are* two witnesses: and not only two witnesses such as their Law requires, but what a Two! viz. (A) God The Son, the Man-God, even He Himself who is bearing witness about Himself,* for no other man can, since no other man knows Him: and (B) God The Father who sent Him."

We must remember that our Lord here is not *arguing*

* "If it be objected that a man could not bear witness in his own cause, the same Rabbinic canon laid it down that this only applied if his testimony stood alone. But if it were corroborated, it would be credited." Edersheim, *Life and Times of Jesus*, etc., vol. 2, p. 169.

with the Pharisees: He is *teaching* any among them who had ears to hear. He is talking to theologians, and He is talking pure theology to them, explaining to them who He really is and what is His relationship to The Father: how it was that He could be God and yet talk of Another than Himself as God: how there can be Father and Son in the Godhead: how The Father is so One in essence with Him The Son, that whatever The Son asserts The Father cannot but assert. He is stating simple dogmatic truths of theology, truths about the nature of Himself and of the Holy Trinity: He is passing on beyond the mere unity of God—a truth familiar to them all—to the more advanced doctrine of the Trinity, three Persons in one Godhead, which was a truth not familiar to them, but one which He came to teach. He is speaking for the benefit of some one or more there present whom He knows to be ready to assimilate His teaching; and He is speaking to Christendom for all time, as John was aware. He never wasted His words, nor yet His works of healing, nor yet His manifestations of the more-than-human that was in Him.

It is a common assertion with a certain school that our Lord's teaching was all simple and easy for the poorest intelligence to grasp: as though He had confined Himself to parables, simple ethics, beatitudes and the like: and in consequence they throw doubt on the genuineness of John's gospel, or, reading it, fail to make anything of it, and close it in impatience: for it does not square with the scheme they have of Christ. They go on to say that the Church is alien in her mind to our Lord's mind, because she has defined dogma after dogma about our Lord's Personality. Is she so alien? Is her dogmatic teaching so unlike His? All her dogmas on our Lord's Personality are in agreement with His teaching as left to us by the N.T. writers, and John's gospel is the principal fount: she has been quick to recognize the sheer theology of much of this teaching; statements requiring intense concentration and abstract thought to grasp them; their simple, bald, formal language clear of all poetry or emotion, hard and luminous as crystal, dry and accurate as all philosophical and theological thought must of its very nature be.

There were assuredly some present whose clear intuition, or trained intelligence, illumined by His Spirit were able to catch sight of His meaning, and for these He is primarily speaking—it may be Nicodemus, or Joseph of Arimathea, or Gamaliel, or John himself.

(19) "Where is thy Father?" *i.e.* 'You say,' say they, 'you are the Light of the world and this and that, and that God is your Father, and that He corroborates you: we are wasting words: you obviously cannot produce God, and we obviously cannot get at Him to question Him: so your statements still remain statements made by yourself about yourself.' 'Ah,' He seems to reply, 'you say you cannot get at Him to question Him: that is exactly the position, and therein lies your condemnation.' How could they possibly get at Him in the mood they and their nation were in and had been in ever since He was born among them? To hear that voice required that a man be seeking to live in unison with Him and to do His will: keeping His Law of Moses (for He is speaking to Jews), yet with ears open to His secret voice lest that Law become a dead ritual: for this all the prophets were sent. Had they sought its spirit beneath its ritual, as the prophets implored them, sought to keep heart simple and hands clean whilst still observing all its ritual, sought to know Him, in short sought to do His will as was said to them last Saturday (John vii. 17), they would have heard His voice within them witnessing to Jesus; they would have leapt to Him, and in Him found The Father's manifestation: 'Had they known The Father they had known Him: and conversely had they known Him they would have known The Father.'

(20) "These sayings He talked in the Treasury." The Treasury was in the colonnade that ran round and gave on to the Court of the Women: this Court of the Women was so called because beyond it no woman might go: it was the most frequented Court—by men and women,

but no Gentile might enter it; its colonnade contained thirteen trumpet-shaped coffers, each of which was labelled with the uses to which the money placed in it would be applied. Along the south side of this Court of the Women ran the Hall of the Sanhedrin. Yet even here, so near His enemies, and although they had given orders for His arrest (vii. 32), He is found teaching: and still "no one arrested Him." It was the same last Saturday (vii. 32), and again yesterday, Tuesday (vii. 44): "for His hour was not yet come"—the hour that He Himself should select six months later.

(21) "Therefore," as knowing none could stop Him, He is again in the Temple, later on on the same day (Wednesday, Oct. 6), probably at the time of the evening sacrifice—about 3 p.m.—when crowds would be again in the courts: "He said again to them: 'I withdraw, and ye shall seek Me.'"

Oct. 6 } Wed.
Tisri 22

"I withdraw (ἐγὼ ὑπάγω)." He could not fall in with their views of Messiah: they would not fall in with His: He therefore must leave them, withdrawing to Him who sent Him, there to finish His work.

"And ye shall seek Me," etc., *i.e.* they should seek their Messiah who was really Himself: but, refusing Him, they should not find their Messiah. To expect any other was vain: and, expecting another, 'they should in that sin meet their death,' viz. at the destruction of Jerusalem by Titus. It was the expectation of a sudden deliverance by Messiah that alone kept up the courage of the defenders (Josephus, *War*, VI. v. 2).

"And whither I withdraw ye cannot come."

(22) "The Jews," therefore, said in mockery, 'What: we to die in our sin? and he to go where we cannot follow? Does he mean to kill himself? then indeed he might go where we cannot follow.' For one who committed suicide was held to be guilty of murder: and to such the darker region of Hades was assigned (Josephus, *War*, III. viii. 5).

(23) In saying "whither I withdraw, ye cannot come," He repeats what He had said yesterday (vii. 33, 34) referring to His withdrawing to The Father and to the

essential divergence of His way from theirs. They had fallen under the domination of the world's spirit, and were content to lie there, deaf to His efforts to raise them to a higher conception of Messiah's office, refusing to accept Him as their Messiah and to allow Him to infuse into them His own nature of perfect Man, or again of perfect God: for that, and no other, was His scheme for lifting His own nation, and by means of them the world, up to heights undreamt of by the race.

(24) In saying "Ye shall die in your sins," He had not been passing sentence of death on them. He was but telling them of the inevitable end for which they, as a nation and as individuals, were making. As they were to-day, there was no living principle in them, not a germ that promised anything but dissolution: how could they be His salt of the earth? "For if ye believe not that I am (He), ye shall die in your sins."

Their only hope lay in an acceptance of Him, and on His terms: there was no national deliverance or empire possible by any such Messiah as they were looking for: true deliverance lay in a regeneration of the individual, and so of the nation: this was only possible to them by a belief in Him at His own valuation. The world-empire promised by all the prophets to their nation postulated an antecedent regeneration of the nation, and that regeneration was to have been the first of Messiah's works on them.

(25) They answer, 'Believe in you? but who are you that we should find in you deliverance? We know all about your history and the hopes that centred round your birth: they have all proved false: we simply do not accept you.'

'Who was He?' The very same that He had been telling them from the very beginning (*Τὴν ἀρχὴν ὅτι καὶ λαλῶ ὑμῖν*, and see x. 25)—telling them ever since He was twelve, and still was telling them, the same that had been foretold in Eden. (26) However, He was far from having finished with them: He had yet many a thing to teach the world about them, the Jews, and many a sentence to pass that would affect them, the Jews, bringing disaster first (though afterwards blessing) upon their nation: but so it must be: such were the Divine decrees, the decrees of Him who is Truth, the decrees of The Father which He The Son makes known through time: the world should hear them and see, for on the stage of the world's history should the drama be played.

(27) "They knew not that it was The Father He was speaking of to them." Such is John's comment as He pityingly looks back on the awful disasters that fell upon that nation forty-two years later. John does not mean that the Jews thought our Lord meant some one else: they knew that *He* meant The Father, but they wouldn't have it that He was right or had any authority to speak for The Father as though He were Himself God. But some day they were to know His true relationship to The Father: and how far they had strayed from The Father.

(28) "Therefore, said Jesus, 'When ye shall have lifted up (*i.e.* crucified) The Son of Man, then ye shall know that I am He.'" Then they should know who He is and what is His mission, and that He The Son of Man is also the eternal Son who in utterance and in history manifests The Father's will: for The Father and He act together.

In the "Then ye shall come to know (γνώσεσθε)" our Lord seems to be alluding to the conversion of the Jews still (1918) in the future, of which all the Prophets assure us. In the word "then" (τότε) He, like His prophets before Him, jumps the secular gap, "the times of the nations," that intervenes between the rejection of Judah and her return.

(29) Also they shall come to know that when He became Incarnate, He did not lay aside His Divine nature: He is still The Son eternally generated by The Father, for as Man no less than as God "I do always the things that are pleasing to Him." The "I" (ἐγὼ, emphatic) calls attention to His Personality which is one only, though working in two natures. His Personality is God. Although they would crucify Him, a day was to come when they would know that, for all that, "The Father left Me not

alone" (οὐκ ἀφῆκέν με μόνον): much the same statement will be repeated on the night of the Agony, "I am not alone, inasmuch as the Father is with Me" (οὐκ εἰμὶ μόνος, ὅτι ὁ Πατὴρ μετ' ἐμοῦ ἐστίν, xvi. 32). It is impossible that The Father can leave The Son for an instant, or The Son The Father: any such separation would be a destruction of the Trinity: it is a contradiction in terms, a contradiction of the eternal, unceasing, entire Generation of The Son from The Father. And this must be borne in mind when we seek to understand that mysterious dereliction on the Cross and the cry, "My God, My God" (not My Father), "why didst Thou forsake Me?" That is not the cry of The Son *quâ* The Son to The Father. Jesus *quâ* the eternal Son of the eternal Father cannot lose consciousness of His union with The Father: nor again can Jesus *quâ* the perfect and sinless Man lose consciousness of His union with His own Divinity, for there is no sin in Him to cloud His vision. It is the cry of the Man Jesus, *quâ the sum of the fallen and sinful race* which in virtue of union with Him the Man-God is being ever re-formed in that living Laboratory His Body into the new creation.

(30) "As He spoke these things (ταῦτα . . . λαλοῦντος) many believed into Him." The "many" who "believed into Him" (ἐπίστευσαν εἰς αὐτὸν) belong to the crowds from the provinces, who were present on this day known as the Feast of the Rejoicing of the Law: they were not Jews proper belonging to the tribe of Judah. The faith of these "many" is a genuine faith.

(31) "Therefore said Jesus to the *Jews* who had believed Him." In the Greek the emphasis is on *Jews*. These "Jews," who had believed Him" (τοὺς πεπιστευκότας αὐτῷ Ἰουδαίους) are clearly distinguished from the "many" who "believed into Him" of verse 30. To "believe into Him" (πιστεύειν εἰς) is a vital process: it is the "credo *in Deum*" of the Creed, a belief implicit, complete, without reservation. To "believe Him" (πιστεύειν αὐτῷ), or credere Deo, which is never used in the Creed, is not necessarily any more than what demons do. It is not a process, it is an isolated fact which may or

may not pass on into growth. Those "Jews who had believed Him" had believed His statement that He was the Messiah, and had believed His claim that He was God: so far, demons did as much: again and again they had cried it aloud, "Jesus, thou Son of God," etc. Something other was needed than such belief. They of verse **30** were on the home track: not so they of verse **31**, as is seen by the sequel.

"'If *ye* abide in My word, truly My disciples are ye:'" *i.e.* if these *Jews* ("you" emphatic) who as yet only believed *ab extra*, without willingness to merge themselves in Him, if these would continue in His teaching, and let Him make their belief a living Faith, then even they would truly be His disciples.

(32) "'Also ye shall know (γνώσεσθε, shall have learnt by process) the Truth,'" the true estimate of all,—of Him, and so of themselves, and so of all ideas. 'And it was this knowledge of Truth that should make them free men.' They were looking for a freedom from the Roman domination: there was a larger freedom than that: it was this larger freedom that He, their Messiah, wished first to give them, 'the freedom born of Truth.'

(33) They reply: 'A very excellent sort of freedom for Greek or Roman: it is not what we want. As Abraham's seed we have an inalienable right to freedom from all domination of the Gentiles over us, nay, a right to world-wide empire: it was promised to Abraham's seed by oath, by covenant, and by all the prophets. It is our destiny: nothing can deflect it. True we have been momentarily in subjection to Egypt and to all the world-powers of Daniel's vision—Babylon, Persia, Greece, Rome—for our sins: but nothing can break us or enslave us; we are God's freemen: soon or late deliverance has ever come to us: it will be the same with this last world-power, Rome. Our claim to world-domination lies in our descent from Abraham. What is this talk of a freedom based on perception of Truth: a Greek philosopher may be content with it: not we.'

(34) He replied that it was the inner freedom that was

the first essential, freedom from sin. "Everyone that doeth sin is a servant—of sin." (35) A servant, not a free man: and how should a servant have permanent dominion? This world was His Father's house, sin should not always dominate in it: only the Son of the house could have permanent dominion in it: He Himself was the Son in this His Father's house, the world: there was no freedom in it, but such as He the eternal Son possesses. (36) As their Messiah He was offering to share the dominion with them, Abraham's seed; but on condition that He first made them really free and Sons indeed.

(37) "I know you are Abraham's seed." Without doubt the promises were made to them: but the promises were made to them on the understanding that Abraham's sons would resemble Abraham: and until that came about, the promises were in abeyance. How little they resembled Abraham was seen by their resolve to put Him to death. "Ye seek to kill Me." Why? "Because My word hath not way (οὐ χωρεῖ) among you." That showed how little affinity they had to Him, for His revelation of Himself found no currency among them.

(38) "What things I (ἐγὼ) have seen with The Father (παρὰ τῷ Πατρὶ) these I talk of": *i.e.* His talk with them was always the expression of what He knew to be His Father's will: for The Son has intimate knowledge of The Father's mind: and was He not here Incarnate in order to reveal His Father to them? Similarly their talk and acts toward Him were the expression of their father's mind toward Him. See how far apart His Father was from theirs.

(39) 'Far apart?' say they. 'Why, our father is Abraham himself, the Friend of God.' He replies that though they descended from Abraham they were not as yet sons of Abraham in the sense that they can claim to inherit from him the promises. If they were Abraham's children, let them act as such. (40) But in their present mood (νυνὶ δὲ)—nothing is said of how it may be toward the end of this Age—they were seeking to kill Him, a Man (for by becoming Incarnate He had deliberately put Himself in their power so far) who had spoken to them as God's

Representative. That was not the way Abraham acted, who won for himself the title of the Friend of God (" My friend," Is. xli. 8). (41) Rather were they acting as genuine children of their genuine father, and they know whom He meant. They object, with a *bonâ fide* surprise, " But *we* are not the offspring of fornication," *i.e.* of idolatrous abandonment of God : 'However our fathers may have erred that way, they paid their penalty under Babylon : *we* cannot be accused of that sin of idolatry : we recognize but one God, and His offspring are we.' He answers—

(42) 'If they were indeed the spiritual offspring of God, they would of necessity instinctively love Him The Son : for He proceeded-out from (ἐξῆλθον ἐκ) The Father by eternal generation. Also from The Father He was come Incarnate (ἥκω) into this world, Man among men : nor in stooping so low was He acting alone : that too was The Father's will : He but echoed The Father's thought.'

We must always remember He is talking to trained theologians, used to subtle inquiries into the nature of God, such as the relationship of *the Word* to God, in that phrase so frequently recurring in the O.T., " *the Word* of God came to," etc., or " spoke to," etc., or, again, the " *finger* of God," or again " the *Glory* of the Lord," etc., etc. We must also remember that the Jewish Rabbis have always had a marked preference for the very simplest anthropomorphical terms in their subtlest disquisitions about God and His actions : in this, differing from the thinkers of Greece who in their attempt to express abstractions sought to divest their language of all metaphor—a vain attempt, for language is of its essence metaphorical. The Rabbis are often despised for what seems their gross anthropological language about God : and it is often assumed that their conceptions of Him are equally gross. The fact is rather that they saw the futility of trying to express anything without metaphor, they boldly went counter to the Greek (and our modern) philosophical terminology, and purposely went out of their way to clothe the subtlest abstract propositions in the most sensuous concrete metaphor. There is much to be said for their method, which has been adopted by adepts of every age. Indeed it may be said to be the true philosophical mode of expressing philosophical or theological thought. Our Lord uses ever the same simple anthropological terms, *e.g.* "heard," "saw," "speak," "came out from," etc., to express abstract conceptions of the essential relationship of the First and Second Persons of the Trinity, which are no *more* inadequate than are "Father" and "Son": but, then, what terms are adequate? When we venture to "explain" our Lord's expressions, we do no more than change the metaphor.

(43) Seeing in them signs of impatience, He adds that they did not understand His talk: did they know why? It was because they had no affinity with His word, *i.e.* with Him as He revealed Himself to them.

The *word* of a man—like the *Word* of God—is ideally the self-revelation of that man: just as the *name* of a man—like the *Name* of God—is ideally the connotation of that man.

(44) It was the old saying, "Like begets like." They, though they were physically the sons of Abraham and ought therefore to be like him, had made themselves sons of the devil, and willed to do his promptings: he was the original murderer, for he deliberately compassed the ruin and death of the first Adam; and they, they were compassing the death of Him, the Second Adam. And the devil, before compassing Adam's fall, had had his own fall: he had not had stability in the Truth, for he had lacked affinity to it: and what affinity to it had they? The Lie, the negation of Truth, had become natural to him. When he talks the lie, he talks out of his own nature (ἐκ τῶν ἰδίων), because he is a liar and the father of it (*i.e.* of the Lie)." All who opposed the Truth were, in so far, his offspring, and all who were his offspring opposed the Truth.

(45) And because He who was very Truth told them Truth in seeking to make them know His relationship to The Father, they did not believe Him: "Ye do not believe Me (οὐ πιστεύετέ μοι)."

The clear soul that seeks Truth leaps to the Truth as to

a magnet, the instant it hears it stated. Only the soul that has the Lie in it fails to respond.

It is evident that those " Jews who had believed Him " (see at verse 31) have definitely fallen away during this discourse which so offended their Pharisaical self-complacency at once national and ritual. For our Lord's words to them now are plain, " Ye do not believe Me."

(46) Was there anything in His actions or in His teaching that ran counter to the Law and the spirit of the Law ? Was He not the very embodiment of the Law and the only One who had ever lived up to it. Why did they distrust Him ? He had not come breaking with their past. " If I say Truth (as I do, εἰ . . . λέγω), why is it that ye do not believe Me ? " To *say* the Truth is, ideally, to *live* the Truth : for action, speech, thought are ideally one and the same, and the same as life.

He does not expect an answer to His question : He answers it Himself :—

(47) " He that is of (ἐκ) God hears the things of God (τὰ ῥήματα τοῦ Θεοῦ)." Ῥήματα (like the Hebrew *debârim*) means equally things said and things spoken about. He was telling them things of God : whoso was born of God, and so had affinity to God, would recognize them and leap to them. " Ye are not of God, this is why *ye* hear not," *i.e.* show no response to Truth.

The whole of the discourse from verse 31 to end of the chapter is carried on between our Lord and " those Jews who had believed Him " (τοὺς πεπιστευκότας αὐτῷ Ἰουδαίους of verse 31); and it shows how worthless had been their belief. His disciples hardly came from among the Jews proper (Judah) : they came rather from Benjamin and Levi, and those descendants, few in number, of the Ten Tribes as were to be found in Palestine. These aforesaid " *Jews* who had believed Him " have been gradually becoming more and more hostile (the change can be followed throughout the discourse) so that now (verse 48) they are called simply " the Jews " without qualification.

(48) " The Jews answered and said to Him " : ' Are we not right in saying, we Jews, that you are a Samaritan

and have a demon? We do not deny that strange signs have been done by you: what of that? they are done not by your own power, but by the power of a demon who dwells in you. Look across the border to Samaria.'

They, of course, knew His parentage quite well, in so far as He passed as the Son of Joseph and Mary: they knew He was a Jew by birth and they never pretended He was by birth a Samaritan. In calling Him, then, a *Samaritan working by means of a demon*, what exactly is their meaning?

They are likening Him to the contemporary Simon Magus the Samaritan, that arch-heretic and arch-deceiver who has ever been regarded as the type of Antichrist. This man was at this very time practising what is known as "black magic" in the city of Samaria, amazing the city and country of Samaria by what seemed to be supernatural control over matter and the laws of physics: deception of the senses, worked (as will be the "lying wonders" and "signs" of Antichrist, 2 Thess. ii. 9) by the aid of demons. That Simon was already at this date at work in Samaria appears from Acts viii. 9, 11 (the date of which is only two years later), where it is said that he "had been already beforetime practising magic in that city" (προϋπῆρχεν ἐν τῇ πόλει μαγεύων), and that he had "for a long time (ἱκανῷ χρόνῳ)" amazed the country of Samaria by his sorceries: so that "all gave heed to him from the least to the greatest." This man (as will Antichrist) "gave himself out to be some great One" (Acts viii. 9)—not a prophet, but, as Irenæus (2nd century) has handed down, claimed to be at once Father, Son, and Holy Ghost, in his own person: those who believed him called him "The Power of God," says Origen (*contra Cels. V.*): see Acts viii. 10.

This is the man to whom the Jews are likening Jesus, accusing Him of working by demoniac agency in the same way as they knew the Samaritan Simon Magus was working in Samaria. All traffic with demons or familiar spirits (*e.g.* by means of mediums) was rigorously forbidden by the Mosaic Law (Lev. xix. 31: xx. 6: Deut. xviii. 10).

(49) "*I*" (emphatic ἐγὼ)—as though He had Simon Magus and his antitype in mind—"*I* have not a demon. But I honour My Father" (viz. God), which no demon would do: "and *you*," because you have no affinity with Him or Me, "dishonour Me" and Him.

(50) But their dishonour of Him was, from one point of view, of no importance to Him. "As for Me (the Man before you) *I* seek not the glory due to Me": it made no difference to Him whether men gave it or no: it made a difference to them, and so to Him as loving them. But though *He* sought it not for Himself, there was One that required it of them for Him, One who passed sentence accordingly: viz. The Father, who willed that all men should honour The Son as they do The Father.

(51) Then recurring to the note on which He had begun this discourse (viz. at verse 31, "If ye abide in My word," etc.), He repeats it, but now for general application and no longer addressed specially to them, seeing that they had fallen away from Him. "Verily, verily, I say to you, If a man keep My word," *i.e.* bear in mind His teaching, "he shall never see Death."

His "*word*," or teaching, is not merely a system of ethics, of conduct between man and man, such as His parables in Galilee and Peræa mainly dealt with. His "*word*" also comprises that vast body of theology and of doctrine concerning His own Personality which John has preserved for us as being addressed to the doctors and theologians of the Law, and to His own inner circle of Twelve which was to replace them. There is no obligation on the individual to understand all doctrine: no religious system has been so senseless as to require that: but there is an obligation on him to implicitly accept all doctrine handed down as being genuine by the successors of the Twelve.

(51) "If a man keep My word, he shall never see Death." The word "Death," from its position in the Greek, is emphatic: it means Death in its essence, that Death which is the negation of Life in its essence. As man's essential Life is the union of his soul with God, so man's essential

Death is the isolation of his soul from God. This Death His true disciples should never see: for this Death was not the death they died in leaving this world of sense.

(52) 'What about Abraham and the Prophets?' say they, 'have not they seen death? *now* we know you are an impostor, like him across the border, and owe your extraordinary miracles to demoniac agency.'

They *said* it: they never thought it: but they had long decided to reject Him; and, as is the way of disingenuous opponents, any quibble served their turn. They knew quite well His meaning when He spoke of "never seeing Death": they are not talking *bonâ fide.*

(53) "What, art *thou* greater than our father Abraham? for *he* is dead." They are not arguing that He cannot be genuine because He claims to be greater than Abraham and the prophets: for if He was Messiah, He must *ipso facto* be greater than Abraham: that they knew. And, moreover, if He was Messiah, His claim to be God was inevitable, for it was known that Messiah would somehow be God. Eve knew that much about the promised Seed, as is seen from Gen. iv. 1, "I have gotten a Man even the Lord," as is the natural rendering of the Hebrew, and see the Targum of pseudo Jonathan: she thought at first that her first-born, Cain, was the promised Seed of Gen. iii. 15.

The point of their argument lies in the venom of the emphatic *thou* (σύ) of verse 53: that this man should say he was their Messiah; that this man should be He who would, of course, when He came, be greater than Abraham; this man be that King of glory whom they had so long expected.

The questions of verse 53 are not put to be answered: there was no doubt what His answer would be. His opponents knew long ago that He claimed to be greater than Abraham or the prophets: they knew long ago that He claimed to be God. He had said it, and they had understood it, at the Feast of Pentecost (v. 18), and before that at the Feast of Passover (iii. 16, and throughout that discourse), and again at ii. 16, at the same Festival. He had been saying it ever since they knew Him. It had been said of Him by John Baptist: it had been said of

Him in His infancy by Anna, Simeon, Zacharias, all speaking in the Holy Spirit as tradition had truly handed down, and as many of them could well remember: on the very night of His birth it had been said of Him by angels to the Temple shepherds: and before He was born it was said of Him by Gabriel in the Temple, as they had learnt from Zacharias.

If He were Messiah, He must be God: they knew that followed. Verse 53 is equivalent to saying 'we will not accept such a disappointing Messiah as you, to be the end of all our glorious hopes: the Messiah-God we have in view is not this.'

(54) Let them remember what He had all along asserted: how He had all along claimed to be God Incarnate, "The Son" of "The Father," using a simple anthropological metaphor to express the Godhead as manifested to Itself. He asserted it here again. 'But if I (ἐγὼ) stood alone making My claims they would be worthless.' In that case He would not be "The Son," for The Son cannot stand apart from "The Father." Though they all shouted assent to Him, that would not make His claim any sounder. There was One corroborating Witness whose witness was, in His cause, alone adequate: even He of whom He was the eternal Son, "It is My Father who glorifies Me, He whom you call your God," not knowing the nature of His unity.

The line of thought is much the same as in verses 16–19 of His discourse of this morning. Again He is talking to them of the nature of God, how that He is not *simplex*, but is "Father" and "Son" (to use the simplest metaphors). How near the Jewish doctors had come to grasping the relation of God to the "Word" of God may be seen in Philo's doctrine of the Λόγος, which is his term for the Hebrew *Dabar*, "Word." The time was ripe for a further revelation. It was part of Christ's mission to reveal the whole nature of God, and that the Λόγος or "Word" of God is God—the Godhead under another mode as it were. To this height of vision, not Philo nor any of them had reached before Christ taught it. John in the prologue of his gospel has stated it clearly for those who could understand. So long as the Jews thought there was but One Person in the Godhead, it was impossible for them to believe aright in our Lord : hence His insistence to their theologians that He has a Father ; that He is not The Father, but is The Son ; that The Son, though He is not The Father, is for all that God : that The Father glorifies The Son and wills that all men should honour The Son as they do The Father : that the Two are therefore co-equal : that He The Son was *sent :* that He *hears* from The Father : that He *sees* The Father doing, etc., etc., all simple anthropological metaphors ; that there are Two who bear witness, Himself and Another. Theology pure and simple is at the bottom of all these discourses. That they should believe in His Godhead was essential : implicit belief in It is as far as most of us get : but to the trained intellect (and He was speaking to trained intellects) He wanted to give more explicit knowledge and insight. There were certainly some (be it but one or two) among them, who were ready to absorb His dogmatic teaching.

(55) And as to this God, " ye have not come to know (ἐγνώκατε) Him : but *I* know (οἶδα) Him." It was part of His mission to reveal Him : and if He failed to insist on the relationship between God (as they understand God) and Himself, reluctant to assert Himself out of false modesty or anxiety not to offend them, He would be failing in the Truth : He would be sinking to their level, instead of lifting them to His. " But I know Him, and His word I keep "—teaching His teaching and acting harmoniously with His will.

(56) Unworthy sons were they of their great ancestor : Abraham had exulted at the vision of the Christ his promised Seed : he had seen the vision and rejoiced. *Exulted at seeing :* such is the meaning of the Hellenistic ἠγαλλιάσατο ἵνα ἴδῃ, where the ἵνα ἴδῃ is an Aramaism representing a Hebrew ל with infinitive (lir'ôth) " to see " or " at seeing."

The Jewish tradition is that in the supernatural darkness of Gen. xv. Abraham saw in a trance the whole future of his descendants, and so "rejoiced with the joy of the Law," as they put it:—The day we are at in this chapter (the *eighth* day since the Feast of Tabernacles began) is known in the calendar of the Jews as the "*Simhaĭ-Torah*" = "Rejoicing of the Law," because on it was read the last lesson from the Law, and they would begin it afresh on the next sabbath. Our Lord seems to accept this tradition as true and to imply that Abraham, as he watched the vision of the Christ, delighted in Him; although he saw his descendants rejecting and crucifying Him.

(57) The Jews must have known that our Lord was referring to this tradition of Abraham's vision: but they have lost patience with Him, and do not want to understand Him. Again, as in verse 52, they seize on a quibble. Dissimulating, they simulate an equivocation that if Abraham had seen Him, He no doubt had seen Abraham, which was obviously impossible, as He was "not fifty years old"—a common way of saying that He was still in the vigour of life: from 30–50 was the only age during which Levites were originally allowed to serve in the Tabernacle (Num. iv. 3, 23, 30, 35, 39, 43, 47).

(58) He accepts the equivocation: in order to insist on His eternal self-existence. "Verily, verily, I say to you, Before Abraham was born, *I* am":—without beginning, without end, God self-existent.

(59) Nor did they misunderstand Him and His claim to the Godhead of Jehovah. It was nothing new, they had often heard it before from Him: but no more to-day than before would they listen. To-day, as four months ago (John v. 18), they took up stones to cast at Him. But Jesus "was hidden" (ἐκρύβη), perhaps by His friends crowding round Him in order to conceal Him, or, as some think, was made invisible by His divine power. For the matter of that, He was perpetually hiding Himself: for His body was essentially dazzling in brilliancy owing to its union with His Divinity in His Personality: the one occasion that He let His body be seen as it really always was, was in the Transfiguration.

The stones they picked up they would have found in

the Court of the Gentiles: for the Temple (viz. its courts) was still building: it was now (Oct. A.D. 28) forty-seven years since Herod had begun it in Oct. of 20 B.C., but Josephus tells us it was not finished till A.D. 64.

"And He went out of the Temple" (ἱεροῦ), *i.e.* out of the Temple courts.

§ XIV

JOHN IX. 1–41

The healing of the man born blind

THE day is still Wednesday, Oct. 6, Tisri 22, the same as that of chapter viii.: the "eighth day" of Lev. xxiii. 36, 39 (p. 198): the day after "the great day of the Feast," vii. 37.

A.D. 28.
Oct. 6 / Tisri 22 } Wed.

The time is afternoon, after the evening sacrifice of 3 p.m. He has recently left the Temple courts by the north gate in the west wall—the regular gate of exit: nor will He again enter the Temple till two months later at x. 22.

(1) "And as He passed along on His way He saw," etc. It is hardly likely that the following incident occurred at the exit gate of the Temple: the excitement that would be caused in the Temple exit by the attempt to stone Him is against our supposing that the scene which follows was anywhere near the Temple, for it is evidently remote from any crowd: so the probability is that the blind man was sitting outside one of the city gates—always the favourite place for beggars in the East—perhaps at the north-east gate of the city known as the Sheepgate.

As the day was a Sabbath (verse 14), the man could not be asking for alms, but he would be able to receive them. Again, here in Jerusalem, he would probably not have made any request to be healed, for that was forbidden by Rabbinical rule on Sabbaths, nor is there any reason to suppose he did so. In Galilee the people were not so amenable to the minute rulings of the scribes as in the city.

(2) "Master (Ῥαββεί), who sinned, this man or his parents, that he was born blind?"

(3) The blindness was not the consequence of any sin

on the part of the parents, nor yet the consequence of any sins of his own foreseen and foreknown by God before his birth. Beyond the answer to their precise question our Lord does not go: He does not give an answer as to the origin of suffering: but He does as to the ultimate issue * of it, viz. the manifestation of the works of God, *i.e.* His glory. In this case the blindness and the cure were to be means by which spiritual light was to come to this man, and no doubt in a measure to others who beheld the cure. An inference may be drawn touching the mystery of suffering, that all suffering will in the long run be found to have helped the human race (and, may be, the rebel host of spirit-intelligences, malignant agents) toward the knowledge of God. And we must suppose that every sufferer will in the long run be made aware of his share in promoting that advance; though to-day he suffer blindly, little conscious of his privilege.

(4) "We must work," etc. The emphatic *We* (Ἡμᾶς) with which this sentence begins in the correct reading is exactly the *We* of iii. 11: it is not our Lord in union with the disciples, but our Lord in union with The Father—He who sent working through Him whom He sent: cf. viii. 16–18, spoken on this same day, where He had insisted on the plurality of Persons in the Godhead, of whom He Himself was One. Had the word "we" been here less emphatic, the statement might have been understood proverbially.

(4) "We must work the works of Him who sent Me, whilst it is day: night cometh when no one can work." Whilst He was on earth, the Godhead worked through His human body as It will never work through any other after He had left. As was evident from the attempt, not an hour ago, to stone Him, He would soon withdraw from this world of men: and when He withdrew, the Light of the World would withdraw. (5) When He manifests His presence in the world, whether at His first Coming—that

* ἵνα φανερωθῇ τὰ ἔργα τοῦ Θεοῦ ἐν αὐτῷ. Here, as is common in Hellenistic Greek, the ἵνα and subjunctive does not signify subjective intention so much as objective result (p. 137). The construction is an Aramaism.

transient appearance—or pre-eminently at His second Coming when He will set up the visible Kingdom, it is as Light that He comes, enlightening darkness, quickening growth. Already this morning (viii. 12) He had called Himself the Light of the World : and in the miracle He is about to do, He will give His disciples an illustration.

(6) The blind man has made no explicit request to be healed : indeed the Rabbinical rules forbade a doctor to practise his healing art on a Sabbath, except in a matter of life and death, where immediate action was imperative : but our Lord, reading all hearts, knew this ground was kindly to His sowing.

" He spat on the ground and made clay," etc. In the mode by which He chose to work this miracle, the making of " clay " and kneading it and applying it, He seems to be pointing to the creative work on Adam ; and to be again asserting as at the Feast of Pentecost (v. 17) that He claims that same right to work on a Sabbath that The Father exercises—the work of maintaining, restoring, readjusting the creation : for The Father and He can neither of Them work independently Each of Other.

(7) " Go, wash in the pool of the Siloam " : *i.e.* the pool formed by the Siloam. " The Siloam " (it always has the article both in Hebrew and Greek) is the *stream* that flows in a rock-cut subterranean channel, 1706 feet long, from the Virgin's Fountain (‘ên Rogel) to issue in this pool. Traces of a covered arcade, thought to be of Herod's time, have been found all round the pool ; and in the 5th century there was a church built, to commemorate this miracle, over the spot where the Siloam issued from the rock-tunnel into the pool. The verb rendered in this verse " wash " (*νίψαι*) and " washed " (*ἐνίψατο*) confines the washing to the eyes.

This silent subterranean stream known as the Siloam is mentioned but once in the O.T. (Is. viii. 6, " the waters of the Siloah which go softly "), where it is used as a type of David's line, from which was to come the Messiah who " shall not strive nor cry " : in opposition to the roaring river Euphrates used as a type of the Assyrian monarchy.

In the very name Siloam (meaning, as John is careful to point out, ἀπεσταλμένος = "sent forth") there must be to John's mind an allusion to Him that was "sent forth" (the same word) by The Father. In John's gospel this verb is used fifteen times by our Lord of Himself as having been "sent forth" by The Father into the world. It was from the Siloam stream that was drawn the water which was poured over the great altar at the Feast of Tabernacles just past, which pouring out was regarded by the Rabbis (and is still) as typical of the pouring out of The Spirit in the "latter days," which are yet to come: thus the ceremony seems to connect the Siloam stream with the Messiah of David's line who pours forth His Spirit. Is. viii. 6 connects the Siloam with the Messiah. And John, by translating the word "Siloam," does the same.

(8–12) Time, the same day. Scene, between the healed man and his neighbours when they see he is no longer blind. His neighbours, and they who used to notice him formerly as being one who begged alms, ask him, "How were thine eyes opened?" He tells them exactly what passed between himself and his healer.

Oct. 6, Wed.

(11) "The man that is called Jesus": the healed man knows Him by report, but has never yet seen Him: it is but an hour or so since his cure; nor does he know where to find Him. It rather looks as though our Lord had left the city after sending him to the pool.

(13–34) Time, the next day. Scene, between the healed man and the Pharisees in their Court of Justice. The Court could not have sat yesterday—the day of the cure—for yesterday was a Feast day.

Oct. 7 / Tisri 23 } Thurs.

(14) The peculiar form of the original, "It was," or "There was, a Sabbath on the day that Jesus," etc. (ἦν δὲ σάββατον ἐν ᾗ ἡμέρᾳ τὸν πηλὸν ἐποίησεν ὁ Ἰησοῦς) strongly makes for the view that the day of the cure had not been a weekly Sabbath (Saturday), but a day of obligatory rest (Sabbath), as being a great festival or day of obligation. The day in question was the eighth day

from the beginning of the Feast of Tabernacles: it is the "Sabbath" (Hebrew *šabbātôn*) of Lev. xxiii. 39–end: this year a Wednesday. A similar remark applies to v. 9, where the same peculiarity is seen in the Greek original: there, as has been seen, the "Sabbath" was the day of the Feast of Pentecost (this year a Tuesday), a day of obligation, just as the word "Sabbath" (Hebrew *šabbāt*) is used in Lev. xxiii. 32*b* for the Day of Atonement, which might fall on any day of the week.

(15) We are not to suppose that the man in his short reply is attempting to shield our Lord from a charge of Sabbath-breaking. For the making of clay and the application of clay or spittle on the eyes, which he admits, as part of a curative process distinctly fell under the Rabbinical definition of Sabbath-breaking. The man speaks simply and straightforwardly, just as did he of v. 11, tersely stating the facts.

(16) "Of the Pharisees," sitting in court as we suppose, "some" argued of Jesus, "This man is not from God (οὐκ ἔστιν . . . παρὰ Θεοῦ)," *i.e.* has not God's sanction or commission, "because he does not observe the Sabbath." Their objection is not to His healing on the Sabbath as it might be by a word, but to His making clay with spittle on a Sabbath and applying it to the eyes—an obviously unnecessary bit of work, a deliberate breach of the Sabbath: cf. v. 16, 17. "Others of them" argued He must be from God, for "'how can a man be a sinner and yet do so great signs?' And there was a cleavage among them." So turning again to the blind man—

(17) They say, "What dost *thou* say of him, as to (ὅτι) his having opened thine eyes?" Could he give any explanation that might make it not so miraculous as it seemed? He has little interest in their discussion: he remembers the voice, the touch, the magnetic power of that sanctity, and replies without hesitation, "He is a prophet."

The man does not say He is the Christ: he may not have been as yet convinced of that: or again, although convinced, he may not have felt any obligation to say all he believed unless they put the question to him point blank, 'did he believe him to be the Christ?' The Pharisees probably purposely did not put the question point blank: the man was not of sufficient importance, nor was the moment sufficiently critical.

(18) It occurs to "the Jews," the extreme party, to say, 'What if the man had never been really blind, but a lifelong impostor living on alms? or perhaps only partially blind? or at least not born blind?' They would summon the parents, perhaps overawe them into some admission.

(19) 'Is this your son? and do you his parents assert he was *born* blind? Did you never see any smallest sign of sight in him that might one day develop into fuller sight?'

(20, 21) 'We know he is our son, and we know he was born blind. How it is he now sees, or who it was opened his eyes, we do not know. Why not ask him?' They are favourably disposed to Jesus, but either timid or cautious (ἐφοβοῦντο).

(22) "*The Jews* had already agreed together with a view to (ἵνα) the excommunication of any one who should confess Jesus to be the Messiah": *i.e.* the extreme party had agreed to secure the excommunication of such a one. Excommunication was doubtless a lengthy process: and was far too serious a sentence to be lightly passed: in any case it would only be pronounced against prominent personages. As a matter of fact it does not appear that excommunication was ever pronounced upon Christian Hebrews in Jerusalem: it is certain that down to the close of the history contained in the Acts, the Christian Hebrews attended all the services of the Temple, and were not considered by the Sanhedrin or any other religious authority to have split off from the mother Church of Judaism: nor did that Christian party imagine themselves to be severed from the community of Jews in Jerusalem so long as the Temple was standing. Only during Saul's persecution, lasting a year, was there a persecution of Christian Hebrews inside and outside Jerusalem; but they were not excommunicated either individually or in block.

(24) As nothing could be got out of the parents, they would have another try with the man.

"Give glory to God" is the formula of solemn adjuration to declare the whole truth (Joshua vii. 19). 'It cannot have been exactly as you say: be careful: you are bringing into contempt the established conception of religion and of God's dealings with men: He does not make use of sinners to be His intermediary with men: this Jesus is a sinner: he breaks the Sabbath by unnecessary work and bidding men carry unnecessary burdens on it. We (ἡμεῖς) the religious authorities and guides of the nation know him to be such: you may therefore be sure of that point. Look about then, and see is there no loophole of escape? Perhaps you were not so totally blind always as you professed to be? we all know there is a good deal of make-believe among those who live on alms. Perhaps even now your sight is not very perfect?'

(25) He replies, 'You are sure he is a sinner?—of that I know nothing, I am no doctor of Law: but what I do know is that I was genuinely blind and that I now genuinely see. There is no escape possible for you there.'

(26) They: 'Well, but what exactly did he to thine eyes? Possibly we have here but a dexterous bit of surgery, which may not require our belief in a super normal interference of God through this man Jesus.'

(27) He: 'Why waste time? You have heard what he did. I have told you already. But—perhaps you are willing, you too, to be his disciples?' Is it sarcasm? efficient weapon to offend, futile instrument to win.

It seems that he has a momentary hope of them. It does not seem to be a fit moment for sarcasm: sarcasm never helped any one yet. Also their answer (28) where "they reviled him and said, '*Thou* art his disciple: *we* are Moses' disciples,'" is perhaps more suitable on the supposition that the man had for an instant thought they might be catching the light that was flooding him.

(29) "*We* (ἡμεῖς) know that to Moses God has spoken: but as for this man, we know not whence he is": 'we do not recognize any divine mission as being his. It is true

there were strange tales current about him at his birth and since : but we have disposed of all that.'

(30-33) He : 'What is that ? . . . you "know not whence he is." And have we not all heard that that is a mark of the Messiah ? ("When the Messiah comes, no one discerns whence He is" : vii. 27) : is it not a maxim of the Schools ? And here are you making that very admission about this man : and look you, he has done such a work on me as never in the history of the world was heard—sight to a man that was *born* blind. Look to yourselves : is He a sinner at all ? we know that God does not hear sinners. Is it not then, the rather, certain that this Man "whom ye know not whence He is" must have a commission from God ?'

It is at this point, perhaps, that conviction came to the man that Jesus was the Messiah and not merely "a Prophet" (17).

(34) They : 'And are we doctors to be taught by such as you ? you who for your parents' sins, if not for your own, were born with the curse of blindness.' He must have been talking with a hope of persuasion, and with no tinge of bitterness.

"And they cast him out (ἐξέβαλον αὐτὸν ἔξω)." The phrase does not mean that they excommunicated him in any way : but rather that they cast him out of their Court-house, and out of their presence, with anger and contempt. It is not the same as the "be made unsynagogued" of verse 22, where indeed we are only told that "the Jews" had agreed to work towards a certain end ; which they never actually compassed in Jerusalem. There is nothing to show that any Christian Hebrew was ever excommunicated in Jerusalem for being a Christian. Rather it seems that there was all along some powerful influence at work in the Sanhedrin that prevented the violent party from having their way. This, it has been supposed, was Gamaliel himself, the President. The story is that he was a Christian (see Baronius, *Annals*, 34, 275, 298), but never let it be known to the Jews nor yet to the Christians except to the heads of Christendom : being convinced he could best serve the cause by remaining unavowed (see Sozomen, *Hist. Eccl.*, ix. 17, a remarkable account).

(35) "Jesus heard they had cast him out" with contempt from their presence for having spoken in His favour: and at once went to find him: for He knew the man's heart, and that he was already convinced of the claims of Jesus who had healed him, but whom he had never seen.

There is little clue to fix the scene that follows. But after his interview with the Jews, the man's chief aim would be to see Jesus, who, we have supposed (verse 11), had withdrawn from the city: perhaps he stationed himself at his old post, say by the Sheep-gate, knowing that this was the gate habitually used by Jesus as He came to and from Bethany or Mount of Olives or Gethsemane. Perhaps it was there our Lord "found" him.

At any rate, having found him, He asks what He already knew. Our Lord never asked for information as one not knowing: He constantly asks, but it is always to bring His listener to a certain mental position. We constantly do the same with children and others.

(35) "Thou, thou believest into (Σὺ πιστεύεις εἰς: see at viii. 30) The Son of Man?" *i.e.* thou believest into the man Jesus, as being the Messiah; the Jesus who calls Himself The Son of Man? (or The Son of God). The MSS. are in favour here of "The Son of Man": it is immaterial which they read: the two terms always mean the same Person, and were interchangeable as being titles of the Messiah and of Him alone. The title "The Son of God" was the declaration formally made by the Baptist as he tells us (John i. 34) after he had seen the official sign of the dove at the Baptism: it had certainly been reported to the Sanhedrin and had become widespread in connection with Him: Nathanael adopts it (i. 49), quoting, of course, from the Baptist's official pro nouncement: and it became an acknowledged title of His for those who recognized Him as the Messiah (see Matt. xiv. 33 (God's Son): John xi. 27: Mark xv. 39 (God's Son): Acts viii. 37: cf. Mark iii. 11: v. 7), though

they who used it had no clear conception of its full meaning. Peter was the first of the Apostles to catch a fleeting vision of the Truth (Matt. xvi. 16), a vision which became permanent with him after Pentecost. As for the title "The Son of Man," it was the title coined by Jesus for Himself, the strange title by which every one knew He called Himself, the strange title which every one associated only with Him (see at i. 51).

(35) "Thou, thou believest into The Son of Man?" Of course He knew that the man did: he had already borne witness to Him before the Jews, and had been in consequence cast out with contempt: but he had never yet set eyes on Jesus, to know Him.

The question is hardly a question. Our Lord has put it rather by way of introducing the subject of Himself, for He is about to make Himself ("The Son of Man") known by sight to this man. The man's position was this:—he knew he had been healed by One who was called Jesus (verse 11), One whom he had since come to believe to be the Messiah and to be "The Son of God" (whatever that might mean) as He had been officially declared to the nation to be by the greatest of the Prophets, John the Baptist: One who habitually called Himself by the title "The Son of Man." But he had never seen Him, did not know by sight who He was: and that is what he is wanting now.

"Thou believest into The Son of Man?" The man answered—

(36) "And who is He, Sir? So that I may believe into Him (*καὶ τίς ἐστιν, κύριε; ἵνα πιστεύσω εἰς αὐτόν*)." The *And* is remarkable: it is as if he had made a sign of assent. 'Yes, I do: and ever since, I want to know who and where that Jesus is whom I believe to be "The Son of Man," "The Son of God," "The Messiah," in order that I may know by sight the Man whom I believe into, and may worship Him: that I may have the concrete individual to believe into. I want to see Him with my eyes.'

(37) "Thou hast seen Him": and then, to be more definite, "and He that is talking with thee is He."

(38) 'And art Thou He!' "I believe, Lord," in Thee: "And he worshipped Him." The rest is veiled. But our Lord has to comment:—

(39) "For judgment I came into this world, in order that (ἵνα) they who see not may see, and they who see may become blind." The necessary outcome of His Coming into this world at this His first Coming in obscurity was a discerning between man and man: it was the touchstone by which "the thoughts of many hearts were brought to light" (Luke ii. 35): it was the test of the bedrock of men's natures. Some would see Him as He was and would leap to Him: others would see nothing in Him to suit their needs and would ignore or scorn Him. Those who, acknowledging no spiritual need, thought they saw, would be hardened in their blindness: those who knew their needs and their own blindness would, like this man here, receive sight. Here again the Hellenistic ἵνα represents not so much the subjective aim as the objective consequence.

(40) Some difference in the look, or in the tone of voice, or in the bearing, as He turned from the worship given Him by the healed man to the Pharisees who were with Him, made them aware that He was talking at them. These Pharisees were some who were favourably disposed to our Lord, perhaps those mentioned in the second half of verse 16, who during that inquiry had demurred on His behalf. On the strength of that they seem to be inclined to patronize Him. The type in all ages is common. Pharisees at heart, with no idea of adjusting their estimate to His.

(40) 'But,' say they, 'you would not say that *we*, who have shown ourselves favourable to you, are blind, whatever you may say of the rest of our party?'

(41) Yes, they too were blind: blind in their patronizing self-esteem: but if they would admit they were blind, they would not have sin: for in Him they would then seek and find a remedy: but, as it was, they were not aware of any need of spiritual light, blind to the Holiest. So long as it was so, there was no remedy: "your sin

remains": *i.e.* they remain in their state or habit of aversion from God.

As the impotent man of chapter v., cured after his thirty-eight years of sickness, may be viewed as a type of the Jews who are yet to be healed: so may this man of chapter ix., blind from his birth, be viewed as a type of the Gentiles whose healing was about to begin and who were about to believe into Jesus as Him who was "the Sent" from God.

§ XV

JOHN X. 1–21

The Sheepfold: the Shepherd. He withdraws to Peræa

(1) THE discourse is continued, with a parable of a sheepfold.

This parable appears to belong to the Christian Hebrew alone: only by analogical application does it belong to the Gentile Christian. The Gentile Christian does not enter into it till verse 16. It is spoken to those "Pharisees who were with Him" (ix. 40), who were half-friendly to Him: but had no doubt that He would have to come to their view.

A.D. 28. Oct. 7 / Tisri 23 Thurs.

(1) "He that enters not by the door into the sheepfold, but climbs up from some other point, he is thief and robber." The "sheepfold" is the Mosaic polity, the Mosaic fold walled round by the precepts and ceremonials of the Mosaic Law.

The door had never been opened till Christ came: and the sheep had remained shut up under the Law, in their fold, expectant.

Many had tried to steal the sheep away (by deceit or by violence) and so make them abandon "Judaism": again and again these deceivers or persecutors had raided the fold:—*deceivers*, mostly from among their own kings and priests inducing the nation to become idolators in pre-Captivity days: and *robbers* mostly from outside, compelling by violence the nation to abandon "Judaism" as did the Macedonians in the days of the Maccabees.

(2) "But He who enters by the door is Shepherd of the sheep. To Him the Porter opens": the Porter being the Guardian of the fold (God The Father) who kept the

door so that until the Shepherd of the sheep came none might enter or lead the sheep out and in.

(3) All the sheep hear His voice when He comes, and ought to recognize Him when they hear His voice, for the sheep are His people of the Old Covenant: but when He comes, the mass of them do not recognize Him. He, however, knowing which of them are willing to listen to Him, calls those particular ones (*e.g.* the healed man of last chapter) individually, and leads them out to pastures, out from the confinement of the typical into the free and open country of the real.

(4) "And when He has put forth all His own," *i.e.* all who recognize Him, "He goes in front of them," lest they should stray in their new-found liberty, and they follow at His call.

(5) And if, out in the open, where they are now Christian Hebrews, false shepherds come to call them and lead them away, they, knowing the One Shepherd's voice, are not seduced, but run from them.

(6) "This parable spake Jesus to them: but they understood not what it was He was talking to them." The *them* to whom He spoke the parable are, as has been said, the half-friendly "Pharisees who were with Him" (ix. 40).

(7) "Again, therefore, spake Jesus"—not merely explaining but re-modelling the parable. Not only is He Shepherd (verse 2), but "I am the Door of the sheep," *i.e.* the Door for the sheep to go out and in by. He the God-Man, the true Janus of two faces or natures is the Door. Directly the Door was opened (*i.e.* when He came into the world) emergence from the fold of the Mosaic Law became for the first time possible. Also through Him alone has any shepherd access to the sheep.

(8) "All [so-called shepherds] that came before Me," *i.e.* before He the Door was opened, before He came into the world, "are thieves and robbers." For till the Door of the fold was opened, the sheep were shut up in the fold, expectant: no shepherd passed in and out with the flock: many self-styled shepherds had indeed entered the fold,

but to do so had had to climb over the fold as robbers, and had come only to steal sheep away. All the Prophets had been born in the Mosaic fold: none of them had sought to burst a way out for the sheep, *i.e.* sought to make the nation abandon the Mosaic Law, but they had all pointed to a future coming of the Shepherd-King, who should be the living Spirit of the Law, without whom the Law and its ceremonial was but a dead form. There had been many thieves and robbers in their history who with much success had sought by deceit or violence to make the chosen People abandon their religion (the Mosaic fold), on the plea that it was played out, antiquated, narrow. Thus their own apostate kings and priests had often done, and also their conquerors—notably Antiochus Epiphanes (see 1 and 2 Maccabees).

(9) If a shepherd enters through Him the Door, he is a genuine shepherd, for entering through Him he has authority to act as His under-shepherd, and with him the sheep shall be secure, and shall pass in at evenings, and shall pass out at mornings and find pasture where that shepherd leads. The subject of σωθήσεται, εἰσελεύσεται, ἐξελεύσεται, νομ. εὑρήσει seems to be τὰ πρόβατα of the preceding verse: just as in vv. 3, 4, τὰ πρόβατα, taken collectively, are the subject of the singular ἀκούει, and ἀκολουθεῖ.

(10) The thief (the self-styled shepherd), not entering through Him the Door, breaks in only to steal sheep by deceiving them, or to sacrifice them (by martyrdom), or to make havoc among them: but "*I* am come that they (the sheep) may have Life (ζωήν) and in abundance," both in the fold, and by being led out of the fold into fresh pasturage. He had no intention of destroying the fold, or of inducing the sheep to abandon the fold, of the Law: these sheep of His are under the Mosaic Law, and are meant to remain so: He was not come to destroy that Law but to quicken it by showing the Living Antitype of all its types: this is "the coming out and finding pasturage" of verse 9, as against the former state of being shut up in the fold expectant until the Door was opened.

There is no abandoning of the fold, for the sheep pass not only out, but " in " and " out."

(11) " I am the Good Shepherd." Not only is He the Door of the fold of verse 1, but He is also the Shepherd of verse 2. And this Shepherd is the Good Shepherd who so loves the sheep (the sheep of the Mosaic Covenant) that He will gladly die on their behalf. (12) It is only a hireling that values his own interests above those of the sheep : as had been so often the case with the shepherds or kings whom He had set over the Nation, who had proved to be the ruin of His people, by their political alliances, and by those religious rites they kept borrowing from the Gentile nations : careless for the people entrusted to them, because at heart apostate from the hope of Israel.

(14, 15) " *I* am the Good Shepherd, and I know My sheep, and Mine know Me, even as The Father knows Me and I know The Father. And I lay down My life (ψυχὴν) for the sheep." The intimacy between The Father and the God-Man is no closer than that between the God-Man and those of the human race who from Age to Age become His : they are generated by Him sacramentally, and in their ultimate perfection and collectivity will reflect Him. They are His not merely as a possession, but as being one with Him living with His Life. The sheep do not choose Him : He chooses them. The life (ψυχὴ) that He lays down on their behalf does not remain a sacrifice external to them, but becomes Life (ζωὴ) moving within them and quickening them by reason of their sacramental union with Him by faith and baptism.

(16) " And other sheep I have which are not of this fold (ἅ οὐκ ἔστιν ἐκ τῆς αὐλῆς ταύτης)." These " other sheep " are the Gentile Christians, " who do not belong to this fold," viz. to the Mosaic fold : they never did belong, and were never meant to belong, to it. " Them also I must *lead* " as their Shepherd,—not " *bring* " *to the fold* of the Mosaic Law : " and they shall hear My voice," and follow where He leads. " And they shall become one *flock* (ποίμνη), *i.e.* along with the Christian Hebrews, under " One Shepherd " : but they (the Gentile-

Christians) shall not belong to the *fold* (αὐλή) of the parable, which is the Mosaic Law, and which is reserved for the Christians of Israelite descent (Jews and Ten Tribes).

It would seem that together with the rebuilt Temple (Ezek. xl.–xlvi.) and the reoccupation of Holy Land by Israel-Judah (Ezek. xlvii. 13–xlviii.), *i.e.* by Representatives of each of the tribes,* the Mosaic Law and ritual will on the conversion of the Jews be re-established in Holy Land for the Jews and Ten Tribes, or rather for their Representatives, and only in Holy Land. The Mosaic Law, as interpreted in Matt. v., is the Nation's charter. But along with the Mosaic ritual and the Temple, Ark, Tabernacle, altar of incense, the Glory of the Lord, and the Cloud (2 Mac. ii. 1–8) there will also be the ritual of the Mass interpreting Melchisedek's sacrifice of bread and wine: Christ Himself being from time to time visibly present there and in the City of Ezek. xlviii. 15–19, 30–35, the world's capital, in the millennial Age. There His deputy, the nation's king (the "prince," *nasi'*, of Ezek. xliv. 3: xlv. 7–xlvi. 18: xlviii. 21), will reside permanently. Outside of Holy Land the Mosaic Law and ritual will not be in force not even for Israelites or Jews, for it was never meant for Gentiles or foreign countries. It is all important to remember that so long as the Temple was standing the Christian Hebrew of Holy Land was in every whit bound by the Mosaic Law and ritual just as much as was the non-Christian Jew. Also, before the rejection of the Jews and the consequent destruction of nation and Temple in A.D. 70, there is not the slightest sign that the

* The English versions (A.V. and R.V.) have made nonsense of Ezekiel's allotment of the Land, by inserting the word *reeds* in xlviii. 8, instead of the word *cubits*, which should be supplied to all the measurements of this chapter. The distance from the altar of Ezekiel's Temple to the centre of Ezekiel's "City" (xlv., xlviii.) is 17,500 cubits=5 English miles (less 50 yards): therefore whilst his Temple is at Jerusalem his "City" is at Bethlehem (accurately, at Migdal 'eder, Tower of the Flock). Had Micah too (iv. 8) a vision of this national capital seated here when he cried, "And thou, *Migdal 'eder*, stronghold of the Daughter of Sion, unto thee shall it come: yea, shall come the chief dominion, the kingdom of the Daughter of Jerusalem"? The "chief" or "first" (in dignity) dominion = the suzerainty of the world. Micah might still be using *Migdal 'eder* as a name for the Messiah, as a rabbinical tradition says.

Temple and its ritual was meant to be superseded at once. That Law and ritual belongs to the Land and to the Race whenever as a Nation they are settled in that their own land as owners and occupiers. The above may be a strange idea to modern ears dulled with the "spiritual" exegesis of the Prophets, but it seems to be plainly stated by the Prophets for those to whom language has any meaning. The present Church is purely Gentile, and its visible head, Christ's Vicar, is Gentile: and his seat is appropriately in Rome the capital of Daniel's fourth kingdom. But the Church of the millennial Age, when the Twelve Tribes are again in possession of Holy Land as the re-united Covenant People converted to Christ, will have its centre at Jerusalem, and its visible head no longer a Gentile vicar. The Temple and Temple precincts of Ezekiel's vision (xl.–xlviii.) is the Jerusalem and Sion and Holy Mountain of the millennial Age.

During this present Age, "the times of the Gentiles" (Luke xxi. 24), there is the Gentile Church, formed by the election of individuals out of the Gentiles, with a Gentile Vicar.

Next, in the millennial Age it seems that there will be a Church embracing, at least nominally, all individuals of all nations, under the protection of Israel's empire and Israel's king acting as viceroy for Christ: its focus in Holy Land, its centre in a rebuilt Temple and City. By that kingdom we may suppose the world's peace will be kept, and security given to every nation to develop unhindered by its neighbours, each nation benefiting from the aid of its own saints who will have risen at the "First resurrection" of Rev. xx. 5. Is not here the meaning of the parable of the Pounds and Cities (Luke xix. 12–27) and of that of the Talents (Matt. xxv. 14–30)? and of the promise to the Apostles in Luke xxii. 29, 30, and Matt. xix. 28, by which they are to sit as Israel's Court of Appeal? Is it asked where are the Ten Tribes of Israel? Look around.

Next, in the post-millennial Age, will be the universal Church in a much purer state, under our Lord's personal visible Monarchy, when not even in any individual is there any opposition to His will: its focus is the New Jerusalem, the Holy City of Rev. xxi.—the outer "nations" being still in process of "healing" (Rev. xxii. 2). This New Jerusalem has a superficies of 12,000 stades (Rev. xxi. 16) and is foursquare: so each side is 109·5 stades in length =12 or 13 English miles, according as the stade is the Attic or the Olympic. "Its length and breadth and height are *even* (ἴσα)," *i.e.* the four sides run straight without sinuosities, and the skyline is level owing to absence of hills or valleys such as exist in Jerusalem to-day. The height is then given, naturally in terms of the city's wall, as 144 cubits = 216 feet. There is nothing in John's account of it that needs "spiritualising" away.

Even that post-millennial Age is but a stage in the history of the race, for it seems to be followed by the yet more perfect state when our Lord "shall transfer the kingdom to God even the Father" (1 Cor. xv. 24–28), and the desire "Thy Kingdom come" shall at last be realized. But be these things as they may.

(17) It is for the whole *flock* (ποίμνη), and not only for those of the Mosaic *fold* (αὐλή), that the Shepherd lays down His life.

"This is the proof that (διὰ τοῦτο) The Father loves Me, viz. that I (ἐγὼ, of My freewill) am laying down My *life*" (ψυχὴν, not ζωήν), "to receive it again (ἵνα πάλιν λάβω αὐτήν)." The ἵνα ("to") in this last clause represents, as frequently in Hellenistic Greek, not so much purpose as consequence, it is the Hebrew ל with infinitive, or *lma'an* with infin. or fut.

If I were not acting in harmony with The Father's will in surrendering My life, I should not receive My life again: but I shall receive it. The crowning proof of My union with The Father will be My resurrection.

(18) "No one takes it from Me, but I lay it down of Myself." Let none think when men shall have slain Him that they prevailed against Him: it is that He has assented to their power, for He became Incarnate in order to be the willing Sacrifice for the whole world, Himself

being High-Priest and Victim. Did any call this suicide? It was not: for "I have authority to lay it down and I have authority to take it again." He is not recklessly throwing life away. He is laying it down with the result that He will receive it again: and in so doing, He is acting in agreement with The Father's command: "This is the commandment that I received from My Father." What The Father orders, The Son also orders: what one Person of the Godhead does *ad extra*, the whole Godhead does.

(19) "A cleavage again was made among the Jews because of these *words* (λόγους)," viz. the whole discourse of verses 1–18. The "again" refers to the previous "cleavage" named in verse 16 of last chapter. This second division arose among "the Jews"—the hitherto violent and extreme party—when the discourse was reported to them by those half-friendly Pharisees to whom it had been spoken. (20) The majority of them, on hearing, summed up, 'he has a demon and is not in his right mind': meaning that yesterday's cure of the blind man was done by Jesus acting as a medium for demonic agency. (21) A minority among them argued, "these *things* (ῥήματα = sayings, and events described) do not belong to one under the influence of a demon (δαιμονιζομένου): a demon cannot open blind men's eyes, can it?"

As suggested at p. 231, the scene of the parable might be at the north-east gate of the city, the Sheep-gate: where could be seen (either just outside the gate, or else on the west slope of the Mount of Olives opposite) the sheepfold for those sheep which were driven up from time to time to Jerusalem for the sacrifices, from the pasture grounds near Bethlehem.

It was during this stay at Jerusalem (Oct. 2–7) that our Lord appointed the "seventy others" (Luke x. 1–16), corresponding to the seventy elders appointed by Moses (Num. xi. 16): just as the Twelve Apostles corresponded to the twelve princes or sheikhs of the Twelve Tribes of Israel. These seventy were not for work in Galilee, which He has abandoned, nor yet for work in Tyre and Sidon or the Decapolis where He has recently been (Matt. xv. 21: Mark

vii. 24, 31), but to precede Him into a new mission field, viz. Peræa, whither He will follow them (Luke x. 1), and where they subsequently rejoined Him (Luke x. 17–24). His charge to them is very similar to His previous charge to the Twelve (Matt. x. : Mark vi.) in May last, which was not given by Luke, just as this charge to the seventy is not given by Matthew or Mark. The "harvest" of Luke x. is the harvest of autumn fruits and the vintage and the beginning of olive gathering.

Here, between verses 21 and 22 of John x., comes an interval of two months (Oct. 8 to Dec. 6). John will resume the story on the occasion of the next visit to Jerusalem, viz. at the Feast of Dedication (verse 22) in December.

These two months seem to have been spent in Peræa (east of Jordan), for after the Feast of Dedication John tells us (x. 40) that He went away *again* to beyond Jordan, *i.e.* to Peræa. The province of Peræa, together with that of Galilee, formed the tetrarchy of Herod Antipas.

Of this two months' interval (Oct. 8 to Dec. 6) no details are given by Matthew or Mark or John : but to it belongs Luke x. 17–24. Then follows chronologically Luke x. 25–37, which seems to have been spoken on the way from Jericho to Jerusalem, as He went up to the Feast of Dedication, say on Monday, Dec. 6 (Kislew 24) : and Luke x. 38–end describes His visit to Martha and Mary at Bethany on the same occasion, say on Monday, Dec. 6, the eve of the Feast. Bethany was on the high-road from Jericho to Jerusalem, and was about one and a half miles from Jerusalem.

Luke xi. 1–13 should also perhaps be placed to this visit to Jerusalem (Feast of the Dedication), for according to local tradition the Lord's Prayer as recorded in Luke xi. 1–4 was taught on the west slope of the Mount of Olives, above the Garden of Gethsemane and near the hill path leading from Jerusalem to Bethany. The site was marked by a church which was already in ruins before the arrival of the Crusaders, so that it probably dated from before the Arab conquest of 636 A.D.

§ XVI

JOHN X. 22-42

Feast of Dedication at Jerusalem. He returns to Peræa.

(x. 22) "AND there took place (ἐγένετο δὲ) the Feast of the Dedication, in Jerusalem." This was one of the minor festivals—not ordained by Moses, but instituted by Judas Maccabæus B.C. 165 (see 1 Macc. iv. 56–59: 2 Macc. x. 6–8). Attendance at the Temple was not obligatory either at this Feast or at that of Purim: but throughout the land the people assembled in their synagogues to keep it. Hence, the notice "in Jerusalem": by which John means that our Lord was at Jerusalem on the date of this festival, although most people were keeping it in their nearest towns. It lasted eight days, viz. from Kislew 25 to Tebeth 2, inclusive; the Julian equivalent this year being Tuesday, Dec. 7, to Tuesday, Dec. 14. Temple and town were illuminated every evening, and every house.

A.D. 28.
Tues. {Dec. 7, Kislew 25} to Tues. {Dec. 14, Tebeth 2}

"And it was winter": rather, "It was stormy weather" (χειμὼν ἦν). There was no occasion for John to tell his readers that it was winter, for every one knew that the Feast of Dedication fell always in winter. Therefore his meaning must be, "it was stormy weather," or "there was a storm blowing" (see Acts xxvii. 20, χειμῶνός τε οὐκ ὀλίγου ἐπικειμένου, "no small storm lay on us"). In consequence, Jesus was in the shelter (23) of "Solomon's portico" in the Temple area: this portico was on the extreme east side (Josephus, *Ant.*, XX. viii. 6) overhanging the Kedron ravine, and would be of especial protection against a storm from the east. The day may be the first day of the Feast, Tuesday, Kislew 25 = Dec. 7.

(24) "Therefore," *i.e.* now that after two months' absence He is in the Temple again, and, because hemmed in by the portico, as they think in their power, "the Jews surrounded Him," as meaning He should not escape them: "and they said to Him, 'How long dost thou hold us in suspense? If thou art the Christ, tell us plainly.'" This does not imply that He had ever left them any ground for doubt, or that He had ever dissimulated His claims to be Messiah. Rather, their question betrays the impatience of men who will not or cannot bring themselves to believe what they do not want to believe. There is at the back of their question the old demand for some external "sign" which may satisfy them.

(25) His answer: "I told you and ye believe not. The works that I do in My Father's name these bear witness concerning Me." Ever since He had been among them they had known His claim: from His birth up, they had never been allowed to lose sight of it: but they would not have it. If they would not accept His spoken word, let them accept the witness of His works. He does not appeal to the events of His Infancy or to the witness of John, or to that of Simeon, Anna, Zacharias, the angels, or Gabriel: these, with which they were well acquainted, could only have value for those whose minds were already attuned: they could be of no avail for those who had all along known of them and had rejected Him.

Miracles have their evidential value, but only in virtue of their ethical quality—some ethical quality which sets forth the nature of Him in whose name they are done, *e.g.* as seen in the healing of sick and maimed and blind, the feeding of the hungry, the raising from death, the ministering to the spiritual needs of those who wait on God ("the poor")—in short, those works of His which He ordered to be reported to John in prison (Matt. xi. 5), because of their evidential value. Mere thaumaturgy has no evidential value: it lacks the ethical quality of God: such is the thaumaturgy of the East: to thaumaturgy Antichrist will appeal "in all power and signs and wonders of Falsehood" (2 Thess. ii. 9). Also, Antichrist will come in his own name: and not as the representative of God, not as The Son asserting the existence of The Father.

(26) "But *ye* believe not, because ye are not of My sheep." The fault lay not in any want of evidence, but in their incapacity to appreciate Truth. To them neither words nor works of His had any evidential value, because their ears were not sensitized to Truth: in other words, "because ye are not of My sheep" which "listen to My voice"—as He had said to them when last here, two months ago.

(27) "My sheep hear My voice, and *I* recognize them (κἀγὼ γινώσκω αὐτά)": the Jews thought they belonged to the Kingdom because they were Jews: but *He* knows whom He calls and who hear Him: between His sheep and Him the Shepherd there exists a mutual recognition: these follow Him where He leads.

(28) "And *I* give them Life eternal." He does not promise them immunity from death; for again, as two months ago, the sheep driven up for the Festal sacrifices give Him His parable. Many of His own sheep too will be sacrificed, but He gives them Life eternal, and living or dying "they shall never perish, and no one shall snatch them out of My hand." They are beyond reach of Death. The transit from this world of sense called death is not Death: the only Death is the being snatched "out of My hand," and that they shall never be.

(29) "That which My Father hath given to Me is greater than all." "That which (ὃ)" = the Divine nature of The Son eternally generated by The Father. So Augustine, "Quid dedit Filio Pater majus omnibus? Ut ipse illi esset unigenitus Filius." "And no one is able to snatch out of My Father's hand."

(30) "I and The Father are One": who then is able to snatch "out of My hand?"

(30) In the sentence, "I and The Father are One," the word "One" (ἓν) is neuter, and means one Essence: it is not masculine, which would have been one Person. He, who was talking to them, is One in Essence with The Father: He is God Incarnate: He is the eternal

Son of The eternal Father—co-eternal, co-equal: two Persons, one Godhead, one Essence.

(31) Again (as two months ago at the Feast of Tabernacles, viii. 59) "the Jews carried stones to stone Him." Before that, also, they had sought to kill Him. On the first occasion, at the Feast of Pentecost (v. 18), because "He kept saying (imp.) God was His own Father, making Himself equal with God." On the second occasion, at the Feast of Tabernacles (viii. 54-58), because He again had plainly said that God was His Father and that He Himself was the self-existent God "I am." On the third occasion, now at the Feast of Dedication (x. 33), because "thou, being a man, makest thyself God." There is no development in His claim: He begins as He ends, claiming to be God: His claim dates from His very birth, though no one at that time understood in what sense He was God. The first to whom He began to teach His relationship with The Father were His mother Mary and Joseph (Luke ii. 40), and even His mother understood but gradually the mysteries of her Son. John the Baptist, the Forerunner, was the next to understand (see under i. 18: pp. 18, 19). And ever since our Lord's public ministry began, it had been His aim to explain to the doctors of theology exactly how He stands to The Father, what is the nature of the Godhead, how The Father and The Son are One in Essence and yet Two Persons. One purpose of His incarnation was to teach the nature of God, and that the unity of God is not the final word of revelation.

(32) 'And why did they purpose to stone Him? Had He done any action worthy of death? Were not all His works good and worthy of The Father, whose indeed they were?'

(33) They reply, Be his actions as they may: "it is not concerning any good action that we stone thee, but concerning blasphemy, and because thou being a man makest thyself God." Even if He were the Christ (it is their last desperate argument) how could He, being a man, be God? how claim God's right to act at will athwart the Sabbath law, and to be equal with God (v. 18)? and to

have been God ages before He came into the world, God the self-existent "I am" (viii. 58)? and to be One Godhead with The Father, though not The Father (x. 30)?

But though a mere man could not be God, God could become Man, whilst still remaining God. Did not the Scriptures plainly hint at it in words with whose meaning they, doctors of the Law, were familiar?

(34) For instance, "Is it not written in your Law,* '*I* said, Gods are ye'?" The quotation is from Ps. lxxxii. 6. The "I," both in the Hebrew and the Greek, is emphatic. This psalm from verse 2 to 7 contains the sentence of God upon the corruption and incompetence of the judges or rulers who held His delegated authority. He says in verse 6 how He had clothed them with His own authority, saying they should sit for Him, even Himself calling them gods and sons of the Most High: alluding to the pouring out of The Spirit upon the seventy elders chosen by lot by Moses (Num. xi. 16, 24–30)—the original of the Sanhedrin: and in verse 8 He sends forth the Messiah to be King, "Arise, O *God*, judge the earth," etc. Our Lord argues:—

(35) If God Himself gives the title of "gods" to their judges unto whom the word of God came marking them out as delegates of His own authority.

(36) It was only because they were vicars, so to say, of the Messiah, the eternal Son, whom the eternal Father was to consecrate as Man and send as Man into the world: sending Him with the words, "Arise, *O God*, judge the earth, for Thou shalt inherit all the nations." That Messiah was Himself God come as Man among men. And yet "Say *ye* (ὑμεῖς λέγετε) of Him whom The Father consecrated and sent into the world, 'Thou blasphemest'?" etc.

"He, a Man, making Himself God." Was not this very thing (viz. an Incarnate God) foreshadowed in their Law? The mere visitation of the word of God to their

* The Hebrew word for the Law, *Torah*, means properly *instruction*. In its narrowest sense, *i.e.* when contrasted with the "Prophets" and the "Scripture," it was confined to the Pentateuch—the five books of Moses, Gen. to Deut.: when not so contrasted, the word included the whole of God's revelation to them, as is clear from Rabbinical authorities.

seventy judges warranted to them the title of gods in God's own mouth, as being His vicegerents: was not that title a prophecy that one day the Judge or King long promised should be One in whose Person the Godhead should unite Itself to Manhood? "Arise, *O God*, judge the earth; for Thou shalt inherit all nations" as universal King. He is talking to adepts in O.T. exegesis, who follow Him.

Seeing then that a God-Man was some day to come, it was not of necessity blasphemy for a Man to call Himself God: for some day that Man will come who has the right to do so. Before they accuse Him of blasphemy let them see whether He is not that very Man who has the right to call Himself God.

His argument is not directed so much toward denying blasphemy on His part, as toward cautioning "the Jews" (*i.e.* the Sanhedrists) for their reckless charge against The Father's Representative. The line taken is not 'since I am God, therefore I am not using blasphemy,' but rather, 'Since I am God, beware how you venture to charge Me.' It has been superficially inferred that He here, for argument, laid aside His claim to the Godhead and placed Himself on a par with those who held a delegated authority: This view seems to miss the point.

(37) They knew He had always claimed to be that Man-God, and from His very birth He had been pointed out to them as that Man by angels and prophets (Luke i. and ii.). If they had found His actions not to correspond with the nature of God, they were right not to believe His claim, He Himself would forbid them to recognize Him.

(38) But if His works did so correspond, then even though they did not straightaway believe His statements (for He knew their ears were dull, else they had leapt to Him), at least let them examine His works, His whole life, in every aspect. They would not then ascribe those works to the agency of demons, but would be led on to the knowledge, and constantly increasing knowledge (ἵνα γνῶτε καὶ γινώσκητε), of the complete harmony and union that exist between Himself the doer of these works and Him whom they called their God.

These are His last warning words to them. He will not appear again in Jerusalem till the week of His Passion some three months later.

(39) They here sought to close in and seize Him: they had already formed a circle round Him (24) to prevent escape.

And He went forth out of that closing circle—the power that emanated from Him preventing their laying hands on Him: it was the same power that He allowed to issue from Him on the night of His arrest (xviii. 6).

(40) "And He went away again beyond Jordan, to the place where John was at the first baptizing." "Again," *i.e.* because He had already been in Peræa for the last two months, the two months before the Feast of Dedication. The "at the first" refers to the time when John *began* baptizing (the time recorded in Matt. iii. 5–17: Mark i. 5–11: Luke iii. 3–18: John i. 19–28) in the lower Jordan opposite to Jericho, and on east of Jordan; as against the time of his baptizing mentioned in John iii. 23, when he was much higher up the river and on the west of Jordan, on the borders of Galilee and Samaria, at Aenon.

Dec. 9, A.D. 28, to early Mch., A.D. 29. (40) "And there He abode," *i.e.* in Peræa: until His visit to Bethany of chapter xi., some twelve weeks later.

(41) "And many came to Him": cf. the "crowd" of Luke xi. 14, 27: Luke xii. 1, 13, 54: Luke xiii. 14, 17. The whole block of Luke xi. 14 to xiii. 21 belongs to these twelve weeks.

"And they kept saying (imp.), '*John* (strongly emphatic in the Greek) did no sign,'" implying that Jesus did many here. And they amplify their implication into "all the things that John spoke of this One (τούτου) were true," *e.g.* when in i. 27 the Baptist spoke in this neighbourhood (lower Jordan) of Jesus as being far greater than himself; so much greater that he, John, whom the whole nation were revering as their greatest Prophet, was not worthy to wait upon Him as a slave: and in i. 33, where he announced Him as "baptizing with the Holy Spirit," and as being "The Son of God": and in i. 36 as being

"The Lamb of God": and in iii. 26–28, where the Baptist recalls how he had witnessed that he himself was but the Forerunner of the "Messiah," who was Jesus. They believed now with John's belief: they believing only implicitly what John had explicitly *seen*.

(42) "And many believed into Him there" and were perhaps also baptized into Him: for that Christian baptism had already begun we have seen at iv. 2.

This stay in Peræa seems to have covered twelve weeks, viz. from about Dec. 9 of A.D. 28, till beginning of March A.D. 29. No details of this period are given by any of the evangelists except Luke. In this period falls Luke xi. 1 or 14 to Luke xiii. 21.

The whole block bears an air of sadness as though it marked the close of a ministry in Peræa as unsuccessful as had been that in Galilee. The section Luke xi. 14 to end of chap. xii. seems to belong to one and the same day, the part beginning xi. 29 being the answer to verse 16. Possibly we may find a clue in xi. 37 as to the actual day of the year. This invitation to the midday meal given by the Pharisee may mark the Feast of Purim (Adar 14 and 15, which fell this year of A.D. 29 on Wednesday and Thursday, Feb. 23, 24) always a festival of social gaiety. The mention of "the sepulchres which appear not" (*τὰ μνημεῖα τὰ ἄδηλα*, verse 44) also points to the Feast of Purim, for Adar 15 was the day on which all sepulchres and tomb-stones had to be rewhitened every year in order to make them conspicuous, so that passers-by might not unwittingly come in contact with them and thus incur ceremonial defilement. In a similar passage in Matt. xxiii. 27 the words are "ye are as whitened tombs": the difference is notable: Matthew's record was spoken in Passover week, when all tombs shone white, having been white-washed but last month. Perhaps also the simile of the marriage-feast in Luke xii. 36 may have been suggested by one actually taking place at this the favourite time for weddings, the Feast of Purim.

The section Luke xiii. 1–21 seems to follow closely on

the preceding, when news came down from Jerusalem of the recent treatment of Galileans by Pilate in the Temple courts—not improbably at this very Feast of Purim. This treatment of Herod's Galilean subjects by Pilate may have been the cause of that "enmity" between the two, of which Luke tells us in xxiii. 12 (a month later): which was ended by the amends Pilate made him over Another of his Galileans (xxiii. 7).

There is a close resemblance again and again in our Lord's sayings here in Peræa to His sayings recorded by Matthew as spoken either in Galilee or during the final week in Jerusalem: it is not that the records are at hap-hazard and show no design: rather, the audience was in the main different in the three localities, also words re-iterated make a more lasting impression: reiteration has always been a note of the oral teaching of the East.

With Luke xiii. 22 we come in touch with John's gospel (see following pp. 252–255), and are in early March of A.D. 29.

NOTE

This note shows how John's account (chap. xi.) dovetails into Luke's (xiii. 22–xvi. 31).

A.D. 29. Early March.

John in chapter xi. resumes the history at about the beginning of March A.D. 29, when falls the journey from Peræa to Bethany for the raising of Lazarus. It is the same journey that begins at Luke xiii. 22 and ends at Luke xvi. 31.

The following remarks may show the connection here between Luke and John:—

The journey will occupy three days (Luke xiii. 32): it begins at verse 22 after the "two days' wait" of John xi. 6; and evidently on a Friday, for of the three days the second is clearly a Saturday (Luke xiv. 1). The position in Peræa was (as we deduce from Luke xiii. 31–33) as follows:—

Luke xiii. 31.

Herod Antipas wishes to get rid of our Lord out of his territory of Peræa, but does not venture to do violence to Him. The people had been already indignant at his murder of John the Baptist last May at Machærus, the southernmost point of Peræa. Herod therefore tries to frighten Him out by the artifice of sending Pharisees to pretend they have wind of a secret plot of Herod's to put Him to death.

A.D. 29.
Luke xiii. 32.

Our Lord sees through the trick, for to Him all minds were open (John ii. 24, 25): and He sends word to Herod that His plans are fixed and unalterable, not subject to compulsion from any one or to any fear from outside (cf. John xi. 9, which was spoken on this same day): that His time, however, is nearly at an end; that in three days His active work will be finished (τελειοῦμαι)—He means with the raising of Lazarus, which will bring about the Sanhedrin's final decision for His death (cf. John xi. 47–53). For after that, He retired to Ephraim (*ib.* 54) on the edge of Samaria, and there waited in seclusion during the last few days until His final journey of six days to Jerusalem (Luke xvii. 11) to meet His death.

Luke xiii. 33.

But He adds that those three days will not be passed in Peræa; for, independently of Herod's wishes, 'I must leave Peræa at once in order to go toward Jerusalem. The Sanhedrin at Jerusalem, and not Herod of Galilee and Peræa, must have their accustomed privilege of slaying the Prophets.' The journey He has in view (viz. to Bethany, only 1¾ miles from Jerusalem) will occupy three days: viz. "to-day" (=Friday), which will take Him to Jericho; "to-morrow" (Saturday), which He will spend at Jericho; and "the next day" (Sunday), when He will arrive at Bethany and end His active work by His crowning miracle, the raising of Lazarus—His final effort to convince the Jews (cf. Luke xvi. 30, 31). The raising of Lazarus will be on Sunday, March 6, A.D. 29.

March 4, Fri.
March 5, Sat.
March 6, Sun.

THE JOURNEY FROM PERÆA TO BETHANY (MARCH 4–6 OF A.D. 29) FOR THE RAISING OF LAZARUS

(John xi. 7–16: Luke xiii. 22–xvi. 31)

The "cities and villages" of Luke xiii. 22 are in Peræa. He had returned to South Peræa in December of A.D. 28 (John x. 40): and has been in Peræa presumably ever since. According to Josephus (*War*, 3, iii. 3) Peræa taken politically, as Herod's province, reached from Machærus (where the Baptist was beheaded) in the south, to Pella in the north, *i.e.* sixty miles north and south by twenty-five east and west. Taken geographically it would be much larger, for it would probably include Decapolis (see Josephus, *War*, 4, vii. 3, where he reckons Gadara to be in Peræa) and all from Jordan to the eastern desert.

The three days of Luke xiii. 32, 33, are the same as the three days He took to get to Lazarus.

A.D. 29.
Mch. 3 } Thurs.
Adar 22 }

He hears of the illness on (say) Thursday morning, (March 3). He stays "two days in the place where He was"

(John xi. 6)—clearly some place in Peræa (John x. 40). The "two days" means till the second day, *i.e.* till the morrow, both terms being counted (cf. iv. 40). Does, then, to "stay two days" mean merely that He left on the morrow? No: it means that, though He left on the morrow, there was a deliberate stay first: thus here He stayed the daylight hours of Thursday, as at iv. 43 He stayed the daylight hours of Monday. He stays until Lazarus is dead and buried. So Lazarus died on Thursday, March 3rd, and is buried on the same day (cf. verse 17 with 39).

A.D. 29. Mch. 3, Adar 22, Thur.

On Friday morning (March 4) our Lord starts to go to Lazarus (John xi. 7), and it will take Him three days (Luke xiii. 32, 33) to get there and do the crowning miracle.

Mch. 4, Adar 23, Fri.

These three days of Luke are checked and verified by John xi. 11, 14: from which we gather that He started the morning after Lazarus was dead-and-buried, and reached Bethany on the fourth day since the death-and-burial. The "four days" of verses 17, 39, of course, include the day of death-and-burial: and are Thursday, Friday, Saturday, Sunday (March 3–6). So, of John's "four days"—

Mch. 3, Thurs.

On the first day, Thursday, March 3, Lazarus died and was buried.

Mch. 4, Fri.

On the second day, Friday, March 4, our Lord starts to go to him (John xi. 7, 11: and Luke xiii. 22). The events of this day are given in John xi. 7–16: and Luke xiii. 22–35. The day's journey would naturally be one of about twenty miles—the regular day's journey whether of ancient Rome, or of the East of then and of to-day. The end of the day finds Him at Jericho, which is seven miles west of the bridge over the Jordan, and on the road from Peræa to Jerusalem. So one may suppose Him to have started this (Friday) morning from some point in Peræa not more than twelve miles or so east of the bridge. This day is the "to-day" of Luke xiii. 32, 33.

Mch. 5, Adar 24, Sat.

On the third day, Saturday, March 5, it being a Sabbath, He, of course, does not travel, but stays at Jericho. The events of this day are given in Luke xiv. 1–24: all of which occur in the dining-hall of the Pharisee's house. We may suppose it was the midday meal of Saturday. This day is the "to-morrow" of Luke xiii. 32, 33.

Mch. 6, Adar 25, Sun.

On the fourth day, Sunday, March 6, He leaves Jericho for Bethany. "Great crowds" were travelling with Him as He was setting out (Luke xiv. 25). The place being Jericho accounts for the great numbers of "publicans and sinners" here (Luke xv. 1): for Jericho was the southern depôt for the collection of customs on exports and imports passing across Jordan; Capernaum in Galilee being the northern.

As for the "sinners" (Luke xv. 1), Jericho was always

notorious for its luxury, for which the enervating heat of its climate was greatly responsible: it is eight hundred feet below the sea. This day is the "third day" of Luke xiii. 32, and equals "the day following" of Luke xiii. 33.

The discourses of to-day (Sunday) are given in Luke xiv. 25 to xvi. 31. Perhaps some of them were spoken in the morning before He began the day's walk. Luke xv. 2 looks as if He had supped on the Saturday evening with some of the "publicans," and they are this (Sunday) morning genial and friendly with Him.

The evening finds Him at Bethany, where John at xi. 17 continues the story.

The distance from Jericho to Bethany is thirteen miles, or by the ancient road fourteen miles.

§ XVII

JOHN XI. 1–57

The raising of Lazarus. The retirement at Ephraim.

THE events of this chapter, as has already been said, seem to belong to the first week of March (as will appear later): and our Lord was crucified some three weeks later, on the 25th of the same month.

The date is early March, A.D. 29.

(1) "And a certain man was ill, namely, Lazarus of Bethany." "Lazarus of Bethany": the preposition (ἀπὸ) here rendered "of" signifies his place of residence: and John names it as being Bethany.

"*Of* the village of Mary," etc. The preposition (ἐκ) here rendered "of" signifies his place of birth, which is not named: John merely says it was the same as the village where Lazarus's sisters Mary and Martha were born. This Mary is, according to all tradition of East and West, the same as Mary *Magdalene* whom, again, the consensus of tradition asserts to be the same as "the woman who was in the city, a sinner" of Luke vii. 37. Thus the birthplace of Lazarus, Martha, and Mary was apparently a village in the township of Magdala of Galilee.

This distinction between the prepositions ἀπὸ and ἐκ has been entirely missed by both A.V. and R.V., which seem to make the "village" refer to Bethany. The A.V. has a similar oversight in i. 44 (nor is the R.V. there clear), where the Greek is exactly the same as here in xi. 1: the Greek has, "Philip was from (ἀπὸ, *i.e.* resident of) Bethsaida, out of (ἐκ, *i.e.* native of) the city of Andrew and Peter," which every one knew was Capernaum. See also at vii. 41.

(2) "It was the Mary who anointed the Lord with ointment and wiped His feet with her hair, whose brother Lazarus was sick."

This is obviously a reference to the incident recorded in Luke vii. 37, where alone in the Synoptics is there any mention of "wiping His feet with her hair"—a story well known, of course, to all the Churches at the time that John wrote his gospel. John cannot be alluding to his own account in chapter xii.: for why should he in xi. 2 tell us that Mary the sister of Martha and Lazarus was the Mary who in the next chapter anoints our Lord's feet, when we have only to wait for his account of that incident to see that she was? Clearly in xi. 2, John is referring *back* to that crisis in her life in this very house some nine months ago, when she came first to love our Lord, and, as Luke had said, "wiped His feet with her hair." See note at end, pp. 441–445.

(3) "Therefore his sisters sent to Him, saying, 'Lord, lo, he whom thou lovest is ill.'"

A.D. 29.
Mch. 2 } Wed.
Adar 21 } evg.

(4) "And Jesus, when He heard it, said, 'This illness is not unto death, but,' etc."

"This illness," etc. This is the message of comfort sent back by our Lord to the sisters; as is clear from verse 40, "said I not to thee . . . the glory of God." John has probably condensed it. The sisters, on receiving it, no doubt took it to mean that their brother should not die, which was not quite our Lord's meaning: for by "not unto death" He meant that the end for which this sickness was sent was not death, but the glory of God: true he will die of it, but only momentarily, for his death will be merely incidental to that end: his death is not meant to be the close of his mortal life, for his mortal life will be shortly resumed. In other words, our Lord meant all along to recall him from the grave. He knew exactly what He was going to do: the sisters did not; they understood that our Lord would not let him die, but would heal him by some startling miracle.

(6) "When therefore He heard 'he is ill,' He *then* (τότε μὲν, at that time) stayed for two days in the place where He was." He stays "two days" in order that Lazarus may die, and that so He may raise him not merely from the grave, but after actual decomposition had set in, which would be a yet more significant sign to the sisters, to the disciples, and to the Jews.

Mch. 3, Thurs., till Mch. 4, Fri. morning.

"The place where He was," viz. some place in Peræa, see x. 40. Say, He heard of the illness on Thursday morning, March 3, the two days would be the daylight hours of Thursday and the beginning of the morning of Friday (see note at iv. 40). They are March 3rd and 4th of A.D. 29. On the Thursday, Lazarus dies and is buried in a rock tomb (buried the day of his death: cf. verse 17 with 39).

(7) "Afterwards, after this (ἔπειτα, μετὰ τοῦτο), He saith, 'Let us go to Judæa again.'" The Greek phrase, μετὰ τοῦτο, "after this," does not express only sequence in time. It always further implies an ethical connection between the two events, and so differs from the very similar μετὰ ταῦτα. Here the subtle connection is that the event (viz. the death and burial of Lazarus) for which He had waited had now occurred. On Friday morning, therefore (March 4), our Lord proposes to start. This, as has been already said, is the journey of Luke xiii. 22. He will take three days to reach Bethany: they are the three days of Luke xiii. 32, 33, and the incidents of this journey are given in Luke xiii. 22 to xvi. 31. The middle day was a Saturday (Luke xiv. 1), and therefore He could not travel that day, but spent it at Jericho. "The place where He was" (verse 6) was not more than a half-day east of the Jericho ford.

Mch. 4 / Adar 23 } Fri.

(8) His disciples, not knowing what was in His mind, why He had waited, or why He now proposed to go again to Judæa (Bethany was in Judæa), recall to Him the recent attempt of "the Jews" to stone Him.

"Of late," viz. at the Feast of the Dedication, Dec. 7

(John x. 31, 39), some eleven or twelve weeks ago, when He was last in Jerusalem.

(9, 10) He replied that there was no cause for fear: that they themselves in full daylight walk securely without fear of tripping, for they can then see: and that they walk insecurely only in the dark, for then only they can see nothing. By which He implied that He walks securely always, for He always sees His way: that to Him there is no darkness, no uncertainty of the future; for He knows every detail of things to come before they come. In Him is no darkness, to Him all is light. (11) He added (μετὰ τοῦτο), as an instance of how all things are to Him in light, "Lazarus, our friend, sleeps: but I am on My way to wake him." (12) They reply, 'Lord, what need? If he is asleep the crisis is over, he will recover.' (14) He explains that by "sleep" He had meant "death."

A.D. 29. Mch. 4 / Adar 23 } Fri.

(15) To their look of astonishment at hearing Lazarus was dead (for they had understood the message of verse 4 in the same sense, as did the sisters when it reached them), He adds, "For your sakes, that ye may believe, am I glad that I was not there." As though, had He been there, He would have held Himself obliged to respond to the appeal of love and distress: not to do so would have had a harsh and ungracious appearance, hard for bystanders to understand, foreign to that tenderness and sympathetic gentleness which He wished all men ever to associate with His human presence. By absenting Himself till the crisis was over, He had made it easier for people not to misunderstand Him: and His delay was only in order to grant a greater boon in His own way.

The raising of Lazarus from the corruption that had already set in (39) was to be the greatest and crowning miracle of His Ministry. It is the τελειοῦμαι (I am perfected, I complete My work) of Luke xiii. 32.

(16) "Thomas, who is called Didymus." See under xx. 24. The Hebrew name Thomas means a Twin: the Greek for "twin" is Δίδυμος (Didymus). There is a very ancient tradition given in the apocryphal gospels that

Thomas's name was Judas—the nickname Thomas, or Twin, distinguishing him from the many other Judases. There seems to be no record as to who was his twin.

Here comes chronologically Luke xiii. 22–xvi. 31. Not, of course, that in the story of Dives and Lazarus the Lazarus is the same as Lazarus of Bethany, but the connection of the raising of Lazarus with that story, and especially with its two closing verses, is obvious. John has no account of the journey up (details of which Luke has given at some length), but he resumes his story with the arrival at Bethany.

Mch. 6 / Adar 25 } Sun.

(17) "So Jesus, when He came (to Bethany), found that he was [already] four days in the sepulchre." It is Sunday evening, March 6, A.D. 29. It seems then that the journey to Bethany had taken three days (cf. Luke xiii. 22, 32, 33): for He evidently started the morning after Lazarus's death (John xi. 6, 7): but the middle day was a Saturday (Luke xiv. 1) and therefore passed in rest. Lazarus dying on Thursday, March 3, and being buried the same day, our Lord started on Friday from Peræa, *viâ* Jericho, and arrived at Bethany on Sunday evening, March 6: the two terms Thursday and Sunday are, of course, both counted in the "four days" of verses 17 and 39.

(18) "Bethany was near to Jerusalem, about fifteen furlongs off": "fifteen furlongs": rather "fifteen *stadia*"* = about $1\frac{3}{4}$ English miles.

(19) "Many from among the Jews had come to Martha and Mary to comfort them about their brother." This and the frequent references to "the Jews" in the scene that follows shows the importance that John attaches to

* A *stadium* (rendered "furlong") was accurately 600 Greek feet = about 200 yards, accurately, 582 English feet, or 630 English feet, according as the Greek foot is taken to be the Attic or the Olympic. The former is the more probable. A "sabbath-day's journey" was 2000 cubits according to the Rabbinical rules: this was equal to 3000 Greek feet, or 5 stadia, = roughly 1000 yards. This notice, coupled with the next verse, shows that the day is at any rate not Saturday: for the distance of 15 stadia puts the village far beyond a sabbath-day's journey from Jerusalem. The πρὸς Βηθανίαν of Luke xxiv. 50 does not mean "to Bethany" (A.V.), but "over against B." (R.V.), and thus Acts i. 12 presents no difficulty.

their presence: for, as we shall see, this crowning miracle was the final act that decided the Sanhedrin to put Jesus to death.

The wording πρὸς τὴν Μάρθαν καὶ Μαριὰμ implies that the house was Martha's rather than Mary's; as indeed we learn definitely was the case from Luke x. 38, where the occasion was the journey from Peræa to Jerusalem (passing through Bethany) for the Feast of Dedication three months ago, in December of A.D. 28.

(20) "Martha, therefore, when she heard 'Jesus is coming.'" The message "Jesus is coming" was given to Martha as the elder sister and the owner of the house. It was no doubt sent by our Lord Himself—He wished her to come to Him: He would not break in upon the sorrow in the house with the crowd of strangers who had come up with Him from Jericho: see the "great crowds" of Luke xiv. 25: xv. 1: and the "crowd" named in John xii. 17 as having been present on this occasion.

"Went and met Him." The traditional place where Martha (and Mary, 32) met Him is half a mile north-west of el Azariyeh (the modern representative of Bethany): the modern village has grown up around Lazarus's tomb, revered alike by Christian and Moslem: the original Bethany was close by it. The ancient road from Jericho passed to the north of the present one, and north of Bethany.

(21) When the sisters received on Thursday noon (March 3) the message of verse 4 (Lazarus being still alive), they had supposed it to mean that Lazarus would not die, but would at the last moment be startlingly healed by our Lord's arrival. When He failed to come and Lazarus died, and He still failed to come and Lazarus was buried, the sisters supposed He had meant to come but had been unavoidably detained, and hence the death. 'But even so,' they would say, 'there is the message He sent us: it may have had a meaning we missed: could it mean that even now He means to bring him back to us?' They knew He had at least twice already recalled the dead to life, though not after actual burial. This is the hope they had scarce dared to name to each other,

and which Martha now but half ventures to formulate in the following words :—

(22) "Even now (καὶ νῦν), I know whatsoever thou shalt ask of God, God will give it thee." Even now at this late hour, if He chose, He might bring her brother back to her : that so, in the words of His message of verse 4, the glory of God would be manifested and He Himself as "The Son of God" be glorified thereby before all present.

(23) "Thy brother shall rise again." He breathes upon that tiny spark of hope within her to kindle it : He means to bring her brother back to life. He does not say "*now*" though He means it : He purposely leaves His words vague, vague as were her own : He will gently blow till He has kindled a flame.

(24) She thinks to herself, 'Can He indeed mean now? I dare not hope it : and yet——' : so she fences with Him as though He must be referring to the resurrection of the just that will precede that setting up of the Kingdom on earth which all the Prophets had foretold : "I know he shall rise-again at the resurrection in the last day."

(25) "It is I that am the Resurrection and the Life : he that believeth into Me, even if he be dead he shall Live," *i.e.* 'but that resurrection of the just is only possible to them because of their union with Me by virtue of their faith in Me'—a faith implicit rather than explicit. He, He that is speaking with her, is that new Life they will enjoy : it is by their faith in Him, which makes them one with Him, that they will Live again. He can as easily call back her brother to life now as He will call the just to Life hereafter : the fact of their being dead, like Lazarus, is of no importance.

(26) "And every one who liveth and believeth into Me, he shall never Die," *i.e.* And in the case of those who like herself are yet alive, whoever of them believes into Him shall never Die. He speaks not of death—the transit from this world of sense, but of Death—the severance from Him who is Life. "Believest thou this," that dead and living alike Live in Him? If so, let her think how easy it is for Him to recall her brother to life now.

(27) "Yea, Lord: I have believed and I do believe that Thou art the Messiah, The Son of God, *He that cometh into the world*"—the title of Him whom man had ever been expecting since the promise made in Eden. 'I believe Thou art He whom these terms denote and art all that these terms connote, though I understand them but dimly.'

To understand is not necessary: implicit Faith carries with it the explicit. No one of them was aware of His eternal Divinity: Peter had had an instant's clear vision in September last, but it stayed not with him: none but the Mother plumbed deep and understood. John the Baptist, who also had understood, was dead.

His aim is won: Martha's faith is now ripe for the amazing work He is about to do, which previously would have been for her but a profitless display of thaumaturgy. Here our Lord bids her call her sister Mary.

(28) "Secretly saying": *i.e.* secretly as was fitting, in that house of sorrow: and so that the news of His presence should not create an unseemly disturbance.

(29) "And she [Mary], when she heard, rose up quickly, and was on the way to Him."

(30) He was still outside the village district of Bethany; and at the spot where (if tradition be accepted) the districts of Bethany and Bethphage touched, the spot where Martha had met Him.

(31) "The Jews which," etc. These particular Jews were friendly to the house of Martha and Mary (19, 33). There is some reason (though not stated by tradition) to suppose that Martha was the wife of Simon the Pharisee of Luke vii. 37, the same as Simon the (one time) leper of Matt. xxvi. 6 and Mark xiv. 3, the same as the leper of Matt. viii. 2: Mark i. 40: Luke v. 12: and the family was of importance. The term "the Jews" in John's gospel always denotes Jews of position, theologians, doctors learned in the Law, and generally even Sanhedrists. These friendly Jews followed Mary, and thus were eye-witnesses of all that follows.

(32) "So Mary, when she came where Jesus was, on seeing Him, fell at His feet, saying," etc. Mary's

repetition of Martha's words (21) shows the keynote of the sisters' talk with each other during the last few days: and, as appears from verse 15, they were right in thinking that had He been there their brother would not have died.

(33) "Jesus, therefore, when He saw her weeping and the Jews weeping who had come with her, groaned in the spirit," indignant at the sight of the triumph of the evil one, who by bringing sin into the world had brought death among men, and all its attendant sorrow. It was the sight of the grief of the mourners that caused His indignation, at the way man's adversary had blinded them. And what is death? a removal to another sphere of conscious continuity. He is about to show how small a thing is death, how completely in His hands are those whom we call dead: for by a word He will recall the voyager to resume the old activities he had left.

"He groaned in the spirit (ἐνεβριμήσατο τῷ πνεύματι)," *i.e.* in His human spirit. The phrase is on all fours with ἀναστενάξας τῷ πνεύματι αὐτου (Mark viii. 12), "He sighed deeply in His spirit": and with ἐταράχθη τῷ πνεύματι (John xiii. 21), "He was troubled in spirit." The τῷ πνεύματι seems to indicate the spiritual or intellectual sphere—the sphere of intellectual emotions, where no disturbance was in His case possible except as He at will summoned and at will dismissed: how should He who lived in untroubled harmony with God know any disturbance except with His deliberate assent? This sphere would be distinguished from the psychic sphere—the sphere of psychic emotions (περίλυπός ἐστιν ἡ ψυχή μου, Matt. xxvi. 38: Mark xiv. 34: and νῦν ἡ ψυχή μου τετάρακται, John xii. 27)—where again no disturbance was in His case possible except as He at will allowed. In both these spheres (as well as in the physical) took place our Lord's Agony, when His human soul and human spirit were almost submerged by all the sinful souls and spirits of the human race that was grafted into Him.

"And troubled Himself." The phrase is remarkable (καὶ ἐτάραξεν ἑαυτον): deliberately summoned up in Himself the feelings of indignation at the havoc wrought by the evil one, and of tenderness for the mourners. As Augustine and John of Damascus, and the Fathers generally, insist, He had no involuntary passions—not even of anger, indignation, sorrow, or wonder: for all were under absolute control. "Thou art troubled," says Augustine, "against thy will: Christ was troubled because He willed." Again, when He is said elsewhere to "marvel at their unbelief," the meaning is not that He unwillingly marvelled as do we, for how could He who knew all men marvel at anything in them: but rather that He called up and expressed in word and gesture such surprise as the occasion warranted human nature in showing. Similarly a philosopher who has mastered all impulse to anger will often deliberately call up within himself the feeling of anger in order to make effect upon some one present, without being in the least perturbed. Even the physical sensations of hunger, thirst, weariness, were entirely under the control of His will, so that He was aware of them only in so far as He deliberately willed to be. Does any one object that this is denying to Him a real humanity? But this mastery of the will over the body has been attained by many ascetics of Christendom and of Hinduism. In our Lord's case, His perfect human nature needed no effort of asceticism in order to attain, for His human will had already and always absolute control. To condemn asceticism because our Lord did not practise it is to ignore the difference between our debasement and His perfection.

(34) "Where have ye laid him?" He does not ask as not knowing: for He knew all things. He asks in order that they may show Him and so assist at the work in hand: as grown-up people constantly act with children. The whole human race were as children to Him the perfect Man: He was constantly putting Himself on their lower level, else they could never get in touch with Him—so high above us is perfect man even apart from the fact that to that particular Manhood the Godhead was united.

This adaptation of Himself to the intelligence He is dealing with is obviously a law that He follows in His handling of all of us always, severally.

(35) "Jesus wept": not involuntarily, as one overcome, but deliberately wept. What at? Certainly not, as the Jews thought, in sorrow at Lazarus's death: for what was death to Him? He wept, not at the cause of the sisters' distress, but at the fact of it; thus showing His tender sympathy for human sorrow. Still, could they but see, there was nothing to weep about: He was Lord of death.

(36) In this scene where all are met together at the spot outside the village where Jesus had halted, as also in the scene at the sepulchre (38) that follows, there are two bodies of Jews to be carefully distinguished.

A. The Jews of verses 19, 31, 33, 45, who are always qualified as friends of the house, and, as such, are not ill-disposed to our Lord who was known to be a friend of the house:

B. A hostile body who (vv. 36, 37) are not qualified as friendly, or (verse 46) are distinguished from the friendly ones. This hostile body do not belong to the Jews who came to comfort the sisters: but they form part of the crowds who came up with Him from Jericho.

"Therefore, said the Jews, 'See, how He loved him.'" These are the hostile body, called simply "the Jews." They misinterpreted our Lord's tears, as though He were weeping at having lost a friend, which, of course, was not the cause. What was death to Him?

(37) "But some of them," *i.e.* some of "the Jews" generically, not some of those Jews who had come to comfort the sisters. These are still hostile Jews (B) who are among the crowd that had come up with Him from Jericho and Peræa. They are the Pharisees and Scribes of Luke xv. 2: xvi. 14, 15. And are the same as the "some of them" of verse 46 of this chapter of John.

These in their bitterness taunt Him with having been unable to prevent His friend's death, though five months ago He pretended to have given sight to a man that was born blind. "This one (οὗτος) who opened the eyes of the blind was not able to cause that even this one (although so dear a friend) should not die." Similar taunts will be shouted at Him on the Cross three weeks hence, "He saved others, He cannot save Himself."

The Greek of verse 37 leaves it quite uncertain whether these words are an ironical statement or a question. The former is perhaps the more probable: for the taunt seems to refer to the message of verse 4, which was known to them: all the crowd that came up with Him knew of it, and had understood Him to mean that Lazarus should not die: and yet here he was dead.

(38) "Jesus therefore again groaning in Himself," etc. "Therefore," *i.e.* the taunts of these hostile Jews are a fresh cause for His sorrow and indignation: indignation not at them, but at the blindness with which the author of all ill had sealed their eyes.

"Cometh to the sepulchre" (rather than "grave"). The Greek word is the same as is always rendered "sepulchre" in chapters xix. xx. "There was a cave, and a stone lay against it," or "lay over it" (ἐπέκειτο ἐπ' αὐτῷ).

This sepulchre (if we may judge from the present remains) appears to have been formed of an open vestibule, and an inner mortuary chamber on a lower level: the whole being cut in the calcareous rock. It is impossible to say whether the mortuary chamber was closed by a vertical stone, as in the case of our Lord's sepulchre and others extant, or by a horizontal slab (over a pit): the Greek text admits of either. In any case the stone of 38, 39, is the stone closing the mortuary chamber and not the vestibule, for the vestibules were always open.

(39) "Jesus saith, 'Take-away (ἄρατε) the stone.'" Although Martha is fully aware that He means to restore her brother to life and that they are all come to the sepulchre for no other purpose, still, as "the sister of the dead man," she naturally shrinks from the unpleasant effects of removing the stone that sealed the body on this the fourth day since the burial.

(40) Our Lord does not deny that decomposition has set in: His very purpose in waiting so long was to ensure it: and here were numbers to be witnesses of the fact,

so that there should be no possibility of doubt about this death. In the other two recorded cases men might have said, and no doubt did say, that Jairus's daughter and the widow of Nain's son were only in a cataleptic trance. This was to be His crowning sign of power. The especial manifestation of the "glory of God" in this miracle was to be the restoration to life *after decomposition had already begun.* They believed in the final resurrection of the body: here they should see that the author of Life and Resurrection-from-corruption was He Himself. Will not all agree with Augustine and the Fathers that He "resuscitavit *fœtentem*"?

"Said I not to thee" is obviously a reference to the message of verse 4. Our Lord is encouraging her, bidding her not shrink from the ordeal. All will be well.

(41) Martha must have here signified her consent, without which He would not have interfered with the tomb. "Therefore they removed the stone": and doubtless all present echoed Martha's words of verse 39.

In figuring the scene one must remember that a crowd was present (see xii. 17, where the Greek has "the crowd," not "the people" of A.V.).

(41, 42) "Father, I thank Thee that Thou heardest Me." These words were, as we are told, used for the sake of the crowd present who heard them. He would not take any glory to Himself apart from The Father: His object is that the crowd may believe that His mission is from The Father. More than that He does not expect from the crowd at present.

"That Thou heardest Me," *i.e.* and that The Father is about to perform the raising of Lazarus through Him. He talks of The Father "hearing" Him: it is only a metaphor suitable to the crowd.

"But I knew that Thou 'hearest' Me always": here is a statement of the truth that there is no possibility of divergence between The Father and the God-Man.

(43) "He cried with a loud voice." The word ἐκραύγασεν, rendered "cried," like its noun κραυγή, means with John

the loud decisive tone of authority. " Lazarus, come forth " (Λάζαρε, δεῦρο ἔξω).

(44) " He came-forth, he that had died, bound feet and hands with bandages." In obedience to a higher volition than his own, Lazarus, now living but bound helpless as a mummy, came-forth : not moving his limbs, for John is careful to say he was " bound, feet and hands, with bandages," as was the custom. The napkin, with which his face was bound around, was not bound over his face hiding it, but served to tie up the lower jaw. Precisely similar bandages and napkin appear again in the case of our Lord's own resurrection.

" Loose him " : here again appears the helplessness of the position in which Lazarus found himself, unable to move a hand with which to unwind his own bandages.

" And let him *go*, i.e. walk (καὶ ἄφετε αὐτὸν ὑπάγειν) " : not till he was unwound could he walk. Therefore he had not come forth walking.

(45) It is important to have the translation of this verse correct : πολλοὶ οὖν ἐκ τῶν Ἰουδαίων, οἱ ἐλθόντες πρὸς τὴν Μαριάμ καὶ θ. = " *Many* therefore from among the Jews, *viz. they who* came to Mary and beheld that which Jesus did (*i.e.* the raising of Lazarus), believed into Him." Thus it would seem that *all* those friendly Jews who had come to comfort Mary and Martha believed into Him after this miracle : for they were not previously blinded by hostility to Him.

(46) " But some of them (τινὲς δὲ ἐξ αὐτῶν) " : some, that is, of the Jews generically, and not of those who had come to comfort the sisters. It is the same distinction as in verse 37, and the words refer to exactly the same body, viz. the hostile Jews who formed part of the crowd that had come up with Him from Jericho (see under 37). These hostile ones went off to the Pharisees at Jerusalem to urge them to take steps against Him, for that there was no gainsaying the extraordinary things He did and the people were sure to follow Him. They would, of course, report also on the cures named in Luke xiii. 32, of which they would have been witnesses.

Epiphanius (380 A.D.) says 'among the traditions, we find that Lazarus was thirty years old when he was raised from the dead, and that he lived another thirty years afterwards.' Did he bring back with him any memory of the spirit-world? rather, was not his mind, as regards that experience, a blank?

(47) "So the chief-priests and the Pharisees gathered a Council." "Gathered a Council": The Greek (συνήγαγον . . . συνέδριον) shows it was a meeting of the Sanhedrin. John's authority for the account of what passed here would be Joseph of Arimathæa or Nicodemus or some other member of the Sanhedrin who later on became a Christian. "And they said, 'What are we doing, that this man is doing many signs?'" They must stir themselves, they could not afford to let things slide any longer.

A.D. 29. Mch. 7, Mon.

(48) "'If we thus let him be, all will believe into him: and the Romans will come and take away'" etc., *i.e.* 'The Romans will not tolerate a Messiah: *we* have no intention of accepting this one: but if the crowd accept him, the Romans will destroy both Temple and city, and destroy the nation from being any longer an organic entity.' Exactly what did happen, after all, 41½ years later, although the Sanhedrin succeeded in setting the nation against Him.

(49) "But a certain one of them, Caiaphas, being Highpriest that year." "That year," *i.e.* that momentous year, the critical year of the human race, the year of the Passion and Resurrection of the God-Man. The fact that marked a priest as the Highpriest of any year was the officiating as Highpriest in the ritual of the great Day of Expiation or Atonement, Tisri 10th (Sept. or Oct.). At this time the office of Highpriest was not hereditary, nor for life.

The reason why John tells us that the speaker was Highpriest of that year is to show him as the *ex officio* spokesman for the nation in matters of religion. Caiaphas speaks:—

"*Ye* know nothing": the "Ye" is emphatic (ὑμεῖς), viz. you chief-priests and Pharisees (verse 47): 'why all this doubt and anxiety ? the thing we must do is quite simple.'

(50) "Nor do ye take into account that it is to your advantage that one man die on behalf of the People (λαοῦ), and not that the whole nation perish." He is urging them to put Jesus to death : but the form of words he uses is unconsciously prophetic, as John goes on to remark.

(51) "And this he spake not from himself, but as being Highpriest that year he prophesied that Jesus was to die on behalf of the nation." The verb προφητεύω ("prophesied") means, not to predict, but to speak as God's spokesman, to speak under the influence of His Spirit : the word is used analogously by pagan writers of the spokesman for pagan gods.

(52) "And not on behalf of the nation only" : not only to save from destruction that political entity known as the Jewish nation (which ceased temporarily to be an organism in A.D. 70, and has never so far been reborn as a nation) : "but in order that He should gather into one the children of God also *who had been scattered abroad* (τὰ διεσκορπισμένα)." It is difficult to believe that this clause refers to the Gentile Church which consists of individuals chosen out of the Gentile nations. Could these individuals be called "the children of God which had been scattered abroad" ? When were they scattered ? The natural allusion seems to be to the Ten Tribes—the old Northern kingdom, the "Israel" of the days of the kings and of the Prophets before "Israel" was lost among the nations. "The children of God who had been scattered abroad" should refer to the Ten Tribes who, as all the Prophets had foretold, should be "scattered" by God to the corners of the earth, but should in the latter days be 'gathered together into one People again with Judah' : a union not, however, to come about till the Kingdom should be ready to be set up on earth : but a union which will usher in the millennial Age.

The mystery of Israel the Covenant People of God (not to be confounded with the Jews who are only a part of them) is vastly deeper, and their destiny vastly greater, than is dreamt of by the present Gentile Church, or by the Jews, or by those lost Tribes themselves living to-day as Gentiles unconscious of their origin or destiny.

A.D. 29.
Mch. 7 / Adar 26 } Mon.

(53) "From that day, therefore, they formed their resolution to kill Him." This was immediately after the raising of Lazarus: so, as we may suppose, they met on Monday, March 7. (The year being 29 A.D.)

(54) It was probably on this same day (Monday, March 7) that Jesus left Bethany: and, to avoid the Jews, "went away into the country near to the wilderness, to a city called Ephraim." This city Ephraim is the Ephrain of 2 Chron. xiii. 19 = the Ophrah of Joshua xviii. 23: it had repeatedly changed hands, between Benjamin and Ephraim, in the old wars. At the time of our Lord it belonged to Judæa, not to Samaria: for it was south of, but close to, the boundary of Samaria as given by Josephus (*War*, 4, ix. 9). It is the modern *et Ṭaiyibeh*, fourteen miles north of Bethany and thirteen miles north-north-east of Jerusalem. We need not suppose that He stayed in the actual city where He scarcely could have remained hidden, but rather in the district belonging to the city, for every city had its own rural district.

The "wilderness" of verse 54 is the barren mountain land along the west of the Jordan valley (Josephus, *War*, 4, viii. 2).

Here our Lord took refuge with His disciples, remaining in seclusion from Monday evening, March 7, when He (hypothetically) arrived, until Saturday evening, March 12. He would be secure even if the Sanhedrin heard of His whereabouts: for, being on the border of Samaria, He could at any moment cross the frontier and His enemies would hesitate to follow. But in view of the order sent out by the Sanhedrists to the public that they should help them in finding His whereabouts (57), we cannot date the raising of Lazarus and subsequent events to a later week than that beginning with Sunday, March 6.

John's account here leaves our Lord at Ephraim,

and when next it brings Him on the scene He is at Bethany again (xii. 1). What of the interval ?

At this point we must turn from John for a moment to follow our Lord's movements on His last journey, from Ephraim to Bethany and Jerusalem. The particulars of this journey will be found in Luke's account: viz. Luke xvii. 11 to xix. 28: Matthew dovetails into it at Matt. xix. 3; and Mark at Mark x. 2.

He seems to have left Ephraim city on Sunday morning, March 13, to go up to Jerusalem for the last time—not, however, by the direct route: for all the Synoptists bring Him to Jerusalem, on this His last visit, *by way of Jericho.* Luke seems further to imply (xvii. 11) that (on leaving Ephraim) He went north first, and then turned east "between Samaria and Galilee," *i.e.* along their common frontier. He would thus cross Jordan into Peræa by the ferry south of Scythopolis: then pass down Peræa (east of Jordan) to the bridge opposite Jericho: and thence ascend to the neighbourhood of Jerusalem, arriving at "Bethany six days before the Passover" (John xii. 1), viz. on Saturday, March 19. Thus, in consequence of the hostility of the Jews in Judæa, and of Herod (Luke xiii. 31) in Galilee and Peræa, during this the close of His ministry, He kept constantly changing the jurisdiction He was under.

A.D. 29.
Mch. 13 / Nisan 3 } Sun.

This last journey from Ephraim to the neighbourhood of Bethany seems to have covered six days: thus—

Sunday, March 13.—Ephraim to, say, Nâblûs (Shechem) in Samaria: on the western pilgrim road. This begins the journey named in Luke xvii. 11.*

A.D. 29.

Monday, March 14.—Nâblûs to Jenîn (on the border of Samaria and Galilee: and on the western pilgrim road. It was at Jenîn (according to local tradition) that He healed the ten lepers. This is Luke xvii. 12–19.

Tuesday, March 15.—Jenîn to, say, Pella in Peræa, on

* Luke xvii. 1–10 I suggest belongs to the five days spent at Ephraim (et Ṭaiyibeh) whence there is an open view of the Dead Sea (verse 6).

the eastern pilgrim road. Crossing the Jordan near Scythopolis, He passed into Herod's jurisdiction. To this day may belong Luke xvii. 20–xviii. 8.

Wednesday, March 16.—Pella to, say, Succoth (still in Peræa, Herod's jurisdiction). He is following the eastern pilgrim road. To this day may belong Luke xviii. 9–17 : Matt. xix. 3–15½ : Mark x. 2–16.

Thursday, March 17.—Succoth to Jericho (by the bridge into Judæa). To this day belong Luke xviii. 18–xix. 7 : Matt. xix. 15½–xx. 28 : Mark x. 17–46½. Luke's blind man was healed whilst Jesus *was drawing near to Jericho* this evening.

Friday, March 18.—Jericho to (perhaps) Bethphage (close to Bethany). To this day belong Luke xix. 8–28 : Matt. xx. 29–34 : Mark x. 46½–52. Mark's blind man Bartimæus was healed as Jesus *was journeying-out from Jericho* this morning. Matthew has perhaps lumped the two cases together, not specifying entry or exit, but merely stating of both cases "hearing that Jesus is passing by."

On this Friday evening, March 18, He must have arrived at some point *close to* Bethany : for He did not enter Bethany till Saturday, March 19, "six days before the Passover" (John xii. 1), and the following day was Palm Sunday. But, as He entered Bethany on the *Saturday*, He must have halted on Friday evening at some point within a Sabbath day's journey of Bethany, *i.e.* under five στάδια = 3000 Greek feet = 2000 cubits, or about 1000 yards. His halting-place for the Friday night was thus not improbably Bethphage, which was half a mile from Bethany and on the old road from Jericho. Bethphage, according to local tradition, was the spot He had halted at outside of Bethany, chapter xi. 30, when He came to raise Lazarus.

Also at Bethphage lived some disciple of His (Matt. xxi. 3 : Mark xi. 2–6 : Luke xix. 30–34), at whose house He may have wished to lodge this Friday, and with whom He seems to have made arrangements about the ass's colt, which He would need on the Sunday following.

(55) After this digression from p. 273, we here return to John's account (xi. 55) of what was happening at Jerusalem. The day will be Thursday, March 17, A.D. 29. Nisan 7. "The Passover of the Jews * was nigh, and there went up to Jerusalem out of the country many before the Passover, to purify themselves": *e.g.* all who when under a Nazirite vow had been Levitically defiled by a corpse would have to be at Jerusalem seven days before a festival so as to be able to take part in it: as in Acts xxi. 23, 27, where we have an instance of the working of Num. vi. 9, 10.

Mch. 17 / Nisan 7 } Thurs.

Among those who came up on this occasion to purify themselves would be a remarkable group, consisting of the ten lepers of Luke xvii. 12–19, who had been healed at Jenîn. We have supposed that cure to have been effected on Monday evening, March 14: these lepers, following His order to show themselves to the priests at Jerusalem, would reach Jerusalem on Thursday, March 17, at noon, according to the common stages of the road from Jenîn to Jerusalem. Presenting themselves to the priests † on duty in the Temple on this Thursday, they would report how they had been healed by Jesus and that they had met Him at Jenîn on Monday evening *coming away* (see His route, p. 273) from the direction of Jerusalem: hence the anxiety expressed (John xi. 46) in the Temple that perhaps He was not meaning to come up on the occasion of the Passover. There must have been received some positive account (such as the lepers would have given of the direction they found Him travelling in) to induce the suspicion that He was purposing to change His life-long habit, and to omit coming up to Jerusalem "for the festival-day" (εἰς τὴν ἑορτήν).

(57) "And the chief-priests and the Pharisees had given commands that 'if any one know where He is' he should tell, so that they may take Him." No doubt these

* This phrase has been already explained at p. 64.

† Luke xvii. 14. Their formal cleansing by the priest (Lev. xiv. 1–11) would require eight days, *i.e.* until Thursday, March 24 inclusive. They would therefore be in time to eat the Passover this year.

orders had been issued (see the pluperfect δεδώκεισαν) by the chief-priests and the Pharisees immediately after the Council of verses 47–53 held some ten days ago. Jesus and His disciples would have left Bethany (54) before that Council had ended.

§ XVIII

JOHN XII. 1–19

The supper at Bethany. Palm Sunday.

(1) " JESUS, therefore, six days before the Passover * came to Bethany." "*The Passover*" is not "the Jews' passover" of xi. 55, but the Passover eaten by our Lord and the Twelve. Such, too, is the view which the Synoptists take of this Passover. The Paschal lamb eaten by our Lord and the Twelve was killed (by Peter and John) on Thursday afternoon, March 24, which this year was (on the Jewish ecclesiastical calendar) Nisan 14—the day commanded by the Law (Exod. xii. 6): it was eaten by them that same night after sunset (as Exod. xii. 8): and the morrow, viz. Nisan 15, would for them have been the Legal "festival-day" (ἡ ἑορτή), but for the archetypal Passover (the Sacrifice of our Lord Himself) that took place that day, Good Friday.

A.D. 29.
Mch. 19 / Nisan 9 — Sat.

The Jews, however, this year postponed the "festival-day" to the Saturday, and the Passover supper to the Friday evening. Thus, in this year A.D. 29, whereas our Lord and the Twelve killed and ate the Passover on the correct Legal day, the afternoon and evening of Thursday, Nisan 14 (March 24); the nation had postponed the killing and eating of their Paschal lambs to the afternoon and evening of Friday, Nisan 15 (March 25), so that the

* It may incidentally be mentioned here that John habitually uses the term τὸ Πάσχα to cover the whole octave of the Azyms or Unleavened Bread, viz. from Nisan 14 to Nisan 21 inclusive, beginning with the day on which the Paschal lambs were killed. This was the common usage of the term. See p. 380.

"festival-day" fell for them on the Sabbath (Saturday, March 26, Nisan 16). See at xiii. 1, pp. 298–302.

"Six days before the Passover" is Saturday, March 19 (A.D. 29), seeing that the Passover was Thursday, March 24; for the ancients, whether Greeks, Romans, or Jews, counted both terms. The phrasing used here by John, "πρὸ ἓξ ἡμερῶν τοῦ Πάσχα," is the equivalent of the Roman form, "ante diem VI.," *e.g.* Id. or Kal.

A.D. 29. Mch. 19 / Nisan 9 — Sat.

"Came to Bethany." Therefore, it being Saturday, He must have passed Friday night somewhere within *a Sabbath-day's journey* (2000 cubits or 1000 yards) of Bethany. We have supposed the halting-place to be Bethphage (see at xi. 54).

(2) "Where Lazarus was . . . whom He raised from the dead. Therefore there they made," etc. The "therefore" (which A.V. omits) points to the gratitude for Lazarus's restoration, which that household now showed by entertaining Him at supper. The supper was given on the Saturday evening. 'It was the custom to provide a more liberal supper at the *going out* of the Sabbath than at any other time,' as J. Lightfoot shows from Maimonides.

The supper was given (Matt. xxvi. 6–13: Mark xiv. 3–9) in the house of "Simon the leper," *i.e.* the *one time* leper, who had been cured by Jesus: but he continued to be thus nicknamed as against all other Simons: he was, not improbably, the leper of Matt. viii. 2: Mark i. 40: Luke v. 12. He seems to be the same as Simon the Pharisee of Luke vii. 37–50: and is conjectured to have been the husband of Martha, and to have died before the time of this supper of John xii. (see note on Mary Magdalene at end of book, pp. 441–445).

Martha serves, as being the hostess: she had also been hostess in this same house in Luke x. 38–42, three months ago. Lazarus, of course, ate with the guests: the house was not his, but his sister Martha's, though still known as "the house of Simon the leper" (her late husband). Her sister Mary Magdalene is now living with her and was with her last December (Luke x. 38–42).

(3) "Mary, therefore, took a pound of ointment," etc. This Mary is Mary Magdalene, sister of Martha and of Lazarus. This is the second time she anoints our Lord in this house: the first time having been nine months ago (Luke vii. 37), when she was not living here with her sister, but *had the right of entry to the house* (pp. 441, 442).

The anointing which John here relates is the same as that related by Matt. xxvi. 6–13: Mark xiv. 4–9. John here, as always, observes chronological accuracy: Matthew and Mark have displaced the supper chronologically, because they only relate it as being the critical occasion which determined Judas Iscariot to the sale of his Master; a sale of which the details were finally settled by the chief priests, during their meeting at the Highpriest's house on Wednesday, March 23. That Wednesday is the "two days" before "the Passover" of Matt. xxvi. 2–5 and of Mark xiv. 1–2, and see Luke xxii. 1–6:—"two days before" being one of their ways of expressing our "the day before."

"*A pound.*" The Greek word λίτρα, taken at its strict Greek value, was equal to eight ounces avdp., but if taken according to its then common usage to represent a Roman *libra*, was equal to twelve ounces avdp.

(4) "One of His disciples." From Matt. xxvi. 8 it appears that others of His disciples agreed with Judas: from Mark xiv. 4 one rather gathers that these other objectors were not of the Twelve.

(5) "Three hundred *pence*," or rather *denarii.* The sum is equal to about £10 if the denarius be valued, as is commonly done, at about eightpence, according to the old ratio of gold to silver, which was 1 to 16. But if we have regard to the fact that one denarius was the wage of a labourer's full day's work (Matt. xx. 2), which to-day must be put at 3*s.* [pre-War rate] at lowest, the value of three hundred denarii may be estimated at £45 of our money.

(6) "Bare what was put therein": and so could pilfer from it unknown. The verb "bare" is in the imperfect tense, showing that he habitually carried it.

(7) The correct reading of this verse seems to be, "suffer her to keep it (ἵνα τηρήσῃ, *i.e.* to have kept it) unto the day of My preparation-for-burial." 'Look upon her, reckon her, as having kept this ointment against the day of My preparation-for-burial, and then you will not think it waste. She has been so keeping it, and has only forestalled the day of My preparation-for-burial by a few days. She has anointed Me with it to-day as knowing she soon must lose Me, for that My end draws near.' The Magdalene knew He was near the end, and in her grief anointed Him as one virtually dead. This is the plain meaning of Matthew's "for in that she poured this ointment on My body, she did it with a view to preparing Me for burial." So, too, of Mark's "she is come beforehand to anoint (lit. she has anticipated the anointing of) My body unto My preparation-for-burial." The word ἐνταφιάζω or ἐνταφιασμός, rendered "burial" or "burying" in A.V. of Matthew, Mark and John, is more accurately "preparation-for-burying," as Westcott on verse 7 of John xii., and as R.V. in Matthew xxvi. 12: although in Mark xiv. 8 and John xii. 7 the R.V. reverts to "burying."

(9) "The common people (ὁ ὄχλος πολὺς) from among (εκ) the Jews," as against their hierarchy of verse 10, "learnt that He was there," *i.e.* in Bethany. "And they came, not only because of Jesus, but that also they may see Lazarus whom He raised from the dead."

"They came": Those of them that came from Jerusalem must have come after sunset: for, the day being Saturday, none might travel more than a Sabbath-day's journey before sunset, viz. half a mile: whereas Bethany was over 1½ miles from Jerusalem (John xi. 18). Of course, immediately the sun set, they were free, like the Moslems to-day at sunset of each day in Ramadan.

(10) "But the chief-priests took counsel to put Lazarus also [as well as Jesus] to death, seeing that because of him many of the Jews were withdrawing and believing into Jesus."

From these notices (9, 10) about Lazarus, it appears

that Lazarus had been absent ever since he was raised from the dead thirteen days ago—no doubt in seclusion with our Lord and others of His disciples at Ephraim, and afterwards with Him on the six days' circuit toward Jerusalem.

(12) "On the next day," viz. Sunday, March 20, Nisan 10. John reckons Days from midnight to midnight, like the Romans, and days as the twelve daylight hours like every one then or now. "The common people (ὁ ὄχλος πολὺς) that were come for the festival-day," *i.e.* who had come from the provinces of Galilee and Peræa: for as John says (xi. 55), "many came up from the country beforehand." This ὄχλος πολὺς from the provinces (always friendly to Him) is to be distinguished from the ὄχλος πολὺς of "Jews" of verse 9.

A.D. 29.
Mch. 20 / Nisan 10 } Sun.

The great mass of the people from the provinces would not normally have arrived at the city yet, for it is only Sunday, and the nation will not be eating the Passover till the latter part of the week: but no doubt numbers had gathered to accompany Him whilst He was following the eastern pilgrim-route through Peræa.

This ὄχλος πολὺς from the provinces, hearing on the Sunday morning that "Jesus is on His way to Jerusalem," determined to give Him a triumphal entry. He had not kept His intention secret: He had meant all along to ride in as King on Sunday, but to ride in in His own way.

(13) "Took the branches of the palm-trees and went-out [of Jerusalem] to meet Him. And they kept crying, 'Hosanna, blessed is He that cometh in the Lord's name, even the King of Israel.'" "Hosanna," meaning *save* (the affix *na* expressing entreaty), is exactly our "God save (the king)."

Mch. 20 / Nisan 10 } Sun.

This entry into the city was that of a King whose kingship lay in His moral and spiritual excellence, and was not dependent on the acclamations or assent of His subjects: King by Divine right. The entry was not suggested to Him by the enthusiasm of His disciples or by that of the crowd. It was an act of His own initiative: and before to-day (Sunday) He had already made His preparations about the ass's colt with its owner—probably on Friday evening or yesterday (Saturday) before leaving Bethphage. He, of course, knew what the crowd would do, and how they were going to acclaim Him King. Nor would He stop them to-day: but by riding on an ass, He would teach them that His Kingship did not lie in pomp, and that He had no mind to claim as yet a visible Kingdom. He set out accompanied by His disciples: and He is met by a crowd from the city (the crowd of John xii. 12, 18) who join in.

This entry into Jerusalem to the acclamation of the enthusiastic mob has been often strangely regarded as the triumphal entry to which Psalmists and Prophets had looked forward. True the crowd which escorted Him thought they were making of it a triumphal procession and entry: and thought this was the Messianic occasion to which the triumphal Psalm cxviii. must refer; and thought He was about to set up His visible Kingdom.

It was no more the triumphal entry referred to in Psalm cxviii. than was His first advent in humility and obscurity and in the cattle stable the advent in triumph and glory that we still await.

As a foil to the enthusiasm of the crowd, our Lord had mounted on an ass's colt: showing He is not entering as the nation's King to-day to take the Kingdom of the world, for the nation has not yet accepted Him. The Sanhedrin, who were at this time the Representatives of the Covenant People, have rejected Him, and they will on Friday carry the nation with them.

The Prophets had foretold His first Coming in humility, ending in His rejection and Crucifixion, though that first Coming looms so small in proportion to the glorious second Coming, that the Scribes, dwelling only on the latter, had neglected to notice the details of the former. And similarly, though there are many prophecies of His yet future manifestation of Himself in power against His enemies, *e.g.* Isa. lxii. 11, as the nation's King, there was one unnoticed prophecy in Zech. ix. 9, of how He would make His entry into His city at His first Coming—an entry in lowliness and humility, for these are the qualities His People must first learn from their King before they are fit for the millennial empire.

(14) " And Jesus." Better " But Jesus." There is a contrast between the crude exultation with which the crowd viewed the entry, and the corrective in our Lord's action.

(15) It is our Lord Himself (Matt. xxi. 4, 5 *) interpreting Zechariah (ix. 9) who, by laying stress on His meekness and lowliness in riding on a young *ass*, makes plain the significance of this His entry to Jerusalem. The horse and mule (1 Kings i. 38) were noble : the ass was despised.

As for the Synoptists' account of this entry : Mark (xi.) and Luke (xix.) are as plain as John that He sat only on the ass's *colt*, and make no mention of the she ass its mother. Matthew (xxi.) is equally plain when correctly translated : for his verse 7 is, " brought the ass (fem.) and the colt (masc.) and put on them their garments, and He sat on them," *i.e.* on the *garments*, and apparently on those only which were on the colt, not on the garments which were on the she ass. Perhaps the disciples did not know which He was going to ride, and so put their garments on both.

As for Matthew's verse 5, which has caused needless difficulty, the *Hebrew* of Zechariah ix. 9 is, " riding upon an ass (masc.), even upon a young ass, a son of she asses " : the *Greek* of Zechariah ix. 9 has " riding upon a beast-of-burden, even a young colt." The Greek of Matthew has " riding upon an ass (the word is indifferently masc. or fem.) even upon a colt, the son of a beast-of-burden." It will be seen that the obscurity is due to rendering by *and* instead of by *even*. The ו of Hebrew and the καὶ of

* Matt. xxi. 4. The perfect tense (τοῦτο δὲ γέγονεν), " this has come to pass," shows that the words are our Lord's comment and not a comment by Matthew. Similarly in Matt. i. 22, τοῦτο δὲ ὅλον γέγονεν, " all this has come to pass," the perfect γέγονεν, shows the words to be Gabriel's and not a comment by Matthew. Again in Matt. xxvi. 56, τοῦτο δὲ ὅλον γέγονεν, " all this has come to pass," the words are obviously our Lord's comment and not Matthew's. Had these comments been Matthew's the second aorist, ἐγένετο, would have been used and not γέγονε, as in John xix. 36, ἐγένετο γὰρ ταῦτα ἵνα ἡ γραφὴ πληρωθῇ.

Greek mean either *and* or *even* (explanatory) equally well.

It is not known by what gate He entered the city on this occasion: certainly not by the Golden Gate which was in the middle of the east wall; for it was not open to the public; and He certainly did not ride into the Temple courts, on to which the Golden Gate opened: He clearly entered the city first and afterwards the Temple (Matt. xxi. 10–12). So He entered either by the Sheep Gate in the north-east, or by the Fountain Gate in the south-east: of these the latter is much the more probable; for by it He would ascend into the original Sion, the old city of David; and thence turning eastward would pass along the causeway which crossed the Central Valley and so into the Temple courts by the main west gate of the Temple area.

The shouts of the multitude are given by Matthew as "Hosanna to the Son of David: Blessed is He that cometh in the name of the Lord: Hosanna in the highest (heaven)," from Ps. cxviii.

Mark has "Hosanna: Blessed is He that cometh in the name of the Lord: Blessed is the coming Kingdom of our father David: Hosanna in the highest (heaven)."

Luke has "Blessed is the King that cometh in the name of the Lord: peace in Heaven, and glory in the highest (heaven)": cf. Luke ii. 14.

John has "Hosanna: Blessed is He that cometh in the name of the Lord, even the King of Israel."

Mark thus most plainly brings out the expectation that the visible Kingdom of Messiah was about to be set up.

(16) It was not till after our Lord's Ascension and that out-pouring of the Holy Spirit, which was the sign of His invisible Triumph (see on vii. 39), that the disciples understood the symbolical meaning of this riding on the ass's colt, or understood how Zechariah's prophecy was to be read: although He had *at the time* called their attention to this prophecy (see Matt. xxi. 4, γέγονε). A very similar position is seen at Luke xviii. 31–34, where, though He quoted to them the Prophets, they failed to grasp the application. Later, they perceived that in acclaiming

Him as King they had been themselves accomplishing a prophecy without thinking of it.

(17) "Therefore" as impelled by the general enthusiasm "the crowd kept bearing witness" to Him. This is the third crowd named, viz. the crowd who had been present at the raising of Lazarus a fortnight ago, and were mainly from Peræa; they were to-day recounting that miracle to the other crowd (verse 12) in Jerusalem, who had come up from the provinces, *e.g.* of Galilee, Peræa, Trachonitis, Syria, etc.

(18) And the hearing this miracle related to them was an additional reason why the crowd of verse 12 went out to meet Him. The place of meeting seems to have been on the crest of the Mount of Olives, where the west descent begins toward the Kedron and Jerusalem (Luke xix. 37).

(19) "The Pharisees therefore spake to themselves, 'Behold, how ye avail nothing: lo, the world is gone off after him.'" In other words: 'There must be no delay in carrying out our decision of a fortnight ago (xi. 47–53) to put him to death as soon as we can safely lay hands on him.' And to-day, Sunday, they make their bargain with Judas Iscariot as told in Matt. xxvi. 14: Mark xiv. 10.

§ XIX

JOHN XII. 20–50

A deputation of Greeks. His last words in the Temple.

BETWEEN verses 19 and 20 is an interval of two clear days, of which the incidents are given by the Synoptists.

During these four days, Sunday, March 20, to Wednesday, March 23, our Lord acts with absolute and supreme authority in the Temple, meeting with no open opposition. On Sunday He cleansed the Temple and had to repeat the operation on Monday. He silenced (1) the chief-priests and elders: (2) the Herodians: (3) the Sadducees: (4) the Pharisees: and taught the people Himself as the supreme Teacher, denouncing the Scribes and Pharisees. On Wednesday, March 23, He left the Temple, as appears from the Synoptists.

This section of John (xii. 20–50) seems to belong to His last appearance in the Temple (see verse 36): and that departure, being His final departure, should therefore be that of Matt. xxiv. 1: Mark xiii. 1: Luke xxi. 5: after which He confined Himself to His disciples, and on the Mount of Olives delivered the prophecy on the doom of the city and on the end of this Age now present (Matt. xxiv. 3–xxv. 46: Mark xiii. 3–37: Luke xxi. 7–36).

(20–33) The deputation of Greeks. Their interview with Him.

(20) "Certain Greeks." These are neither Jews nor pagans: but belong to that class of foreigner known by the technical term "devout" or "who feared God" (constantly in the Acts, etc.): they had come "to worship on the festival-day" (ἐν τῇ ἑορτῇ, *die festo*), *i.e.* the natural day following the paschal supper. This class worshipped in Temple and synagogue,

A.D. 29. Mch. 23 Nisan 13 } Wed.

and observed certain of the Mosaic precepts, without, however, submitting to the initiatory rite of Judaism. They could not, of course, eat the Passover.

(20) These "Greeks" have certainly not come to see Jesus merely to satisfy a curiosity: for that, they would not have applied to Philip: also they might have seen our Lord freely in the Court of the Gentiles. Rather they seem to be a formal deputation, hence their ceremonious introduction of themselves (21), "Sir, we wish to see Jesus." Philip, again, applies with ceremony to one of the four who form the inner circle round our Lord. The four are Peter, James, John, Andrew—the first four to be called: they appear again as an inner circle later on this same day (Mark xiii. 3), as He delivers His eschatological prophecy. (22) The formality with which the introduction is made is marked also in the language, "Philip cometh and telleth Andrew: Andrew cometh, and Philip, and they tell Jesus."

As to who exactly these "Greeks" were, probably they are right who regard them as the embassy sent to Jesus by Abgarus, king of Edessa. Edessa (the modern Urfa) is the traditional "Ur of the Casdim" (Gen. xi. 31) in Mesopotamia. Eusebius (*Hist. Eccl.*, i. 13) gives at great length the history of the conversion of Abgarus, the king of Edessa: he also gives the translation (A) of a Syriac letter which was sent by that king to Christ in which he offers Him a refuge in his city of Edessa from the malice of the Jews; and (B) of the letter which Christ sent him in return, which letters Eusebius says he himself took from the archives of Edessa and had them translated out of the Syriac in which they were written. 'And not only,' he says, 'were the letters preserved in the archives; but also in the public registers at Edessa which embrace the times of Abgarus these details respecting him are preserved down to this day' (*i.e.* 325 A.D.). 'After Christ's Ascension' (he continues), 'Thaddeus (one of the seventy, not Thaddeus of the Twelve) was sent by Thomas to Edessa to King Abgarus, as Christ had promised by letter to Abgarus: and the king and the city of Edessa were thus converted':

"And this" (he adds) "was in the 340th year,"* *i.e.* of the Seleucid era: viz. the year from Oct. 1, A.D. 28 to Sept. 30, A.D. 29.

The term "Greeks" (Ἕλληνες) does not require them to be true Greeks by birth: for the word is frequently used in N.T. as synonymous with Gentiles, *i.e.* non-Jews: *e.g.* Rom. i. 16: ii. 9: x. 12: 1 Cor. xii. 13: Gal. iii. 28.

It is not without significance that Philip and Andrew are the only two of the Twelve who have Greek names. Were these two at first the recognized channels for communication with the foreigner as here?

However the above may be, our Lord was probably in the Treasury (by the Court of the Women) when the news of the deputation was brought to Him—the last incident perhaps having been that of the widow's mite (Luke xxi. 1–4).

The Greeks could not enter beyond the Court of the Gentiles: we may, therefore, suppose that on receiving their application our Lord went out into the Court of the Gentiles, and there had them presented to Him by Andrew and Philip.

(23–33) This section gives His interview with the Greeks—but greatly abridged by John. As our Lord, of course, spoke to be understood by them, it is evident from His language that these Greeks are not strangers to the Jewish hope of the Messiah: and that they know the Messiah, as all Jews for the past year knew him, by the title of The Son of Man: nor yet are they strangers to our Lord's claim to be that Messiah. *And they know Him to be the Messiah* Our Lord's words to them suit well with the assumption of some such offer by these Greeks of a refuge and escape as that contained in Abgarus's letter.

(23–26) He speaks to the deputation and explains to them that He of whom they had heard so great things was near His hour of glory. But what glory? The pomp of earthly courts? No: a glory the road to which lay through death—the glory of Resurrection, Ascension, and an invisible kingdom in a visible Church (for the present). (24) As, on nature's plane, the grain of wheat must be

* For this the correct reading see Pagi on Baronius, *Annal.* xli. 18.

buried and die (undergo seed change) if it is to bring forth fruit: so is it with all who follow Him who is the Seed of the new Creation. Death is the door to Life. (25) There is a love of life (ψυχὴ, the lower, sensuous, psychic life), which operates at the cost of all that makes life worth having: and there is a generous surrender of this same psychic life, which surrender is the condition on which depends the preservation of the germ of true and lasting Life (ζωή). With this thought all philosophy is familiar.

(26) This is a law of Life: and "If any one serve *Me* (emphatic), it is for him to follow Me," *i.e.* in this law of Life at the cost of life: "and where I am" (for even then He Lived eternally in a superhuman state), "there shall also My servant be"—his, too, shall Life be: "if any one serve Me, him will The Father honour" (see x. 17, 18).

To these Greeks the term "The Father" would mean God, the universal Father of all. To our Lord's mind and to any who might have insight, the term means not only that but also the full mystery of the Trinity—the eternal Father of the eternal Son who is speaking. We must never imagine that the Synoptists give us a representation of the theology of the early Church: that was not the aim the editors of those gospels had in view. Of that theology and dogmatic development we shall find glimpses, incidentally preserved, in the epistles: some of which at any rate antedate those gospels. But nowhere is the implicit Faith of the early Church made so explicit as in the gospel of John the Theologian and contemplative.

(27) "Now is My soul troubled." To say that the "trouble" of His soul here, or the Agony in Gethsemane, was caused by the vivid picture of the personal sufferings and shame to be inflicted upon Him by human hands in the near future is nonsense, and is as insulting to our Lord as is the patronizing sympathy with which so many have reviewed Him. The contemplation of those sufferings would have been nothing to Him the perfect Man, indeed would have been waste of time and vitality to any philosophic mind. Many a mere man would be beyond the touch of "trouble" from such external agencies: philosophers

and martyrs by the thousand have risen superior to pain and insult as they wrapped themselves in the contemplation of God, or of any other ideal for which they gloried to suffer torture and death. What could the uttermost of physical and psychical suffering have been to Him in comparison with the sight and knowledge of *sin* around Him ?

The " trouble " here, and the Agony in Gethsemane, and the dereliction on the Cross, are the same at bottom in varying intensity. None of those who heard Him here or who watched Him had the slightest true conception of what He meant. We must always except the sinless Mother. His agony is a mystery, as the Catholic Church knows ; a mystery into which none but some rare contemplative spirits have had the privilege to enter. It had nothing to do with any sufferings that met the eye. It lay in the consciousness of all the sins of all the world, and of the consequent abandonment by God, which in a sacramental reality were laid upon Him the Man as upon our scapegoat.

(27) " And what am I to say ? Father, save Me from this hour ? " (*i.e.* of suffering which has begun and is soon to culminate). " But for this object I came to this hour," *i.e.* No. For the very object of His Incarnation, the reason of this His Coming into the world and of His continuance to this hour was to meet this Suffering.

The words do not imply that He was in any hesitation Himself ; but they are spoken for the sake of the Greeks, to explain to them how He views His coming death, that He faces it voluntarily and that it was one of the purposes of His Incarnation.

(28) " Father, glorify Thy Name." This is the perfect prayer : it embraces the height of the passive virtues—self-renunciation, and the height of the active virtues—craving for His glory with every energy. But it has its theological meaning as well, which must have been present to our Lord's mind : ' Glorify Thy Name, glorify Thy Name as Father by manifesting Me as the eternal Son, that those here may believe in Me and so in Thee.'

" There came, therefore, a Voice out of heaven." " A Voice out of heaven " : not a mere thunderclap, although to most present it sounded as that and no more : to others it sounded as though articulate, but not intelligible. To those, however, for whom it was meant (here, the " Greeks "), the thunder-voice was articulate and intelligible, but to them alone.

So the Rabbinical tradition of the Voice of God speaking to Moses and others : its physical reverberation might be heard by many, but the Voice itself, *i.e.* its meaning, was known to those only for whom it was meant, *e.g.* Moses, the Prophets, etc.

So in Acts ix. 7, xxii. 9, Saul's companions heard the physical reverberation, but not so as to understand the Voice, for it was not meant for them.

" I glorified It before," viz. when at His Baptism the Voice pronounced His Sonship, so that John the Baptist might announce Jesus to the nation as the Messiah and The Son of God (cf. Matt. iii. 17 with John i. 31–34) : and again when at the Transfiguration the Voice announced His Sonship, so that Peter, James, and John might know that compared with Him Moses and Elijah were but servants.

" And I will again glorify It," *i.e.* now. For the Voice came now for the sake of the Greeks, as being the representatives of the non-Jewish nations ; and the Voice was distinctly heard by them and articulately, and the words understood by them.

(29) But by "the crowd " (ὁ ὄχλος) of Jewish nationality it was heard as mere sound, a portentous thunder roll, " they said ' it has thundered ' " : by others there it was felt to be articulate though they caught no sense, and by these it was ascribed to an angel talking with Him, " they said ' an angel has talked to him.' "

(30) " Jesus answered and said " : answered, that is, to the expressions of wonder of the Greeks at the Voice. Verse 29 (the effect on the Jews) is parenthetical.

Jesus is still talking to the *Greeks :* ' This Voice you have heard (and understood) was not sent for My sake as though I needed encouragement or enlightenment: it was sent wholly for your sakes, to help you Greeks toward Me.' And for that reason it was only the Greeks who were meant to understand it: it was not meant for the Jews, and therefore to them was unintelligible.

(31) "Now there is judgment on this world." The hour was approaching when judgment was to be passed upon this world, the world (ὁ κόσμος) viewed in its acme, man the microcosm; but man as alienated by sin from God and under subjection to the devil.

"Now shall the ruler of this world be cast out." Man had not developed on the lines that his Creator had laid out: his ideals had been warped aside: moral disease was making for ruin: his Creator was come to head back the ruin that awaited His world and give it a fresh start: and He began by reversing men's ideals.

(32) "And I, if I be lifted up, will draw all men to Myself." Men would crucify Him their Creator, but from the Cross He would win the whole human race, non-Jews as well as Jews. The Cross and its attendant disgrace marks, by its "lifting up," * a severance from all worldly ideals and release from all earthly allurements.

Here ends His talk with the Greeks. They withdraw here, having received His gracious promise with regard to non-Jew as well as Jew.

(34–36) The effect on the Jewish crowd.

(34) But "the crowd" (*i.e.* of Jewish nationality) on hearing Him talk of being "lifted up from out the earth" were amazed. He had meant He was to be crucified. Though "the crowd" misunderstood Him, the Sanhedrists

* The verb (ὑψοῦν) here used for to "lift up," whether in its active or passive mood, is used only five times in John's writings, and every time in the sense of *lift up on a cross*: viz.—

iii. 14, "As Moses *lifted up* the serpent in the wilderness."
iii. 14, "So must The Son of Man be *lifted up*."
viii. 28, "When ye have *lifted up* The Son of Man."
xii. 32, "And I, if I be *lifted up*, will draw all men to Myself."
xii. 34, "Thou sayest, 'The Son of Man must be *lifted up*'": which is an exact repetition of His words to Nicodemus in iii. 14.

It is also remarkable that nowhere outside John's gospel does the word bear this meaning.

and Scribes who had determined on His death could not fail to catch His meaning—no more than they had failed at ii. 19. 'Lifted up from the earth?' say the crowd, 'but we have heard out of the sacred Books that the Messiah, when once He comes, abides with us for ever on earth, a glorious King. If you are the Messiah, why do you say that "The Son of Man must be lifted up" from the earth? Who is this Messiah? Who is this "The Son of Man"? This is not the Messiah we thought we were acclaiming when we went but last Sunday to bring you in in triumph.' They are using His own phrase, "The Son of Man," quite simply as being synonymous with "the Messiah." They are in difficulty, not about the title, but about the prospect of Messiah leaving the earth.

That "The Son of Man" had become, though recently, a recognized title of Messiah, see under i. 51 (pp. 46, 47).

The crowd are full of disappointment, and disillusioned. They probably objected also to the promise which seemed to put the Gentiles on a par with the Jews (cf. Acts xxii. 21, 22). The chief-priests and scribes have been busy among them during these last four days: and now the climax is reached. The crowd has turned against Him, as is clear from the rest of this chapter, and have sided with the chief-priests and His enemies.

(35) "Therefore" (such being the revulsion of their feelings) "Jesus said to them, 'For yet a little while is the Light with you,'" etc. It was for them to learn and Him to teach: He was the Light, and for but a little while was He still among them. When once the Sun should be set, what Light would there be? blind would be leading blind. As they had (36) still the Light among them, let them believe in the Light and trust Him for guidance: and so become sons of Light having Light in themselves.

But He spoke to dull ears. He departed from the Temple: their Sun was set. Thenceforth "He was hid from them," not again appearing to them.

This is the departure from the Temple of Matt. xxvi. 1: Mark xiii. 1: Luke xxi. 5: and the day is Wednesday, March 23.

Mch. 23 / Nisan 13 } Wed.

(37–41) Here follows John's comment on the national rejection of Him :—

(37) 'That when the crisis came to the nation, they were found wanting : that in spite of the many signs He had done among them they did not believe into Him—

(38) 'And so was fulfilled (ἵνα πληρωθῇ, see p. 308) Isaiah's prophecy (liii. 1), "Lord, who has believed our report," *i.e.* the report we brought them ? Isaiah identifying himself and all the Prophets with our Lord. "To whom has the arm of the Lord been revealed ?" *i.e.* who has discerned Him in the mighty works He did among them ?

'They did not believe because they could not : the failure was the result of long neglect to respond to their opportunities, a neglect spread over centuries, bewailed by every Prophet that had been sent to them, as he saw the canker at work around him and foresaw what the end inevitably must be.

(39) 'And the reason why they could not believe was because, as Isaiah (vi. 9, 10) had foretold, (40) "He has blinded their eyes and hardened their hearts." Divine warnings persistently and wilfully ignored could not pass by as though they had never been.'

(41) "These things said Isaiah *because*" (not "when") "he saw His glory" in vision (Isa. vi. 1–4), and heard the "Holy, Holy, Holy is the Lord of hosts," and saw (verse 5) how little were the nation in the mood or on the way to meet that searching sanctity.

"And he" (Isaiah) "talked of Him," *i.e.* the Lord of Hosts of that vision was no other than Jesus.

(42–end)

The timid believers among the Sanhedrin : and His last words to them, and to the nation.

(42) "Nevertheless" (*i.e.* in spite of the general unbelief just commented on), "even among the rulers many believed into Him (ἐπίστευσαν εἰς αὐτόν), but because of," etc.

There is no stronger phrase used anywhere to express

genuine belief in Christ than πιστεύειν εἰς, the phrase used here: so we must suppose their belief was genuine and of the kind that later on would grow to fruition: it only lacked *at present* (notice the imp. tense, ὡμολόγουν, "were not as yet confessing Him"), the robustness to face persecution.

(43) "For they loved men's glory rather than God's glory," *i.e.* loved man's purblind estimate of what constitutes glory rather than God's estimate. The commentators are hard on these timid ones. Are all Christians heroic? is there no smoking flax?

(44) "And Jesus (as He was leaving the Temple courts as told in verse 36) cried aloud." Here as elsewhere in John the word rendered "cried aloud" marks the decisive tone of authority which exacts attention.

These parting words are meant for the ears of the timid believers of verse 42, and also for the unbelieving nation—to awaken them to the gravity of the situation. Let them (44) remember, belief or non-belief into Him involves belief or non-belief into God who sent Him: for (45) whoso sees Him aright sees God who sent Him. (46) His Incarnation was the coming of Light among men: on the belief into Him depends the issue whether a man lives henceforth in Light or remains in the darkness He came to dispel.

(47) "And if any one hear My message and observe it not" (like those timid ones assenting to it, but not conforming with it) "I do not judge him" (*i.e.* at this His first Coming), "for I came not to judge the world but to save the world." He became Incarnate not as a judge, but He came as a helpless Child, that none might be afraid.

(48) "He who rejects Me and accepts not My teaching" (τὰ ῥήματά μου = teaching by Me or about Me) "has one that judges him: the word that I spoke, that will judge him in the last day." The judgment is automatic. How far was he responsible for that teaching having met with no response in him? It should have found a response in every heart.

(49) "For I spoke not from Myself" (ἐξ ἐμαυτοῦ, apart from The Father); "but The Father who sent Me,

Himself has given Me commandment what to say and what to speak": *i.e.* the message which was embodied in His words and in His life is from The Father: both its subject matter (τί εἴπω) and the form in which He delivered it (τί λαλήσω) have The Father's authority behind—and if The Father's, then the whole Godhead's.

(50) "And I know that His commandment is Life eternal": *i.e.* both the subject matter of the message and the form in which it was delivered is Life eternal to all who accept it. And what was it? A message concerning the Godhead, The Son's Incarnation, the sacramental system, faith, and ethics. "Therefore what things I speak, I speak them even as The Father has said them to Me." Let them therefore know that His message to them is as though The Father Himself were speaking to them.

They are His last words: and here closes His public active Ministry. He passes out from the Temple enclosure.

Here follows Matt. xxiv. 1: Mark xiii. 1: Luke xxi. 5: and then His long discourse on the Mount of Olives this evening (Matt. xxiv. 3–end of xxxv.: Mark xiii. 3–37: Luke xxi. 7–36).

§ XX

JOHN XIII. 1–30

Our Lord's last Passover. The Eucharist instituted.

(1) "AND before the festival-day of the Passover" (πρὸ δὲ τῆς ἑορτῆς τοῦ Πάσχα), or, as it should be rendered, "*on the eve of*," or "*on the day before* the festival-day of the Passover," *i.e.* on Thursday, Nisan 14 (as explained in the note to ii. 23).

A.D. 29.
Mch. 24 / Nisan 14 } **Thur.**

This was the eve of, or the day before, the correct festival-day, Nisan 15. The words πρὸ δὲ τῆς ἑορτῆς here do not mean simply and vaguely "*before* the festival-day" of the Passover, but "*on the day before*," etc. It is the Latin "pridie": and is otherwise expressed by πρὸ μιᾶς τῆς ἑορτῆς = "one day before the festival-day." Neither Greek nor Latin ever uses "two days before" for yesterday, though they use "after two days" for to-morrow. For the phrase πρὸ τῆς ἑορτῆς as meaning the eve of, or day before (a festival), cf. Philo, ii. 481, προεόρτιος, and the common ecclesiastical term, τὸ προεόρτιον. Cf. also προσάββατον, the day before Sabbath, as a name for Friday. See pp. 379, 380.

In A.D. 29 (the year of the Crucifixion), ἡ ἑορτὴ, "the festival-day" would have been (Friday) Nisan 15, for our Lord and the Twelve, for they had eaten the Paschal supper on Thursday, Nisan 14, as the Mosaic Law enjoined (Exod. xii. 8), *i.e.* on the eve of the 15th: and thus ἡ ἑορτὴ means Nisan 15 in xiii. 1 (above), and 29, "what we have need of for the festival-day" (εἰς τὴν ἑορτήν, viz. the morrow). But the event that happened on Good Friday changed the character of that day from a festival to the saddest day in man's history. For it became the day of the archetypal Passover, the Sacrifice of the true Paschal Lamb, the

God-Man; and from *its* day of the *'omer* Pentecost was this year reckoned.

But in this same year, A.D. 29, the festival-day for the nation and for every one except our Lord and the Twelve was Saturday, Nisan 16, for in this year the nation had postponed the celebration of the Passover by one day. Thus this year the nation killed and ate the Passover on the afternoon and night of Friday, Nisan 15, instead of on the afternoon and night of Thursday, Nisan 14: and the festival-day thus fell for them on Saturday, Nisan 16.

This postponement of the Passover seems to have been made by the Sanhedrin suddenly on Wednesday evening, March 23 (Nisan 13), at the meeting mentioned by Matthew (xxvi. 1–5) and Mark (xiv. 1, 2), when they decided that for fear of "an uproar among the people" our Lord's death "must not occur on the festival-day (μὴ ἐν τῇ ἑορτῇ)" (Friday, Nisan 15), the day fixed by Pilate for the public execution of Barabbas and the two brigands. Those words (μὴ ἐν τῇ ἑορτῇ) give the very substance and sum of the decision of that conference. They argued thus:—He must be put to death along with Pilate's malefactors—that is, the day after to-morrow: but that will be the festival-day, and the people (λαὸς)—the mass of pilgrims who arrived to-day—may prove dangerous, for they are madly in his favour: we will postpone the whole Feast one day, and use the interval in an energetic counter propaganda among them.

John, like the Synoptists, recognizes the Paschal supper eaten by our Lord and the Twelve on Thursday after sunset as the genuine Paschal supper: and Friday as its proper festival-day. The Synoptists take no notice of the Paschal supper eaten this year by the nation on Friday, Nisan 15, after sunset, and it is not until John xviii. 28 that we learn definitely that the nation had not eaten their Paschal supper on the same night as did our Lord. Once we have learnt this fact from John, we see how to read the Synoptists: *e.g.* Matt. xxvi. 2, "ye know (οἴδατε) that after two days (*i.e.* to-morrow) is the Passover and The Son of Man is delivered over to be crucified": this "ye know" shows that at the time He was speaking, viz. Wednesday afternoon, March 23, it was assumed by every one that the Passover was to be killed and eaten by every one on the following day, viz. Thursday, March 24, Nisan 14: and it is Matthew's three next verses which tell us how and when it was (viz. that very Wednesday) that the Sanhedrin determined to postpone the Passover: for the word τότε (verse 3) synchronizes this meeting of the Sanhedrin with our Lord's words in verse 2. He, and He alone, foreknew that they were about to postpone the Feast, and He knew their reason for doing so, viz. to push through His death first. But He had no intention of recognizing the postponement.

Again, Matt. xxvi. 17, "Where wilt Thou that we prepare for Thee to eat the Passover?" The question spoken on the Thursday will imply that *they saw a difficulty* in preparing and eating the Passover on a day when no one else was doing so, for in the interval between verse 5 (Wednesday) and verse 17 (Thursday) the Sanhedrin had proclaimed the postponement.

Again, Matt. xxvi. 18, "The Master (ὁ διδάσκαλος) saith, 'My time is nigh: at thy house I keep the Passover with My disciples'": the message will imply that *the circumstances had required* some special arrangements to have been *already* made by our Lord privately with one of His influential disciples in the city—perhaps Joseph of Arimathæa.

Again, Mark xiv. 12, "On the first day of the Azyms when they-used-to-sacrifice (ἔθυον, imp.) the Passover." The ἔθυον will refer to the Jews' normal custom of killing the Passover on the 14th of Nisan: it will not state that the Jews did so on this occasion. Mark, writing for Gentile Christians of Rome, saw no necessity to go into the details that made this year exceptional: for the only Paschal supper he means to notice is the one eaten by our Lord and the Twelve on the correct night, viz. after the sunset of Thursday, Nisan 14.

Again, Luke xxii. 7, "The day of the Azyms on which the Passover was-due (ἔδει) to be sacrificed": the ἔδει will refer to the Mosaic ordinance which named the afternoon of the 14th as the day for killing the Passover (Exod. xii. 6 : Lev. xxiii. 5 : Num. ix. 3) : it will not refer to what the Jews actually did that year : it seems rather to emphasize the fact that the day Peter and John prepared this Passover was the strict legal day—the 14th.

Again, Luke xxii. 15, "I have greatly desired to eat this Passover with you before I suffer." The *with you* will acquire a new force, as though in antithesis to with the rest of the nation. Unless He kept the Passover on the 14th He would not have opportunity to institute the Eucharist as a supplement to (or, in the case of Gentiles, a substitute for) the Paschal supper.

If the nation had this year eaten the Passover on the same night as did our Lord and the Twelve (viz. Thursday, Nisan 14, after sunset), we should have to believe that on the night of the arrest in Gethsemane the whole city was joyfully eating the Passover in every house and every open space of the city, and that all the details of the trial and the Crucifixion took place on the great national Holy Day of obligation—a day kept more religiously than even our own Easter Sunday. It would also follow that the Sanhedrin failed to carry out their decision (Matt. xxvi. 5 : Mark xiv. 2) not to put Him to death on the festival-day (μὴ ἐν τῇ ἑορτῇ), for had they eaten the Passover on Thursday night their festival-day would have been Friday : whereas it seems clear that the reason why they hurried the arrest and trial and death with such unseemly haste and postponed the Passover was to secure His death with the malefactors, and to get the whole thing over and done with before their Paschal celebration this evening (Friday) and their festival-day to-morrow (Saturday).

Although John does not name the Festival of *the Azyms*, i.e. *the Unleavened*, it is so closely associated to this Passover by the three Synoptists that it requires some explanation. *The Azyms* (τὰ ἄζυμα = the Unleavened), or *the Festival of the Azyms* (ἡ ἑορτὴ τῶν ἀζύμων), was strictly the seven days Nisan 15–21 inclusive (Lev. xxiii. 5, 6 : Num. xxviii. 17–25), beginning at sunset of

Nisan 14 and ending at sunset of Nisan 21. But as the Passover lambs had to be killed on the afternoon of the 14th, and not only eaten without leaven but also killed without there being any leaven in the houses (Exod. xxiii. 18), all leaven was removed from the houses on Nisan 14, viz. on the morning of the 14th. Thus the 14th came to be included in *the Festival of the Azyms*, which was thus extended to cover the eight days, Nisan 14–21 inclusive: beginning at morning of the 14th and ending at sunset of the 21st.

And these *eight* days came to be known as *The Azyms* (τὰ ἄζυμα), or *the Festival of the Azyms* (ἡ ἑορτὴ τῶν ἀζύμων), or again as Πάσχα = *Passover* (Luke xxii. 1): but not as ἡ ἑορτὴ τοῦ Πάσχα, which meant the one day, Nisan 15.

That at the time of our Lord the 14th of Nisan had come to be habitually reckoned as part of *the Festival of the Azyms* is clear from Mark xiv. 1, "After two days was the Passover and the Azyms" (ἦν δὲ τὸ Πάσχα καὶ τὰ ἄζυμα μετὰ δύο ἡμέρας), where the Azyms begin on the same day that the Passover is killed on, viz. Nisan 14. Again, verse 12, "On the first day of the Azyms when they used to kill the Passover" (τῇ πρώτῃ ἡμέρᾳ τῶν ἀζύμων ὅτε τὸ Πάσχα ἔθυον). Again, Luke xxii. 1, "The Festival of the Azyms which (festival) is called Passover" (ἡ ἑορτὴ τῶν ἀζύμων ἡ λεγομένη Πάσχα). Again, verse 7, "The day of the Azyms on which the Passover was due to be sacrificed" (ἡ ἡμέρα τῶν ἀζύμων ἐν ᾗ ἔδει θύεσθαι τὸ Πάσχα). Also Josephus (*War*, V. iii. 1), "The day of the Azyms being come, on the 14th of the month Nisan" (τῆς τῶν ἀζύμων ἐνστάσης ἡμέρας, τεσσαρεσκαιδεκάτῃ Ξανθικοῦ μηνός).

Where ἑορτὴ is used of Pentecost, as in John v. 1 (ἑορτὴ τῶν Ἰουδαίων, "a Festival of the Jews"), it means the one day, normally Sivan 6, the fiftieth day after the day of the *ʿomer* (Lev. xxiii. 15, 16), both terms included. But where, as in A.D. 29, the nation had postponed the Passover one day, Pentecost also had to be postponed one day, and thus fell on Sivan 7, which was Sunday, May 15, in A.D. 29.

Where ἡ ἑορτὴ is used of the Festival of Tabernacles, as in John vii. 2, 8, 10, 11, 14, 37, it means the whole seven days, from Tisri 15 to 21 inclusive—much as it means the whole eight days of the Azyms.

In this double celebration of the Paschal supper, viz. by our Lord and the Twelve on Thursday, Nisan 14, and by the rest of the nation on Friday, Nisan 15, lies the explanation of the otherwise difficult anomaly that, whereas from time immemorial western Christendom uses for the Eucharist unleavened bread, eastern Christendom has from time immemorial insisted on the bread being leavened. The East asserts, and rightly, that the Last Supper was eaten on the night before the nation ate the Passover, and infers that it was, therefore, eaten with ordinary leavened bread. The West asserts, and rightly, that the Passover eaten by our Lord and the Twelve was a genuine Passover, as He Himself calls it (Luke xxii. 15) and as all the Synoptists agree in calling it, and infers that it was, therefore, eaten with the full Mosaic ritual and therefore with unleavened bread, and eaten on the strict legal day the 14th of Nisan after sunset. Thus, what to many seems discord between John's gospel and the Synoptics finds an echo in the immemorial rituals of West and East: and what explains the gospels explains the rituals.

(xiii. 1) "Jesus, knowing that His hour was come to depart out of this world" (κόσμου) . . . whilst leaving His own ones behind still in the world . . . "loved them to the end" (εἰς τέλος): (A) *to the uttermost measure*, by dying for them (cf. "greater love hath no one than this"): and by rising again for them. (B) *unto the end of time*, by making provision for them in the Eucharistic sacrament. With the institution of the Eucharist and with its meaning John's readers were, of course, familiar, for he writes as late as 101 A.D.: he proposes only to add certain details of that last Paschal supper which shall help to bring out the *love* which characterized every action of our Lord in those His last hours.

As to the scene of the following "supper," "the Passover" of Matthew (xxvi. 17–19), of Mark (xiv. 12–16), and of Luke (xxii. 7–13), it is described (see Mark and Luke) as a "large upper-room (ἀνάγαιον μέγα)." The local tradition of all the denominations of Christendom is agreed that the building known to-day as the Cenácolo ("Supper-room") occupies the site of the ἀνάγαιον of the gospels. It is on the traditional ancient Mount Sion and well within the old city walls, though five hundred feet south-south-west of the present Sion Gate. This original Cenâcolo became the seat of the first Christian Church, the Church of Mount Sion, the mother Church of all Churches: from here the risen Lord led forth the Apostles on Ascension Day, here Matthias was chosen in place of Iscariot (Acts i.), here the Holy Spirit descended at Pentecost (Acts ii.), and here was held the first œcumenical Council (Acts xv.). The house escaped destruction at the siege of Titus, A.D. 70, and had become a church before the time of Hadrian. The building that to-day occupies the site is part of the church built by the Crusaders in the 12th century, and is in the hands of Moslems.

Tradition is singularly silent as to the owner of the original Cenácolo, but according to the most probable opinion it belonged to Joseph of Arimathæa.

Mch. 24 / Nisan 14 — Thurs. after sunset.

(2) "During supper" (δείπνου γινομένου seems to be the correct reading), *i.e.* during the ritual of the Paschal supper.

The following remarks * on the Paschal ritual will be here to the point. The ritual required that all should eat reclining upon couches about a low table, each resting on his left arm so as to have the right hand free. It was the same attitude in which Greeks and Romans ate habitually at table. The original Passover had been eaten standing: the later ritual required the Passover to be eaten reclining as symbolical of the security into which the people had been brought by God into the Promised Land.

The supper begins (and cf. Luke xxii. 15, 16) by the head of the company taking the first cup and speaking over it the blessing, "Blessed art Thou, Jehovah our God, who hast created the fruit of the vine." . . . This is immediately followed by the thanksgiving over "the day," that they had been "preserved alive, sustained, and brought to this season." This first cup is the "cup" of Luke xxii. 17, 18. Our Lord drank of it and said He would "not (again) drink of the fruit of the vine until the Kingdom of God shall come": all the company drink of it.

The next part of the ritual is that the head of the company should

* Repeated from my book, *The Crucifixion and Resurrection of Jesus Christ* (Murray).

rise alone and wash his hands. This washing of hands by him alone is, according to the rubric, followed by the dishes being placed on the table: he then dips some of the bitter herbs into the salt water and vinegar, speaks a blessing, eats of them, and hands them to each of the company.

Next, he breaks one of the unleavened loaves, and puts half of it aside for after supper: this latter half is called the Aphigomon,* or "after dish": and this was probably the bread of the Holy Eucharist—of which see below. Then the half-loaf (not the Aphigomon) is elevated, and the words spoken, "This is the bread of misery which our Fathers ate in the land of Egypt: all that are hungry, come and eat: all that are needy, come, keep the Passover."

Next, the second cup is filled, and the youngest in the company is told to make formal inquiry as to the meaning of all the observances of the night (Exod. xii. 24-27). The youngest at the Last Supper would be John, and no doubt all this was done. The cup is then elevated, and the service proceeds lengthily: the cup is again elevated, certain prayers are recited, and Psalms cxiii., cxiv. (cxii., cxiii.*a*) are repeated: the cup is elevated the third time, and a prayer is recited, and then the cup is drunk by all. This ends the first part of the service.

Then follows a general washing of hands: and then the Paschal lamb was eaten. After eating the lamb the *third cup* was filled.

At this point in the Paschal ritual they had arrived when occurred the incident which John begins to relate at verse 2 of this chapter.

(2) "During supper." Although aware that Satan through Judas was scheming His betrayal, and that all would soon forsake Him, He still washed the feet of all and ministered as a servant to all in the scene that follows.

The strife as to "which of them is accounted greatest" (Luke xxii. 24) had already begun, probably started by Judas Iscariot who might base his claim upon the considerations that the couch of honour at this supper had been assigned to him and not to Peter, that he alone of the Twelve belonged to the royal tribe of Judah, and that to him had been entrusted the finances of the Community (xii. 6: xiii. 29). To end it, our Lord will show them that the greatest among them should be the humblest: and with this aim He made Himself their servant.

(3) Although aware that He, *quâ* Man, had been made Lord of all things, and although aware that He was God Incarnate, or, as John puts it, "that He came forth from

* Perhaps represents a Greek ἀφιέμενον = put aside, as ἄφετον, consecrated.

God and was withdrawing again to God"; yet He made Himself a servant.

(4) "He riseth from the supper," *i.e.* from the Paschal supper. The Eucharist has not yet been instituted. The precise point in the ritual of the Paschal supper at which our Lord rose seems to be immediately after the Paschal lamb had been eaten and the *third cup* had been filled. The ordinary ritual of the Passover continued thus: After filling the third cup, the blessing or grace after meat was said, then the third cup was drunk—hence its proper name, "the cup of the Blessing"; and then followed the final washing of hands. See Lightfoot, *Hor. Heb.* But on the night in question, after the filling of the third cup, our Lord seems to have modified this ritual: the grace after meat was suspended, and the final washing of hands He changed to a preparatory washing of feet—preparatory, that is, to the new rite and the new Sacrifice He was about to institute.

(4) "He riseth from the supper." John's account reads like that of an eye-witness who had watched with wonder and suspense—short staccato sentences: "He rises from the supper: and He lays aside His garments: and taking a towel He girds Himself: then He puts water into the bason: and He began to wash the feet of the disciples, and to wipe them with the towel with which He was girded."

(6) "Therefore (*οὖν*) He cometh unto Simon Peter." He began with Peter as occupying the lowest place near the door: and because occupying the lowest place, therefore deserving to be first served: and Peter, as spokesman for the Twelve, shrinks from being waited on by the Lord.

At first Peter's mind seized only on the humility and self-abasement in this action.

(7) Jesus answered him, "What *I* am doing *thou* knowest not at this moment, but thou shalt understand hereafter." The emphatic pronouns imply the different planes of thought on which the two were moving: for Peter does not discern as yet the meaning of the washing.

(8*a*) Peter still seeing in the action only an act of

self-abasement on our Lord's part, still protests that he can never allow Him to so demean Himself for him, Peter.

(8*b*) Jesus replied by calling Peter's understanding to quite another meaning in His action. It must be noticed that our Lord's action was symbolic and had a twofold meaning. There was—

A. The washing their feet *as a servant*—to teach them humility: and unless He carried the lesson into explicit action they would never lay it to heart and learn so to act. And this is the meaning He mainly dwells on in the subsequent comment in verses 13–17. But there was also, and primarily—

B. *The washing:* which had its meaning also.

Every rite of cleansing by water under the Law was a type of the true cleansing, which is only to be found in that sacramental system which has its fount and flow in Jesus Christ. And that our Lord had this symbolism in His mind is evident from verses 8*b*, 11. John's habit, however, of abridging his accounts makes it difficult to follow him: he presumes in his readers a certain familiarity with doctrine and ritual: his gospel will not be understood by any chance reader who takes it up ignorant of, and impatient of, the mind of the Church.

Again, John's mind is one that works by intuition, not by syllogism: his contemplation is so intense and his vision so quick, that it is often hard to track his line of thought: but that is the man: that is his style, which makes him at once the most arresting of the N.T. writers and the most entrancing.

In the section 8*b*, 11, "If I wash thee not," etc., the main idea is fastened not to the humility shown in our Lord's action (that will be brought out later on, in verses 13–17), but to the washing as *washing*. Without the *washing*, Peter can have no part with Him. What washing? The washing from sin, which all ritual cleansing symbolized.

(9) Now suddenly Peter understands. 'Washing from sin? ah, then, Lord, cleanse me wholly: it is more than feet: for I am wholly sinful.'

(10) 'Nay: thou hast been already wholly bathed in the waters of baptism: and they that have been once baptized need only to have from time to time removed those defilements which will inevitably attach to all in their passage through life.'

In this verse, the rendering should be, "he that has been *bathed*" (λελουμένος, one of the common words used thenceforth by the Church for the "baptized") "needeth not save to *wash* his feet" (this word νίπτειν, "wash," is never used of bathing, nor yet of Christian baptism, but only of partial washing, *e.g.* of feet or hands or face or eyes) "but is (thus) wholly clean," *i.e.* being once bathed wholly (sc. baptized),* a man to keep thereafter wholly clean has but to have removed the dirt of the road from his feet (sc. subsequent sins incidental to the frailty of mankind).

And this washing of their feet, preparatory to the communion of His Body and Blood in the Eucharist which is about to follow, symbolized that washing (preparatory to the same mystery), which all receive who come worthily to it.

(10*b*) "And ye are *clean*" (κάθαροι, another common ecclesiastical term thenceforth for the *baptized*): "but not all of you"—though they had all of them been baptized. This was said for Judas Iscariot's ears, to let him know that our Lord was not deceived about him, but knew what he was scheming.

(12) Having washed their feet, He resumed His garments, took His place again at the table, and continued His discourse.

(12–17) Now our Lord dwells on another aspect of His action, not now on the symbolism of the *washing;* but on the symbolism of His acting for them as *their servant*, although their Lord.

* As to the baptism of the Apostles: according to Baronius (*Ann.*, xxxi. 40), Evodius (1st century, and made bishop of Antioch by Peter himself) says in his treatise τὸ φῶ, "that Christ baptized only Peter: that Peter then baptized Andrew and the two sons of Zebedee: and that these baptized the rest of the Apostles. But the seventy were baptized by Peter and John." So, too, says Clement Alex. (not about the seventy). Tertullian and Augustine lay great stress on the fact that the Apostles were baptized.

(17) 'If they have now learnt this lesson of humility, blessed are they if they carry it into practice: but only so.'

(18) "Not concerning all of you am I speaking: I know whom (plural) I chose out" to the apostolate that day upon the mountain. All were selected in full knowledge by Him of their characters, and among them was one selected to be a type of future traitors in His Church, and in its high places. As was long ago foretold in type concerning him and his like—

(18) This phrase (ἵνα πληρωθῇ), "that it may be fulfilled"—commonly used in the gospels where a fulfilment of prophecy is noticed—means "*and so is fulfilled*": it represents, not purpose, but consequence, and is the Hellenistic rendering of the Hebrew conjunction *lma'an* with infinitive or future, expressing that which answers to, responds to, an impulse; hence (subjectively) end aimed at, or (objectively) result come at. Other instances in this gospel are xii. 38: xv. 25: xvii. 12: xviii. 9, 32: xix. 24, 36: in all of which the meaning is objective result, and consequence.

The Psalm xli. here quoted is one of David's, written just after the outbreak of Absalom's rebellion, when David fled from Jerusalem weak and ill. The treachery of Ahitophel, his friend, to king David is here used as an acted parable of the treachery of Judas, a familiar comrade, to that Son of David and King of whom David was a type.

"To lift up the heel against" indicates the malice of the blow.

(19) "Now," better "From now" (ἀπ' ἄρτι): an emphatic term marking the crisis (viz. this Supper) dating from which He no longer will keep secret the *name* of the traitor. He had long ago (vi. 70) told them what was the nature of *one* among them, but never till this Supper had He even hinted which was that one. And Iscariot is listening.

(20) Verses 18 and 19 are almost parenthetical. He now (20) returns to His line of thought at verse 17, "Blessed are ye if ye do them." And lest they should be tempted at any time to be slack in doing, He bids them remember

whose ambassadors they are: they represent Him the Lord, and He represents The Father who sent Him. The very honour of God is placed in the hands of these His ambassadors. And Iscariot was one of them.

(21) At the contemplation of the treachery of Judas—treachery to the cause of God due to self-seeking, "He was troubled in spirit." His "trouble" is due to a consciousness of all the future treachery in His Church; treachery of which the guilt and horror was piled upon Him to bear in that mystery of Expiation which none can fathom.

(21) As for the position of our Lord and His guests at the table this evening. At a Roman or Greek dinner

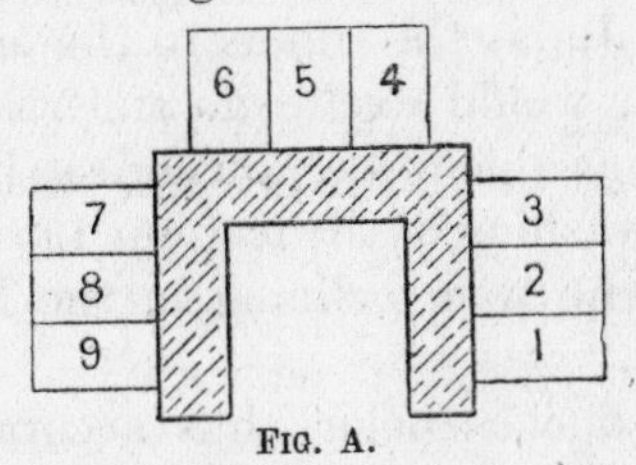

Fig. A.

(and similarly with the Jews), where the number at table rarely exceeded nine, the arrangement of the table and the couches was commonly as in the figure A. The host usually occupied the corner divan marked 7 on plan: the place of honour (*ὑπατικός*, *consularis*) was that marked 6 at the same corner: and the lowest place was that here marked 1.

It has been suggested that the system was extended on this occasion, so that the thirteen divans were arranged as in figure B. The host (our Lord) occupying the divan in the proper corner: the place of honour being at the same

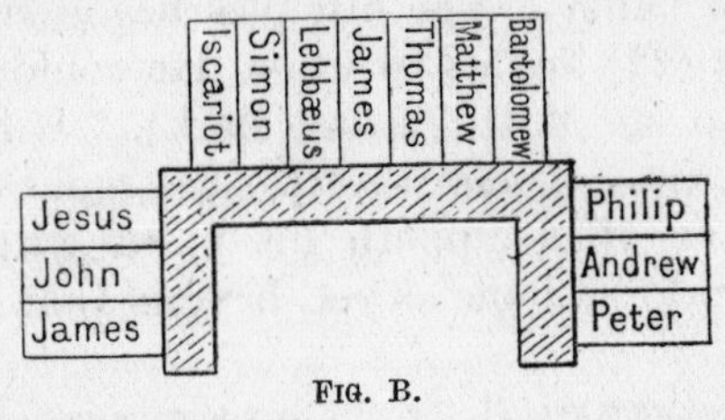

Fig. B.

corner and occupied by Judas Iscariot: John occupying the divan below (*infra*) the host, *i.e.* on his right, for the person reclining on the right of another was technically "below" him, and "*infra aliquem cubare*" was the same as "*in sinu alicujus cubare*," "to recline in the bosom of" that person: Peter occupying the humblest couch of all. To Peter as chief of the Twelve, our Lord not improbably assigned on this occasion the lowest place, having in view the lesson of humility that He meant to teach them on this the last night.

These positions explain how it was that Jesus whispered to John how to recognize the traitor, without the others hearing Him: and how, when Judas asked, "Is it I?" he received his answer unheard by the others: and how Jesus, in giving Judas the sop as to the one occupying the place of honour, would excite no surprise in the others: and how Peter was able to beckon across the table to John: and how at the washing of the feet our Lord came naturally first to Peter, who was reclining in the lowest place and nearest the door.

These four couches being thus accurately assigned, it is easy to assign the remainder with approximate security, bearing in mind the order and coupling observed in the lists of the Twelve in Matt. x. 2–4 and Luke vi. 14–16, checked with Mark iii. 16–19: Simon Peter and Andrew, James and John, Philip and Bartholomew, Matthew and Thomas, James of Alphæus and Judas Thaddæus, Simon the Zealot and Judas Iscariot.

(21) He tells them that one of them should betray Him.* The warning was perhaps meant specially for Judas, to make him think again before he joins in the approaching Sacrament of Unity. The disciples began to look one at another, at a (22) loss as to whom He could mean: each one asking (so say Matthew and Mark), "It is, surely, not I, Lord?" (*μήτι ἐγώ εἰμι, κύριε;*). He replies, "It is one of the Twelve, that dippeth his hand with Me in the dish." He specifies none as yet, beyond that the treachery

* Matthew's notice xxvi. 21, "whilst they were eating" (*ἐσθιόντων αὐτῶν*), and Mark's xiv. 18, "whilst they were reclining and eating" (*ἀνακειμένων αὐτῶν καὶ ἐσθιόντων*) merely mean that the ritual of the Paschal supper was as yet unfinished.

is from one of them, one of His intimate associates, alluding to Psalm xli. 9 (xl. 10), to which John had already referred in verse 18. But to Judas who put the similar question, "It is surely not I, Rabbi ?" the answer is given, "Thou hast said," a Hebrew idiom for "It is thou": an answer meant for him alone and heard by him alone.

(23) The disciple is, of course, John himself.

(24) Peter beckons across to John (because John was next to Jesus and "reclining in His bosom"—a technical phrase), to the effect that John should find out who it was. "Say (*i.e.* to Him), 'Who is it ?' of whom He speaks" (εἶπε τίς ἐστιν περὶ οὗ λέγει).

(25) John "leant back with-this-purpose (οὕτως) upon the breast of Jesus" (in order to ask Him privately, and privately to get the answer), "and says to Him, 'Lord, who is it ?'"

(26*a*) And the answer is given him privately, in a low voice: "It is he for whom I shall dip the sop (τὸ ψωμίον) and give it to him."

The sop will, of course, not be dipped and given yet—not till the end of the ritual.

Here,* at 26*a*, followed the institution of the Eucharist, which John does not relate, as being already familiar to Christendom.

Matthew (xxvi. 26) and Mark (xiv. 22) record the institution of the Eucharist as being "whilst they were eating" (ἐσθιόντων αὐτῶν), *i.e.* because the Paschal ritual was not finished till after the fourth cup, to which we have not yet come. Luke (xxii. 20) and Paul (1 Cor. xi. 25) say "after supper" (μετὰ τὸ δειπνῆσαι), *i.e.* after the lamb and the bread and bitter herbs had been eaten.

Matthew xxvi. 26–28: Mark xiv. 22–24: Luke xxii. 19, 20: 1 Cor. xi. 23. For the Eucharistic bread our Lord seems to have taken the half-loaf or Aphigomon which had been put aside (see p. 304): He "blessed" (Matthew, Mark), and "gave thanks" (Luke), and broke it into as many parts as there were people to receive it, and handed one to each.

He then took the cup, *i.e.* the third cup of the ritual (see p. 305), which had been filled before the washing of the feet. This is "the cup" of

* In the ancient MSS. there are no divisions into chapters or verses or sentences or even words: and the divisions when made, some centuries after our era, were often unfortunate and misleading.

Matthew xxvi. 27, Mark xiv. 23 : it is "the cup" "after supper" of Luke xxii. 20 and of 1 Cor. xi. 25 : it is "the cup of the blessing" (τὸ ποτήριον τῆς εὐλογίας) of 1 Cor. x. 16 : "and when He had given thanks He gave it to them" (Luke).

Mark (xiv. 23) says "they all drank of it," which seems to include Judas, for he has given no hint of Judas's departure : nor does any of the four gospels make it clear as to when (with reference to the Eucharist) he went out. It is the general opinion of the Fathers (*e.g.* Augustine, Chrysostom, Cyril of Jerusalem) that Judas received the Holy Communion.

The third cup ("the cup of the blessing") being finished, the Paschal ritual requires the rest of the Hallel to be sung, viz. Psalm cxv.–cxviii. (cxiii.*b*–cxvii.) : this is the "hymn" of Matt. xxvi. 30 and Mark xiv. 26. The two first Psalms of the Hallel, viz. cxiii., cxiv. (cxii.–cxiii.*a*), had been sung before the second cup (p. 304).

Lastly the ritual requires the fourth cup to be drunk : this cup is probably the wine He speaks of in Matthew's (xxvi. 29) and Mark's (xiv. 25) accounts, using virtually the same words as He had used at the first cup (Luke xxii. 18) : after so long and momentous an interval He perhaps repeated the words He had used of the ordinary wine on the table to draw attention to the promise they conveyed for a yet future Age.

The ritual of the Paschal supper is now completed. Into it, at the third cup, has been inserted the ceremony of the Eucharist.

(26*b*) As a sign that all is over, Jesus "dipped the sop and taketh and giveth it to Judas, son of Simon Iscariot." By this act John (but no one else) knew at last for certain who was to be the traitor. The giving of the sop was a mark of honour shown by the host to the chief guest of the evening. And Judas consented to receive this last mark of favour though meditating his treachery. It is the climax. Hitherto his fate had hung, as it were, in the balance. The special favours shown him by our Lord to-night have served not to mollify but to intensify his self-esteem. Henceforth he is given over. "After the sop, then Satan entered into him."

(27) "Entered into him." How did John know? unless from our Lord Himself after His resurrection. The Eleven must in those forty days have discussed that act of Judas, and learnt then how Satan had really been the moving spirit in it. After this entering in of Satan, who shall say how far Judas was thenceforth responsible ?

"Jesus therefore saith to him, 'What thou doest, do quickly'" : as though signifying to Judas that He knew his purpose : also as bidding him leave them. These words were spoken aloud to Judas and heard by all.

(28) " But no one at the table knew with what purpose He said this to him " : no one, not even John ; for John would not connect this public exit with the treachery.

(29) Some at the table thought that as Judas was the treasurer Jesus was bidding him either " Buy what we have need of for the festival-day" (εἰς τὴν ἑορτήν), viz. to-morrow, Nisan 15,* which for the Twelve (so they thought) would be the festival-day, but not for the nation, seeing that the nation would not eat the Paschal supper until to-morrow (Friday) evening, and so would have their festival-day on Saturday : or, " that " on behalf of them all " he (Judas) should give something to the poor," *i.e.* to enable the very poor to buy Passover lambs for to-morrow, when the nation would eat the Passover. This helping of the poor to rejoice in the Law was a well-recognized and common act of charity.

(30) " Having therefore taken the sop, he straightway went out. And it was night." The moon was nearing her last quarter, and would not be rising till after midnight : for the evening is Thursday, March 24, A.D. 29. Judas probably went straight to Annas or Caiaphas.

* Whether we reckon by the civil day of twenty-four hours beginning at midnight, or by the natural day of twelve hours beginning at sunrise six hours later. In the former case there were but a few hours before Nisan 15 would begin ; and, as it would be for the Twelve a day of solemn-rest, all buying and selling would be prohibited for them once it began.

§ XXI

JOHN XIII. 31–XIV. 31

The traitor being gone, our Lord continues His last talk with the Eleven.

(31) "Now was The Son of Man glorified." The *now* is emphatic in the Greek. *Now*, *i.e.* an instant ago, at the moment He had told Judas to do his work quickly: for by that self-surrender to Judas's treachery He had, so to say, put the seal to His acceptance of the final act of Redemption: and in that glad acceptance which carried with it the world's expiation, The Son of Man, the Messiah, He that was to come as the world's hope, the one true Representative of humanity, received glory and approbation from God; and God received glory and adoration from Him, the second Adam, the Father of the new race.

Mch. 24, Thurs., about 8.30 p.m.

And we must not forget that this Man is Himself eternal God and all the while fully conscious that He is so.

(32) Seeing that God was glorified in The Son of Man by the action of the latter, The Son of Man shall also be glorified in God by God's action, viz. by the Resurrection and Ascension. And the manifestation of that glory is close at hand. They should see it begun on Sunday next.

(33) "But a little while yet am I with you": for this was His last evening with them. "And whither I withdraw (ὑπάγω) you cannot come." They should search for Him: but just as He had told "the Jews" repeatedly, *e.g.* six months ago (vii. 34: xiii. 21), that they were not able to reach His plane of being, so He says to His Apostles that they also are not able at present (ἄρτι): for they are but "little children."

(34) And how should they fit themselves to follow where He goes? By adherence to this new commandment "to love one another even as He loved them." Wherein, it may be asked, was this commandment *new?* is it not already recognized in the Law, "Thou shalt love the Lord thy God with all they heart, etc., and thy neighbour as thyself"?

But the pith of the *new* commandment lies in the "even as I loved you," which is added as the definition of the *new* sort of love (ἀγαπή). Henceforth they should love each other with the same love that He had for them, viz. as being brethren of the eternal Son of God and co-members of His Body: and no longer as being merely brethren of each other because sons of Adam, or even because the chosen people, adopted sons of the Covenant of Sinai. So, virtually, says Augustine.

But His hearers do not, of course, as yet understand all He means.

(36) Peter, struck by the announcement that He was leaving them, and understanding He was to be crucified, and none the less that somehow He was yet to end in triumph, asks, 'Whither goest Thou? to death, I presume: but even so——?' Jesus answers in effect: 'To the Cross, yes, and beyond: and thou, Peter, are not yet fitted to follow Me there: but later on thou shalt follow Me'—alluding to Peter's martyrdom by crucifixion on the Janiculum of Rome.

(37) Peter asks: 'Later on? but why not now, now? My very life I will lay down for Thee.'

(38) Jesus replies: "Thy very life thou wilt lay down for Me?" "Cock shall not crow till thou hast denied Me thrice." *Cock shall not crow* is, of course, a reference to the third watch of the night, that from midnight to about 3 a.m.: this watch was known as *Cock-crow* from the habit ascribed to cocks of crowing during this part of the night and more particularly at about three hours before sunrise. See Mark xiii. 35, where the four night watches are severally named, viz. 1. ὀψέ (evening) = from sunset to 9 p.m.: 2. μεσονύκτιον (midnight) = from 9 p.m to

midnight: 3. ἀλεκτοροφωνία (cock-crow) = from midnight to 3 a.m.: 4. πρωΐ (morning) = from 3 a.m. to sunrise.

Is this warning to Peter the same as that mentioned in Luke xxii. 31–34? or is that of Luke's distinct from it —making three warnings to Peter? for certainly that given by Matt. xxvi. 34 (and Mark xiv. 30) was given after leaving the house; see Matt., verse 30, and Mark, verse 26. Many have thought that as Peter denied thrice, and was thrice reinstated (John xxi.), so he had been warned thrice.

(XIV.) (1) Again recurs the note of His departure from them. Let not their heart be troubled at it, nor dismayed. They believe into God as ever present, let them believe similarly into Him.

(2) "In My Father's house are many mansions (μοναί), and if there were not, I would have said to you that * I go to make ready a place for you": so dear were they to Him and to The Father.

The word μονὴ (Lat. *mansio*) was the technical term for the nights' halting-places, or stages, along the imperial highways: and there may be here implied the idea of gradual advance toward the ultimate goal.

(3) "Even if I did go and make ready (ἐὰν πορευθῶ καὶ ἑτοιμάσω) a place for you, still I am coming again and I will take you to Myself." We must not miss the hypothetical aor. subj. ἐὰν πορευθῶ καὶ ἑτοιμάσω, nor render as if it were εἰ πορεύομαι ἑτοιμάσαι = if I go to make ready, *as I am about to do.* His meaning rather is that He is *not* going away to make ready a place for them, for there is already large accommodation for them in His Father's house. It is they who have to be made ready for mansions in that house: and that is why He is going, (to send the Holy Spirit). And even if He were going away to make ready a place, in any case "I am coming again and will take you to Myself, that where I am you also may be"—

* εἶπον ἂν ἡμῖν ὅτι . . . It is strange that the A.V. and the R.V. render "I would have told you: for," etc., instead of the obvious "I would have told you that," etc. There is not a single instance in the N.T. where, after the verbs of speaking, the word ὅτι means anything else than "that": nor are Mark i. 34, Luke iv. 41, exceptions, although there again both A.V. and R.V. oddly render "because" or "for."

alluding to the Coming which ushers in the millennial age, when the dead in Christ shall rise, and the living "saints" are caught up to Him (1 Thess. iv. 14–17).

(4) "And where I am going, you know the Way." The words are difficult for them to understand, and are purposely such, in order to make them ask for further explanation: which Thomas does.

(5) 'Lord, as we know not where Thou goest, how do we know the way?'

(6) "I (ἐγὼ) am the Way and the Truth and the Life." The Way He spoke of (in verse 4) is no other than He Himself. It is the Person of our Lord that is the Way, the Truth, the Life. By union with Him, Christians advance to the goal which is God: and the normal mode of union with Him is a Sacramental one, such as the Sacrament just instituted: but no one will say He has bound Himself to win no souls except by the Sacramental system.

In union with Him lies union with Truth, and with Life, in every aspect: for He is the Microcosm of evolution, or of creation-with-a-purpose, whether on the physical, psychical, or intellectual planes.

"Except by means of Me no one comes to the Father," *i.e.* (A) except through His humanity no one has access to the Godhead: and (B) except through His divinity—Him *quâ* Second Person of the Trinity—there is no access to the First Person of the Trinity. It is the Second Person of the Trinity, The Son, who has relinked the human race to the First, The Father, by the link of the human nature which He assumed. He is the supreme Pontifex or bridge-maker between the Creator and the created. Thus Christendom rejects "theosophy," "Christian science," and all other forms assumed by that old deception "pantheism."

(7) "If you knew (ἐγνώκειτε, had learnt) Me," the Man-God, under His two natures, "you would have known My Father also. Henceforth you recognize Him and you have seen Him." Again, as in verse 4, these last words are difficult for them to understand, and are purposely such;

in order to make them ask for further explanation: which Philip does.

(8) 'Seen the Father? When? Lord show us The Father and we ask no more, for then our faith were unshakable.' Perhaps Philip has in mind a theophany such as the elders of Israel experienced on Sinai (Exod. xxiv. 10, 11): or again as Moses (Exod. xxxiv. 5–8).

(9) "So long a time have I been with you, and thou hast not learnt Me, Philip? He that hath seen Me hath seen The Father: how is it thou sayest, 'Shew us The Father'?" The true Theophany is our Lord Himself, for He is the Godhead manifested in the flesh: a manifestation, not indeed of the splendour or power of God, but of His holiness and love, under the only form in which man could adequately apprehend. Our Lord's words here imply that He had often taught the Twelve the truths of His own Personality and of the Trinity, just as we have often seen Him teaching them to the Jewish doctors.

(10) "Dost thou not believe that I am in The Father, and The Father is in Me?" Philip was forgetting that in all the words and actions of Jesus, in everything whereby Philip was learning to know Him, he was learning to know The Father also: for The Father and He are one and the same Godhead. When the Man-God speaks or acts, The Father also speaks and acts.

(11) Then turning from Philip to all of them, for all were in like case: 'Believe Me (πιστεύετέ μοι, plur.) when I say that I am in The Father and that The Father is in Me: or at least let My life and my works make you believe the Godhead to be inherent in Me.' The signs or miracles of our Lord have their evidential value (see under x. 25), for they are true to type.

(12) "He that believeth into Me the works that *I* do *he* too shall do, and greater ones than these shall he do, because I go to the Father." How far is this promise general? In other words, how far does it depend on the quality of faith? how far on times and seasons? how far on the general health of the Christian community?

can it be expected to be fulfilled whilst Christendom is torn by schisms, and ugly for want of mutual charity ?

That the Church did even " greater works," in a way, than our Lord did when present in this world of sense, seems sure : for whereas He, when on earth, did not feel Himself at liberty to make the Faith widely spread, directly the Spirit was poured out at Pentecost " men of Israel " flocked into the Church by thousands : and a few years later were followed by a host of Gentiles : and this was only possible because He had " gone to the Father " and sent the Holy Spirit to witness in men's spirits to Him.

Yet, for all that, the words, " greater than these shall he do," seem to point to a time yet future, when Christendom shall more nearly resemble that ideal He has in view.

(13, 14) " And whatever you ask in My name I will do it, so that The Father may be glorified in the Son. If you ask a thing in My name, I will do it." The asking " in His name " seems to be the one necessary condition : but to ask " in His name " or do anything " in His name " argues a unity of mind with His, a unity of aim and of motive, that can hardly be reached as yet. To ask or act " in His name " must be done objectively so : no merely subjective intention can be sufficient. Prayer is not the persuading of God to adopt our views. Meanwhile the Church's prayer works at low pressure.

(15) Love (ἀγαπὴ) is the great requisite : love to Him which should involve love to each other. " If you have love for Me you will keep My commandments," of which the most recent was to " love each other even as I love you." (16) And He, on His part, will see that the Holy Spirit is sent to them to enable them to attain. We hardly realize that we of this Age are but the infancy of Christendom compared to the maturer Christendom of the millennial and post-millennial Ages of mankind on earth.

(16) " And I (ἐγω) will request The Father, and another Comforter will He give you, to be with you for ever." That our Lord here calls the Holy Spirit " another Comforter (ἄλλον παράκλητον)" implies that He Himself claimed

to be also a παράκλητος, as John in his first epistle (ii. 1) calls Him.

This word παράκλητος occurs in the N.T. in the writings of John alone. In his gospel he has it four times (xiv. 16, 26: xv. 26: xvi. 7), always as spoken by our Lord and always as signifying the Holy Spirit. In his epistles he has it once (1, ii. 1), and uses it not of the Holy Spirit, but of Jesus Christ.

As to the actual word used by our Lord (speaking, of course, in Aramaic) in the gospel where John's Greek word is παράκλητος, the probability is that He used this Greek word, for in all the versions, even in the Syriac (itself an Aramaic dialect), Old Latin, Vulgate, Arabic, Memphitic, Thebaic, Ethiopic, the Greek word Paráclitus has been retained. Also in the Targums and the Talmud the word appears in the form, פרקליטא, as though the Greek word was well recognized in the Aramaic dialects, where it is used in two senses, viz. sometimes in that of a *helper* (generally), and sometimes in that of an *advocate* (specifically). Philo also, contemporary with our Lord, uses the word παράκλητος in the sense sometimes of a helper (general) and sometimes of an advocate (specific).

The meaning of παράκλητος is quite simple, it is *one who is called up to one's side* to help: hence a helper, a strengthener or comforter, using "comforter" in its proper sense of *strengthener* (*con*, intensive, and *fortis*, strong): the legal meaning of *an advocate* (one called in to aid in a court of law) is but one form of helping or strengthening, and is too specialized to serve as a universal rendering.

The least unsatisfactory rendering of παράκλητος, if we must translate it, is *Helper*, or *Comforter* in its proper sense of *Strengthener*: the mode in which the help or strength is given being determined according to the circumstances; *e.g.* as an advocate or as a champion, or as infusing strength. As applied to The Spirit (as our Lord applied it) the idea is naturally of a Comforter, *i.e.* Strengthener, as infusing strength and counsel—being summoned to our aid not so much by us as by The Father. As applied to Christ (as John in his first epistle uses it) the idea is naturally of a Champion or Advocate.

(17) "The Spirit of Truth, whom the world cannot receive."

The Holy Spirit was not "sent" into the world, but to the Church.

The Son was "sent" into the world.

The Holy Spirit works powerfully in those only who are members of Christ, and but weakly in those who are not members of Christ. If the world cannot receive the Holy Spirit, shall we wonder that we in our collective worldliness see and show collectively so little of His power ?

The Holy Spirit was to be given to them, His Church, at Pentecost, and would always be witnessing to the presence of Christ. And thus—

(18) "I will not leave you reft of My presence (ὀρφανούς): I come to you," *i.e.* ever present to their spirits, by virtue of the Holy Spirit.

(19) "Yet a little while, and the world beholds Me no longer, but *ye* behold Me." After His death, now close at hand, He passes out of the mind of the world: it will give no further heed to Him: it will think He is dead and done with. Not so with them, for after His resurrection they shall behold Him: and yet again after Pentecost, after that effusion of The Spirit just promised, shall they behold Him with the eyes of faith.

(19*b*) "Because I Live, you too shall Live": viz. at the resurrection.

(20) "In that day." It is the regular formula of prophecy to denote a later and better Age. Here the Day or Age meant seems to be that of the millennium, which will be preceded by "the first resurrection" (Rev. xx. 5). "In that Day *you* shall know (γνώσεσθε as against the present stage of faith) that I am in the Father, and you in Me, and I in you": shall know, that is, that I am the link between The Father and you.

(21) And this promise of knowledge is made not only to His Church collectively, but to the individual also, for "he who has and observes My commandments," which

are summed in that new commandment to love one another in the same way as I love you, "he is the man who loves Me" (ὁ ἀγαπῶν, the spiritual love, not ὁ φιλῶν, the psychic love): he has already the Holy Spirit in him, his obedience is the proof of it. "And he who loves Me shall be loved by My Father: I too will love him and will manifest Myself to him": not merely as loving him, but will make clear to him My personality, making gradually explicit what before was implicit in his faith in Me.

(22) Judas (Lebbæus, also called Thaddæus) asked, "Lord, what is come to pass that *to us* Thou wilt manifest Thyself and not to the world?" How to us only?

(23) The answer to Judas's question is, in effect, 'You eleven, and those in the Church who resemble you, love Me and observe obedience to Me: therefore My Father and I will come to you and such as you, and will make our abode with you—thus manifesting to you the Godhead.'

(24) 'But the world, and those in the Church who resemble it, do not love Me nor observe obedience to Me: and thereby they shut themselves against The Father and Me; for in neglecting My words, they neglect The Father's.'

(25) "These things I have talked to you whilst (yet) abiding with you" here on earth: and you understand but little of what they mean.

(26) "But the Comforter, the Holy Spirit, whom The Father shall send in My name": Just as (v. 43) our Lord said, "I am come in My Father's name," *i.e.* as the representation and the revelation of My Father to make Him known to men, so will the Holy Spirit come as the representation and the revelation of Christ, to make Him known to men's spirits.

"He shall teach you all things," etc. The revelation made by Christ was absolute and complete. Thenceforth, all dogmatic development is the making explicit what at the first lay implicit. The Holy Spirit brings to the full light what before lay latent: brings to the general consciousness out of subconsciousness: brings into focus what was seen hazily: puts in clear formula what was indefinite. No dogma can contradict another: but a later dogma will sharply define what an earlier one left vague, and will thus show an opinion to be erroneous which formerly was held by many as true—and held blamelessly so, because the teaching had on that point lain indeterminate. As a good instance, Catholics are still waiting for a dogmatic definition of the exact meaning of the "Inspiration of the Bible": we all hold the belief, but there are various theories at present current about it among us.

(27) "Peace I leave to you: My peace I give to you." This is His solemn farewell to them. *Peace:* that inward tranquillity, peace with neighbour, peace with self, peace with God, which has ever been held by philosophers to be the highest good. *My peace*, that tranquillity which I the Man-God enjoy and which nothing can disturb.

When He talks of His soul being "troubled" (xii. 27; cf. xi. 33, etc.) He never means His soul *quâ* Jesus Christ the perfect Man, but His soul *quâ* the expiatory Scape-goat of the race. The soul of Jesus Christ the perfect Man is not subject to perturbation or temptation: but only in so far as He was the sum of the *fallen* race of man that is grafted into Him. See note on *The Agony of our Lord* at end of book, p. 446.

(27) "Not as the world gives." The world would give "peace" and wish "peace" when there is no peace possible: for the only true peace is the consciousness of union with God which became possible by the Incarnation. Therefore it was at His birth that the Heavenly Host shouted, "Peace on earth to the race which is henceforth reconciled to God" (Luke ii. 13, 14).

"Let not your heart be troubled, neither let it be afraid (δειλιάτω)": *i.e.* at His going away. The fear here named is the craven, abject fear that paralyzes or makes servile: it has nothing in common with the "fear" (φόβος) of God.

(28) "If you loved Me, you would have rejoiced at My going to The Father"; for in proportion as they loved Him they would have understood what that going

to The Father meant. "For The Father is greater than I," *i.e.* in so far as He the eternal Son became Incarnate, linked to Himself a created though perfect human nature, in that far He made Himself lower than The Father. But He stooped far lower than that: for He gave that immaculate human nature of His (spirit, soul, body) to have grafted into it, by faith and by the sacraments which He instituted, the whole of sinful humanity. In His holy organism as in an alembic all the sinful race is gradually sublimated and glorified into His own perfection. By His Passion, Resurrection, and Ascension the purgation and re-formation of the human race was consummated, done with and "finished" on the timeless plane. It is still in process of elaboration on the time plane, according as each individual becomes taken in hand. The Sacraments are not empty symbols: they are mighty forces operating on the spiritual plane. He returned to The Father, His work done, bearing the human race living and dead one with Himself, a holy offering to The Father.

(28) For this reason His "going to The Father" should be to them a subject of joy: for in that, His Ascension, they all were sharers—sacramentally and substantially now, though the physical limitations of to-day obscured the truth. The "going to" The Father, or again the "Ascension," are but metaphors of language. Place cannot be predicated of the spiritual body until it materialises itself to our senses. Our Lord's risen human body is "everywhere," but becomes manifested to us necessarily in place. Heaven is not a place, but a mode of being. The farthest star of the zenith and the farthest star of the nadir are no nearer, in place, to the "Throne" of God than is the room where we sit. But some day that "throne" and "the New Jerusalem" will materialise on earth.

(28) In the "For The Father is greater than I," He is, of course, speaking of Himself *quâ* Incarnate, *quâ* linked to the creature. Only *quâ* Incarnate does He "come from" and "go to" The Father: for *quâ* eternal Son He never left The Father: to conceive of such a

thing would be to conceive of the Trinity as dead. The Son *quâ* eternal Son is everyway equal to The Father: for if it be said that without The Father no Son were possible, it must also be said that without The Son no Father were possible: time is, of course, eliminated: neither mode of the Godhead is conceivable without the other. Our difficulties lie in that we being finite can form no conception of That-which-has-no-beginning. The Son has not a beginning any more than has The Father: neither language nor thought rises to it: we have to use sign-posts on either hand with warnings of trespass.

The Ascension of our Lord, the "going to The Father," is the first step in the eventual "handing over of the Kingdom to God The Father" (1 Cor. xv. 24)—the delivery of all creation over unto God The Father in its redeemed or glorified state: and who shall say what Age upon Age shall be requisite for that to come about? The Apocalypse of John brings us into the post-millennial Age, and still the Race is left in process of being "healed" (Rev. xxii. 2).

(30) "No longer will I talk much with you": for the end is near: "for the prince of the world is coming": *i.e.* the hour of Satan's seeming triumph but real defeat is near.

"And in Me he has nothing." Satan has no power over Him, there is nothing in Him on which Satan can lay a hold, or by which he can come in contact with our Lord. But, voluntarily, (31*a*) will Jesus yield Himself to his malice, in order that the very world of which Satan is now the prince may hereafter come to recognize that He, Jesus Christ, loves The Father even unto death, and that He submitted Himself to death because and only because it was The Father's command that He should so submit. Always The Son's action manifests on the time-plane The Father's thought. Without His death—and in Him die all those who thereafter will be united to Him—how shall the old Adam be transformed and glorified? for in His glory (Resurrection and Ascension) are glorified all who shall thereafter be united to Him. He is the germ of the new creation: He is the new Man, the second Adam, the Father of the Age to come.

(31*b*) "Rise, let us go hence." At this point He and the Eleven rise from the table to leave the room and house. He did not wish His capture to be effected here. He knew exactly how the enemy's plot was meanwhile advancing: also He had determined the exact place and hour of His arrest.

Perhaps it was as they rose that He foretold the danger threatening, in the words Luke (xxii. 35–38) has preserved.

It must occur to all who read these discourses preserved by John how simple the text looks, and yet how transcendant is the thought when it is even dimly understood. John is sailing sky-high: are we? It is the strongest food in the Bible.

The key to all these discourses preserved by John is the prologue of his gospel. In so far as those opening fourteen verses are understood and assimilated, John's gospel becomes intelligible. His object is to explain the *Person* of our Lord: that He is very God of very God, the eternal Son of the eternal Father, the eternal Word of the eternal Mind: and that He became Flesh—took to Himself in time what before He had not, viz. human nature, but a human nature perfect as was Adam's before the Fall. Never for an instant did He cease to be conscious that He is also God: for He has but one Person.

And only through John's gospel does the story of His infancy as given by Matthew and Luke become reconcilable with His public ministry as given by the Synoptists.

(31*b*) On leaving the house it is probable He led the way to the nearest eastern gate, which would have been the Fountain Gate near to the Pool of the Siloam at the south-east corner of the city. The distance from the Cenácolo (Supper-room) to the Pool is six hundred yards, and it would be another hundred to the gate.

A SYNOPTICAL TABLE OF THE EVENTS IN THE "UPPER-ROOM," *i.e.* THE SUPPER-ROOM OR CENÁCOLO.

	Matt. xxvi.	Mark xiv.	Luke xxii.	John xiii.
Passover Supper	20	18	14–18	—
Dispute "who is greater"	—	—	24	—
Washing of feet	—	—	—	1–11
Explanation of the act	—	—	25–27	12–17
They are His and God's representatives	—	—	28–30	20
"As they did eat," *i.e.* the Passover ritual being still unfinished He foretells His betrayal. Their dismay	21–24	18–21	21–23	21–22
The answer given secretly to Judas Iscariot	25	—	—	—
Peter beckons to John to ask . .	—	—	—	23–25
"It is he for whom I shall dip the sop"	—	—	—	26*a*
"As they did eat," *i.e.* the Passover ritual being still unfinished, the Eucharist instituted . . .	26–28	22–24	19–20	—
"I will not drink," etc.	29	25	—	—
The "hymn" is sung. It is the end of the ritual	30*a*	26*a*	—	-
He dips the sop: gives it to Judas Iscariot, who at once goes out .	—	—	—	26*b*–30
Discourse to the Eleven . . .	—	—	—	31–35
Warning to Peter	—	—	31–34	36–38
Further discourse	—	—	—	xiv. 1–31*a*
"When I sent you," etc. (spoken perhaps as they leave the room)	—	—	35–38	—
They leave the room and house .	30*b*	26*b*	39*a*	31*b*

In the above table, the time-sequence seems to be not observed by Luke: that is only because in the matter of sayings related by him (verses 21–38) Luke has lumped them together at the end. They represent certain salient points of the discourse that took place this evening in the "Upper-room."

Of the sayings thus lumped together by Luke—

Verses 21–23 (corresponding with Matt. 21–24 and Mark 18–21) were spoken during the Paschal Supper and before the Eucharist.

25–27 (corresponding with John xiii. 12–17) were also spoken before the Eucharist.

28–30 (corresponding with John xiii. 20) were also spoken before the Eucharist.

31–34 (corresponding with John xiii. 36–38) were spoken after the Eucharist.

35–38 spoken as they leave the room at John xiv. 31*b*.

In harmonizing the four gospels, it will be found that without exception John throughout observes accurately the chronological sequence. The same cannot be said of any of the Synoptists: for they, while keeping the main stream of time-sequence, constantly turn aside into lateral channels in order to follow out and finish with subordinate currents of thought.

§ XXII

JOHN XV. 1–XVI. 33

His last talk with the eleven before leaving the city.

SOME have supposed the following discourse (xv. 1–xvi. 33) and the prayer (xvii. 1–26) to have been spoken in the Temple area. This, however, is hardly possible, for the gates of the Temple area were not open to the public at night. It would, therefore, seem that the figure of the vine with which the discourse opens (xv. 1) was suggested, not by the great gold vine sculptured over the entrance to the ναός, but by the vines growing in the neighbourhood of the Pool of the Siloam. March is the month for the spring pruning of vines throughout the countries of the Mediterranean: and at this corner of the city near the "king's Garden" (Jer. lii. 7: "the king's wine-vats," Zech. xiv. 10) the newly lopped vine branches were perhaps lying gathered into heaps for burning (xv. 6).

The long discourse and the prayer can hardly have been spoken whilst our Lord and the Eleven were actually walking: hence it seems probable that they paused somewhere in this neighbourhood within the city walls. It was not till the end of the prayer that He "went forth" (xviii. 1), *i.e.* from the city—as we suppose by the Fountain Gate, at the south-east corner close to the Pool of the Siloam.

Verses 1–11

(XV. 1) Under the ancient Covenant (O.T.) God had planted Israel to be His vine (Isa. v. 1–6) whose husbandmen had been the Levitical hierarchy and the national kings. The failure of these husbandmen to give Him returns from this vine

Mch. 24, Thurs. evening, about 9.15 p.m.

had been on Tuesday last (Matt. xxi. 33–44) denounced in the parable of the Vineyard.

Now our Lord announces that He Himself is the ideal Vine: and that the Husbandman of this Vine is no other than God. True, that ancient vine (Israel) had been united to Him as type to antitype, for by faith in Him the saints of the old Covenant had lived (Heb. xi. 8–40): but henceforth the Antitype was here, and they, the eleven Christian Israelites, to whom He is speaking, are the branches of that Vine which is Himself: from them, as the main branches, shall ramify the vast growth which shall spread over the earth: but the principle of Life lies in the Vine Stock whence the sap flows to the furthest grape.

(2) "Every branch in Me not bearing fruit" the Husbandman takes away; as He recently cut away Judas Iscariot from among them (xiii. 27–30).

(2) "And every branch that bears fruit He cleanses it (καθαίρει) that it may," etc. Instead of "cleanses" we perhaps should have expected "prunes," having in mind the very heavy pruning to which all vines are subjected: but a vine is pruned for fear of the stock being exhausted by the great growth, and so the notion of pruning is alien to the inexhaustible vitality of the Vine in question. But it is of great moment to *cleanse* the branches, to keep them clean of outside pests which harbour in the bark and eat into the wood so that the branch decays: hence the whitewash with which vines (trunk and branches) are covered in spring.

(3) 'Already you (emphatic, ὑμεῖς), you eleven, are clean (καθαροὶ) for the reason (διὰ τὸν λόγον) I have given you'—referring to the *cleansing* He had spoken of when talking of the symbolism of the washing of their feet—that removal of the outside dirt which alone was necessary (but was necessary) for those who had been once baptized (see on xiii. 8*b*–10). And in speaking to the Eleven He speaks to all who through them and their successors should ever believe.

"Abide in Me": continue in union with Him by such

from-time-to-time washings: for, as He said, "if I wash thee not thou hast no part in Me." 'Abide in Me, and so I abide in you and the sap flows freely in you.'

(4) "Unless the branch abides in the Vine" stock, etc. It is only by union with Him that any branch can bear fruit: once that union is broken, the sap no longer flows; and *fruit* in that branch is no longer possible, though the remains of the sap that lay in it may be enough to bear leaves and so for a time give semblance of life.

(5) "It is he who abides in Me" (and it needs will and effort on his part) "and I in him, that bears fruit in plenty: for severed from Me you are not able to do anything," *i.e.* to bear any fruit.

(6) The simile of the severed branch ready for burning is taken from the newly lopped prunings of the vines which grew in the gardens here at the Fountain Gate of the city.

(7) "If you abide in Me and My sayings abide in you, ask whatso you will and it shall come to pass to you." Asking in this condition of constant union with Him, what is it but the asking "in My name" of xiv. 13, 14, to which a similar promise was attached? And again, if they abide in Him and He in them, what are the things that they will wish to ask for?

(8) He seems to answer: "That you may bring forth much fruit and become My disciples." Why? Because "in that lies The Father's glory," as at xiv. 13. Branches and clusters have no self-seeking, no aim outside the Vine and the Husbandman's glory: all other aims are cast out as unworthy.

(9) "Even as the Father loved Me, so I loved you: abide in My love." The love (ἀγαπὴ) which binds Him the God-Man to The Father is the same as that with which the God-Man binds them to Himself. He is always the link. By His humanity He lays hold of man to lift him into His own Divinity and on into The Father.

"Abide in My love." This is the one condition in which He is able to pour His life-giving blood (like vine-sap) through them. Sanctification is not done sudden in a minute; it is a long process: only begun here, has it ever an end?

(10) And how shall they abide in His love, so that His union with them may do its perfect work? By keeping His commandments. "Even as I," etc.—not that they can ever keep them as He the perfect Man has kept The Father's: but in so far as they do keep them, in that far they abide in Him. And they know what He said about the washing, how that the travel-stains must be constantly removed.

(11) And the result will be that the joy that is His, and which springs from a perfect conformity to The Father's will, will be in them and will grow on to perfect fulness. Down the long vista of the Ages that end is seen.

This verse, and its ταῦτα λελάληκα, belongs to the section preceding, beginning at verse 1, and closes it.

Verses 12–17

(12) And what again is the supreme commandment that they are to keep, in order to abide in His love? It is, as He said before at the table (xiii. 34), that "you love (ἀγαπᾶτε) one another even as I loved you": and to this love there is no limit.

(13) "Greater love (ἀγαπὴν) has no one than this love, that he lay down his life for his friends"; sc. for those whom he loves (verse 12), for none ever loved Him but had been first loved and drawn by Him. The ἵνα . . . θῇ means a love *making for* (whether subjective aim or objective result) his laying down, etc.

(14) "You are My friends" (sc. those whom I love), "if you do what I command you": viz. (above all) love each other even as He loved them (verse 12)—with a divine love that has no limit and no self-seeking, and has its source in God.

(15) "No longer I call you servants, for a servant knows not what his master is doing," *i.e.* has not his intimate confidence, is not informed of his intentions immediate or remote. "But you I have called friends,

because all things that I heard from My Father, I made known to you." The deposit of Faith left by our Lord with His Apostles was a complete whole, as is a seed. But the early Church was not conscious explicitly of all that that deposit implicitly contained: nor, we may assert, is the Church of to-day conscious explicitly of all its implications: for we need time and circumstance to unfold to us all that that deposit means. A seeing eye might, and the Apostles might (we do not know that they did), from the beginning have seen the whole as not even yet does the Church see it, for Truth is not in itself dependent upon time for an unfolding: it is our vision that is so dim and slow that we need time to purge it before we can see Truth. There is obviously a plane, could we but reach it, where there is no past, no future, no There, but all is Now and Here.

(16) With regard to this term, "My friends" (14): He calls them so, "not because you chose Me" to love, "but because I chose out you": the initiative was on His side, therefore they shall fear no fickleness: it was He who sought them out and chose them out and appointed them to the Apostolate 'to go and bring forth fruit and a fruit that should endure.' The sap is His, and from Him flows into them: the only love that is worthy and lasting starts from Him and circulates back to Him, doing its work on the way: it is the Holy Spirit, which circulates throughout His mystical Body, the Vine. In so far as this circulates in them and "informs" their requests, their requests shall be granted.

(17) Again He insists, "This is My commandment to you, to love one another (ἵνα ἀγαπᾶτε ἀλλήλους)" (reiterating xiii. 34: xv. 12). Jerome tells how John in his old age used to be carried into church and, being too old to speak to the people at any length, used to repeat to them, "Little children, love one another. . . . For that," he said, "is the Lord's commandment: and if that be done, it is of itself enough (et, si solum fiat, sufficit)."

This verse, and its ταῦτα ἐντέλλομαι, belongs to the section preceding, beginning at verse 12, and closes it.

Verses 18–*xvi.* 1

(18) "The world" (ὁ κόσμος) in the proper sense of the Greek word, means the created earth in all its ordered beauty, and viewed in its sum or acme, man the microcosm. But, owing to the Fall of man, the world, thus intimately bound up in man, is regarded as alienated for the moment from God, and as having to be won back to God through the return of man to His allegiance: so that the whole shall be again brought back to the line of harmonious evolution. Thus the "world" (κόσμος) becomes a term for mankind *quâ* alienated from God, off the track of development, and on the road to dissolution.

(18) "If the world hates you," as it will, "know," etc. The world will hate them because they are not of the world's mind: but let them reflect that "it has hated Me before it hated you, and that I am the first it ever hated." *

(19) And they are not of the world because *He* (ἐγὼ) chose them out of it and made them dissatisfied with, and averse to, the world's spirit. He and the world are antagonistic. The world is glad to forget God: He came to bring men back to God.

(20) "Remember the word I said to you," viz. when they were appointed to the Apostolate (Matt. x. 24, 25), and which He had recently repeated to them at table (xiii. 16), "'a servant is not greater than his Lord': if they persecuted Me," as they had, "they will persecute you too: if they kept My word," which they did not, "they will keep yours too": but they will not.

(21) "But all this they will do to you because of My name," *i.e.* because they represent Him: and He represents The Father, and of that Father the world has no knowledge, little though it thinks so.

(22) "If I had not come and talked to them, they would not have had sin." 'If I had not become Incarnate, and come amongst them, and talked with them, their sin (sc. their state of radical alienation from God) would

* Such is the meaning of the superlative πρῶτον joined with the genitive (ἐμὲ πρῶτον ὑμῶν): it is not synonymous with πρότερον. See also at i. 15, 30.

not have been proved against them: but, as I did come among them, they have no cloak to hang up and cover their sin and pretend it is not there.' They might else have said, "Had He but come among us, we should sure have recognized Him": just as they did actually say, "Had we lived in the days of our fathers, we would not have been partakers with them in the blood of the Prophets" (Matt. xxiii. 30).

(23) "He that hateth Me hateth My Father also." 'In this their hate of Me they have shown their essential state of hostility to My Father,' whom they call their God of Sinai. For Jesus is the one and only revelation of The Father. Men may prefer to evolve an idea of the universal Father, but that idea of theirs will take their own colour and the colour of their Age. The only true idea of Him is to be got from The Son.

(24) "If I had not done among them the works which none other did," *i.e.* if He had not lived the perfect life which they had watched from His infancy and in which they could find no sin (viii. 46) (for they never lost sight of Him, only His ideal did not jump with theirs); if He had not done superhuman miracles which revealed the power and the ethical quality of the Godhead; "they would not have had sin": their state of sin—of aversion from God—would not have been proved against them: 'But, as things are, they have seen Me in the Flesh, and seen My Father revealed in Me, and they have hated Us both. (25) It is but what was written * in their Law (see under x. 34), "they hated Me without a cause," or "gratuitously."' The words are taken from Ps. lxix. 4, written by David in the time of Absalom's rebellion, where David is a type of our Lord: and his favourite son Absalom is a type of the Jews.

(26) "When the Comforter (ὁ παράκλητος) is come," He who will side with the disciples and take their part, pleading with their better selves, strengthening them (which is the root meaning of comforting); He "whom I (ἐγὼ)

* For the Hellenistic phrasing ἵνα πληρωθῇ at the beginning of this verse, see at p. 308.

will send to you from The Father's presence (παρὰ τοῦ Πατρός), the Spirit of Truth who comes forth from The Father's presence; He will bear witness concerning Me," both in their hearts and in the hearts of those who will hear them. And because He is the Spirit of Truth, He can witness only to Truth. Though the "world," *i.e.* man *quâ* alienated from his Creator, has swerved from the axis of true development, the Spirit of Truth secures that His Church shall not—in spite of many set-backs due to human frailty.

(27) "And," along with the Holy Spirit, "you too," you Eleven, "are to bear witness (μαρτυρεῖτε, imperative) concerning Me: for you have been with Me from the beginning," *i.e.* of His public ministry. The Holy Spirit shall witness in men's hearts, in conjunction with the Apostolic message to their ears. They, the Eleven, as first-hand witnesses, supply the material facts, the body of Faith: the Holy Spirit concurrently supplies the quickening intelligence in their hearers, by which the facts live and are apprehended.

(XVI. 1) "These things I have talked to you that you may not be offended" (σκανδαλισθῆτε = be made to stumble). This verse belongs to the section preceding beginning at verse 18 of chapter xv., and should form the closing sentence of chapter xv. It refers to the hatred that the "world" will show to His Apostles and to His Church in proportion as they are not conformed to the "world." That hatred was not to make them swerve or think they must be wrong.

Verses 2–5*a*

(2) "They will put you out of the synagogues." Formal excommunication from the Temple worship in Jerusalem was never passed on the Christian Hebrews: but in the provinces and in foreign countries Christian Hebrews were no doubt gradually cut off from worship in the synagogues, according as the animosity of the Jews increased against the new movement.

"Yea, an hour is coming that every one that killeth

you will think he offereth service to God." Allusion is to their treatment by Jews, *e.g.* by the Sanhedrin (as in Acts iv. 5: vi. 12): by Saul as prime mover (Acts viii. 3: ix. 1, 2): by Herod Agrippa (Acts xii. 1–3): by provincial Jews (Acts xiv. 19, etc.): by Ananus (Annas) the High-priest (Josephus, *Ant.*, XX. ix. 1): and their persecution by Roman and other Gentile secular powers. Our Lord tells them that their persecutors will be acting conscientiously as thinking they are pernicious to the cause of God: therefore let His hearers bear with them.

(3) "These things they will do because they had not come to know (οὐκ ἔγνωσαν) The Father nor Me." Those persecutors would be acting in ignorance, for they knew not the nature of the God whom they thought they served: the Jews knew not that in that Godhead there are Father and Son, and, therefore, they could not believe that He the Man is God incarnate: the Gentiles knew God still less.

(4*a*) "But these things I have told you so that when their hour comes, you may remember," etc. He had said (verse 1) that His reason for talking to them of the world's hatred of them was that they might not find it a stumbling-block. But (ἀλλὰ) His reason for talking to them of the conscientious motives (verse 2) of their persecutors is that when the persecutions come, "you may remember these things, how that *I* told you," *i.e.* may remember what He had told them of those motives, and how it was *He* who had told them, He who knows all hearts. Therefore they should bear with those persecutors. The emphatic ἀλλὰ calls special attention to this important statement of motive, which they might otherwise have found hard to believe.

(4*b*) 'Of these future troubles I did not tell you at the beginning of My ministry.' When He commissioned them to the Apostolate (Matt. x. 1–42) He had indeed foretold persecution for them ultimately (Matt. x. 16–39): but with regard to that their first mission, where Gentiles and Samaritans were excluded (verse 5) and only the ruined house of "Israel" (not Judah) favoured, He had evidently given them to understand that all would be smooth and easy for them : and so it had been (Luke xxii. 35).

" Because I was still with you " : and therefore would not spoil their joy (Matt. ix. 15).

(5) But now that the Bridegroom is shortly to be taken from them, the time is come to prepare them for evil days, for persecution is now imminent.

Verses 5b–15

(5*b*) " And no one of you asks Me, ' Whither goest Thou ? ' "

(6) " But because I have told you these things sorrow has filled your heart." Though He is leaving them, let them not therefore assume that His absence is all loss to them, let them remember whither it is that He withdraws : remember what He told them at the table (xiv. 28), viz. that He is going to *The Father*, returning triumphant, the economy of servitude being ended. Under the circumstances of His rejection by the nation and the consequent delay in the coming of the visible kingdom, (7) it is to their advantage that He goes away.

(7) " If I go not away," ascending to The Father, bearing with Me human nature glorified, " there will not come to you the Paraclete," *i.e.* the Comforter, the Strengthener. Can we say why a further access of the Creative Spirit pleading with men's hearts and strengthening them into a new creation was only possible when the new Germ, the new Man, withdrew from our plane of matter ? As the Fall of Adam was the Fall of all his descendants, the Ascension of our Lord was the ascension of all the sons of God who were, or shall be, grafted into Him. It would seem that so far as concerns mankind it is only throughout our Lord's risen and " ascended " body, into which Christians are sacramentally grafted, that the Holy Spirit has perfect freedom of action.

(8) " And He, when He is come " at Pentecost, taking up His perpetual presence in them the members of the mystical Body, " He will convict the world "—not indeed in its own eyes, but in the eyes of those whose vision is purged.

(9) "He will convict" it (A) "in the matter of *sin*": convict it, that is, of being in a state of alienation from God, in that it refuses to believe into Jesus, viz. into God who had come incarnate among them. Had it not been for its acquiescence in "sin," the world must have leapt to the God-Man for release.

(10) "He will convict" it (B) "in the matter of *righteousness* in that I go to The Father and ye-behold Me no more." Convict it, that is, of holding false views of what Righteousness is: for the One righteous Man has come among them and left His record, and withdrawn to The Father because they would have nothing to do with Him. And mankind are so gone away from Truth that, He being withdrawn to The Father, they cannot behold Him as being yet alive, but rather think of Him as dead.

The verb θεωρεῖτε used here = to behold with the mind's eye. Even the disciples had, until He re-appeared to them after His death, ceased to consider Him (θεωρεῖν) as living. In the word θεωρεῖτε, "ye-behold," the disciples are included with the world, in that, until the Holy Spirit came to them collectively after His resurrection and comes to the individual down the centuries, all alike were and are unable to behold Him with the eye of faith as being living and present. The Greek original shows, by the absence of the pronoun ὑμεῖς before this verb θεωρεῖτε, that there is no distinction drawn here between the disciples and the world, such as there was in xiv. 19.

(11) "He will convict" it (C) "in the matter of *judgment*": convict it, not in its own eyes, but in the eyes of those whose vision is purged: convict it of holding false standards of success and failure. 'For My cross and passion, the measure of the world's opinion of Me, is the measure of the judgment and sentence passed by the All-seeing on the world: and not only on the world and its body of opinion, but also on its prince, Satan, who has led it astray after false ideals (see under xii. 31).

(12) "I have yet many things to tell you." Not that He had anything materially new to tell them, for (xv. 15) He had told them all: but as to what He had told them whether by hint or parable, by plain statement or obscure, He had much to interpret and make clear to them, much to carry out to logical issues which at present they did not, nor were able to, understand.

(13) "But when He, the Spirit of Truth, is come, He will guide you to all the Truth," *i.e.* it was the office of the Holy Spirit, the Spirit of Truth, to be their guide into all the ramifications of that body of Truth once for all delivered by Christ Himself and into which they were baptized, but which as yet they could not appreciate or estimate. The Holy Spirit, during His economy between Pentecost and the second Coming of our Lord, would add no new truth, 'for He only speaks from Me, and I have told all'; but He would constantly show them fresh values, the full meanings, and the logical issues inherent in the premises. Here is the statement of the development of Catholic doctrine.

"And the things that are coming He will announce to you," *i.e.* 'He will declare to you the future, the eschatological events (Luke xxi. 26, "the things that are coming on the earth") before they are upon you.' Not that the Gentile Church has ever yet understood the full meaning of the Hebrew prophets or of the Hebrew Apocalypse, nor has she pretended to officially: but the Church will understand them when the time draws near, when the things "are coming" and before they are upon her: but probably not till the Jews are converted, for the Books are the national Books of Israel and Judah.

(14) "He will glorify Me, because He will take of Mine (ἐκ τοῦ ἐμοῦ λήμψεται) and will announce to you." 'The Holy Spirit's work will be to glorify Me in your understandings: for He issues from Me, takes of Mine, and will unfold to you a clear perception of Me: and that you have not yet.'

(15) In saying, "He will take of Mine and will announce to you," our Lord declares that the Holy Spirit issues not

only from The Father but also from Him The Son, for The Father has nothing that The Son has not: "for all things that The Father hath are Mine."

Verses 16–*end*

(16) 'Yet a little while elapses (*i.e.* till His death to-morrow), and then no longer *ye-behold Me* (θεωρεῖτέ με),' *i.e.* with the eyes of faith or mental contemplation. For during the interval between His death and resurrection the disciples lost their faith and spiritual vision, and no more *beheld* Him than did the world.

'And again a little while shall elapse, and then *ye-shall-see Me* (ὄψεσθέ με), *i.e.* with bodily eyes.' When the short interval between His death and resurrection had elapsed, then they should see Him with their bodily eyes.

(17) His disciples, or rather some of them (ἐκ), repeating His words of verse 16, ask each other what does He mean by them and also by those other words (from verse 10), "because I withdraw to The Father."

(18) And they sum up the matter (ἔλεγον οὖν) by particular stress on the meaning of that phrase, "a little while," as though to understand that might give them the clue.

(19) Jesus, aware that they wished to question Him, forestalls them. 'You are asking each other about My words, "a little while and *ye-behold Me not* (οὐ θεωρεῖτέ με), and again a little while and *ye-shall-see Me* (ὄψεσθέ με)."'

(20) He gives no explanation of the phrase, "a little while": but as to the words, "ye-behold Me not," viz. in that short interval between His death and resurrection, during which their eyes of faith were dimmed so as to see no better than the world, He explains that His absence, or rather the inability to behold Him, would affect them in one way and the world in another way: for they and the world were already sundered from each other. "*You* (emphatic ὑμεῖς) shall weep and lament" at having lost Me: "but the world shall rejoice" at being, as it will think, rid of Me. "You" (emphatic ὑμεῖς) who will be sorrowful at My absence, "shall have your sorrow

turned into joy": for (as He explains in verse 22) "I will see you (ὄψομαι) again," *i.e.* see with bodily eyes, and, by implication, they will again see Him with bodily eyes: as happened after His resurrection.

(21) Their sorrow would be sharp, but again it would be soon forgotten. As a woman has sorrow when her hour comes, but forgets her travail pangs when her child is born: so would His disciples have sorrow when their hour came. But as soon as their agony was over and they had given birth to Him and borne Him into the world,* they would remember no more their anguish. It was not till they saw Him after His resurrection that the Apostles fully believed into Him.

(22) "Therefore," to apply the simile, "*now* you have sorrow: but" I will come to the birth in you, you shall be delivered of a man-child even Me on the day I see you again: for "I will see you again with bodily eyes (ὄψομαι)" and you shall see Me: "and your heart shall rejoice, and your joy no one shall take from you."

Although the first application of the πάλιν ὄψομαι ("again I will see" you with bodily eyes) is to His appearance to the disciples after His resurrection, the second and fuller application is probably to an Age yet future.

(23*a*) "And '*in that day*'" (ἐν ἐκείνῃ τῇ ἡμέρᾳ, the regular formula of prophecy for a future Age, and so used again by our Lord in verse 26 and in xiv. 20) "you shall ask no question (οὐκ ἐρωτήσετε οὐδέν) of Me" (as they had wished to do in verse 19), for before they asked He would answer—so complete would their union then be. For though the union is already real during this the time of His absence, this the time of the economy of The Spirit, it is as yet very imperfect owing to the imperfections of men's natures with which The Spirit is ever striving. But "in that day" they shall not feel that He is outside of them.

* For this simile of a woman bringing forth a child applied to the birth of the Christian Faith in a community, see Rev. xii. 2, where the conversion of the Jews to Christ at the end of this Age seems to be figured.

(23*b*) And, whether "in that day" or in the present time, "Verily, verily, I say to you, if ye shall make any petition (ἄν τι αἰτήσητε) of The Father He will give it to you—in My name." Although the union is as yet imperfect, it has already begun: it is as true of this Age as of the future one that whatever petition the Church makes of The Father now or then He will give it: but it must be made, as it will be given, "in My name." See at xiv. 13: xv. 7.

(24) "Hitherto you have asked nothing in My name": for as yet they could not fully ask "in My name," *i.e.* with His singleness of desire for The Father's glory. "Ask, and you shall receive": the nearer they approached to asking "in My name," the nearer they approached to receiving "in My name," *i.e.* to receiving as fully and as surely as The Father gives to Him. And when they have attained to fully asking "in My name," as they will "in that day," then "your joy will be filled." As at xv. 11.

(25) "These things I have talked to you in *parables* (παροιμίαις)," or similes or metaphors, such as the parables by which He taught, and such as the metaphors of His "coming from" and "going to" The Father; of The Spirit "speaking not of Himself" but "speaking what He hears"; of The Spirit "taking of Mine"; of The Father's "sending" Him; of Himself as "sending" The Spirit, etc. But "an hour is coming" (viz. a yet future Age) "when I shall no more talk to you in proverbs" or metaphors, "but shall report to you plainly concerning The Father": through the medium, that is, not of our present imperfect language which by its metaphor often obscures, but of that perfect language by which the resurrection bodies communicate.

(26) "In that day" (again as at verse 23 the regular prophetic formula for a future Age: it is the *bayyôm hahû'* of the Prophets) "ye shall ask in My name": ask as He asks, and asking receive: "and I do not say to you that" in that day "I will request (ἐρωτήσω) The Father concerning you" (περὶ ὑμῶν, in anything to do with you).

(27) "For The Father, of Himself, loves you." That

He does so is seen "from the fact (A) that you have loved Me": for this they could never have done unless God had first poured His love into them (1 John iv. 10), so that it circulates back to Him from them like sap in a vine, or as blood in a body: "and from the fact (B) that you have believed that I came forth from The Father's presence"; and this Faith again, like Love, is the gift of God.

(28) Here is the sum of the Christian Faith in four fundamental propositions, which, with their several *why* and *how* and *result*, form the whole body of Christian verity:—

1. "I came forth from out * The Father": sc. My eternal generation as God The Son.
2. "I am come into the world": sc. My incarnation, and My revelation of the Godhead to men.
3. "I am leaving the world": sc. My rejection by the world, My passion and death.
4. "I go to The Father": sc. My resurrection from the dead, and ascension to The Father in glory, and My effusion of The Spirit.

(29) His disciples grasping the four propositions think they understand the whole—knowing as yet little or nothing of what any of the four propositions mean, or how they stand related each to other, nor of the vast body of Truth which lies implicit in those four.

'Now, now we understand Thee: there is no need to talk of speaking plainly to us in some future Age.'

(30) 'Thou sayest that in that future Age (verse 23) we shall have no need to ask questions of Thee: but now, already, we know that Thou seest all hearts and hast no need that any of us should formulate questions to Thee,

* ἐκ τοῦ Πατρός, not ἀπὸ τοῦ Πατρός, as the disciples misunderstood Him to mean (see verse 30, ἀπὸ τοῦ Θεοῦ): ἀπὸ would merely mean having a mission from God. The misunderstanding was possible because the Aramaic language (in which the conversation was carried on) has, like the Hebrew, only the one word *min* to express two distinct ideas which Greek renders by ἐκ and ἀπό. John, translating the conversation into Greek, took advantage of the niceties of the latter in order to show that the meaning which our Lord here attached to *min* had been misunderstood by the disciples. He meant ἐκ (essential origin): they understood ἀπὸ (mission or accidental origin).

inasmuch as Thou knowest our thoughts before we put them in words.'

"Hereby (ἐν τούτῳ) we believe that Thou camest forth from (ἀπὸ) God": they have in mind how easily and correctly He had read their difficulties in verse 19, although they had not put them in words in His hearing. This knowledge of all hearts (ἐν τούτῳ) seemed to them a sign that He was no common man, but had a mission from (ἀπὸ) God. The same effect had been produced on Nathanael when he found that his thoughts were all known to Jesus (i. 48, 49); and again the same effect is seen in the case of the woman of Samaria on finding all her past life was open to Him (iv. 16–19 and 29). The Eleven do not as yet think habitually of Him as being very God, but as being some great one worthy to be called, figuratively, the Son of God though only human: as Nathanael (i. 49) and others had called him. Peter had once, for a moment last September, risen to the heights of clear vision of His Godhead (Matt. xvi. 16): but not until Pentecost did the vision become permanent with him.

(31, 32) "Do ye *now* believe? lo, the hour cometh, yea, is come, for your being scattered each to his own home and for your leaving Me alone." They thought that already, at that moment, they had a faith full and firm: little they knew themselves and the frailty of their confidence.

(32) Of this verse 32 and the incident immediately connected with it a fuller account is given in Matt. xxvi. 31–35, Mark xiv. 27–31. John saw no need to repeat the prophecy of Peter's denial. "And I am not alone because The Father is with Me": *i.e.* so utter will be His desertion by all of them, that except The Father none will stand by Him. He is not alone, only because The Father is with Him.

(33) "These things I have talked to you, that in Me ye may have peace." "These things," *i.e.* all the discourse since the close of the ritual and Judas's departure, *i.e.* all from xiii. 31 to here. Only in unity with Him will they find peace, and His peace: xiv. 27.

"In the world ye shall have tribulation: but be of good cheer, I have overcome the world": and in His victory, they, and all who through them shall hereafter become members of His mystical Body, are of necessity victors. The victory is His: none else could conquer: and by their sacramental union with Him, His victory becomes theirs in the process by which He assimilates them, body, soul, and spirit, into Himself—an assimilation which confirms rather than obliterates each individuality.

The discourse of John xv., xvi. divides into—

XV. 1–11. The living union that exists throughout His mystical Body: its element (like sap in a vine) is Love (ἀγαπή) which starts from Him and courses through them, bearing fruit with their co-operation—the co-operation of, at least, their will. The process of transforming their alien human nature into complete harmony and union with His perfect and glorified human nature is slow but it is certain.

XV. 12–17. Repeats the "new commandment" of love (of xiii. 34), and describes the nature of that love.

18–XVI. 1. The world's treatment of them because of their witness to Him: for it hates Him. The Holy Spirit's witness to Him will concur with their own.

XVI. 2–5*a*. The world's treatment of them, due to its false idea of God.

5*b*–15. The promise of The Spirit, during our Lord's absence (5*b*–7): the work of The Spirit as affecting A, the World (8–11); B, the Church (12–15).

16–end. The immediate future for the latter is dark, but will be succeeded by one of joy: and there will be a yet more perfect union with Him in a later Age and later Ages.

Here follows the request of our Lord for His Church (xvii. 1–end): the communing of The Son-Incarnate with The Father.

§ XXIII

JOHN XVII

The request of Jesus Christ for His Church.

(1) "AND He lifted up His eyes to heaven and said, 'Father, the hour has come: glorify Thy Son'": *i.e.* make plain to these there that the Man Jesus is also the God-Man: make it plain by His resurrection and ascension. Thus, by their having a true knowledge of The Son they may advance to a true knowledge of The Father: for to know The Son is to know also The Father. Every religion that acknowledges a God but ignores the Trinity, becomes, when handled by its own philosophers, pantheistic. The sum of created things takes the place of the Second Person, and the act of creation becomes an act of generation: see Gnosticism, Brahmanism, Buddhism, and even Mahommedanism. Fortunately the masses do not and cannot deal in abstract thought, and so can still worship God as a Being apart from themselves.

March 24
Nisan 14
Thurs. evening, about 10 p.m.

(2) "That The Son may glorify Thee even as Thou gavest Him authority over all flesh: authority, as regards the whole mass which Thou hast given Him (πᾶν ὃ δέδωκας), to give them individually (ἀυτοῖς) Life eternal." A similar analysis of the neut. sing. ὃ (the mass) into the masc. plur. ἐκεῖνοι (the individuals) forming it occurs in verse 24. This "authority to give" cannot be fully exercised by The Son till He be glorified, *i.e.* risen and ascended, for not till then is the power won: and the gift, viz. Life eternal, will be the glorification of The Father by The Son.

(3) For "eternal Life is this, the recognising or

learning-to-know (ἵνα * γινώσκωσι)," (A) "Thee," *i.e.* 'that Thou art The Father': (B) "The only true God," *i.e.* 'that the only true God is triune, viz. Thou The Father, I The Son, and the Holy Spirit': (C) "Him whom Thou didst send—Jesus Christ," *i.e.* 'that I, Jesus Messiah, sent by Thee, am God The Son and also Man. And this full but gradual knowledge will only be given after the resurrection and ascension of The Son: for not till then will The Spirit be given in abundance so as to have a full flow in His mystical Body.

(4) Here our Lord changes from the indirect mode, "The Son," "He," "Jesus Christ," to the direct, "I" and "Me."

"I," the God-Man, "glorified Thee on the earth," *i.e.* during and by means of His life on earth He made The Father known, revealing Him as eternal Father, revealing also His love and His holiness: "having finished the work which Thou hast given Me to do," *i.e.* the work for which He became Incarnate.

He speaks from the standpoint of some seventeen hours later, when His death shall have been consummated. True, very few had accepted His revelation of the Godhead; and they, very imperfectly until Pentecost; but, so far as His part was concerned, His work on earth was done: the rest belongs to His work in Heaven and the economy of the Holy Spirit on earth.

(5) "And now glorify Me Thou, Father, alongside Thee with the glory which I had alongside Thee before the world was," *i.e.* make it clear that I, the Man, am eternal God, ascending to Thee, alongside of Thee, co-equal with Thee, and co-eternal. And the object of this glorifying of Him by The Father is not that anything may accrue to Him Jesus, but that the disciples, by learning that He is Divine, may pass on to know The Father (as in verse 1).

(Verses 6–8) The present state to which He has brought the Church which He is leaving.

(6) "I manifested Thy Name," *i.e.* I revealed Thy

* A Hellenistic Hebraism: it is exactly the Hebrew ל with infin. const., meaning *position of*, or *for*, *recognising*.

nature. For any adequate *name* of a person or thing is the complete connotation of that person or thing. Thus the eternal Son is called the "Name" of the eternal Father.

To set forth this relationship of Jesus Christ to The Father is the main object of John's gospel. Whilst our Lord was yet with the Eleven, they did not take the full meaning of His talk concerning His own transcendental nature: nor again was it a fitting subject to be handled in the Synoptic gospels which were mainly for popular use and for exoteric teaching. John's gospel gives our Lord's esoteric teaching, such as He spoke to the theologians of Jerusalem, or to the inner circle of His disciples—*arcana*, reserved for such as should be able to understand.

(6) "To the men whom Thou gavest Me out of the world," *i.e.* primarily the Eleven whom God had chosen by preparing their inward dispositions, and had then given to the Man-God to be taught by Him.

"Thine they were, and to Me Thou gavest them," *i.e.* 'Thou didst begin the work in them: I continued it in them at Thy bidding': "and they have kept (τετήρηκαν) Thy word": *i.e.* they on their part have given attention to The Father's message as given by the God-Man, and have laid it up in their hearts for further meditation and fuller insight into its meaning later on. This laying up in the heart of things not clearly apprehended, in order for further meditation, is twice noticed in the case of the Virgin Mother as her constant habit (Luke ii. 19, 51).

(7, 8) 'The result is that now' (when He must leave them) 'they have learnt that all that I say or do or am is but a manifestation of Thee: for the things' (ῥήματα, the several teachings) 'which I had from Thee I have passed on to them. Thus they on their part have accepted as truth and learnt as truth' (though they are far, as yet, from understanding them) 'the formal propositions that'—

(A) "I came-forth from Thee" (παρὰ σοῦ = from Thy presence): and (B) "*Thou* didst send Me." This was what they thus far had learnt and believed: but they would come later to see all that lies implicit in these bald statements, they would see that A means that His coming "from Thy presence" is the Incarnation of the eternal Son: and that B means that the scheme of redemption is the will of the whole Godhead, Father, Son, and Spirit. We shall remain on only the outskirts of knowledge unless we endorse that axiom of theology that "the operations of the Holy Trinity *ad extra* (*i.e.* with reference to that which is created) are common to all the Three Persons of the Trinity," Each in His several mode.

Verses 9–end. The request in behalf of His Church.

(9) "I (ἐγὼ, emphatic) make request (ἐρωτῶ) concerning them," *i.e.* the Eleven; "not concerning the world am I making request." His concern as yet is directly with these Eleven. It is through them that He means to work indirectly on the world.

Then follow three pleas in support of His request:—

(A) 'They are Thine: in that Thou didst predispose them toward Me.'

(10) (B) 'They are Thine as being Mine and taught by Me, just as being Thine they are drawn to Me.' Thus intimate is the union between The Father and The Son in His double nature.

(C) 'And I-have-been-and-am-glorified (δεδόξασμαι) in them,' *i.e.* the work in them is well advanced; for by them He is acknowledged and confessed to be what He is: although as yet with imperfect vision, still as far as their present capacity admits.

(11*a*) Here follow three circumstances which induce the request:—

(A) "No longer am I in the world," *i.e.* He is about to leave this hostile world and to be locally parted from them.

(B) "*They* are in the world," *i.e.* *they* remain alone in the midst of a hostile world.

(C) "*I* am coming to Thee," *i.e.* they will think He is not at hand to aid them: and this is in a measure true, cf. verse 12: although His absence is really gain for them: for it means a closer union with Him in the Holy Spirit than that which they have now.

(11*b*–26) Here follows the request proper :—

(11*b*) "Holy Father, keep them in Thy Name which Thou hast given to Me" (*Πάτερ ἅγιε, τήρησον αὐτοὺς ἐν τῷ ὀνόματι σου, ᾧ δέδωκάς μοι*). If this be the correct reading (Westcott and Hort have no doubt of it), the "which" must refer to "name" and not to "them." The meaning will be 'keep them in Me who am Thy name, Thy connotation, revelation, manifestation : keep them in unity with Me, and therefore in unity with and in knowledge of Thee.' The words "Thy name which Thou hast given to Me" recall that other cryptic saying at x. 29, "that which My Father has given to Me is greater than all," viz. the Godhead, as Augustine there comments : "What is that 'greater than all' that The Father has given The Son ? That He should be His only-begotten Son."

"That they may be one (ἓν = unity) even as are We," *i.e.* 'that their unity with Us and among themselves may be preserved and perfected.'

(12) "Whilst I was with them," *i.e.* the Eleven, "*I* kept them in Thy Name," etc., *i.e.* in the knowledge of Thee, and so in unity with Me : "and I guarded them" from Satan's attack : "and none of them perished, but the son of perdition," *i.e.* Judas. The phrase, "son of perdition," is a Hebraism for *the lost one*, cf. "son of strength" = *strong one :* "son of wickedness" = *wicked one :* "son of possession" = *heir :* "son of pledging" = *hostage.*

"That the scripture may be fulfilled" (ἵνα πληρωθῇ, see p. 308) = and so the scripture is fulfilled. Our Lord is perhaps referring to Ps. cix. (cviii.) 8, as does Peter in Acts i. 16–20.

(13) "But now I am" leaving them and "coming to Thee : and these things I speak in the world," etc., *i.e.* whilst as yet with them. In saying that He is coming to The Father, He means that He is not lost to them, so that they may not be sad, but may rejoice, as He does, at His going : seeing that it means a stage further for them toward the goal.

(14) "I" (ἐγὼ, The Son) "have given to them Thy word," *i.e.* not merely the oral teaching, but the whole revelation of The Father as manifested in the words and acts and personality of Jesus Christ: and they have embraced it: "and," in consequence, "the world hated them, because they do not belong to the world, even as I do not belong to the world."

(15) "I am not making request that Thou shouldst remove them out of the world, but that Thou shouldst keep them out of the power of evil" (ἐκ τοῦ πονηροῦ. Better, "out of the power of the evil one").

(17) Not only keep them out of the power of the evil one, but "Hallow them (ἁγίασον αὐτοὺς) in the Truth," *i.e.* by keeping them apart in the Truth. "Thy word," *i.e.* Thy doctrine as revealed to them by Me, "is Truth." If they are kept apart, *i.e.* from error, and kept in the Truth, they will become closer knit to God. For Truth absolute (and not what men are pleased to-day or to-morrow to call truth) has a transforming power.

The word ἁγιάζω (rendered "sanctify," "hallow," "consecrate") means to set-apart-and-devote-to-God: whether it be things, or sacrificial animals, or men for His service: the more thoroughly men are set apart to God in the sphere of Truth, both intellectual and moral, the more closely are they knit to the Deity, and made holy.

(18) "As I was sent by Thee," as Thy representative, "into the world, so send I them" as Our representatives "into the world."

(19) And in His complete and unceasing consecration of Himself lies the power that they also become wholly consecrate: for He transfuses His own sanctity into them by virtue of His sacramental union with them.

(20) "And I make request not about these only," *i.e.* the Eleven, "but also about those who shall believe in Me by means of their word," *i.e.* their teaching, both of dogmatic truth and of historical truth, concerning the facts of His Godhead and of His life on earth.

(21) "That all of them may be a unity—even as Thou, Father, art in Me and I am in Thee, that they also may be

in Us: so that the world may believe that My mission was from Thee" (σύ με ἀπέστειλας). The faith of this Age of the Gentile Vicariate affects but a handful in comparison with the harvest of the world in the millennial and post-millennial Ages.

'Not only did I deliver to them Thy word (14) and sent them as Our representatives into the world (18), not only do I consecrate Myself for their sakes that they too may be wholly consecrate (19)'—

(22) "Also I have given to them" mystically in the recent Holy Communion, and to be theirs ultimately, "the glory which Thou hast given Me" (*e.g.* that glory which for want of better words or metaphors we call His "ascension to Heaven," and "sitting on the right hand of God the Father"; all of which belongs to those who form His mystical Body): "so that they may be Unity, even as We are Unity: I being in them and Thou in Me." Our Lord, by His two natures, is the Ladder (Gen. xxviii. 12: John i. 51) of which one end—His Divine nature—is in Heaven, and the other end—His human nature—is on earth.

(23) "That they may be perfected into Unity": it is a matter of gradual realization, this Unity: "and the result will be that the world will know that My mission was from Thee, and that Thou didst love them with the same love with which Thou lovedst Me"—so close will their union with Him be seen to be. We may suppose that in the millennial Age, those who shall have been found worthy of the first resurrection (Rev. xx. 5), and those who while yet living were assumed to Christ (1 Thess. iv. 17), will be in mature immortality and will be visible to those who shall be still on earth: these last, not having yet died, will not have reached the stage of resurrection and immortality. Besides all these, there will be those dead who shall not have been found worthy of the first resurrection, but who will be awaiting the Judgment Day beyond the Millennium (Rev. xx. 12), many for Life and many for a second period of death, until after another Age, or other Ages, all shall be gathered in.

(24) "Father, with regard to that which Thou hast given Me" (ὃ δέδωκάς μοι), *i.e.* the final sum of His Church, "I will that where I am they also (κἀκεῖνοι) may be with Me," viz. "sitting on the right hand of God the Father," as we call it. Nothing short of His own fulness—the Godhead—has Jesus decreed to give to men when they shall have advanced through the successive stages (μοναὶ) that await them in His Father's house, xiv. 2. The collective mass (ὃ) given by The Father to The Son is analyzed into the individuals (ἐκεῖνοι) forming it, as at verse 2.

"In order that they may behold My glory which Thou hast given Me." "Behold My glory," a Hebraism for "share My glory," as in the phrases, "to see Death," viii. 51: Luke ii. 26: Heb. xi. 5: to "see Life," iii. 36: to "see the Kingdom of God," Luke ix. 27: John iii. 3: to "see corruption," Acts ii. 27, 31: xiii. 35–37: to "see grief," Rev. xviii. 7: to "see good days," 1 Pet. iii. 10.

"My glory"; sc. My glorified Humanity and also My Godhead as the eternal Son: "because Thy love to Me" as eternal Father to eternal Son "is from before the world's foundation," *i.e.* is from before time and had no beginning.

(25) "O righteous Father, and the world knew Thee not": for man had become alienated from God's Fatherhood and God's righteousness by the Fall: "but *I*," The Son who became Incarnate, "knew Thee: and" the result is that "these knew that My mission is from Thee"—a mission to bring back the human race to Him. (26) "And I made known to them Thy name," *i.e.* His nature to which man had become blind, "and I will make it known," *i.e.* yet more, according as He makes their capacity greater: 'so that ultimately the Love wherewith Thou lovedst Me may have free course in them, as it has between Thee and Me, I being always in them.'

This request of our Lord thus given in John's seventeenth chapter is clearly no prayer of an inferior to a superior: constantly there is seen in it the co-equality of the Speaker with The Father. They Two have but one mind. Neither can have a desire apart from the Other. Also as God Incarnate, the harmony between our Lord's Human nature and His Godhead (His Divine nature) was utter.

Where The Son speaks He is not seeking to bend The Father to Him: rather is He voicing the purpose of the Godhead. This soliloquy or intercessory communion of The Son, the God-Man, with The Father was uttered aloud for the sake of the Eleven who were with Him: perhaps more especially in order that John the mystic who had lain on His breast might afterwards, plumbing the deeps of memory, recall its salient sentences and record it for the Church. The object being not so much to let us know what He said on a special occasion, as to show the constant attitude of His mind, the informing idea of His unceasing "intercession" for us during the time of His absence.

The "mediation" or "intercession" of our High-priest, the God-Man, is not a modifying of the Father's position as regards us: that idea is due to our anthropomorphic images which at once aid and hinder thought: rather is it a modifying of our position as regards The Father, in the Living Laboratory Jesus Christ.

The "mediation" of our Lord is not a thing external to us: it is, as it were, a chemical change that is ever going on in His mystical Body, precipitating and purging out our dross, vivifying and sublimating what remains.

His "mediation" or "intercession" for us is not words: it is a process by which all that is alien to the Godhead's sanctity is gradually eliminated from those who form our Lord's mystical Body: it is ever going on in Heaven (as we call it) before The Father, by the alchemy of the Holy Spirit who is the Godhead flowing through It as sap in the Vine: so close is that mystical Body knit to our Lord's risen Body.

But there: is the metaphor of a chemical process any better than that of intercessory words? Indeed it is not as good, for it seems to lack the interest of the Personality of the medium.

This and the other long discourses of our Lord's preserved by John, are they to be considered as given to us in the very words of our Lord rendered into Greek? The form in which these discourses are presented to us shows that we have but fragments of a larger whole: but John, sounding in his memory, could recollect much of our Lord's very wording, phrase by phrase, and how one thought led on to another. The procession of thought was doubtless marked more explicitly as the discourses flowed from His lips: John has not attempted to do more than present the salient thoughts in their consecutive order, recalling the actual Aramaic words in which they were uttered: he must leave much of the connecting links to be supplied by such of his readers as should be able to follow him. These discourses, preserved by John, spoken to Jewish theologians or to the inner circle of the Twelve can never have been meant for popular reading: we seem to require the mystic's vision, or intellects trained in dogmatic theology, to expound them to us. And this not so much because dogmatic theology has its roots in the written records of John, as because the mind of the Church moves of necessity in harmony with the written records.

When our Lord spoke to the people and to the untrained intelligence, He spoke as the Synoptic gospels represent Him. When He spoke of the deep mysteries or to trained theologians, He spoke as John has recorded. John has not recast in his own style our Lord's discourses; but rather those discourses, by long meditation upon them, have become John's habitual language as the only language adequate to express the transcendental vision. The same thing has happened with John the Baptist: he sees as John the Evangelist sees, and as our Lord's own language had taught them both to see. The Baptist's language (John i. 15–18: iii. 27–36) is that of our Lord's discourses as preserved in the fourth Gospel, and is that of our Lord's uttered communion with The Father as preserved by Matthew (xi. 25–27) and by Luke (x. 21, 22).

§ XXIV

JOHN XVIII. 1–27

The arrest in Gethsemane. The inquiry in Caiaphas's house.

(1) "HAVING spoken these things Jesus went forth with His disciples," etc., *i.e.* with the Eleven. "Went forth," *i.e.* from the city, and probably by the Fountain Gate at the south-east corner of the walls, near the Pool of the Siloam. Then turning northward they would ascend the Kedron ravine for 1000 yards or so to the lower bridge that stood by the "Tomb of Absalom": here crossing the torrent to the east side and following up the valley for another 400 yards they would come to Gethsemane.*

March 24, Thurs. night, about 10.30 p.m.

"A garden," viz. that of Gethsemane. It lay at the foot of the western slope of the Mount of Olives and on the left bank of the Kedron torrent.

John makes no mention of the Agony in the garden: that had already been related in the three synoptic gospels: but he will add a few details of that night.

(2) Judas not only "knew the place," but knew that our Lord and the Eleven would be passing the night there as was His habit. Though Saturday and Sunday nights were spent at Bethany, those of Monday, Tuesday, Wednesday, and to-night He passed on the Mount of Olives (Luke xxi. 37, "during the nights, going out (of the city), He used to lodge in the mount which is called the Mount of Olives" (τὰς δὲ νύκτας ἐξερχόμενος ηὐλίζετο εἰς τὸ ὄρος τὸ καλούμενον Ἐλαιῶν)). Another notice of His passing a night

* From this point onwards fuller notes will be found in my *The Crucifixion and Resurrection of Jesus Christ;* but advantage of this opportunity has been taken to make some corrections and additions.

here is in John viii. 1. Tradition shows still the large natural grotto here used by Him.

(3) "Judas therefore having received (A) the band of soldiers (τὴν σπεῖραν) and (B) officers from the chief priests and the Pharisees." This is the first notice we have in the four gospels of any Roman infantry having taken part in the arrest. The article in τὴν σπεῖραν points to the battalion which garrisoned the Antonia fortress in Jerusalem. The "officers" (ὑπηρέτας) are members of the Temple police, a body of men drawn from the tribe of Levi.

"With cressets and torches" (μετὰ φανῶν καὶ λαμπάδων): an incidental touch that shows it was not the time of full moon. The details given by the Mishna and other Rabbinical books about the fixing of the Paschal month by observance of the moon's phases belong either to an ideal system of Rabbinical fancy, or, more probably, to a change of system adopted by the Jews in the latter half of the first century of our era when they abandoned their 84-year cycle as being unsatisfactory, and began a long series of experiments to obtain a calendar which should keep months and moons concurrent—experiments which resulted in their present luni-solar calendar at the time (early 4th century) that the Council of Nicæa gave Christendom an amended Paschal canon.

The moon had been full last Friday at 9.16 p.m. Jerusalem time, and would hardly be up as yet—say 12.30 a.m.

Mch. 25 } Fri.
Nisan 15
12.30 a.m. about.

(4) "Jesus therefore, knowing all the things that were coming upon Him, went forth." John is careful to mark the divine omniscience of our Lord. "Went forth," not from the garden, but from the grotto, where He and the Eleven had had a brief rest after His agony.

Here comes the kiss of Judas (Matt. xxvi. 47–50*a*: Mark xiv. 43–45: Luke xxii. 47, 48) at the entrance of the grotto: and Judas drops back into line with his party who had now come up.

"And He saith to them," *i.e.* to those in command of

the soldiers, "Whom seek ye?" knowing it was Himself they sought.

(5, 6) They answer, "Jesus the Nazoræan" (ὁ Ναζωραῖος),* and they know He stands before them, for Judas has already given the sign agreed on and is standing with them. He replies, "I am He": and in order that His disciples, as well as His captors and Judas, might know that He was not forcibly taken but deliberately surrendered Himself, a sudden power went forth from Him before which His enemies retreated and fell to the ground.

(7) He repeats the question to make them recollect that they had no warrant to arrest the Eleven which perhaps they were inclined to do. As they admitted they had only orders to arrest Him, He puts it to them,

(8) "'If therefore it is Me ye seek, let these go.' (9) Thus was fulfilled (ἵνα πληρωθῇ, the ἵνα of result) the word which He had said (xvii. 12), 'Of those whom Thou has given Me I lost not one.'"

(10) "Peter therefore," *i.e.* touched by this loving care of our Lord for them all, and remembering how vehemently he had protested a few hours ago that he would die with Him, "having a-long-knife (μάχαιρα) drew it," etc. This long-knife was one of the two long-knives (μάχαιρας) or "short-swords" which had been produced by the Apostles in the "Upper Chamber" (Luke xxii. 38). They are probably the two long double-edged knives which Peter (the Levite) and John (the priest) had used in the slaying and preparing of the Paschal lamb in the afternoon (Luke xxii. 8). The word μάχαιρα is used by the LXX for the sacrificial knife of Abraham (Gen. xxii. 6, 10) and for that of the Levite in Judges xix. 29—the Hebrew in all three instances being *hamma'akeleth*, "the knife."

(11) To Peter's vehemence Jesus answered by bidding

* "The Nazoræan," ὁ Ναζωραῖος. This is the form that Matthew (twice) and John (three times) invariably use: so too Luke in the Acts invariably (eight times), but in his gospel only once as against Nazarene (Ναζαρηνὸς) twice. Mark uses Nazarene (Ναζαρηνὸς) invariably (four times). The Syriac Version does not vary: throughout the four gospels and Acts its *Noṣroyo'* favours the form Ναζωραῖος.

him sheathe his knife, "The cup which The Father hath given Me, shall I not drink it ?" He intended to accept to the full what The Father (and He Himself *quâ* The Son) had put on Him. From this moment the disciples would understand that He forbad them to interfere in any way on His behalf. Thus John during the scene in Caiaphas's house to-night will not make any protest: he will watch, and seek to understand.

(12) The Roman soldiers "therefore" * and the Jews' police "officers" (ὑπηρέται) arrested Jesus and bound Him: whilst He pointed out (Luke xxii. 52) to certain of the Sanhedrin and magistrates of the Temple (στρατηγοὺς τοῦ ἱεροῦ) who were present the uselessness of this armed force: 'Did they not know that He could not be taken unless He assented ? Had they not discovered that, during their many futile attempts to arrest Him in the Temple ?' Cf. John vii. 32, 44: viii. 20: x. 39. 'But now their hour was come'—the hour that He and The Father had fore-ordained for the seeming triumph of evil.

The three Synoptists record our Lord's remark to these His enemies, "As against a robber are ye come out with swords and staves to take Me." In the words, "As against a robber" (ὡς ἐπὶ λῃστὴν). He seems to be alluding to the recent capture of the notable robber (λῃστὴς) Barabbas and his band who had made an insurrection in the city accompanied with murder (see Matthew, Mark, Luke, and the contrast Peter draws (Acts iii. 14, 15) between Barabbas the "murderer" and Jesus "the Prince of Life"). We may conjecture that the capture of Barabbas had very recently been made. Some such political crisis seems required to account for the readiness with which Pilate had furnished the soldiers for this raid upon Jesus; and would also explain why so strong a force as ἡ σπεῖρα had been put at the disposal of Caiaphas: for it needs an explanation. The governor, determined to show a strong hand in dealing with Barabbas's insurrection, had purposely

* The "therefore" implies that, with those last words to Peter, our Lord withdrew that power by which He had (verse 6) prevented the advance of His captors.

fixed the public execution of that ringleader and of his two accomplices to Friday, Nisan 15, knowing that that was the festival-day. It was only at the last moment, viz. on Wednesday afternoon (p. 298), that the Sanhedrin, determining that Jesus should be executed along with those malefactors, postponed the Paschal celebration by twenty-four hours: for they feared a riot unless they could secure time to divert the current of popular enthusiasm that had set so strongly in His favour these last four days: and it is surprising to find how successful they proved to be. Such postponement would further, incidentally, serve them as a counterblast to the governor's challenge.

Thus, that our Lord was crucified on Friday, Nisan 15, was due to Pilate's having fixed Barabbas's crucifixion to that the proper festival-day: whereas that He, the Paschal Lamb, was crucified at the very hour that the nation were sacrificing the Paschal lambs was due to the Sanhedrin's action under Caiaphas in postponing the Passover by one day.

The whole narrative of the occurrences of to-night and to-morrow argues an agitation throughout all classes—Pilate and the garrison, the Sanhedrin, the crowds—that is hardly accounted for by the mere arrest of One who had spent the last four days openly and peacefully in the city and Temple. Fanatical outbreaks such as that of Barabbas habitually coincided with the great annual festivals.

(13) "And they brought Him before Annas first." * Not to Annas's house, but before Annas as magistrate sitting in Caiaphas's house: for Luke (xxii. 54) says, "they brought Him into the house of the Highpriest," (εἰσήγαγον εἰς τὴν οἰκίαν τοῦ ἀρχιερέως), viz. of Caiaphas: and the three denials of Peter are, according to the Synoptists, clearly in one and the same house, viz. Caiaphas's. Here Annas was waiting, perhaps having come over from his own house (180 yards to the north) as soon as he knew that the detachment from the Antonia garrison had started to make the arrest.

* ἀπήγαγον πρὸς Ἄνναν, cf. the Attic law term, the ἀπαγωγὴ πρὸς τοὺς ἕνδεκα = the carrying off a prisoner before the magistrates.

With the safe transfer of Jesus to Annas at the High-priest's house the work of the Roman soldiers ended for the night. The time may be about 1 a.m. Friday.

Fri., about 1 a.m.

"Caiaphas, who was Highpriest that year." The force of "that year" seems to be "that, the most momentous year in the history of the human race," as at xi. 49.

(14) "Caiaphas was he who had counselled the Jews, 'It is expedient that one man die in behalf of the People.'" John here repeats what he had already told us at xi. 50. This repetition shows John's desire to make it clear that it was Caiaphas, the People's representative before God, who was mainly responsible for the death of Jesus. Also, it was Caiaphas's house that was the scene of what follows.

(15) Though all His disciples had fled at the time of our Lord's arrest, there followed Him at a distance Simon Peter and "another disciple" who no doubt was John himself. On arrival at the house of Caiaphas, John, being an acquaintance, or more probably a relative (ὁ γνωστὸς), of Caiaphas, had passed in with Jesus and the Temple police into the hall * (αὐλὴ) of the house.

(16) But Peter, as being unknown, was stopped at the outermost door (*i.e.* the door leading from the street into the courtyard in front of the house), till John went out and by a word to the woman who kept that door procured his admittance.

(17, 18) *Peter's first denial.* The servants of Caiaphas, and the Temple police (ὑπηρέται), had made a fire of charcoal in the centre of the hall (Luke xxii. 25) on one of the portable braziers commonly used for charcoal, and were sitting round it warming themselves, and Peter was sitting with them warming himself. Luke is quite definite that they and Peter were *sitting:* so too Matthew as to Peter. John seems to speak of them and Peter as *standing* (εἰστήκεισαν, and ἦν ἑστώς): but these words used by John are so frequently idiomatic to mean merely "to be

* The αὐλὴ, or hall, of a large house was commonly surrounded by a roofed colonnade which left the centre of the hall open to the sky.

stationary," "to continue," "to be there," "to be," exactly like the Italian *stare*, that the *standing* cannot be pressed—no more here than *e.g.* in the other nineteen places where they occur in John's gospel.

Here, then, at the fireside Peter was questioned by the maid-servant who had admitted him at the street door of the courtyard and had brought him in: "Can it be that thou too (μὴ καὶ σὺ) art of this man's disciples?" Her tone is one of contempt at such silliness. And Peter made his first denial "before them all" (ἔμπροσθεν πάντων, Matt.). And he went out from the hall into the porch (εἰς τὸν πυλῶνα, Matt., εἰς τὸ προαύλιον, Mark), *i.e.* the porch between the hall and the courtyard. And a cock crew.

(19–23) Then followed a short preliminary examination before Annas whilst the rest of the Sanhedrin are assembling in the house. This examination is reported by John alone, who may have been present.

That Annas is here (19) called by John "the Highpriest" (ὁ ἀρχιερεύς), and that Caiaphas is given the same title (τὸν ἀρχιερέα) in verse 24, is not extraordinary, for in Acts iv. 6 the title is again given to Annas, and the date is only two months later. They both bore the title. The nationalist and religious party probably refused to recognize the deposition of Annas by the Roman power, and continued to regard him as Highpriest *de jure* for life, although they recognized Caiaphas as Highpriest *de facto*. Both are recognized as together bearing the title in Luke iii. 2, ἐπὶ ἀρχιερέως Ἄννα καὶ Καιάφα. Though the title ὁ ἀρχιερεὺς (singular with the article) was confined to the Highpriest acting or deposed, that of ἀρχιερεὺς was extended to other members of the great sacerdotal families and to heads of the various departments connected with the Temple service (see the usage of the N.T. writers and of Josephus).

(24) "Annas, therefore,* sent Him before Caiaphas the Highpriest bound." The word here rendered "before"

* The correct reading, ἀπέστειλεν οὖν αὐτὸν ὁ Ἄννας, "Annas, *therefore*, sent Him," etc., prevents this verse being regarded as a deferred parenthesis, such as the A.V. (omitting οὖν) assumes it to be.

is πρός, the regular word for transactions before magistrates. The scene is still in Caiaphas's house, to which the Sanhedrin meanwhile had assembled. It is the dead of night: but, for all that, they are all present (see "where the scribes and the elders assembled," Matt. xxvi. 57: "the chief priests and all the Sanhedrin," do. 59: "all the chief priests and the elders and the scribes come together," Mark xiv. 53: "the chief priests and all the Sanhedrin," do. 55): we may, therefore, picture their agitation throughout that night. Caiaphas as the *de facto* Highpriest was to act as president of this informal meeting in his own house: he is the leading spirit in the movement. He no doubt received from Annas a summary of his preliminary interrogatory and our Lord's demand that witnesses against Him should be produced (John xviii. 21).

(25) *Peter's second denial.* It was during this inquiry before Caiaphas that occurred Peter's second denial. We saw (p. 363) how after his first denial he had gone out from the hall (ἀυλή) into the porch. There he was seen, by another maid (ἄλλη, Matt. xxvi. 71): she is Mark's "the maid" (ἡ παιδίσκη, xiv. 69), *i.e.* she who kept *the porch*, not she of the street door of the courtyard who had been concerned in the first denial. This maid of the porch says "to the men there" (τοῖς ἐκεῖ, Matt., τοῖς παρεστῶσιν, Mark), viz. at the porch, "This one was with Jesus the Nazoræan" (Matt.). Thus it was that on his return to the fire in the hall, and whilst he "was there warming himself" (ἦν . . . ἑστὼς καὶ θερμαινόμενος, John xviii. 25), another person, a man (ἕτερος, Luke), said to him, "Thou also art of them." Peter said, "Man, I am not": or as Matthew has it, "he again denied, with an oath, 'I know not the Man'": or as John has it, "he denied and said 'I am not.'" The time may be about 2 a.m.

Fri., about 2 a.m.

(24) For this examination before Caiaphas and all the Sanhedrin this night we are dependent on Matthew (xxvi. 59–66) and Mark (xiv. 55–64), for neither John nor Luke give any details of it. To what I have said in *The Crucifixion and Resurrection of Jesus Christ*, pp. 43–47,

which deal with this examination before Caiaphas, I wish here to add that Matthew (xxvi. 61) seems to be giving the words of one of "the two false witnesses," and Mark (xiv. 58) seems to be giving those of the other one. It is the word ἀχειροποίητον ("not-made-with-hands") used by this latter witness that was fatal to their agreement: for it showed that our Lord had not been talking of rebuilding the *stone* temple, as indeed the chief priests and theologians had all along known.

Having failed to establish any charge of innovation on the Law, or of contempt for the Temple and its ritual, the Highpriest adopted another course. 'We can dispose of the Prisoner on the simple charge of blasphemy: for if he claims to be the Messiah, he must also claim to be The Son of God.' It was John the Baptist (as we saw at p. 27) who had coined this title for *the Messiah in the Person of Jesus.* The scribes or theologians had accepted it from the Baptist as a title belonging to Messiah, but refused it to Jesus as not being Messiah (see at p. 42, "Son of God"). The "blasphemy" was not that He who claimed to be Messiah claimed also to be "The Son of God," the two titles went together: but that this man before them, whom they denied to be the Messiah, should be claiming Messiah's highest prerogative. Had He consented to be the sort of Messiah they wanted, there would have been nothing heard about blasphemy.

It was this Man's personality that they hated. There was no room for them and Him: one or other must go: nor was the position obscure to the Roman governor—"he knew that it was owing to envy (διὰ φθόνον) that they delivered Him to him" on the morrow (Matt. xxvii. 18).

The conditions under which the examination in Caiaphas's house was conducted, viz. (A) after sunset, (B) in a private house, make it impossible that any one present supposed it to be a formal trial: it was rather an unofficial inquiry held by Caiaphas to take the sense of the Sanhedrin, and to decide on the definite line they should take to-morrow in the Council Hall of the Sanhedrin.

They showed a practical unanimity * and condemned Him to be worthy of death (ἔνοχον εἶναι θανάτου = to be liable to the penalty of death). Thereupon, no doubt, the Sanhedrin dispersed to their several homes: after arranging to meet at daybreak in their Council Hall.

Then followed the ill-treatment of our Lord mentioned by the three Synoptists (Matt. xxvi. 67, 68: Mark xiv. 65: Luke xxii. 63–65). Luke specifies the actors as being "the men who held Jesus," where the words rendered *the men*, οἱ ἄνδρες (not οἱ ἄνθρωποι), point to men of some authority and probably are equivalent here to Mark's οἱ ὑπηρέται, viz. the Temple police.

(26) *Peter's third denial.* It was about now, "about an hour" (Luke, 59) after Peter's second denial, that he was again accused by one of the Highpriest's servants—a kinsman of that Malchus whose ear Peter had cut off (John). "Did not I myself (ἐγὼ) see thee in the garden with him (Jesus)?" (27) "Again Peter denied. And straightway a cock crew." The time may perhaps be 3 a.m., Friday—the close of the third watch, known as Cock-crow. See at xiii. 38.

Fri., 3 a.m. about.

All the eleven Apostles could have been easily identified by the hostile party, had the latter cared to inquire: but they were looked upon as of no account and not worth hunting down. In the Highpriest's hall Peter had been in danger, not of violence, but rather of ridicule, as being a weak-headed fellow led astray by an enthusiast.

For the short remainder of the night (two or three hours) our Lord must certainly have been locked up by the Temple police, in Caiaphas's house. Local tradition shows the place of this His detention in the present Armenian church which occupies the site of Caiaphas's house.

* Mark's "all" (πάντες), in verse 64, will mean *all who were present.* In view of Luke xxiii. 51 it is probable that neither Joseph of Arimathæa nor Nicodemus had received summons from Caiaphas to this meeting in his house, they being known to be favourably disposed to Jesus. In that case, it is probable that neither, again, were present at the Sanhedrin's meeting in their Council Hall that followed at daybreak, for that meeting can only have been arranged overnight.

§ XXV

JOHN XVIII. 28–XIX. 16

Jesus and Pilate

THE last two or three hours of the night being over (and before John resumes at xviii. 28), with the early morning of Good Friday, March 25, A.D. 29, the narrative is taken up by Luke (xxii. 66–71), who tells how our Lord was led away from Caiaphas's house to the Council Hall of the Sanhedrin, thus—

"At daybreak, the assembly of elders of the People, chief priests, and scribes, was gathered together. And they led Him away to their Council Hall" (Luke xxii. 66, εἰς τὸ συνέδριον αὐτῶν): the word means, indifferently, "the Sanhedrin" or "the Hall of the Sanhedrin." This official Hall was still, and until the end of this year A.D. 29, the *Hall of Polished Stones:* it stood at the south-west angle of the Court of the Women. Luke alone (xxii. 66–71) gives any details of this formal meeting of the Sanhedrin, though both Matthew (xxvii. 1) and Mark (xv. 1) mention it. John wholly ignores it.

Fri., shortly before 6 a.m.

The proceedings were short and summary, confined to putting formally, at 6 a.m. (the earliest legal hour), in this the official Council Hall, the question which they had last night in Caiaphas's house decided on as the one that best met the case, or at least the one they could best make serve their turn. It is drawn out syllogistically, "Art thou the Christ (the Messiah)? tell us." To our Lord's indirect reply in the affirmative, in which He calls Himself "The Son of Man" who was to "sit henceforth at the right hand of the power of God," the Council themselves (πάντες, all of them,

6 a.m.

as by previous agreement) draw the certain inference, and add, "Therefore (sc. being the Christ) thou art The Son of God ?" in order to get home the charge of blasphemy. They all knew that "The Son of Man" and "Messiah" were used synonymously by our Lord. They also knew that the Messiah must also be the "Son of God" in some special way, though there was doubt as to the exact connotation of this latter title. He answers, "Yourselves say, I am"—a Hebrew idiom for "You are right: I am." And they, "Why have we still need of witnesses? Ourselves have heard from His own mouth," *i.e.* have heard to-day in the Court formally what they heard last night informally in their inquiry in Caiaphas's house. But here again no sentence of death was pronounced by the President formally against Him. According to the Gemara, "Sentence of death could not be pronounced till the day after the trial": and He had not yet been formally tried.

The object of this Council was not to pass a sentence that they themselves would have to carry out, but to make a pronouncement that would justify them in procuring the Prisoner's death at the hands of Pilate. The pith of their scheme was to compass His death *to-day* and by *crucifixion*: neither of which ends could they attain except through Pilate.

That to-day cannot have been the national festival-day of the Passover, *i.e.* the day (whether we reckon the civil day of twenty-four hours beginning at midnight, or the common day of twelve daylight hours beginning at sunrise) following the Paschal supper of the nation, is clear from the fact of this sitting of the Sanhedrin to-day: for the Mishna (Beza) expressly declares that on a festival-day no Court of Law may sit, no more than on a Saturday.

(XVIII. 28) It is at this point, viz. *after* the Friday morning's meeting of the Sanhedrin in their Council Hall, that John resumes the narrative. "Therefore they lead Jesus from Caiaphas to the Prætorium."

Fri., shortly after 6 a.m.

John was aware that the meeting in the Sanhedrin's

Council Hall intervened between the meeting in Caiaphas's house overnight and the scene in the Prætorium. The force, therefore, of "from Caiaphas" in this passage seems to be to emphasize again the fact that Caiaphas, in the Council Hall no less than in his own house, was the head and front of the hostility to Jesus (see at verse 14). The President of the Sanhedrin was rarely, if ever, the Highpriest: at this date Gamaliel was President.

"The Prætorium" (τὸ πραιτώριον) is the official residence *for the time being* of the governor,* viz. on this occasion the Castle of Antonia, which was also the Roman barracks: it adjoined the north-west corner of the Temple cloisters.

"And it was morning" (ἦν δὲ πρωΐ). The hour is vague. It may be about 6.15 for the Sanhedrin had wasted no time and the proceedings had been merely formal—a ten minutes' affair.

"They themselves went not into the Prætorium, in order not to be defiled, but to eat the Passover." The defilement here meant is probably that caused by entrance into a Gentile house *whence leaven had not been removed* for the Paschal festival. By the word αὐτοί ("they themselves") in this verse John draws distinction between the Jews who had yet to eat the Paschal lamb and therefore could not enter the Prætorium, and Jesus who as we know had already eaten it. It has been argued that to "eat the Passover" cannot here mean to *eat the Paschal* supper seeing that the defilement caused by entering the Prætorium (a Gentile house from which leaven had not been removed) would last only till sunset, and so would not prevent their eating the Paschal supper to-night, which, anyway, would not be eaten until after sunset.

But is it strange that the Sanhedrists should refuse to wantonly incur any defilement on the day of the year when every individual was specially bound to purify himself before coming this evening to the Paschal celebration? Would not every one, Sanhedrists and all, be specially

* As is fully explained in *The Crucifixion and Resurrection*, p. 54.

careful to-day to incur no defilement that could possibly be avoided ? Translate literally the words ἵνα μὴ μιανθῶσιν ἀλλὰ φάγωσιν τὸ Πάσχα, "with a view to not being defiled, but to eating the Passover," and we shall see that the English "but might eat" is misleading, for the Greek has no suggestion that their eating the Passover would be impossible if they incurred this particular defilement.

"But to eat the Passover": for, as explained on pp. 297–302, the nation were going to kill their Paschal lambs this afternoon, Friday, Nisan 15, and to eat their Paschal supper after sunset—our Lord and the Twelve having killed their Paschal lamb yesterday, Nisan 14, and eaten it last night. To "eat the Passover" (φαγεῖν τὸ Πάσχα) means invariably to eat the Paschal lamb: see Matthew xxvi. 17: Mark xiv. 12, 14: Luke xxii. 11, 15. So too in the O.T. (where, however, the phrase is rare), 2 Chron. xxx. 18 (Exod. xii. 11: Num. ix. 11). Nor has any warrant been produced to make it mean anything else; much less any instance given where it does mean anything else. Wieseler has done the best to make out a case, but without success.

Verses 29–32

The Trial before Pilate. It was held "outside" the Prætorium building, and in the open: it is described by Luke (xxiii. 1–4), who also shows (verse 14) that it must have been outside the Prætorium, for Pilate there refers to this trial as having been held "before you" (ἐνώπιον ὑμῶν), viz. the Sanhedrists. The pith of it is given by Luke (xxiii. 2, 3), Matthew (xxvii. 11–14), and Mark (xv. 2–5).

(30) The charge brought was that of inciting to rebellion and claiming to be Himself King (see Luke). The Prisoner admitted to Pilate that He claimed to be "the King of the Jews" (Luke, Matt., Mark), and obviously Pilate must have been satisfied (verse 4 of Luke) that there was in that claim no taint of treason against the emperor.

To the accusations of the members of the Sanhedrin the Prisoner gave no reply (Matt. verse 12): He knew they did not believe their charge that "He forbade to give tribute to Cæsar," for it was to their own envoys that He had given the exactly opposite decision two days ago (Luke xx. 19–26): and as for their charge that "He calls Himself Messiah and therefore King," if that were valid as a crime in His case, it would be valid as against any Messiah, so that they were making themselves apostates from the very hope of Israel.

When Pilate with some duplicity called His attention to the mass of testimony brought against Him by His accusers He made no defence to Pilate on even one single point (Matt., Mark), for He knew that Pilate was aware of the flimsiness of the charges. His silence was no discourtesy to Pilate: it was rather, as Pilate knew, a protest against the disingenuousness of the prosecution, and a reproof to the conscience of Pilate the judge who was dissembling knowledge.

Pilate's decision is given us by Luke in verse 4, "I find no fault in this man," and it is again referred to by Pilate in verse 14 (Luke). Pilate had known all along that there was nothing in the charge: he understood the position perfectly (Matt. xxvii. 18, "he knew that for envy they had delivered Him up"). As governor of the province Pilate had long had his attention turned to this religious reformer, had long ago decided that there was no danger to the public peace from that quarter: Jesus must have been frequently the subject of discussion in the governor's house, and the governor's wife (Claudia Procula) seems to have been strongly impressed in His favour. She, knowing the weakness of her husband's character, had sent to him the first thing in the morning, whilst he sat on the judgment-seat (Matt. xxvii. 19), to caution him against interfering with "that just man," telling of a painful dream-vision she had had that morning connected with Him, and probably warning Pilate not to let himself be over-ridden by what he knew to be a base scheme against an innocent man. The "judgment-seat" (βῆμα) was a portable seat, and had of course been set up outside the Prætorium when Pilate went "outside" (John xviii. 29) to hold the trial; just as it was again set up outside each time Pilate went outside later on to speak to the people, *e.g.* xix. 13, where it is again mentioned as being "outside."

Pilate's decision (Luke xxiii. 4) that so far as Roman law went he found no fault in the Prisoner was met by vehement disapproval from the Sanhedrist party. "If he was not a malefactor it is not to thee that we would have handed him over," *i.e.* it is just because he is guilty of treason to Rome that we have transferred him to your Court.

(31) Pilate: 'Take him and judge him yourselves according to your own law: you have full powers there.'

The Jews: But "*we* have not the power to put any one to death (ἡμῖν οὐκ ἔξεστιν ἀποκτεῖναι οὐδένα)": *i.e.* 'our Court has no jurisdiction in cases under Roman law involving capital punishment. We charge the prisoner with treason against Rome. It is a matter for your Court, not ours.' They expect Pilate will find himself bound to pronounce the penalty of crucifixion against Him. They do not mean that they had not the power to put to death offenders against their own Mosaic law: for all Rabbinists allow that the Sanhedrin had the power of capital punishment until they abandoned their Council Hall of Gazith, *i.e.* Hall of Polished Stones, "forty years before the destruction of the temple," *i.e.* they had it until A.D. 30. They mean they had no power to crucify; and crucifixion was what they were bent on securing as being the most ignominious form of death—the very death Jesus had often foretold as awaiting Him. (For the Hellenistic ἵνα πληρωθῇ = and so was fulfilled, see p. 308.)

They continued in their violent insistence on the mischief that was out over the whole province (Luke), and on how it had its origin in that hotbed of fanaticism, Galilee: it was from Galilee that those frenzied zealots had come whom Pilate had recently put to death in the Temple courts (Luke xiii. 1), p. 252.

Hearing (Luke xxiii. 6) that the Prisoner was a Galilæan and therefore belonged to Herod's jurisdiction, Pilate sent Him to Herod for trial: Herod and his court being at the time in Jerusalem, having come up probably for the festival.

Between verses 32 and 33 of John xviii. should be placed the removal of the Prisoner to Herod's house, the scene there, and the return to Pilate (Luke xxiii. 5–12).

Verses 33–38*a*

(33) "Therefore Pilate entered the Prætorium again and," etc. This is an interview between Pilate and the Prisoner after the return of the latter from Herod: it was held inside the Prætorium, and therefore no other Jew was present at it.

Pilate recurring to the pith of the accusation, repeats, "Thou art the king of the Jews?" was it so?

(34) "Of thyself art thou saying that or did others speak to thee about Me?" This reply asks what exactly is the meaning that Pilate intends to attach to that term. Does he purpose to treat the charge of treason at what he personally knows it to be worth, and so dismiss it with contempt? or will he pretend to take it seriously and treat it as the Jews hoped to compel him?

(35) Pilate scouts the latter alternative: "Am *I* a Jew?" *i.e.* like these your despicable accusers, of whose disingenuousness I am fully aware? *I* am not accusing you. "It is thine own nation and their chief-priests that handed thee over to me. What didst thou?" *i.e.* to embitter them so against thee?

(36) He replies that His offence is that "My Kingdom is not of this world (ἐκ τοῦ κόσμου τούτου)" and therefore not to their liking. Κόσμος is here used as at xii. 31 (p. 292)—the created world viewed in its microcosm, man: but man in his present state of alienation from God owing to sin: for by sin he dragged creation back into its evil rut whence it had for a moment been lifted, and been given a fresh start along with himself, in Eden. His Kingdom does not owe its origin to, nor is it based on, the maxims and ideals that govern this world.

"If My Kingdom were of this world, My servants would fight that I should not be handed over to the Jews" —as saying that "the Jews," and their then conception of

Messiah's Kingdom, were the embodiment of all that on earth was most alien to His Kingdom.

"But now (νῦν δὲ) My Kingdom is not from here (ἐντεῦθεν)": perhaps implying that in a later Age His Kingdom would be from here, in that then the Jews will be converted to Him, and this world will grow to be after His own pattern, till He be the one Lord of all in the New Jerusalem come down from Heaven and set up on earth (Rev. xxi., xxii.).

(37) Pilate: "So then, a king thou art?"

Jesus: "Thou sayest that I am a king"—Hebraism for "thou art right in saying that I am a king." "*I* to this end have been born and to this end have come into the world, viz. to witness to Truth," *i.e.* to witness to true ideals of thought; to true values of desires, aims, conduct; to the true nature of God both in Himself and as regards His creation. Such is the first work of this King. And—

"Every one who is of Truth (ἐκ τῆς ἀληθείας) hears My voice": *i.e.* His appeal is to the conscience of man, and in so far as conscience (that mirror in man that reflects God) is not wholly obscured His appeal finds response. Our Lord who never wasted words would hardly have spoken thus impressively to Pilate had He not detected in him that which would one day respond.

(38) Pilate: "What is truth?" *i.e.* there is no such conception to which man can attune himself: is not all in flux? What is true to-day is not true to-morrow: what is true for you is not true for me.

(38*b*) And without waiting for an answer nor admitting that there might be room for one, "he again" (for the previous exit see verse 29) "went out to the Jews" (John), whom meanwhile "he had summoned together" (Luke): there he harangues them, saying (39) he himself could find no fault in the Prisoner in the matter of any of the charges brought against Him, nor yet had Herod found Him guilty of any capital crime: he proposed, therefore, to scourge Him and then release Him in accordance with the Passover custom of releasing one prisoner: the

Luke xxiii. 13–19; Matt. xxvii. 15–21; Mark xv. 6–11.

choice was to be left to the crowd: should it be Jesus who was called "Messiah" (Christ), the "King of the Jews"? or that notable prisoner and rebel called Barabbas? whose name also was Jesus according to a very early tradition.

This is Pilate's first attempt to secure the release of Jesus: it fails: for—

(40) The crowd, at the instigation of the chief-priests and elders (Matt., Mark), "cried out, saying, 'Not this one, but Barabbas.'" John says "they *again* cried out" (ἐκραύγασαν οὖν πάλιν): he has perhaps in mind the previous shoutings of "the chief-priests and the crowds" which had greeted Pilate's first announcement to them (as we learn from Luke xxiii. 4, 5) before he sent the Prisoner to Herod.

John's account, from beginning to end of his gospel, always in the minutest details, preserves the strict chronological sequence of events: whereas the three Synoptists frequently prefer to follow a sequence not of time but of idea.

(XIX. 1) So at this point our Lord was taken and scourged at Pilate's order by the Roman soldiers. The scourging was meant by Pilate to save the Prisoner from death: it was meant to put such an indignity upon Him that "the Jews" would be satisfied that the people would no longer want Him for a king. No doubt too the mocking by the Roman soldiers that immediately followed the scourging, and which John alone (xix. 1–3) describes, was carried out at Pilate's orders, and was part of Pilate's not ill-meant attempt to make the Prisoner appear contemptible. For that is the line Pilate is taking in his second attempt to save Him.

Fri., March 25, about 7.30 a.m.

(2) After the scourging "the soldiers plaited a crown out of thorns and put it on His head, and put around Him a purple cloak: (3) and they kept coming (ἤρχοντο) before Him and saying, 'Hail, king of the Jews!'" And after this prolonged mock obeisance "they smote Him with their hands."

"A crown of thorns": it was made probably of the

flexible twigs of the *Zizyphus Spina-Christi*, known locally to-day as the *nebq* or *sidr*, as are the plaited crowns of thorns commonly sold to-day to pilgrims at Jerusalem.

"A purple cloak" (ἱμάτιον πορφυροῦν), *i.e.* a long cloak of royal colour (see at p. 386).

(4) "And Pilate" (aware of the condition of the Prisoner) "came out again" (it is his third exit), "and he says to them, 'See, I bring him outside to you, that you may know that I find no crime in him'": *i.e.* otherwise he would not have brought Him out again.

(5) "Therefore Jesus came out outside, wearing the thorn crown and the purple cloak." This crown He continued to wear to the end: both Origen and Tertullian, two of the earliest Fathers of the Church of east and west, assert that He was crucified with it on His head.

"And Pilate says to them, 'Behold, the man!' (ἰδοῦ, ὁ ἄνθρωπος)." There is the man whom you, the Sanhedrin, pretend to fear the people will insist on making their king. Look at him: the poor torn buffoon. After this public exhibition of him, you will admit he may safely be released.

It is Pilate's second attempt to secure His release: it is Luke's (xxiii. 20) θέλων ἀπολῦσαι, "willing, or meaning, to release" Him. Again he fails: for—

(6) "When the chief-priests and the officials" (οἱ ὑπηρέται, viz. the Temple police) "saw Him, they shouted 'Crucify, crucify,'" thus anticipating any possible cry of indignation or pity from the crowd, and showing them how a righteous people must steel themselves in a righteous cause. It is the first overt demand for crucifixion from the Sanhedrists, but that was the mode of death they had been working for from the beginning: it would be the ordinary death for treason under Roman law.

Pilate answers ironically, "Take him, you, and crucify him"; knowing that they could not, however much they wished it: "for *I* (ἐγὼ) do not find crime in him": before Roman law he is not guilty: and there is the end of it.

(7) The Jews replied that if innocent before Roman law, He was guilty before their Law: that His life was forfeit

in any case, even though Pilate would not let Him suffer by crucifixion. That His guilt for them lay in blasphemy, in that "He claimed to be God's Son."

(8) Pilate, on hearing this, "became the more afraid." Impressed already by the Prisoner's personality and moral aura, he was aware of a stronger fear and anxiety on hearing of this strange claim.

(9) "And he entered again into the Prætorium," followed by Jesus, "and he says to Him, 'Whence art thou?'" "And Jesus gave him not answer": because Pilate's question had no bearing on the case before Pilate. The Prisoner stood before Pilate as a Son of Man, not as The Son of God.

(10) Pilate asks, had He no reply for him the judge? "Knowest thou not I have authority to release thee and I have authority to crucify thee?"

(11) Jesus: "Thou wouldest have no authority against Me had not a grant been made to thee from above": *i.e.* it is only as the representative of Supreme Authority that Pilate has any: he is not there to act on caprice nor yet as the convenience of the moment may suggest. "For this reason he who handed Me over to thee hath a greater sin": *i.e.* the Highpriest who handed Him over to Pilate, he too sits as the delegate of Supreme Authority: but inasmuch as the Highpriest's jurisdiction lay on a higher—the spiritual—plane, and inasmuch as the Highpriest had or should have had a fuller knowledge of the Hope of Israel as centred in a Messiah, the Highpriest was more to blame than was Pilate.

(12*a*) "Upon this Pilate sought to release Him": it is his third attempt. The ἐζήτει . . . ἀπολῦσαι used here by John is stronger than the θέλων ἀπολῦσαι used by Luke of Pilate's second attempt. A further detail of this third attempt we have in Luke xxiii. 22, how Pilate again protesting to the people that he found no cause of death in the Prisoner, added that *as he had chastised* (*scourged*) *Him* he would now let Him go. For this is the meaning of Luke's second (xxiii. 22) παιδεύσας οὖν αὐτὸν ἀπολύσω, literally, "having, therefore, chastised him I will release him."

The A.V. and R.V. by rendering, "I will, therefore, chastise him and release him," needlessly insert difficulties: for the scourging has certainly already taken place (John xix. 1). Where Luke first uses this phrase (verse 16), it would be more proper to render again literally with "having, therefore, chastised him I will release him"—the meaning on that occasion being that he *proposed* to chastise Him and then to release Him. By a literal rendering on both occasions, the English would preserve exactly the same ambiguity as the Greek possesses, and a misleading gloss would be avoided.

A very similar case occurs in Matt. xxvii. 26, φραγελλώσας παρέδωκε, and Mark xv. 15, παρέδωκε τὸν Ἰησοῦ φραγελλώσας, where the A.V. and R.V. render "*when he had* scourged Jesus, he delivered Him to be," etc., as though the scourging only took place immediately before the delivery to be crucified. But as the scourging had taken place long before, it would be better to render here again literally, "having scourged Him, he delivered Him to be," etc., thus preserving in English the same vagueness as exists in the Greek as to the length of time between the scourging and the delivery to be crucified.

(12*b*) To this third attempt by Pilate the Jews cried out, "If thou release the accused, thou art no friend of Cæsar's," implying that for favouring the Prisoner they would impeach him for high treason, and would have in his conduct a justification for the sedition that was inevitable if he continued to thwart them. At this—

(13) Pilate (still not without hope) "led Jesus out and sat down on the judgment-seat in a place called Lithóstroton, but in Hebrew (Aramaic) Gabbathá." Not that Gabbathá is the Aramaic (ἑβραϊστὶ) for a *tessellated pavement* which in Greek is Λιθόστρωτον, Lithóstroton: but this particular place bore two names, the Greeks calling it Λιθόστρωτον, "the tessellated pavement" on which the judgment-seat was placed, whilst the Jews called it Gabbathá="the jutting-rock (or brow) of the House," *i.e.* the projecting scarped rock upon which the keep of

the Antonia Castle was built (and on which still stands the Turkish barracks), overhanging the Temple courts.

(14*a*) " And it was Preparation-day of the Passover" (ἦν δὲ Παρασκευὴ τοῦ Πάσχα). There is no doubt but that the more proper rendering of this clause would be, " And it was Friday of the Passover." Παρασκευὴ was the common term for Friday among all Greek-speaking Jews, and is to this day the Greek name for the sixth day of the week wherever Greek is spoken—as universally as is Σάββατον (Sabbath) the name for Saturday, and Κυριακὴ (Lord's-day) for Sunday. The meaning of Παρασκευὴ is " Preparation (day)," but it always meant the Preparation-day for the *weekly Sabbath*, the day (Friday) on which provisions, etc., were prepared, so as not to break the holy Sabbath; and, more technically, the day (Friday) on which the twelve loaves of Shewbread had to be baked every week so as to be ready for exposition on the Saturday In other words, it meant the week-day preceding Saturday: and it is never used to mean the preparation-day (or day preceding) any other festival than Saturdays. Perhaps the earliest instance found so far of the word in this sense of Friday is preserved in Josephus, *Ant.*, XVI. vi. 2, where a decree of Augustus, inscribed in the *Augusteum* at Ancyra in Galatia, is quoted, in which occur the words that the Jews shall not be compelled to appear in court, ἐν Σάββασιν ἢ τῇ πρὸ ταύτης Παρασκευῇ ἀπὸ ὥρας ἐννάτης, " on Saturday, or on the Preparation-day before this day after the ninth hour," *i.e.* they were exempt from 3 p.m. of Fridays till sunset of Saturdays.

See again how Mark (xv. 42) explains the word, ἔπει ἦν Παρασκευή, ὅ ἐστι προσάββατον, " because it was Preparation-day [*i.e.* Friday], which is the-day-before-Sabbath": Luke (xxiii. 54) similarly explains incidentally, καὶ ἡμέρα ἦν Παρασκευή, καὶ Σάββατον ἐπέφωσκε, " and the day was Preparation-day, and Sabbath was drawing on." In the recently discovered *Teaching of the XII. Apostles* (viii) (dating A.D. 80–100) Παρασκευὴ is the regular name for the *weekly Friday*. It appears then that, among the Greek-speaking Jews, beside the more technical name,

Παρασκευὴ, another name for Friday was Προσάββατον, "the day-before-Sabbath" (plural, προσάββατα): see Judith viii. 6, "she fasted all the days of her widowhood except days-before-Sabbaths, and Sabbaths, and days-before-new-moons, and new-moons, and feast-days, and rejoicing-days, of the House of Israel," ἐνήστευε πάσας τὰς ἡμέρας χηρεύσεως αὐτῆς χωρὶς Προσαββάτων καὶ Σαββάτων καὶ προνουμηνιῶν καὶ νουμηνιῶν καὶ ἑορτῶν καὶ χαρμοσυνῶν . . . This weekly Προσάββατον, "day-before-Sabbath," is the same as the weekly τῇ πρὸ τοῦ Σαββάτου of Josephus, *Ant.*, III. x. 7, where he is describing the baking of the Shew-bread every Friday. See also the title to Ps. xcii. (xciii. Heb.) in the LXX version, which runs εἰς τὴν ἡμέραν τοῦ Προσαββάτου ὅτε κατῴκισται ἡ γῆ, κ.τ.λ., "for the day of the day-before-Sabbath," etc., clearly meaning Friday; and this Psalm was, according to the Talmud, Friday's psalm: just as Ps. xci. (xcii. Heb.) has for its title, εἰς τὴν ἡμέραν τοῦ Σαββάτου, "for the day of the Sabbath," viz. Saturday.

The meaning of Παρασκευὴ being thus settled as Friday, there remains still tne question, What does "Friday of the Passover" (Παρασκευὴ τοῦ Πάσχα) mean? The answer is quite simple: John is using τὸ Πάσχα in the sense of the ***Paschal octave, i.e.*** as the equivalent of τὰ ἄζυμα = ἡ ἑορτὴ τῶν ἀζύμων = the festival of Unleavened Bread: viz. the ***eight days*** from Thursday, Nisan 14, to Thursday, Nisan 21, inclusive, as explained at xiii. 1 (p. 301). In so doing, John is using the term τὸ Πασχα precisely as Luke has explained it in xxii. 1, "the festival of Unleavened Bread which (festival) is called Passover": and in Acts xii. 3, 4, "intending after the Passover (μετὰ τὸ Πάσχα) to," etc. So, too, Josephus, ***War***, II. i. 3, "the festival of Unleavened Bread having come (it is called Passover among the Jews)," τῆς τῶν ἀζύμων ἐνστάσης ἑορτῆς (Φάσχα παρὰ τοῖς Ἰουδαίοις καλεῖται): and in the parallel passage, ***Ant.***, XVII. ix. 3. John's habitual use of the term τὸ Πάσχα covers *the whole eight days of Unleaven* (see especially at ii. 23, "at the Passover, on the festival-day" (ἐν τῳ Πάσχα, ἐν τῇ ἑορτῇ) where the words τῇ ἑορτῇ select Nisan 15 out of the whole eight days: for, as shown at p. 115, ἡ ἑορτή, in connection with Πάσχα, always means the morrow of the day on which the Paschal lambs were killed. The sole exception to this extended use of τὸ Πάσχα by John is in the phrase, "to *eat* the Passover" (φαγεῖν τὸ Πάσχα), which means with him as with every other writer, "to eat the Paschal lamb" or Supper (see p. 370).

Thus, Παρασκευὴ τοῦ Πάσχα, "Friday of the *Passover*" (or *Paschal octave*), is analogous to Ignatius's Σάββατον τοῦ Πάσχα, "Saturday of the Paschal season."

It may be added that "to prepare the Passover" was not παρασκευάζειν τὸ Πάσχα, but ἑτοιμάζειν τὸ Πάσχα, see Matt. xxvi. 17, 19: Mark xiv. 12, 16: Luke xxii. 8, 9, 12, 13.

But we are not yet at the end of the difficulties connected with this verse 14. For the next clause, "It was about the sixth hour" (ὥρα ἦν ὡς ἕκτη), has been the despair of commentators. If John's notation of hours were the same as that of the Synoptists, viz. from sunrise to sunset—the night being marked by the four watches of three hours each—"the sixth hour" must mean 12 o'clock midday. But this is impossible in view of all that has yet to take place before the great darkness which did not begin till our Lord was on the cross and lasted "from the sixth to the ninth hour" (Matthew, Mark, Luke), *i.e.* from noon till 3 p.m.

It has been already shown (pp. 34, 98, 118) that John's notation of hours is different from that of the Synoptists, and that he reckons, as we do, from midnight to midday and again from midday to midnight. "About the sixth hour" will therefore be "about 6 a.m." We must remember that John reckons all days, except the Jews' Sabbath, to begin with midnight (as did the Romans) and not with sunset; he has just told us the day was Friday, and immediately adds that the hour was about the sixth"—obviously meaning "about the sixth hour" of *his* Friday, *i.e.* "about" 6 a.m.

But Luke (xxii. 66) has told us that at daybreak this morning (ὡς ἡμέρα ἐγένετο, *i.e.* at actual sunrise) the Sanhedrin assembled and Jesus was brought to their

Council Hall. This was shortly before they brought our Lord to Pilate: and John himself has told us already (xviii. 28) that it was "early" (πρωΐ) when they so brought Him. How then can it be only "about the sixth hour" (=shortly after 6 a.m.) at this late stage of the proceedings reached in xix. 14—after, that is, the tedious trial before Pilate, the transfer to Herod, the examination by Herod, the return to Pilate, the scourging and the first mocking by Pilate's soldiers, the exhibition to the people, and the further examination by Pilate? The hour 6 a.m. appears to be as impossible as 12 noon.

The only tolerable hypothesis seems to be that the first half of this verse 14 (viz. the double notice as to the day and the hour, "and it was Friday of Passover: the hour was about the sixth") was a late additional note by John, or by his Ephesian amanuensis, written in the margin between two columns of his scroll*: that it really belongs to the very beginning of the trial before Pilate, and that John meant it to be inserted after the word "early" in xviii. 28, where it fits aptly and where indeed John saw he had omitted to give this very important notice of the day and hour—after his account of the preceding night's events. But the copyists outside of the small province of "Asia," not understanding John's notation of hours, and thinking that "the sixth hour" must mean "noon," as was its common meaning with Jews, Romans, and Greeks, inserted the note into the corresponding line in the other adjacent column, arguing that the notice of "noon" was less unreasonable at this point than at xviii. 28, where indeed it was impossible. The distance between xviii. 28 and xix. 14, will be the equivalent of one column of John's autograph. Thus, too, is explained the incongruity of this clause 14*a* with its present context.†

* On papyrus scrolls the columns of text were always written at right angles to the scroll-length: on either side of every column was a wide margin, purposely left for corrections, or additions, or what we may call footnotes.

† Further remarks on this and on Mark's notice of "the third hour" will be found on pp. 89–94 of *The Crucifixion and Resurrection of Jesus Christ.*

The hour reached thus far by the trial is little more than 8 a.m., for we learn from Mark (xv. 22–25), when rightly understood, that the hour at which our Lord arrived at Golgotha and was offered the soporific was "the third hour," *i.e.* 9 a.m. That note of time by Mark refers backwards to his verse 23, not onwards to the words, "And they crucified Him" in verse 25. Verse 24 is not in chronological order, and owes its place to force of association with verse 23. Mark knows by heart, or has before him, the account embodied in Matthew's gospel: in verses 23, 24, he finishes the two quotations from Ps. lxix. 21 and Ps. xxii. 18, just as Matthew had given them in xxvii. 34, 35: Mark then resumes his narrative by naming the hour at which the events of verses 22, 23, had occurred, viz. "the third hour," *i.e.* 9 a.m. Verse 24 is parenthetical and anticipatory, as is clear from the *σταυρώσαντες δ' αὐτόν*, "having crucified Him," for in the direct course of the narrative the fact of the crucifixion is not told till 25*b*, "And they crucified Him" (*καὶ ἐσταύρωσαν αὐτόν*). There should be placed a full stop after "and it was the third hour." And a colon should be placed after verse 24. For "the third hour" has nothing to do with the "And they crucified Him."

8 a.m. about.

(14*b*) Pilate has sat down (verse 13, p. 378) on the judgment-seat (*τὸ βῆμα*) which had been again brought outside the Prætorium. "And he saith to the Jews, 'Lo, your king.'" Pilate is not speaking in contempt of Jesus. From the beginning of the day his sympathies have been with the Prisoner, whilst for the Jews he has had only contempt tempered with a fear of a renewal of the insurrection that was but recently suppressed by the capture of Barabbas and his band.

It is probable that even before the arrest of Jesus Pilate had been predisposed in His favour through Claudia Procula his wife. This Procula seems to have been, like many Roman women, a proselyte to Judaism, and already a believer in Christ: her dream-vision of last night (Matt. xxvii. 19) will hardly be the first occasion on which she has heard of Him, rather that vision was due to her intense preoccupation with the outcome of His arrest and of His trial on the morrow before her husband. She is the S. Procula of the Greek hagiology.

Pilate may well have learnt that this Man, whose dignity and Personality had so strongly appealed to him, was the king of the Jews by right of descent from David. Any intelligent governor must have acquainted himself with the causes of last Sunday's extraordinary enthusiasm of the crowds for this Man whom they had hailed as "The Son of David" and as "He who comes in the name of the Lord": Pilate knew, from what this Man had just told him, that He was not claiming an earthly throne to-day, that in no case would He consent to take His throne by violence: he must have known from his agents that herein lay the very root of the Sanhedrin's hate of Him; nor could he fail to draw the contrast between the simple majesty of this Man as against the ugly religiosity of the hierarchy and their hypocritical professions of loyalty to Cæsar.

Hence his taunt to "the Jews," *i.e.* the Sanhedrists, "Lo, your king." 'See how you treat your king, a Man of whom not one of you is worthy. Did ever nation prove itself so blind.'

(15) "They (ἐκεῖνοι) therefore cried out, 'Away, Away with him: crucify him.'" To their renewed frenzy Pilate's renewed taunt. 'Your king, shall I crucify your king? The last of your royal line. I have heard what he has done amongst you. Is this your recognition: this the estimate you make of him? a felon's death for him, and pardon for the rebel murderer. Did ever a nation so condemn themselves?'

(15*b*) "The chief-priests answered, 'We have no king but Cæsar.'" This answer has been called "the formal abdication of the Messianic hope." It was rather an abdication of any such hope then and there: a rejection for that time of Jesus as the Messiah: but never have the Jews abandoned the Messianic hope: and it is certain that toward the close of this present Age they will turn and adore Him before His second Coming. For neither Judah, nor yet Israel, were permanently divorced for all their infidelities: there is no such a thing as divorce recognized: long ago He chose the nation Israel (the Ten Tribes and "Judah") to be His bride. He has never divorced, nor ever can divorce her. Matthew (xxvii. 24) tells how Pilate, finding his efforts vain and the tumult increasing, made one last protest against the crime to which he was being forced: calling for water, he washed his hands before the crowd, by this symbolic act visible to all of them, as well as by word of mouth, solemnly disavowing all responsibility for the Prisoner's death, whose innocence he once more affirmed. Let those whose violence had forced his hand accept the guilt: "See *ye* to it." To which "all the People" assented saying, "His blood be on us and on our children."

(16) "Then, therefore, he delivered Him over to them to be crucified." Pilate's "determination to release Him" (Acts iii. 13) yielded to his fear of a popular outbreak with bloodshed, such as he knew the chief-priests might easily, and certainly would, at this crisis foment.* And releasing Barabbas the rebel and murderer for whom they petitioned, he handed Jesus over to their will.

8.15 a.m. about.

(16) "Therefore they received Jesus": *i.e.* it was because Jesus had been handed over to them for crucifixion that they received Him to themselves (παρέλαβον): on no other terms would they take Him. The subject of the verb is "the chief-priests" of verse 15*b*, inasmuch as they were the principals acting for the Jews.

Here followed the third scene of derision: viz. the mocking by the soldiers of the Antonia garrison, on their own initiative and without official supervision. The Prisoner having been condemned to a felon's death, none cared how He is handled now, provided He is not so

* Traditions as to Pilate's end vary. That he died a Christian is in agreement with Tertullian (*Apolog.* 21), and Augustine (*Serm.* 3 *de Epiphan.*); also with the Coptic and Abyssinian Churches, who commemorate him as even saint and martyr.

maltreated that He cannot live to be crucified three hours or so hence. This scene is not mentioned by either John or Luke, but is described by Matthew (xxvii. 27–31) and Mark (xv. 16–20). These two Evangelists, as they mention only this third scene, relate at this point the scourging: they do not, however, say that the scourging took place at this point. It had certainly occurred long before (John xix. 1). Their words are φραγελλώσας παρέδωκε (Matt.): παρέδωκε . . . φραγελλώσας (Mark): "having (*i.e.* already) scourged Him, he delivered Him to be crucified." Had He not already been scourged, He would in accordance with Roman custom have been scourged at this point—on His condemnation to death: this is the reason why Matthew and Mark mention *at this point* of the proceedings the fact that He had been scourged. Barabbas and his two associates had been doubtless scourged at the time of their condemnation.

It should be remembered that there were three scenes of derision, and in each case our Lord was differently vested: nor perhaps is the fact without prophetic significance: at this crisis in human history every detail was pregnant with mystery. Thus He was vested—

Firstly, by Herod Antipas (recounted by Luke alone, xxiii. 7–11), who put on Him a *white robe* (ἐσθῆτα λαμπράν) as though He were a *candidate* soliciting the kingship of His nation. These words, λαμπρὰ ἐσθὴς, are those used by Polybius (X. v. 1) to render the Roman *toga candida* worn by candidates for office: it was specially whitened-with-chalk (cretata) by the fullers. Its symbolism has been interpreted of this present Age in which He still awaits recognition by His nation as King.

Secondly, at Pilate's order, carried out by his soldiers of the Antonia garrison (recounted by John alone, xix. 2, 3). Pilate put on Him the *long-cloak of royalty* (ἱμάτιον πορφυροῦν) worn by national kings under the emperor, such as were Herod the Great, or the king of Pontus, or the king of Cappadocia, or Herod Agrippa, etc. Its symbolism has been interpreted of the millennial Age in which He will be visibly recognized as King of His united nation (Israel and Judah): but reigning by deputy in Jerusalem. This deputy (the *nasi'* of Ezek. xliv.–xlviii.) is "My servant David" of Ezek. xxxiv. 23: xxxvii. 24: Jer. xxx. 9: Hos. iii. 5. The imperial nation of that Age is United Israel.

Thirdly, by the whole garrison of the Antonia (ὅλην τὴν σπεῖραν) at their own initiative (recounted only by Matthew xxvii. 27–31 and Mark xv. 16–20), after His condemnation to death. They stripped Him of His garments and clothed Him with what Matthew calls "a scarlet mantle" (χλαμύδα κοκκίνην). The χλαμὺς is the *short mantle* worn by Roman soldiers and generals, and especially by the Roman *emperors*: it is the Latin *sagum* and *paludamentum*. In the case of soldiers its colour was scarlet (as here), in the case of the emperors it was purple (porphyry), to which Mark here alludes in his ἐνδιδύσκουσιν αὐτὸν πορφύραν (purple). This πορφύραν is Mark's gloss "imperial purple" to explain to us what the soldiers meant by the χλαμύς. The scarlet χλαμὺς was the nearest approach they could lay hands on to the *imperial* χλαμύς. The point lies in the χλαμύς, which no Greek writer could be using vaguely. On this occasion our Lord is being derided not as the *candidate* for a throne, nor yet as the *national* king, but as the *imperial monarch* of the world. Its symbolism has been interpreted of the post-millennial Age, the Age of the two last chapters of the book of Revelation, after the final suppression of Satan and of the last rebellion of man under Gog's captaincy: that long Age when Jesus reigns as visible Monarch of the whole earth, before He yields all up to God having uplifted the whole human race into the Godhead.

The following is a synopsis of the four accounts of Good Friday morning from 6 a.m. to about 8.45 a.m. :—

	Approximate hours. a.m.	
1. The two brief questions put, and the answers given, in the Sanhedrin's official Hall in the Temple area. The Temple area adjoined the Prætorium.	6.0	Luke xxii. 66-71. Matt. xxvii. 1. Mark xv. 1.
2. The trial before Pilate, "outside" the Prætorium (J. 29); with which agrees Luke (see L. 14, "before you"). Prisoner not guilty (L. 4 and again 14).	6.15	John xviii. 28–32. Luke xxiii. 1–4. Matt. xxvii. 11-14. Mark xv. 2–5.
3. Pilate sends Jesus to Herod Antipas: Herod sends Him back as not guilty (L. 15), Herod and his soldiers having made a mock of Him.	6.40	Luke, vv. 5–12.
4. First private interview between Pilate and Jesus inside the Prætorium.	7.15	John, vv. 33–37.
5. Pilate goes out and talks to the People, and makes his first attempt to save Jesus: neither he nor Herod had found Him guilty. "Will scourge Him and then release Him." The Jews cry, "Not this one, but Barabbas."		John, vv. 38–40. Luke, vv. 13–19. Matt., vv. 15–21. Mark, vv. 6–11.
6. The scourging: the mocking by Pilate's soldiers, done, of course, by order, and under official supervision.	7.30	John xix. 1–3.
7. Pilate goes out to the People: "Behold, the man": makes his second attempt to save Jesus. The Jews cry, "Crucify Him."	7.45	John, vv. 4–7. Luke, vv. 20–21. Matt., v. 22. Mark, vv. 12–13.
8. Second private interview between Pilate and Jesus inside the Prætorium.		John, vv. 8–11.
9. Pilate's third attempt to save Jesus: the Jews insist, "Crucify Him."	8.0	John, v. 12. Luke, vv. 22, 23. Matt., v. 23. Mark, v. 14.
10. Pilate takes his seat "outside," upon Gabbathá: makes yet a final appeal: washes his hands of the crime.	8.10	John, vv. 13–15. Matt., vv. 24, 25.
11. Pilate hands Him over to be crucified.	8.25	John, v. 16. Luke, v. 24. Matt., v. 26. Mark, v. 15.
12. The mocking by the whole garrison of the Antonia, on the soldiers' own initiative, and without supervision, now that the Prisoner is condemned.		Matt., vv. 27-31. Mark, vv. 16-20.

§ XXVI

JOHN XIX. 17–42

The Crucifixion. The Burial.

THREE crucifixions had already been ordered for to-day by Pilate, viz. those of Barabbas and two of his band. Barabbas being now released, there remained but to transfer the cross that had been meant for him to Jesus.

A.D. 29.
Nisan 15 } Fri.
Mar. 25 }

(17) "And bearing for Himself His cross He went out (viz. out of the city) to the place called Skull's Place, which in Hebrew is called Golgotha." * The distance from the Prætorium (the present Turkish barracks north of the Temple) to Golgotha (in the Church of the Holy Sepulchre) is about six hundred yards. Along the traditional route (the "Via Dolorosa") excavations made at several points have laid bare the Roman pavement of the road of our Lord's time, at a depth of many feet below the present surface.

About 8.45 a.m.

The name Golgotha, or Skull, was not given to the place because of any physical resemblance to a human skull, for there was no detached hillock then as there is now. There was, rather, the brow of a hill of calcareous rock ; the hill dipped to the east : the brow ended abruptly on the west like a terrace, with a vertical drop of some fifteen feet. In this vertical rock-face was a small cave. The present form of Golgotha is apparently due to the Empress Helena (*c.* 325 A.D.), who seems to have cut away the northern, southern, and eastern sides of the slope in order to make the exact spot of the Crucifixion stand

* The meaning of Golgotha is "a skull" : in classic Hebrew the word is Gulgoleth. I have dealt with the very remarkable tradition connecting this place with Adam's burial in pp. 80–84, 177–183, of *The Crucifixion and Resurrection of Jesus Christ.*

out in bolder relief, whilst also giving room for the southern colonnade of Constantine's vast basilica, the *Martyrium:* the vertical western rock-face and its cave was left untouched. The ascent to the top of Golgotha is to-day by two stairways. On the top, which is some fifteen feet above the surrounding pavement of the Church of the Holy Sepulchre, the native rock crops out; in it is seen the "rent" made at the moment of our Lord's death: three holes are also seen here cut in the rock which mark the traditional sites where the three crosses were fixed. Immediately underneath the "rent" and the middle hole is the small cave above mentioned.

With this cave was connected the strange legend that it was the spot where Adam had finally been laid. This was a belief held in the Church from the earliest times: not only so, it was a Hebrew tradition handed down to the earliest Christians of Jerusalem.

So Origen (Migne's *Patrol. Græca,* XIII. col. 1777); Athanasius (*ibid.* XXVIII. col. 208); Basil Seleuc. (*ibid.* LXXXV. col. 409); Ambrose (Migne's *Patrol. Latina,* XV. col. 1832).

It was thus Adam's skull that gave the place its name: and on the spot where in the First Adam was the death of all, there in the Second Adam was the life of all. It is remarkable that all four Evangelists have been so careful to name the exact spot where our Lord was crucified—a detail that were trivial if no special "mystery" were attached to it, but a detail of vast significance if there is truth in this local tradition.

The hour of arrival of the procession at Golgotha seems to have been 9 a.m. (see p. 383): and He was offered, but did not accept, the customary soporific of wine and *opium,* for opium is the "bitterness" or "gall" of Matt. xxvii. 34. By χολή the LXX frequently render the Hebrew *ro'sh,* "poppy-*head*" (the globular capsule) and its bitter narcotic juice * (see Gesenius's *Heb. Dict.*).

9 a.m.

* As *e.g.* in Ps. lxix. 21*a* (Greek, lxviii. 22) to which Matthew (*l.c.*) is no doubt alluding, as also is Mark in his parallel (xv. 23). Opium was at this time

Here was a long delay: the exact places for the three crosses had to be chosen; their footings had to be cut in the rock; the three crosses were then laid by the three holes: Jesus and the two robbers were brought forward from the stocks, and fastened to the crosses: His title was affixed: His cross was hoisted up and shot into its socket. The time was shortly before midday. (18) The other two crosses were then raised and shot home. Our Lord's cross was the first to be lifted up, if we may trust the relative position of the present three holes; for the middle one is distinctly in advance of the other two, and yet the three are so close that the middle cross must have been raised first.

Shortly before midday.

(19) The "title" was written by Pilate and affixed to the cross by his orders: John says (verse 20) it was written in Hebrew (Aramaic), in Roman (Latin), and in Greek. John, writing for Greeks, has probably given it exactly as it stood in the Greek, "Jesus, the Nazoræan, the king of the Jews": Matthew, writing for Palestinians, has probably given it as it stood in the Aramaic, "Jesus, the king of the Jews": Mark, writing for Romans, probably gives it as it stood in the Latin, "the king of the Jews" (Rex Judæorum): and Luke agrees with Mark, "the king of the Jews." The words οὗτος, or οὗτος ἐστιν, "this is," were not part of the title. "Hebrew" (*i.e.* Aramaic) was the national language; Latin the official; Greek the international for the races of the East, from Egypt to the Black Sea and from the Adriatic to Persia. The city would be thronged by Jews come to the festival from all parts of the Roman empire, so that—

(20) This title written in the three common languages was read by many of the Jews, for "the place where He was crucified was nigh to the city": and, of course,

unknown to the Romans and western Greeks, though familiar to Asia. Hence the difficulty the LXX translators of the O.T. had in rendering the Hebrew *ro'sh*. Matthew's Greek translator ("wine mingled with *gall*") has simply followed the LXX's rendering (Ps. lxix. 21*a*) of *ro'sh* by χολὴ: Mark (xv. 23) has rendered by ἐσμυρμισμένον οἶνον, vinum *myrrhatum*, "*embittered* wine" (wine mingled with *myrrh* or *bitterness*), thus, like the LXX, expressing the *bitterness* of the mixed wine and opium.

outside the walls. Golgotha is about ninety yards west of the line of the old western wall known as "the second wall" (Josephus, *War*, V. iv. 1) which is to-day marked at this part by the street *Khan ez Zeit:* even nearer to Golgotha and on the south, was a westward turn of this same wall. The "second wall" was the west wall of the northern half of the city until A.D. 43, when Herod Agrippa I. built his new wall very much further west, including the site of Golgotha.

Our Lord was crucified with His face to the west, the city being at His back and on His left.

(21) "The chief-priests of the Jews," objecting to the wording and publicity of the title, said to Pilate, "Write not 'The king of the Jews,' but that 'he said, I am king of the Jews'" (ἀλλ' ὅτι ἐκεῖνος εἶπεν βασιλεὺς τῶν Ἰουδαίων εἰμί). They were indignant that strangers coming to the Passover should infer that the man whom the Romans had hung up was one whom the nation had wanted to be their king. 'It was not we who said he was our king, but he.'

(22) Pilate's answer, "What I have written I have written" was an abrupt refusal to yield to any further request from the Sanhedrists. They had caused him mischief enough already: he was still smarting from having been driven by them.

(23) The four soldiers who had charge of the crucifixion of Jesus, having raised up the cross into its socket, divided His clothes, which were their perquisites, into four portions:

(24) But being unwilling to cut up what they would consider the only valuable garment, viz. the long seamless tunic, they made a fifth portion of it and then cast lots for it. "That the Scripture might be fulfilled" is for most readers a misleading English rendering of the Hellenistic ἵνα πληρωθῇ, which here, as commonly in the N.T., represents the Hebrew *lmallo'th*, lit. "toward the fulfilling of," etc., or a Hebrew *lma'an* with infin. or fut., all of which represent rather an objective result than a subjective aim, and would be more idiomatically rendered "and so was fulfilled."

Luke (xxiii. 36) adds that "The soldiers also mocked

Him, drawing nigh, and setting before Him vinegar, and saying, 'If thou art the king of the Jews, save thyself'" —their exact meaning being 'for thou art in evil case: it is now or never: thou hast come to thy last draught—the felon's vinegar.' On this vinegar see further, p. 398. As is seen in Luke's Greek, the stress is on the word ὄξος (vinegar), the regular accompaniment and "note" of a crucifixion. This vinegar is quite distinct from the soporific of wine and opium, mentioned by Matt. xxvii. 34 and Mark xv. 23, which had been offered three hours before, on arrival at Golgotha.

Thus far the soldiers.

(25) This group of women standing "*by* the cross of Jesus" (παρὰ τῷ), *i.e.* as near as the soldiers would allow, consisted of—

1. His mother Mary. 2. His mother's "sister" Salome. 3. Mary the wife of Clopas. 4. Mary the Magdalene. And with them was John the Evangelist (son of Salome).

2. Salome is called His mother's "sister" as being her nearest living blood-relation, her first cousin (their mothers being sisters): just so James the Little, Joses, Simeon, Jude (sons of Clopas) are called our Lord's "brethren," as being His nearest relations, for Joseph and Clopas were half-brothers. John does not give the name of this his mother Salome, but from Mark and Matthew we know she was present. Salome was wife of Zebedee and mother of James and John the Evangelist, two of the three chief Apostles. John as being the son of Salome was thus the natural, as well as the elected, person to be entrusted with the care of the Blessed Virgin.

3. "Mary the (wife) of Clopas" is the same as "Mary the mother of James the Little, and of Joses" (Mark xv. 40: and Matt. xxvii. 56). She is also called "the other Mary" (ἡ ἄλλη Μαρία), *i.e.* "other" to the Blessed Virgin and the Magdalene, in Matt. xxvii. 61; xxviii. 1. She is also called "Mary the (mother) * of James" (Μαρία ἡ Ἰακώβου) in Luke xxiv. 10, and "Mary the (mother) of

* The word *mother* is supplied here in the Syriac.

Joses" in Mark xv. 47. Her two younger sons were Simeon and Jude, the first and second successors to their eldest brother in the bishopric of Jerusalem. These four sons are called "the brethren" of our Lord: none of them was of the Twelve Apostles. Their father Clopas (Κλωπὰς) was the half-brother (on the father's side) to Joseph our Lord's foster-father (see Hegesippus, who says that Simeon the second bishop of Jerusalem was the son of our Lord's *uncle* (πατρώου)). This Clopas is almost certainly the same person as Cleopas (Κλεόπας) of Luke xxiv. 18. He is not the same person as Alphæus (Matt. x. 3: Mark iii. 18: Luke vi. 15: Acts i. 13) father of the James who is ninth on the list of the Twelve Apostles; nor do any of the versions confound the two names Κλωπας and Ἀλφαιος, though many moderns pretend that they both represent the Aramaic Ḥalphai.*

4. Mary the Magdalene, native of a village in the Magdala township, as were her sister Martha and her brother Lazarus (see at xi. 1). She is the same as the "woman who was in the city, a sinner" (Luke vii. 37), and is the Mary of Luke x. 39.

(26) He gives the Mother He loved to the care of the disciple He loved, and the disciple to the Mother, making tender provision for the one as for the other, and showing John how complete was His confidence in him.

* It is quite clear that Αλφαιος (Alphæus) represents the Aramaic Ḥalphây, for wherever Αλφαιος occurs in the Greek, the Syriac version (itself an Aramaic) has Ḥalphây: and Αλφαιος should probably be read with the soft breathing, for the initial guttural Ḥ (ḥeth) was habitually so rendered in Greek, and not by the rough breathing: sometimes by Χ (chi): never by Κ. For instance, out of a total 135 proper names in O.T. beginning with Ḥ, the LXX, or the Alexandrian grammarians, render 106 with the soft breathing, 21 with Χ, 5 with either of these indifferently, 2 with rough breathing, 1 with doubtful Χ or Γ. As to Κλωπας (Klopas) and Κλεοπας (Kleopas), the Syriac version renders both forms by one, viz. *Qleyôpha'*. The Semitic initial Q (Qoph) and the Greek initial Κ are the regular equivalents in transliteration. Kleopas is possibly a purely Greek name, a short form of Kleopatros (cf. Antipas for Antipatros). Klopas has nothing to do with the Aramaic Ḥalphây, which could not be transliterated with Κλπ, but would require either Αλφ(π) or Χλφ(π). Nor is Κλωπας (Klopas) or Κλεοπας (Kleopas) a Greek transliteration of any Hebrew name; for there is no proper name in Hebrew with the combination Qlp or Klp, one or other of which is required by a Greek Κλπ.

(27) "From that hour the disciple received (ἔλαβεν) her to his own home." Not that he then and there led her away to his home: but from that hour John's home was hers. Tradition is quite certain that the Blessed Virgin stayed until the end, as did John.

Between verses 27 and 28 occurred the three hours' darkness from midday till 3 p.m. mentioned in the three synoptic gospels. The "darkness" was certainly not caused by a normal eclipse of the sun, which can only occur at the new moon: and the darkness of even a total eclipse of the sun lasts but a few minutes. Nor was there any normal eclipse of the sun with which this darkness can possibly be identified (see Pingré's *List of eclipses* since A.D. 1). The darkness was due to some derangement of the earth's atmosphere, which caused the sun to suffer eclipse, and was no doubt connected with the earthquake which followed on it (Matt. xxvii. 51).

At about 3 p.m. as the darkness within and without lightened, our Lord spoke for the fourth time from the cross, this time crying with a loud voice (ἀνεβόησεν . . . φωνῇ μεγάλῃ, Matt. xxvii. 46). "My God, My God, why didst Thou forsake Me?" quoting the opening of Ps. xxii. (xxi.). The rendering "why hast Thou forsaken Me" seems to be faulty, for the dereliction is just ended: nor is the perfect tense a correct rendering of the Greek aorist.

3 p.m.

The Greek of both Matthew and Mark gives the words not from the original Hebrew of Ps. xxii., which are *'Elî, 'Elî, lâmâ 'azabtânî*, but from the Aramaic, in which our Lord uttered them. This is certain from the change of the Hebrew *'azabtânî* to the Aramaic *šebaqtani*. The Aramaic, however, is much obscured in the Greek transliteration, ἐλωί, ἐλωί, λεμὰ σαβαχθανεί. It is only in the Aramaic that the cry "My God" ('Elâhî) and the cry "Elias" ('Elîyâhu) could be mistaken one for the other. In a loud shout and heard from a distance the resemblance would be great. There would be no resemblance between the Hebrew 'Elî (My God) and the Hebrew 'Eliyâh or 'Eliyâhu (Elias).

"Some of them that stood there," Matthew tells us, said "He is calling Elias" (Ἠλίαν φωνεῖ): so too says Mark. These bystanders are not deriding Him; they misunderstood Him. There was no derision left in any now present after that mysterious three hours' darkness and hush of nature. Nor again are the speakers Roman soldiers, for what knew they of Elias? Rather, the speakers are in sympathy with Him, and are some who had believed in Him and were still hoping against hope, half expecting yet that at this the last moment Elias would appear to save Him.

Among these bystanders the talk was still going round, "He is calling Elias," when there came from the Cross the one word διψῶ, "I-thirst." * It is mentioned, significantly, by John alone. The mystery of His suffering has ended with the end of the darkness. The reconciliation of man with God is, potentially, finished. As pledge of it He the God-Man wills to make for man one last chance to serve Him. And some one, whose name has not come down to us, snatched that opportunity and so sealed the repentance of the race. Who was this man? None but John himself: who thus did the last service to the Man he loved,—John the adopted brother (verse 27) of the dying God who loved him.

The scene is rarely understood correctly: consider it further:—

(28) The μετὰ τοῦτο ("After this") with which John connects verses 27 and 28 is remarkable. The phrase (unlike the very similar μετὰ ταῦτα) always implies an ethical connection, and not merely a sequence in time. Observe that John has gone straight from the second utterance, "Woman, behold thy son": "Behold, thy mother," to the fifth ("I thirst"): he has omitted all mention of the intervening three hours' darkness and of

* It is the verb of the noun used in Ps. lxix. 21, "in My *thirst* they-gave-me-to-drink vinegar": for to this "scripture" John evidently refers in this verse 28. It would seem, then, that in Ps. lxix. 21, David is likening his own misery to the plight of one crucified, who has already been offered the narcotic of wine and opium, and is afterwards given vinegar to refresh him in his thirst as he dies. A "blind" prophecy.

that fourth cry which some of the bystanders had misunderstood to be a call on Elijah and which immediately preceded the "I thirst": by the *μετὰ τοῦτο* he has connected the request "I thirst" with that gracious bequest "Behold thy son . . . Behold thy mother."

This word "I thirst" was not shouted loud as was the cry immediately before, for John describes it simply as λέγει, "He saith": it was in fact *addressed to John*, and was heard by none but John and the Blessed Virgin, who were watching every motion of those lips and eyes. These two, it seems, were now—after the three hours' darkness—the only bystanders near the cross. When, *before* the darkness, our Lord committed these two to each other, the other three women (Mary the Magdalene, Mary Clopas, and Salome) who had hitherto been with them (verse 25) reverently withdrew, recognizing that those two were now apart from all. That those three women did so move away we infer from Matt. xxvii. 55, 56: Mark xv. 40: Luke xxiii. 49, where we find them *after* the three hours' darkness no longer "near the cross," but "beholding from afar off."

The two synoptists (Matthew and Mark) who mention the cry "My God, My God," etc., and the incident of the sponge and vinegar, had not heard the word "I thirst": nor did they originally know of that appeal addressed to John. They, and every one else, had only heard the loud cry "My God," etc., and many had put a wrong meaning upon it; and seeing John run for the sponge and vinegar, all thought that that was the cry that had started him. They describe exactly as they or their informers saw. It is only John who knew that the critical word which had decided him to run for the vinegar was this "I thirst."

Matthew and Mark both say it was *one*, "a certain one" (τις), of those standing there, who ran and filled the sponge, etc.: they have omitted the name of that man, because, no doubt, he (John) so wished it; but, in their account, that *one* man has the credit, for the initiative was his. But in John's account observe how he hides himself; he says nothing of this *one* man: he makes the action shared by those who ran in to help him when they saw what he was doing, for he says, "They-surrounded with hyssop a sponge full of the vinegar and put it to His mouth" (σπόγγον οὖν μεστὸν τοῦ ὄξους ὑσσώπῳ περιθέντες προσήνεγκαν αὐτοῦ τῷ στ.).

It would seem that John at this moment shared the hope of others that Elias would yet come at the last moment and bring in a great deliverance: for Mark says that the unnamed one, "having put a sponge of vinegar on a reed, gave Him to drink, saying, 'Let be, let us see if Elias comes to take Him down'" (Ἄφετε, ἴδωμεν εἰ ἔρχεται Ἠλείας καθελεῖν αὐτόν): where the plural "Let be" is his request to the soldiers for permission to do what they themselves ought to have done and had not done. Matthew's account is slightly different in that he describes not the unnamed man but "the rest" (*i.e.* the bystanders) as asking for the permission (οἱ δὲ λοιποὶ εἶπαν Ἄφες, ἴδωμεν, etc.): where the singular "Let be" is their request no doubt to the centurion in command.*

(29) But what is this vinegar? The common opinion in England seems to be that it is the rough wine of the soldiers' food. But what is this sponge doing here, lying so handily? And what of the hyssop? Just a handful of weed that chanced to be growing around?

There is no doubt Baronius (*Annales*, 34, § 120) has the truth of it in saying, "The vinegar, sponge, hyssop, reed were all regular accompaniments of a crucifixion." He quotes Pliny (*Nat. Hist.*, xxiii. 1) as saying that "vinegar flavoured with a bundle of hyssop (fasciculo hyssopi conditum) has the power of staunching blood, whether it be put on a sponge and so applied, or whether it be drunk." The vinegar and hyssop were there to be given by the soldiers to the crucified ones by means of a sponge put on the end of a reed. That the soliders had not as yet carried out this duty was due to the three hours' dense darkness, which had lasted ever since the three crosses

* The ἄφετε and ἄφες, "Let be," are certainly requests for permission to give the drink. They do not govern the ἴδωμεν, "allow us to see if Elias," etc., for in that sense ἄφετε always takes the infinitive.

were set up. And that they had not as yet done so is evident, for John and his helpers had themselves to wrap the sponge round with the bundle of hyssop and put it on the reed; also the vessel was still "full" (σκεῦος οὖν ἔκειτο ὄξους μεστόν).

The "hyssop" (ὕσσωπος) is the *'ezôb* of the O.T. Hebrew, used in sacred purifications (Exod. xii. 22: Lev. xiv. 4, 6, 49: Ps. li. 7) which the LXX always render by ὕσσωπος; see also Heb. ix. 19. It was used like the Catholic aspergill, which is said to have been originally a fascicle of hyssop. The plant seems to be the *Origanum maru* (Linn.), a low-growing herbaceous marjoram which grows in crevices of rocks and walls in Sinai, Palestine, and Syria. The bundle lying with the vinegar and sponge was perhaps dried, of last year.

The "reed" (κάλαμος) mentioned by Matthew and Mark, but not by John, is no doubt the *Arundo donax*, which is ubiquitous over the Mediterranean basin. The same word is used again by Matthew xxvii. 29 for the "reed" that was put "in His right hand" by way of a sceptre. It grows from ten to eighteen feet high.

Shortly after 3 p.m.

(30) This last service of vinegar and hyssop, from John acting for the human race, He gladly received: and by receiving it He showed He had forgiven us all we had done to Him. Then followed the sixth word, "It-is-finished": His work on earth was for the moment done; just as on the Friday ("sixth day") of the Mosaic cosmogony God's work is represented as finished, preparatory to the "seventh" day or Sabbath of rest. "And He bent His head and gave-up (παρέδωκε, gave over as a deposit) His spirit" with the seventh utterance from the cross, which Luke has preserved, "Father, into Thy hands I commend (παρατίθεμαι =I place as a deposit) My spirit": that is, of course, His human spirit such as all men have. No one took His life from Him: His death was a voluntary surrender: a surrender which He had authority to make, because the authority to surrender His life was accompanied with an authority to resume it (x. 18).

(31) "The Jews, therefore, *because it was Friday*" (ἐπεὶ παρασκευὴ ἦν). The true meaning of παρασκευὴ has been shown at p. 379. The word simply means the weekly Preparation-day for the weekly Sabbath, hence is equivalent to our "Friday." *

"In order that the bodies should not remain upon the cross on the Sabbath, for great was the day of that Sabbath" (ἦν γὰρ μενάλη ἡ ἡμέρα ἐκείνου τοῦ σαββάτου). It was "great" as being a Saturday or Sabbath of more than ordinary ceremony. It began, as did all Saturdays of the Jews, at sunset of Friday: the nation were to eat the Paschal supper at once after sunset, and the morrow, reckoned from sunrise to sunset (twelve hours), would be the nation's Passover festival-day, as has been explained at p. 298.

If the nation had eaten the Passover on the Thursday (when our Lord ate it), as many contend they did, their festival-day would have been the Friday; and the Saturday could hardly have been called particularly "great," for it would have coincided merely with the day of the "wave-sheaf," which was not in itself one of the days of obligation.

The Mosaic Law (Deut. xxi. 23) required the removal beford sunset, Sabbath or no Sabbath, of any dead body from the tree or cross on which it had hung. Now, ordinarily death would not follow on a crucifixion until after very many hours—even a whole day or more. The Jews were anxious that this high Sabbath of theirs should not be marred by the sight of living bodies hanging on the crosses. Hence their request to Pilate to have the deaths hastened by breaking the legs, so that they might be able to take

* See the Διδαχὴ τῶν ιβ ἀποστόλων (viii. 1), a Church manual dating of the late first century or early second century of our era. "Let not your fasts coincide with the hypocrites" (unbelieving Jews): "for they fast on the second and fifth days of the week (δευτέρᾳ σαββάτων καὶ πέμπτῃ)" = Mondays and Thursdays, "but do *you* fast the fourth day and Preparation-day (τετράδα καὶ Παρασκευήν)" = Wednesdays and Fridays. The days of the week bear invariably the same names to this day in modern Greek. Thus Sunday is Κυριακή = Lord's day, Monday is Δευτέρα = Second day, Tuesday is Τρίτη = Third day, Wednesday is Τετάρτη = Fourth day, Thursday is Πέμπτη = Fifth day, Friday is Παρασκευή = Preparation-day, Saturday is Σάββατον = Sabbath.

down the dead bodies and bury them before sundown this evening as their Law commanded.

(32) It must not be supposed that the two robbers were conscious at the time their legs were broken. They had, of course, been given and had taken the strong narcotic of wine and opium on their arrival at Golgotha. The effect of a strong dose of opium is firstly insensibility to pain, a sense of well-being, activity and clearness of the brain. The two were therefore insensible to the pain of being fastened to the cross, but their minds were abnormally clear. The later effect of the opium would be a state of coma, passing to complete unconsciousness, accompanied by slow stertorous breathing: this unconsciousness would last until death ensued, due to paralysis of the brain.

The soldiers coming to them would see by their respiration that they were still alive though unconscious. The shock caused by the breaking of the shin-bones would hasten death.

(33) But coming to Jesus, they saw He was already dead, and so did not break His legs.

(34) This stab with the lance may have been to make sure, officially, that He was dead. Anyway, there was left no possibility of maintaining that He did not actually die but was buried in a cataleptic trance. According to all tradition the lance entered on the *right* side, it traversed into the heart. In a normal case of death there could not have been any flow of blood or water, for "blood" will not flow after death: and what of the "water"?

The phenomenon was in no way natural: it was something wholly beyond nature—as much beyond nature as are the sacramental virtues attaching to the water of Baptism and to the wine of the Eucharist. The "blood and water" were visible symbols of the cleansing power of the water of Baptism and the invigorating power of the blood of the Eucharist. They flowed from His body to show that it is from His body that the sacraments originate and draw their virtue.

That body upon the cross was no lifeless corpse. Though dead in the sense that His human spirit had temporarily left it, it was alive in that His Divinity was inseparably united with it: so inseparably that that body was not only impassible of corruption, but was the source of Life for the new creation.

(35) "And it is he who has Seen that has borne witness" (καὶ ὁ ἑωρακὼς μεμαρτύρηκεν), *i.e.* he John the eye-witness to the phenomenon, the man who Saw and Sees (perf.), the man whose eyes were opened to the significance of that phenomenon, it is he who has borne witness. See the same words used by John the Baptist in i. 34.

"And his witness is true" (ἀληθινή). The words seem to be those of some one or more corroborating John's testimony: as it might be Simeon and Jude (see p. 439) saying, "John's testimony is true (ἀληθινή), as we can attest who also were present (cf. Luke xxiii. 29) and saw the wonder."

"And he" (ἐκεῖνος, emphatic: viz. John as against his attestors who had not his spiritual keenness of vision) "*knows* that he says true things" (ἀληθῆ), *i.e.* that his account is true not only verbally but in its essence; *i.e.* that he has grasped the meaning of what he saw, that he sees it in true perspective and proportion, and is not making more of it or other of it than it was meant to convey. The "blood and water" had momentous significance, as the oral teaching of the Church ever explained.

(36) "For these things came to pass" (ἐγένετο, the aorist as being the historian's comment, see p. 283, note) "that the scripture should be fulfilled" (ἵνα . . . πληρωθῇ, see at verse 24). This prohibition concerning the Paschal lamb's bones (Exod. xii. 46) found its ultimate significance in that Paschal Lamb, of whom all others were but types.

(37) "And again a second (ἑτέρα) scripture saith," etc. This scripture ("They shall look on Him whom they pierced," Zech. xii. 10) has not yet been fulfilled, nor does John say it has. The *piercing* has been done, but the "looking upon" with "mourning" and "supplication," such as Zechariah foretells, lies in the yet future.

(38) Joseph of Arimathæa was not a native of Arimathæa (which would have been expressed by ἐξ 'Αρ.),

but a *resident* there (ἀπὸ), as all four Evangelists agree. The town seems to be the same as the modern Ramleh, which was built by the Saracens on the site of the old town. Arimathæa is the Ramathaim of 1 Macc. xi. 34, one of the three towns taken from Samaria and added to "Judæa" by Demetrius Nicator about 146 B.C.

This Joseph was at the time "a disciple of Jesus": "but he had been so secretly (κεκρυμμένος δὲ, plup. part.) for fear," etc. John's purpose in these words is to show the change that has come over Joseph. No longer has he any fear of the Jews, but now boldly (cf. Mark xv. 43) shows his love and reverence for the dead Man: his boldness the more remarkable now that to all appearance the dead Man's cause was lost.

"After these things," *i.e.* after the death of our Lord and the piercing of His side, and after the breaking of the legs of the two robbers, but before the actual death of these two, Joseph of Arimathæa went to Pilate and asked "that he might take the body of Jesus"—in order to save it from a felon's burial. Pilate had already given permission for the breaking of the legs in order to hasten death, but was surprised (Mark xv. 44) at hearing from Joseph of the so early death of Jesus, viz. that He was dead before they came to break His legs. On requiring, and receiving, from the centurion a verification that He had *already* (or, if we take the reading πάλαι, *some time ago*) died, Pilate gave the permit to Joseph.

Joseph, and all the Evangelists, use the word σῶμα for our Lord's "body." Only when expressing *Pilate's subjectivity* does Mark use the word πτῶμα, "corpse," "made a present of the corpse to Joseph" (ἐδωρήσατο τὸ πτῶμα τῷ Ἰωσήφ, xv. 45).

So Joseph came and took (ἦρεν) the body, or, as Mark and Luke say, "took it down" (καθελών), *i.e.* from the cross. We are, of course, to understand that Joseph directed and assisted in the taking down.

Friday, 5 p.m.

(39) When Joseph had got his permit from Pilate, he probably at once arranged with Nicodemus to bring the

spices and bandages for laying out the body, whilst he himself bought a fine linen sheet (σινδόνα, Mark) and returned to take the body down.

"Nicodemus too, he who came unto Him *by night at the first*" (νυκτὸς τὸ πρῶτον): John's purpose in these words is to mark the change in the action of Nicodemus also. At the opening of the Ministry a year ago (iii. 2) he had thought it wiser to come by night, thinking that by not openly avowing his beliefs he might have wider opportunities to help the cause; now that there is no longer good reason for concealing his mind, he openly avows his love and reverence for the dead Rabbi. He comes openly bringing a vast quantity of myrrh and aloes to enwrap the body.*

(40) We may safely assume that these resinous gums brought by Nicodemus, and the rolls of linen bandages, were carried by professional layers-out of the dead. The intricate process of swathing a body and binding in the resins and spices could be properly done only by skilled hands; and the time was short. This was no case for bungling hands, however loving.

(40) How intricate the process was may be seen from Egyptian mummies. Each toe and finger, each limb, the whole body, was to be separately wound round with narrow linen bandages (ὀθόνια of John xix. 40: Luke xxiv. 12) such as surgeons use, such as are found also swathing mummies. After the body had been washed and anointed, in among the bandages was bound the mass of spices (verse 40) over the whole, to prevent corruption setting in, for the body was torn with wounds. The eyes were closed: the jaw was bound up with a napkin. Lastly the whole was wrapt in the winding sheet of fine linen

* The English equivalent of the amount brought, "about a hundred, λίτρας," is uncertain. If the λίτρα be taken at its strict value of 218 grammes or 8 oz. av., the total amount will be 50 lbs. av. or about 3½ stone. If, however, the λίτρα be taken loosely, according to its common usage, to represent the Roman *libra* of 327 grammes or 12 oz. av., the total will be 100 lbs. Roman=75 lbs. av., or about 5⅓ stone.

The swathed Body with all the resins and spices bound in around would be as bulky as Egyptian mummies when freshly swathed are known to have been.

(σινδόνα) which Joseph had bought for the purpose (Mark xv. 46). That this was the customary mode of burial among the Jews may also be seen from the account of the raising of Lazarus (xi. 44): see how he "had been bound hands and feet with grave-clothes," and "his face had been bound round with a napkin," and he had to be "loosed" so as to be enabled to "go." The laying-out of our Lord's body seems to have been done in the most elaborate and costly mode, thanks to the wealth of both Nicodemus and Joseph.

(41) "And there was in the place where He was crucified a garden, and in the garden a new sepulchre." The garden belonged in all probability to Joseph of Arimathæa: the sepulchre certainly did, as we learn from Matthew (xxvii. 60): he had hewn it out of the live rock, and it had never yet been used. It was customary for rich Jews to be buried in their own grounds and not in a common cemetery.

The name of the place where He was crucified, viz. Golgotha or Κρανίου Τόπος (verse 17), means "a skull" (sing.): it was not so called as being a place of skulls (plur.), or place of execution, or place of common burial, as many think. Perhaps they also think skulls were lying there in the open as may be seen in the *ossuaires* of Brittany. That was not the mode in which Jews disposed of the bones of the dead. The place owed its name to the *one* famous skull laid there, the skull of Adam according to the ancient Hebrew tradition: we may compare the Capitolium of Rome, so called from the *one* famous skull found there when digging the foundations for a temple. The semi-sanctity attaching to this resting-place of Adam's skull seems to have been the reason why this place had so long been left outside the city walls, which here made a re-entrant angle. We can only conjecture Pilate's motive in ordering the Crucifixion to take place at this exact spot (if it was his order): there was no recognized place for Roman executions (crucifixions); the place for Jewish executions (stonings) was outside the Damascus-gate, away on the north of the city.

The presence of this private garden, where Joseph the wealthy Sanhedrist had had his own sepulchre hewn, is alone enough to show that Golgotha was not a place of public execution.

(42*a*) "There, therefore, owing to the Jews' Friday, because the sepulchre was near at hand they laid Jesus."

Friday, shortly before 6 p.m.

This sepulchre was not meant by the mourners to be His permanent tomb. They laid His Body here temporarily, intending to remove it on Sunday (after the festival-day) to its final resting-place—probably in the Garden of Gethsemane, which many think belonged to His mother, and there she herself was buried twenty-two years later. They were pressed for time on this Friday evening, anxious to have the sepulchre closed before the Sabbath began at 6 p.m.

"Owing to the Jews' Friday" (*διὰ τὴν Παρασκευὴν τῶν Ἰουδαίων*). At the time John wrote his gospel (100 A.D.) the word Παρασκευὴ had been adopted by Greek Christendom, from Greek-speaking Jews, as the common name for the weekly Friday. This, long suspected, has been made certain by the recent discovery of a MS. of the Διδαχὴ τῶν ιβ ἀποστόλων (see p. 400, note). A MS. of this long-lost treatise was discovered in a Greek monastery in Constantinople in 1875, and was first published to Europe in 1883. The treatise is generally admitted to date from the first century of our era: its great value is no less generally recognized. In this treatise the word Παρασκευὴ is seen to be the common word for the weekly Friday. Hence the reason for John speaking here of the Friday "of the Jews." Gentile Christians (for whom John writes) might not understand why the fact of the day being a Friday should have hurried Joseph and Nicodemus to get the burial over before sunset. By saying "Friday *of the Jews*" John directs his Gentile readers to the peculiarity of a Jewish Friday, viz. that all work must cease that day at 6 p.m. John in his gospel reckons days as the Romans reckoned the civil day, viz. from midnight to midnight: hence his notice of *the Jews'* Friday, which of course ended at sunset because their Sabbath began at sunset; whereas John's Friday, as he reckons it for his Gentile Ephesian readers, did not end till midnight.

"Because the sepulchre was near at hand." The sepulchre lies west by north of Golgotha, and is forty-five yards distant from it. Placing the swathed body in the winding-sheet they carried it and laid it in the rock-hewn *loculus*, or grave, in the inner or mortuary chamber of the double cave. They did not place the stone slab or lid over the *loculus*, because they meant to remove the body on Sunday morning: but they closed the entrance to the inner chamber by rolling-to the large flat circular stone which ran in a socket like a sliding shutter widely overlapping the opening. This inner rock chamber opened out of the outer rock chamber by a low entrance in the curtain of rock: it was *this entrance* that was closed by the great stone being rolled. Of this inner chamber the northern half was occupied, as may still be seen, by the rock bench which was hollowed out to form a *loculus*, so that the body might be laid down in it as into a sarcophagus or coffin.

(42*b*) It is important to notice the terminology used by the four Evangelists in describing this sepulchre. All four employ the term μνημεῖον: and all four mean by it specifically the *inner chamber*, which was closed by the stone and in which was the *loculus*. See especially Matthew xxvii. 60, "rolled a great stone to the door (or entrance, θύρα) of the *sepulchre* (μνημείου)": Mark xiv. 46, "rolled a stone to the door of the *sepulchre* (μνημείου)": xv. 3, "who will roll . . . from the door of the *sepulchre* (μνημείου)": Luke xxiv. 2, "the stone lying rolled away from the *sepulchre* (μνημείου)": John xx. 1, "sees the stone lifted out away from the *sepulchre* (μνημείου)": 5, 6, John coming to the *sepulchre* (μνημεῖον) did not enter it but stooped and looked into it, and sees the bandages; but Peter entered into the *sepulchre* (μνημεῖον), and John afterwards entered it. It would be well to retain "sepulchre" exclusively for this word μνημεῖον: for the "Church of the Holy Sepulchre" has never contained the original outer chamber, but only the original inner one (see p. 409).

John speaks only of the μνημεῖον throughout his account. Not so the Synoptists, for Matthew uses also another word, τάφος, in three places, viz. xxvii. 61, (women) "sitting over against the *burial-place* (τάφου)": 66, "the Jews made safe the *burial-place* (τάφον) by sealing the stone along with setting the guard": xxviii. 1, "came to look at the *burial-place* (τάφον)." By this word τάφος as against μνημεῖον Matthew seems to mean the place of burial, *i.e.* the whole tomb consisting of the outer chamber and of the μνημεῖον or inner chamber.

Mark, again, uses a second word in one place, xv. 46, "laid Him in a *tomb* (μνήματι)": and Luke in two places, xxiii. 53, "laid Him in a *tomb* (μνήματι)": xxiv. 1, "came to the *tomb* (μνῆμα)." This word μνῆμα as against μνημεῖον Mark and Luke seem to be using exactly as Matthew uses τάφος—to express the whole two-chambered tomb. As everywhere else in their accounts the three Synoptists use μνημεῖον, they must mean to distinguish the latter from the μνῆμα, or τάφος: and the English version should do the same.

We learn from Eusebius (*Life of Const.*, iii. 25, etc.) and Sozomen * (*Eccl. Hist.*, ii. 1) and Socrates * (*Eccl. Hist.*, i. 17) that in consequence of the devotion shown by the earliest Christians to the Holy Sepulchre, the enemies of Christianity covered the two sites, of the sepulchre and Golgotha, with one great platform of earth enclosed by a wall and paved with stone, and upon this vast *podium* they built a temple to Venus. When Helena and Constantine, some two centuries later, in 325 A.D., removed this great mound of earth and the temple in order to bring to light again these two sacred sites, they did not include either of these sites (viz. the sepulchre and Golgotha) under the roof of the great basilica they built, known as the Μαρτύριον (the Witness, *i.e.* the Cross): for this basilica was slightly to the east of the sepulchre and of Golgotha, and was directly over the pit where the three crosses had been found buried. The sepulchre and Golgotha were

* These two writers belong to the early part of the fifth century, Sozomen being a native of Palestine.

separately treated, as two distinct shrines: they stood within the τέμενος or porticoed enclosure that surrounded the basilica. As for the sepulchre, Helena cut away the whole of the outer chamber as well as the live rock from around the inner chamber so as to leave this latter standing out as a solitary cone of rock above the levelled ground (see Cyril Jerus., *Catech.* xiv. 9): this cone she then adorned with marbles and columns.

It was the Crusaders in the twelfth century who first included the three sites (the sepulchre, Golgotha, and the pit where the Cross had been found) in one and the same building, viz. that vast church known ever since as the "Church of the Holy Sepulchre," so called from the most important of the three sites it embraces.

Between chapters xix. and xx. is an interval of about thirty-five hours, viz. from 6 p.m. of Friday to 5 a.m. of Sunday, March 27.

Sat., March 26, after 6 p.m.

During this interval, on the Saturday, March 26, but after sunset, "the chief-priests and Pharisees," as we learn from Matthew, got permission from Pilate to seal the great stone, and obtained from him a guard of soldiers to watch the place of burial (τάφος) during the Saturday night. After sunset, therefore, of Saturday they affixed their official seal—of course first having rolled back the stone for a moment to see that the body was still there—and then left the guard there on duty.

Sat., March 26, after 6 p.m.

Also after sunset of Saturday (Mark xvi. 1), Mary Magdalene and Mary Clopas (who is the same as "the other Mary" = "the Mary the mother of James the Little" = "Mary the mother of Joses" = "Mary the mother of James") and Salome bought spices for the purpose of anointing the Body on the Sunday morning: for it is evident that Joseph and Nicodemus and others of His relatives and friends had arranged to meet at the tomb on Sunday morning to remove the Body to its permanent resting-place. The "women" of Luke xxiii. 49, 55, 56 no doubt includes Mary Magdalene, Mary Clopas, Salome, Joanna, Susanna, and many others: we need not assume from verse 56 that they bought their spices immediately they returned, on the *Friday* evening, for there would not have been time before sunset: they bought them, as Mark tells us, on the *Saturday* evening, after sunset (xvi. 1, διαγενομένου τοῦ σαββάτου).

Meanwhile, though our Lord's Body lay in the sepulchre dead in that His human soul was parted from it, but alive in that not for an instant was it bereft of His Godhead, He in His human "spirit" had passed to among the dead and "preached to the spirits who were in ward, who aforetime were disobedient when the long-suffering of God waited in the days of Noah whilst the ark was a-preparing" (1 Pet. iii. 19, 20). Not that it was only to these spirits that He preached, but these are specially named by Peter as representing the most stubborn disobedience and the greatest wickedness: as Bellarmine says, "these are named as seeming to be *the most unlikely ones* to have had forgiveness held out to them." If these, then all. And, as we may suppose, that ministry in the underworld thus begun continues still. Hence the importance of that article of the Creed, "He descended into Hades": it assures us that the resting-place of the dead is warm with the memory of that presence of Christ. Does it not also assure us that those who fail to know Him here are there taken in hand by a secondary ministry—wiser and more experienced from having lived and passed on from here?

Fri. evening, March 25, to Sun. morning, March 27.

§ XXVII

JOHN XX. 1–31

The Resurrection

THE date is Sunday morning, March 27 (Nisan 17), A.D. 29.

Before chapter xx. opens our Lord had risen and the events had taken place which Matthew relates in xxviii. 2–4. These Matthew introduces by Καὶ ἰδού, "And lo!" as describing *the scene which met the eyes* of Mary Clopas and her companions when they arrived at the tomb.* The account given in those three verses of what had already happened came, it would seem, from one or more of the guard, for none else had been present.

March 27, Sunday.

Local tradition asserts that the Blessed Virgin passed the night in the house in the garden, not thirty yards distant from the tomb. She, we imagine, knew the hour when He would rise. To her He appeared first of all, and at once, according to the tradition of the Church east and west recorded by Ambrose. The πρῶτον "firstly" of Mark xvi. 9 is only relative to the "afterwards" (μετὰ ταῦτα) of

* Viz. the scene of the stone lying rolled away and an angel sitting on it. All the aorists in these three verses (Matt. xxviii. 3, 4) have the force of pluperfects, ἐγένετο, καταβάς, προσελθών, ἀπεκύλισε, ἐσείσθησαν, ἐγένοντο. But what the women saw is given by the imperfects, ἐκάθητο, "was sitting," ἦν, his appearance "was" . . . and his raiment, etc. The Hebrew language has no pluperfect tense, and the context alone decides whether the perfect tense is a past or a present or a future perfect: nor does our Greek Matthew anywhere use a pluperfect form. The Greek translator of the original Aramaic has preferred to render the Aramaic vague perfect tense by the Greek vague aorist rather than gloss it by a pluperfect: perhaps it seemed to him that thus was better preserved the Hebrew idiom whether of language or of thought. Other instances in Matthew of a Greek aorist used as a pluperfect are ii. 16, ἠκρίβωσε; xiv. 3, ἔδησαν; xxvi. 48, ἔδωκε (where Mark has δεδώκει); xxvii. 18, παρέδωκαν; 31, ἐνέπαιξαν.

verse 12 and to the "later yet" (ὕστερον) of verse 14. The adverb πρῶτον has not the same meaning as the adjective πρώτῃ would have had. It has been objected that any such appearance to His mother must have been recorded in the gospels, had it occurred. It is from reverence for the Virgin Mother that all four Evangelists have kept her name out of this morning's scene, knowing they could not associate her with the otherwise universal disbelief of this Easter Day. Again, her certitude that He would rise, as He had said, would be known to all the disciples: so that His appearance to her might have carried little weight with any one: it might have been regarded with suspicion as a case of self-hypnotism. Except the Mother, not one had the tiniest expectation of ever again seeing alive the Man they had buried: this is a strong point in the evidence for the Resurrection.

However that may be, before Mary Clopas (="the other Mary") arrived at the tomb (with her companions) as recorded by Matthew, the Magdalene had already been there alone: also Peter and John had been there: also our Lord had appeared to the Magdalene there—in short, all the events had occurred which are contained in John xx. 1–17, as we shall see.*

(1) Mary Magdalene was the first of any of the disciples to arrive at the tomb. The other women who had bought spices had no doubt arranged together over-night to meet this morning at the sepulchre: they will naturally come in different groups as they come from different parts of the city: and, as naturally, the groups will not all arrive at quite the same time. The Magdalene is first: she comes alone: "she comes (ἔρχεται) early *whilst it was yet dark*" (σκοτίας ἔτι οὔσης, *i.e.* an hour before sunrise) "to the *sepulchre*" (μνημεῖον).† Whilst

5 a.m.

* A fuller treatment of this chapter and of the Synoptists' accounts of the Resurrection will be found in the writer's *Crucifixion and Resurrection of Jesus Christ*, pp. 129–176.

† ἔρχεται . . . εἰς τὸ μνημεῖον = "is on her way *to* the sepulchre (*i.e.* inner chamber)." In Hellenistic Greek εἰς must not be pressed to mean *into*, unless used with a verb compounded with εἰς or ἐν, *e.g.* εἰσῆλθεν εἰς (vv. 6, 8). See p. 433 note.

entering the outer chamber, which was always open, she sees the stone lying lifted out and away from the *sepulchre* (μνημεῖον, inner chamber). The stone was lying there on the floor of the outer chamber. She goes no further; she does not advance to the entrance of the inner chamber to look in: she jumps to the natural conclusion that the Body has been removed.

(2) Running she comes "to Peter" as the head of the Twelve, "and to the other disciple whom Jesus loved": these two, Peter and John, were probably together (and see verse 3). Local tradition says they were in the cave of the "Gallicantus" two hundred yards east of Caiaphas's house, and hardly half a mile south of the sepulchre.

5.10 a.m.

"The other disciple whom Jesus loved" (τὸν ἄλλον . . . ὃν ἐφίλει ὁ Ἰησοῦς), *i.e.* John the writer, not hereby distinguishing himself from Peter, but including Peter with himself as being beloved by Jesus as His friends. The word ἐφίλει represents a more tender personal love than ἠγάπα. Elsewhere John uses this latter word to express the love our Lord bore to him himself: perhaps he so uses it rather in disparagement of himself, as though saying, 'it was not, as you all seem to think, that I was in any way worthy of His tender personal love (φιλεῖν), but only that He showed to me especially that large general love (ἀγαπᾶν) which He has equally for all.'

The Magdalene's words to Peter are, "They-have-taken-away" (ἦραν, the subject of the verb being vague) "the Lord, and we-know not where they-have-laid Him." In this "we know not" she does not imply that any one else had been with her; she had been alone: she is rather including in one camp Peter, John, herself, and all who loved Him, whilst opposing to them all others, viz. the hostile or indifferent Jews, whom she suspects of having removed the Body.

(3) The Greek original by using the singular ἐξῆλθεν gives to Peter the initiative of the start for the sepulchre: the two, Peter and John, were running together: the Magdalene no doubt following.

(4) John as being the younger (he was 30 or 31 years of age) ran ahead towards the end—it shows the impatient eagerness of the two—and "was the first to come to the sepulchre" (μνημεῖον, the inner chamber). The words are ἦλθεν πρῶτος εἰς τὸ μνημεῖον, from which it appears that the Magdalene had not gone as far as the μνημεῖον on her first visit: for πρῶτος must refer to more than two. If the comparison were only with Peter, the Greek would be πρότερος. John means to say that he was the first of any one that day to reach the μνημεῖον.

5.20 a.m.

(5) "And he *stooped-down-to-enter*" (παρακύψας, more commonly *stooped-down-to-look*), "and *he sees* (βλέπει) the *linen-bandages* (ὀθόνια) lying: he did not, however, enter in." The entrance in the rock-curtain to the inner chamber was so low that it was impossible to enter that chamber or to get a full view of it without stooping low down.* John did not enter further as he had meant to do, because on catching sight of the ὀθόνια he naturally thought *the Body was still within them*, and reverence withheld him.

(6) But Peter coming up "went-in into the sepulchre (εἰσῆλθεν εἰς τὸ μνημεῖον)," *i.e.* into the inner chamber through the low entrance,† "and he gazes at (θεωρεῖ) the linen-bandages (ὀθόνια) lying, (7) and at the napkin that was on His head not lying with the linen-bandages but apart rolled up in a place alone." John had not seen the napkin, because, not entering, he had not been able to see far enough round to the right where the napkin lay on the spot where the head had lain. This napkin had been bound round the head so as to tie up the lower jaw.

(8) "Then, *therefore*" (οὖν, *i.e.* as seeing Peter's start, or hearing his cry of amazement), "went-in also the other disciple, he who was the first to come to the *sepulchre* (μνημεῖον), and he saw and believed." What was it

* The entrance to the inner chamber is similar to-day, the original shape being more or less preserved through the changes of centuries.

† See Luke xxiv. 12, where Peter ran to the μνημεῖον, and then παρακύψας, *i.e.* stooped-down-to-enter, and then sees, etc.

exactly that they saw to make such an impression on Peter and to bring Faith to John? Was it the sight of bandages unwound and lying carefully folded as by angelic hands—no trace of haste or of hurried removal, but every sign of power, of calm, of order? It was something far more strange.

The bandages they saw were lying *precisely as they had lain when swathed* round the Body and limbs. It must be remembered that the bandages (rolls of long strips of linen like surgeon's bandages) had been wound in a practically unbroken length round Body and limbs, beginning at the toes and ending at the neck—just as mummies are swathed. During the process the 3½ stone of resinous gums had been bound in, giving to the linen a firm and rather sticky consistency. It was this *stiff* casing of bandages that Peter and John now saw, lying empty like a cocoon from which the chrysalis has escaped, preserving the exact shape of the Body and limbs that had once lain within. It was a physical impossibility that the Body should have been drawn forth through the narrow opening at the neck: yet the Body was gone: the bandages were undisturbed: and the napkin that had been wound round the head, tying up the jaw whilst leaving the face exposed, lay just as it had lain slightly parted necessarily from the Body bandages, but it too empty.*

The Body of our Lord had simply passed out of the stiff casing of bandages, as from a matrix, without displacing them, as easily as He passed through the rock walls of the sepulchre.

There fell upon John the echo of words heard on many occasions but never apprehended or assimilated: "The Son of Man is delivered into the hands of men, and they shall kill Him, and after that He is killed He shall rise the third day" (Mark ix. 3): "After that I am risen I will go before you into Galilee" (xiv. 28): "Destroy this Temple, and in three days I will raise It up" (John ii. 19). "There

* The winding-sheet (σινδὼν) which had been folded over all (Matt., Mark, Luke) must have been unfolded and laid back along either side so as to leave the bandage-casing exposed.

shall no sign be given to it (this generation) but the sign of the prophet Jonas: for as Jonas was three days and three nights in the whale's belly, so shall The Son of Man be in the heart of the earth three days and three nights" (Matt. xii. 39, 40).

To John flashed the conviction that the Lord was indeed risen (John xx. 8) as He had foretold. Peter was as yet in amazement at the thing that had happened (Luke xxiv. 12).

(9) "For as yet they knew not the Scripture that He must rise from the dead." In this John is explaining how it was that he could say, only now, that he "believed": so great was the extension of insight that he now received into the vast scheme of the Christian Faith—the redemption of the race by the death of the God-Man and the regeneration of the race in His risen life.

Never hitherto had he or any of them understood that the Law and the Prophets and the Scriptures foretold that Messiah must literally die and literally from the dead rise. John recollects his own expectations of Friday last, as he ran for the vinegar and sponge, that Elijah would come to deliver the crucified Messiah *before* He died.

(10) "They went away, therefore, again home—the disciples." These two last words he has added at the end to mark the cleavage between his and Peter's experience on the one side, and that of the Magdalene's on the other to which he at once passes.

(11) Having thus ended with Peter and himself, he resumes Mary Magdalene's story. As they two went away from the tomb, she came back: and she was standing "near the sepulchre" but "*outside*" of it, "weeping" (*πρὸς τῷ μνημείῳ ἔξω, κλαίουσα*), *i.e.* she was standing in the outer chamber and near the inner chamber.

5.30 a.m.

"Therefore whilst she wept she stooped-down-to-enter the sepulchre," i.e. *the inner chamber* (*παρέκυψεν εἰς τὸ μνημεῖον*). But was arrested by what she saw within, viz. two angels.

(12) "And she gazes-at (*θεωρεῖ*) two angels in white

sitting one at the head and one at the feet where the body of Jesus had been laid." The word rendered "had been laid" is ἔκειτο, the imp. of κεῖται. Just as the present tense κεῖται, he "lies," serves also for he "has been laid," acting regularly as the perf. pass. of τίθημι, to "place," to "lay," so the imp. ἔκειτο, he "was lying," serves also for he "had been laid," acting as the pluperf. pass. of τίθημι. From the matrix of bandages and the rolled napkin (not folded flat, but stiff, as though the head were still within) she could talk of "the feet" and "the head."

(13) It is the angels who break the intense silence (see the emphatic ἐκεῖνοι), for she is too absorbed in amazement to speak. With gentle courtesy, they ask, "Woman, why weepest thou?" She says to them, "They-have-taken away my Lord, and I know not where they-have-laid Him"—the "they" in both cases being indefinite in the Greek, exactly as in verse 2.

(14) "Having said this she turned backwards," as no longer minded to enter the inner chamber: "and she gazes-at (θεωρεῖ) Jesus who is standing there: and she did not know it is Jesus." Her failure to recognize was not due to any want of daylight, nor (in face of the word θεωρεῖ) to any want of concentration of thought. The cause of it must have been that Jesus was deliberately withholding Himself from being known, until she was prepared to recognize Him without the sudden shock affecting her mind injuriously. She had been already partly prepared by the sight of the two angels: directly she saw Jesus standing, it had occurred to her, "Can that be He?" hence her long gaze at Him: but as He still withheld Himself and said kindly to her—

(15) "Woman, why weepest thou? whom seekest thou?" she supposed He must be the gardener, and says, "Sir, if (as seems now probable) it is thou that hast borne Him away, tell me where thou hast laid Him, and *I* will take Him away"; and as she speaks she naturally turns to the sepulchre to make her meaning clear. The moment for recognition has come.

(16) "Jesus says to her, 'Mariàm,'" the Hebrew name, of which the Greek form is Maria.

At that word in His natural voice, "she turned and says to Him in the Hebrew (*i.e.* Aramaic), 'Rabbûni,' that is to say, Master." Here she evidently was about to cling to Him; her joy and affection outstripping her reverence: for she is not aware, nor ever has been aware, of His absolute Divinity.

(17) Tenderly He checks that unrestrained emotion which is too psychical to be wholesome, and too familiar for the new conditions:—"Touch Me not: for not yet have I ascended to The Father": as saying He is no longer mingling as a man with men upon earth: but henceforth resumes His place as God in Heaven. The economy of servitude is over, the economy of triumph begins. Though this may seem for the moment to be a loss to the disciples, it is the beginning of a new order: for to Heaven He purposes to lift them all, and on a higher range of life they shall meet Him. Though the Magdalene may not touch Him thus familiarly, let her take this His assurance of innermost union with Him, "Go unto My brethren and say to them, 'I ascend unto Him who is My Father and your Father and My God and your God.'"

The message is to "My brethren," which will primarily mean, not the eleven Apostles, but those habitually called His "brethren," *i.e.* His nearest relatives—the children of Clopas and Mary Clopas, viz. James the Little, Joses, Simeon, Jude, and their sisters: secondarily, no doubt it means all His disciples including the Eleven.

(18) "Mary Magdalene cometh announcing to the disciples" (not merely to the Eleven), "'I have seen the Lord,' and that He spake these things to her."

The confusion that we find in the accounts of Easter morning as given by the four Evangelists is due to the concise brevity of the three Synoptists. Not one of them imagined he was *proving* the resurrection for his readers, any more than that he had proved the birth, or life, or public ministry, or the humanity, or the divinity of our Lord. Faith, in the readers, depended not so much on the written word as on the oral teaching of the divinely constituted society called the Church, complemented by the co-operation of the Holy Spirit enlightening the minds of the hearers.

With regard to the visits of the women to the sepulchre on Easter morning, there are four distinct sources from which the four Evangelists have drawn. All four Evangelists have named Mary Magdalene as one of the women who went to the sepulchre, for she was notably the first there, and the first recorded appearance of the risen Lord to any of the disciples was to her: but only John has described her visit at any length: he does so because he saw that the synoptic accounts were imperfect and easily misleading.

Matthew (xxviii. 1–10) has evidently given us Mary Clopas's (=" the other Mary's ") account of the visit of herself *and her companions* who are referred to in " the women " of verse 5 (see Luke xxiv. 10 for the presence of other women with the different leaders). None of her companions is named. The Magdalene did not come with her, but had been there before her. There may be a hint of this in the singular *ἦλθεν Μαρία ἡ Μαγδ. . . . καὶ ἡ ἄλλη Μαρία* instead of the plural *ἦλθον*.

Luke has given us (xxiv. 1–10) Joanna's account of the visit of herself and her companions, none of whom is named: but they are referred to in " the rest of the women with them " (verse 10), *i.e.* in the different groups.

Mark (xvi. 1–8) has given us Salome's account of the visit of herself and her companions, none of whom is named, for Mary Magdalene, and Mary the mother of James, and Salome, named in verse 1, did not come together.

The times at which the Magdalene and the three groups arrive are all different: also the experiences of all the four parties are quite different.

In the local tradition there is no confusion of our Lord's appearance to the Magdalene (as told by John) with His appearance to " the women," *i.e.* to Mary Clopas and her group (as told by Matthew). For whereas in the former instance the site is marked near the entrance to the outer chamber of the tomb, in the second instance the site is marked as four hundred yards to the south of the sepulchre and close to the English church on Mount Sion —the exact spot used to be marked by a chapel known as that of *The three Marys.* Did this name commemorate the fact that here He appeared to the *third* Mary? for so far He had appeared only to Marys, viz. *Mary* His Mother (recorded by tradition though not in the Gospels), *Mary* Magdalene (near the sepulchre, see John), and now to *Mary* Clopas and her group (Matthew).

The events of Easter morning may be roughly timed as follows:—

It was at the hour when life's tide is at the lowest ebb, viz. at 3 a.m., "cockcrow,"* of Sunday, March 27 (Nisan 17) of A.D. 29, that our Lord rose from the dead, passing through the rock walls of the sepulchre, and appeared to His mother. At the same instant "there was a great earthquake, for an angel of the Lord descended out of heaven and came near and rolled away the stone from the sepulchre," "and from fear of him the watchers quaked and became as dead men."

5 a.m. Mary Magdalene comes whilst it is yet dark (σκοτίας ἔτι οὔσης): sees only that the stone has been rolled away from the inner chamber: goes no further: sees no one: jumps at an inference: runs to Peter and John (John).

5.10. Tells Peter and John (John).

5.20. Peter and John arrive at a run: enter the inner chamber: see no one: gaze at the bandage-matrix lying empty: leave, having seen no one (John).

5.30. The Magdalene again at the tomb: sees "two angels" in the inner chamber sitting at

* This is the tradition of the early Church: and cf. Prudentius's hymn, *Ad galli cantum*:—

"... Inde est quod omnes credimus
Illo quietis tempore
Quo gallus exultans canit
Christum redisse ab inferis."

Hence the cock, as symbol of the resurrection, tops the steeples of our churches.

head and foot of the bandage-matrix. Jesus appears to her, outside: she leaves with a message to " My brethren " (John).

5.40. Mary Clopas and her group arrive at the tomb " as it was gathering light to the first day of the week " (τῇ ἐπιφωσκούσῃ εἰς μίαν σαββάτων). They see an " angel " sitting on the stone which is lying on the ground in the outer chamber: this angel shows them the very spot in the inner chamber where the Body had been laid, *i.e.* shows them the bandage-matrix. They leave quickly with a message to " His disciples." On the way they are met by our Lord: they lay hold of His feet without rebuke and worship Him: He specifies particularly that the message is to " My brethren." His first care is His nearest relatives, and to their mother (Mary Clopas) He is talking (Matthew).

5.50. Joanna and her group arrive " when the dawn was full " (ὄρθρου βαθέως). They found the stone lying rolled away: evidently no angel sitting on it: they entered into the inner chamber: evidently saw no one there: in their perplexity at seeing the matrix of bandages without the Body in it, suddenly two " men " (ἄνδρες) stood over them in dazzling raiment and spoke to them. They leave, and report " to the Eleven and to all the rest " (Luke).

6.5. Salome and her group arrive " very early," but " after the sun was risen " (λίαν πρωῒ . . . ἀνατείλαντος τοῦ ἡλίου): they see with astonishment that the stone has been rolled away: evidently no angel sitting on it: they entered into the inner chamber and saw " a young-man " (νεανίσκον) sitting on the right-hand (*i.e.* on the north side where the

Body had been laid) clothed in a white long robe. He shows them "the place where they laid Him" (pointing to the matrix of bandages): he gives them a message to His "disciples and to Peter." They fled in terror and "told no one anything" (Mark).

It is obvious that these different accounts represent so many different visits and different experiences. As for the various manifestations from the spirit-world, we know nothing of the laws that govern them. But assuming the fact of the resurrection and its doctrinal value, we should expect on that day just what we find—an extraordinary lifting of the veil that normally hides from our eyes spiritual agents and their activities.

Besides these manifestations on Easter morning, there occurred also to-day "the resurrection of the bodies of many of the saints who slept; and they (the risen saints) came forth out of the sepulchres after His resurrection and came into the holy city and were manifested to many" (Matt. xxvii. 52, 53). Though Matthew has recorded this in connection with the moment of our Lord's death, he expressly says that they did not rise until after He had risen: we may therefore suppose they appeared on this Easter Day. They represented that *Wave-sheaf* of the new harvest which was being offered in the temple on this day—the day after the nation's festival-day of the Passover: see Lev. xxiii. 10–14.

5 p.m.

6.30 p.m.

On this same day He appeared in the afternoon to the two disciples on the way to Emmaus (Luke xxiv. 13–33), made Himself known to them about 6.30 p.m.: and appeared afterwards about 6.30 p.m. to Peter (*ib.* 34: 1 Cor. xv. 5) as to the head of the Church.

8 p.m.

(19) Later yet, on this same evening, "He came and stood in the midst" of the "disciples" gathered together within closed doors. This is the manifestation which is also described by Luke (xxiv. 33–43) and by Mark (xvi. 14). We learn from Luke

that the two disciples had returned already from Emmaus, so that the hour can hardly be earlier than 8 p.m. Also Luke adds that there were others present besides "the Eleven." It appears from Mark (xvi. 14, "as they sat at meat") and incidentally from Luke (xxiv. 41–43) that the owner of the house (as we suppose, Joseph of Arimathæa) had provided a supper for all who assembled on this occasion, the first of the suppers afterwards known as *agapæ*. It is at this point, during this supper, that John resumes the story, at about 8 p.m.

(19) "It being, therefore, evening (ὀψίας) on that day, the first day (τῇ μιᾷ) of the week," etc. The word ὀψία, "evening," occurs fourteen times in the N.T. It has two distinct meanings:—

1. The evening that begins about 2.30 p.m. and lasts till sunset: this according to the Rabbinists is the "first" evening. In this sense the word occurs in the N.T. three times only (Matt. xiv. 15: xxvii. 57: Mark xv. 42).
2. The evening that begins with sunset and lasts on into dark: this is the "second" evening of the Rabbinists. It is the common meaning and occurs eleven times in the N.T. This is the meaning in the passage in question: for it had been the time of the evening meal (after sunset, say 6.30 p.m.) when our Lord had made Himself known to the two at Emmaus (Luke xxiv. 29, 30), and the village of Emmaus is "60 stades" (=6½ miles) distant from Jerusalem where the two afterwards found "the Eleven" and others gathered together (*ib.* 33–36). Luke never uses the word ὀψία. For the No. 1 meaning he has ἡ ἡμέρα ἤρξατο κλίνειν, "the day began to decline" (ix. 12): and for No. 2 meaning he uses ἑσπέρα (xxiv. 29: Acts iv. 3; xxviii. 23), and κέκλικεν ἤδη ἡ ἡμέρα, "the day has already declined" or "set" (xxiv. 29).

To these two distinct "evenings" is due the curious phrase in the O.T. "between the two evenings," marking the time for the killing of the Paschal lambs and for the offering of the evening sacrifice. The Rabbinists interpret it as the time between the beginning of the "first" evening (about 2.30 p.m.) and the beginning of the "second" evening (sunset).

(19) As we have seen, it is long after 6 p.m. of Sunday, March 27, and yet John distinctly says it was still the Sunday. It is therefore clear that he reckons days as the Romans did, and as we do, from midnight to midnight (just as he does his hours): and not from sunset to sunset. Of course, when he is writing of the Sabbath *of the Jews* (xix. 31) he has to reckon that as they did, viz. from sunset to sunset, but he is careful to explain (xix. 42) that it was only "*the Jews*' Friday" that ended at sunset: the Friday of the Greeks, for whom he is writing, ended at midnight (p. 406), as did all their days. See at iv. 52: p. 118.*

About 8 p.m.

Not only John, but Mark also (who according to all tradition writes for Romans) evidently reckons days from midnight to midnight. This will be seen from a careful examination of his iv. 35, where the ὀψία, "evening," will be found to be the evening beginning with sunset (not the evening beginning at 2.30 p.m.), and yet he calls it "on that day," *i.e.* the same day. Like John, he of course recognizes that *for Jews* a Sabbath begins with sunset.

(19) "It being therefore evening on that day, the first day of the week, and the doors being shut where the disciples were for fear of the Jews, Jesus came and stood in the midst." The room in which the disciples were assembled is identified unhesitatingly by all tradition with that "Upper-room" where our Lord and the Twelve had supped seventy-two hours before, commonly known as the *Cenácolo*, "Supper-room," where the Eucharist was instituted. See at p. 303.

* Throughout the Roman empire, since the introduction of the Julian calendar in B.C. 45, the official civil day began at midnight. It seems that this official notation of the civil day was observed by all the nationalities of the empire including the Jews: but these latter made exception for Sabbaths and other holidays of obligatory rest just as they do to-day, for these they reckoned (and still reckon) as beginning at the preceding sunset.

And He says to them, "Peace to you" (εἰρήνη ὑμῖν, Hebrew *shâlôm lâkem*). The greeting occurs four times in the O.T. (Gen. xliii. 23 : Judges vi. 23, xix. 20 : Dan. x. 19). In the O.T. it is never the equivalent of the modern Arabic greeting, "The peace be with you": but is always an assurance of safety, an assurance that there is nothing to fear. Even in Judges xix. 20 it is so, with the condition added that 'you put yourselves under my charge and that you do not pass the night in the street.'

So, too, this greeting of our Lord in verses 19, 21, "Peace to you," is an assurance that there is no cause to fear, and that all is well: for they (Luke xxiv. 36) were alarmed by His manifestation. But coming from Him the phrase is also a sacramental bestowal of "peace." The phrase preserves the same meaning in the Apostolic salutation, "Grace to you and peace," which is not a pious hope but an authoritative assurance: it is also a blessing, which is not an empty form but a sub-sacramental form conveying an objective grace if the receiver is worthy.

(20) "He showed them His hands and His side. The disciples therefore were glad," etc. See the fuller account given by Luke (xxiv. 37–43), where we find that before the disciples were convinced that He was not a spirit, they saw Him eat part of a roast fish.

(21) "Even as The Father has sent Me, I too send you." The commission of the Church has the same warrant or authority as His own commission had. And as authority alone would be insufficient, He next bestowed on them an enabling Power:—

(22) "He breathed into them" (ἐνεφύσησεν), thus informing them with the Holy Spirit that proceeds from Him and is the Giver of Life. But The Spirit was not with them as with Him: for whereas the whole Spirit, the whole Godhead, was in Him autogenous and not communicated, He merely "breathed a breath into" them—a single act (ἐνεφύσησεν). This Greek word is the same as is used by the LXX in those two pregnant phrases of the O.T., viz. Gen. ii. 7, "the Lord God *breathed into* man's

nostrils the breath (or The Spirit) of Life"; and Ezek. xxxvii. 9, "*breathe into* these slain and they shall live" (the vision of the Dry Bones).

(23) "Receive ye the Holy Spirit: whosesoever sins ye remit, they are remitted to them: whosesoever sins ye retain, they are retained." This is the institution in the Church of the Sacrament of Penance. This power of remission and retention of sins of individuals is thus made inherent in the whole Church collectively: for this in-breathing of the Holy Spirit by our Lord and this bestowal of enabling Power were not confined to the Eleven Apostles (or rather Ten, for Thomas was absent), but extended to all the disciples present. The Church collectively declares the conditions on which sins are remitted, and with the plenary powers of an ambassador pronounces their remission or their retention.

It is certain that different sections of the Church have from the first interpreted the external conditions of this Sacrament differently. Some, for instance, in the early centuries required individual, public, confession of specialized sins to the assembled Church: but this for obvious reasons became disallowed.

Other Churches, again, have been satisfied with a general confession, either individually to a priest, or collectively in public assembly.

The Church of Rome, again, has gradually insisted on individual confession of specialized sins to a priest as part of the normal conditions. If the Church of Rome for disciplinary reasons has seen fit to confine, in practice, this absolving power to a certain body of officials, well and good: it is but part of the discipline which binds together the members of that the most vital of the Christian denominations. Or the philosophy of this phenomenon may be that a power at first inherent in the general organism has, by the inevitable law or formula of that organism's development, become specialized into a function of a definite part of that organism. Just so the power of infallibility in doctrine, at first known to be inherent somehow in the Church collectively, has by the law of development become specialized into a function of the visible head of the Church. All will agree that every living organism must develop, and development is specialization of parts and functions; any difference of opinion that may arise will be confined to whether certain specializations are morbid or healthy.

(24) "But Thomas, one of the Twelve, he who is called Didymus," etc. The meaning of the Hebrew *Thomas* is *Twin*, which in Greek is *Didymos*. No less than three times (xi. 16: xx. 24: xxi. 2) does John insist on this Greek name Didymos. The reason here, as in similar cases, was perhaps that the Greek name was the name by which the Apostle Thomas was best known to the readers for whom John is writing. See note to iv. 25.

It was after our Lord disappeared from the room that Thomas entered it, and on the same evening.

March 27. Sunday, say 8.30 p.m.

(25) The rest of the disciples, therefore, who were present tell him that they have but just now seen the Lord (ἑωράκαμεν, perfect), and no doubt also that He had shown them the marks in His hands and side (verse 20). Thomas protests that he *will be unable* to believe (οὐ μὴ πιστεύσω)—not that he *refuses* to believe—unless he not only sees the marks (as the others had seen), but feels with his touch that the holes are real—as the others had not felt, although they had probably felt His flesh and bones (Luke xxiv. 39) to satisfy themselves that He was not a phantasm.

(26) On that day week (for that is the exact equivalent of the Greek "after eight days")—and the date is Sunday, April 3—"again His disciples were within, and Thomas was with them." They were no doubt assembled in the same room as before. Already it seems that Sunday is becoming the day for Christian Hebrews to meet together to commemorate the Resurrection, the central fact of Christianity.

April 3. Sunday, say 7 a.m.

(27) Jesus becomes present under the same conditions as before and with the same greeting, "Peace to you." Next (εἶτα) He offers Thomas the very test which Thomas

had said could alone convince him. "And be not faithless but believing" (καὶ μὴ γίνου ἄπιστος ἀλλὰ πιστός). The γίνου, "become," is not to be joined so much to ἄπιστος, "faithless," which Thomas already was, as to πιστὸς, "believing," which he now becomes.

(28) There is every reason to suppose that Thomas did as he was invited to do ("Reach thy finger hither and see My hands, and reach thy hand and place it in My side"): just as there is every reason to suppose that on Easter Day the other ten Apostles and the disciples with them had done as they had been invited to do, and handled Him (ψηλαφήσατέ με, Luke xxiv. 39), verifying flesh and bones. Their difficulty of belief, though in a measure reprehensible in them, was salutary for those who were to believe through their testimony: for no room for doubt was left—so far as human testimony could be adequate.

"Thomas answered and said to Him, 'My Lord and My God.'" Thomas's belief was not solely nor mainly the result of his touch and vision: for the physical senses alone can never be sufficient to produce faith—no more than can miracles. But no doubt the physical senses helped Thomas, just as the sight of our Lord's miracles helped others before. The main factor, however, of his faith, as of all faith, was the power emanating from the Personality of the risen Lord, a power that leaves no doubt as to that Personality.

(29) "Because thou hast seen Me thou hast believed," *i.e.* 'Could you not believe without seeing Me?' He implies a certain hardness of heart in Thomas in that he had needed the aid of the physical senses: for that aid ought not to be necessary; and is not necessary where the heart is in touch with God's spiritual world that exists behind the veil of God's material world.

"Blessed are they who without seeing believed." The primary application of this Beatitude will be to the Blessed Virgin, and to John who alone of the Apostles or of the disciples (as far as we know) believed on Easter Day without seeing (see verse 8). But we may suppose that during this last week, on the testimony of those who had seen

Him last Sunday, many had believed and were present to-day and heard this blessedness pronounced on themselves. This Beatitude abides for the Church of this Age, which must be content with faith alone. In a yet future Age ("after eight days") faith and physical sight will go hand in hand for the then Church upon earth.

(30, 31) "Therefore, whilst many and other (πολλὰ μὲν, οὖν, καὶ ἄλλα) signs Jesus did in the presence of His disciples which have not been written in this book, *these* (ταῦτα δὲ) have been written that ye may believe that Jesus is the Messiah, The Son of God, and that believing, ye may have Life in His name." The force of the "therefore" is 'Because of this blessing, just recorded, upon those who believe without the aid of physical sight, I John have selected and recorded what I have recorded, in order that you, my readers, who cannot possibly "see" Him with physical eyes may believe without seeing and thereby may come under this Beatitude.'

John thereupon goes on to amplify the word "believe," by defining what our Lord meant by it in His Beatitude, viz. the belief that "Jesus is the Messiah, The Son of God," with all that is connoted by these terms, and all the inferences that necessarily derive from them,—connotation and inferences that the Church has ever been more and more clearly visualizing and in her creeds and dogmas has ever been more and more accurately defining.

Next, he goes on to amplify the word "blessed," also by defining what our Lord meant by it here: viz. "the having Life in His name." "In His name," *i.e.* in the name just given, *i.e.* in Him *quâ* "Jesus the Messiah (Christ), The Son of God." Explicit understanding of all that the Name connotes is not necessary: implicit belief in what is meant by it is enough to begin with.

§ XXVIII

JOHN XXI. 1–END

The government of the Church is vested in Peter.

It has been held by many, perhaps by most, commentators since the sixteenth century, that this last chapter of John's gospel is an appendix added as an afterthought either by the author of the gospel (John) or by some later hand. But this opinion is due solely to the assumption that John in writing his gosepl can have had no other object in view than those named in the last verse of chapter xx., viz. " that ye may *believe* that Jesus is the Messiah, The Son of God: and that, believing, ye may *have Life* in His name."

There can be little doubt that with the end of chapter xx. ends the main purpose and the main body of John's gospel: he had, however, a second purpose in view and a last message before his death. It concerned the new Society formed of these believers. Was it to be an amorphous body without visible head, such as organisms belonging to the lowest order of zoology? Undoubtedly to Peter had been given the keys of government for his life: but after Peter's death, was there thenceforth to be no visible head or guiding hand? Had our Lord made no provision for His Church down the ages, by which she might voice herself, thus realizing to herself her own unity, and to all outside of her her entity?

John's purpose in this last chapter is plain. It is to show what provision our Lord had made for carrying on until His second coming, viz. that He had vested in Peter acting through his successors the government of the universal Church.

(1) " After these things " (viz. the last recorded incident—that of April 3—of verses 26–29 of chapter xx.) " Jesus manifested Hinself again to the disciples on the Sea of Tiberias." The day is probably Sunday, April 10 : all His previous manifestations had been on Sundays, viz. March 27 and April 3.

A.D. 29. April 10, Sunday.

Peter and others leaving Jerusalem on Monday, April 4, would arrive at Capernaum on the evening of Thursday, April 7. After the Sabbath was over, at sundown of Saturday, April 9, he resumed his old occupation of fishing on the lake of Tiberias, whilst awaiting that great manifestation of our Lord in Galilee to the assembled Church, which had been promised to the Apostles on the night before His Passion, " after I am risen I will go-before you to Galilee " (Matt. xxvi. 32). The promise had been repeated to the disciples, through Mary Clopas and her group, by the angel on Easter morning, " He goeth-before you to Galilee : there shall ye see Him " (Matt. xxviii. 7) : and was sent a few minutes later by our Lord Himself to His brethren, " Tell My brethren that they go to Galilee, and there shall they see Me " (*ib.* verse 10).*

(2, 3) With Peter in his ship are six others, viz. Thomas called " the Twin," Nathanael who resided at (ἀπὸ) Kana of Galilee (he is generally allowed to be the same as Bartholomew of the Synoptic gospels), James and John, the sons of Zebedee, and " two others of His disciples." The five named belonged to the number of the Twelve Apostles. The " two others " were not improbably Simeon and Jude, two of the " brethren " of our Lord (and not of the Twelve).

They are using the long seine net (δίκτυον), which is paid out by the ship's boat and afterwards drawn round

* That great official manifestation to the assembled Church was made on Mount Tabor, " the mount " (τὸ ὄρος) of Matt. xxviii. 16 : it is the occasion named in 1 Cor. xv. 6, when " He was seen by above five hundred brethren at once " : it occurred at a later date than that with which we are dealing in John xxi. (see verse 14), and probably on the following Sunday, April 17 : and was marked by a formal act of adoration of Him by all the assembled Church.

in a sweep by the boat back to the ship, where it is hauled on board.

(4) After a fruitless night's work, early on Sunday morning, April 10, " as the morning was now breaking " (πρωίας ἤδη γινομένης, as is probably the true reading), (5) they hear a stranger hailing them from the shore as one wishing to buy their catch, " O my men, have ye no fish to sell me ? " (παιδία, μή τι προσφάγιον ἔχετε) : and so Chrysostom understands it. He addresses them not as a Father by the endearing τεκνία, " little children " (as in xiii. 33), but in the guise of a stranger by παιδία, a term marking inferiority in age, or, as here, in rank : it is the Latin *pueri*, the English " my men." They answered " No."

5.30 a.m.

(6) He shouted back, " Cast the net on the right side of the ship, and ye shall find "—as though He, standing on higher ground, could see a shoal of fish there. This would be in accord with a common habit among the fishermen of the Levant to-day, who station one of their number on a cliff and take his signals as to where the shoals are.

They did as advised by the stranger, paying out the net by the boat ; and as the boat brought round the far end of the net, those in the ship were no longer able to haul it on board, so great was the multitude of the fishes (ἰχθύων).

(7) Meanwhile John, " that disciple whom Jesus loved (ἠγάπα)," has recognized the Stranger, as the morning light increases or perhaps by some gesture made to him (John) and seen by him alone : and he says to Peter, " It is the Lord." Peter had been superintending the operations, too busy to think of much else, and like the rest of them is lightly-clad (γυμνὸς) at the work. But on hearing " It is the Lord," he looks up, recognizes Him, casts all other care aside, slips on his outer-garment (ἐπενδύτην),* for no Oriental would appear in undress before

* ἐπενδύτης. A garment put on over other garments. The word γυμνὸς, rendered "naked," commonly means merely lightly clad, *e.g.* in tunic only. So also *nudus* in Latin, *e.g. nudus ara, sere nudus*, Virg. *Georg.* 2, 299.

his superior, girds it to him, and casts himself to the sea,* so eager is his love for the Lord.

It is clear he does not mean to swim ashore in the cumbersome cloak: it is clear he does not mean to wade ashore, for he is "about 200 cubits" (100 yards) off, and the shore nowhere shelves so gently. What then? He means to walk upon the water—he had made trial of that once last year at our Lord's bidding, and had failed only from want of faith (Matt. xiv. 28–31). To-day he goes, not as a private individual, but in his official capacity as head of Peter's Barque, head of the infant Church: there is no flicker of doubt about Peter to-day: he knows to-day the omnipotence of the risen Lord: he knows something of the destiny of the new Community: he knows he had been appointed head of it, that to him had been given the keys of it (Matt. xvi. 18, 19: Luke xxii. 31, 32), and that death ("the gates of Hades") should never prevail against it.

Peter was no doubt the first to reach the land: but his meeting with our Lord is passed over.

(8) The rest of the disciples (the other six) came on slowly in the ship's boat (πλοιαρίῳ), dragging the net of fishes (ἰχθύων): the ship being left in charge of the hands.

(9) As soon as these six reached the shore, they would naturally at once leave the boat to go to our Lord to worship Him, rather than wait to haul in the net: and on the shore "they see charcoal laid" (but not kindled), "and a fish laid upon it" or "by it" (ready for cooking) "and a loaf of bread" (ὀψάριον ἐπικείμενον καὶ ἄρτον).†

* ἔβαλεν αὑτὸν εἰς τὴν θάλασσαν. The Hellenistic εἰς need not be pressed to mean "into" unless used with a verb compounded with εἰς, *e.g.* εἰσῆλθεν εἰς τὸν οἶκον, Matt. xii. 4, entered into the house. But ἐλθὼν εἰς τὴν οἰκίαν, Matt. ix. 23, came to the house, ἀνέβη εἰς τὸ ὄρος, Matt. v. 1, went-up on the mountain, πορευθεὶς εἰς τὴν θάλασσαν, Matt. xvii. 27, went to the sea, ἤγγισαν εἰς Ἱεροσ., Matt. xxi. 1, drew-nigh to Jerusalem, κηρύσσων εἰς τὰς συναγωγάς, Mark i. 39, preaching in the synagogues, καθημένου εἰς τὸ ὄρος, Mark xiii. 3, sitting on the mountain.

† ἐπικείμενον, "lying by it." Cf. αἱ ἐπικείμεναι νῆσοι, Thuc. II. 14, "the islands lying *near* the coast": ἐστάθη ἐπὶ τοῦ θυσιαστηρίου, (an angel) "stood *at* the altar," Rev. viii. 3. The fish was not yet cooking, for a long time must elapse yet before the midday meal (ἀριστήσατε, verse 12).

(10) After an undetermined interval, but which may have been of considerable length, Jesus says to them, " Bring of the fishes (ὀψαρίων) which you just now caught." He of course knew exactly what was there: His object was to call their attention to the quality and quantity of the catch: He does not mean, " Bring of them that we may eat of them," for the account that follows leaves it quite clear, in the Greek, that the food they ate later on consisted of the one fish and the one loaf of His providing which they had seen (verse 9) on the shore.

(11) At this command of our Lord, " Simon Peter went-up " into the boat—followed of course by the rest, for the order was given to all (ἐνέγκατε)—and with their help " he hauled the net ashore full of great fishes (ἰχθύων), a hundred and fifty-three: and though they were so many, the net rent not." Many have been the attempts by the Fathers to elucidate the mystery hidden in the number 153: for that it contains a mystery has been felt by all. If the explanation was given to the disciples it has not come down to us: when time is ripe, no doubt the veil will be lifted.*

(12) " Jesus saith to them, ' Come, dine ' " (Δεῦτε, ἀριστήσατε). The ἄριστον is always the Latin *prandium*, the midday meal: it is not the early breakfast (ἀκράτισμα). Therefore many hours must have passed since He was first seen by them in the dawn, as it is now midday. The fire has been kindled, and the fish (singular, ὀψάριον) cooked. Our Lord's invitation to them is to a meal of His own providing, and, of course, He will eat with them.

Midday.

" Not one of the disciples ventured to ask Him, ' Who

* Some have seen in the hauling of the net to shore the end of this Age of the Church, the close of Peter's vicariate, the close of " the times of the Gentiles," and of the purely Gentile Church. The 153 great fishes are interpreted to be a cycle of 153 solar years. The Gentile number being 13—Paul the 13th apostle being the apostle of the Gentiles—153 × 13 = 1989 years for the Gentile Church. Reckoned from Jan. 6 of B.C. 3 (the day and year of His epiphany to the Gentiles), 1989 years run out in Jan., A.D. 1987. This is the same year that the 70 " hebdomads " of Dan. ix. 24 run out, viz. with the 70th Jubilee year which begins in October of 1987 A.D. But——.

art Thou ?' for they knew it is the Lord." The phrase is remarkable. Why should they have been expected to ask ? Peter, James, John, Thomas, Nathanael (assuming him to be Bartholomew) can have had no doubt of Him : these five had already seen Him at least once, and (except Thomas) twice. It seems to point to some one or two present who had not yet seen Him and had refused hitherto to believe He was risen, saying, 'It must have been an hallucination or a phantom from the spirit-world that you all saw on those two last Sundays in Jerusalem.' It seems as though John's remark had reference solely to the two unnamed disciples of verse 2, whom we have reason (p. 439) to identify with Simeon and Jude, His "brethren"; thus we may infer that this was the first time Simeon and Jude had seen Him since His resurrection : now they also are convinced.

(13) "Jesus cometh and taketh *the loaf* (τὸν ἄρτον) and giveth to them, and likewise *the fish* (τὸ ὀψάριον)," *i.e.* the single fish they had seen lying ready for cooking when they came ashore and the single loaf: one loaf, one fish, to signify Unity.

(14) "This was already the third time," *i.e.* the third separate day, "that Jesus was manifested to the disciples as risen from the dead": the two other days being Sunday, March 27, and Sunday, April 3.

(15) After they had dined, Jesus says to Simon Peter, "Simon, son of Jonas, lovest thou Me more than do these ?" *i.e.* 'lovest thou Me (ἀγαπᾷς με) with that divine and supernatural love which ought to be the one principle of the Pastorate which I am about to vest in thee ?' Peter says to Him, "Yea, Lord, Thou knowest that I love Thee (φιλῶ σε)." Peter perhaps missed our Lord's full meaning; he says nothing about the divine love (ἀγάπη), only with humility and self-distrust claims to love Him with a human and natural love (φιλῶ). Yet, even so, to him is given the charge, "Feed My lambs (βόσκε τὰ ἀρνία μου)": provide food for the little ones in Christ.

(16) "He saith to him again a second time, 'Simon,

son of Jonas, lovest thou Me (ἀγαπᾷς με)? ' "—again insisting on the divine and supernatural love. Peter answers in the same words as before, " Yea, Lord, Thou knowest that I love Thee (φιλῶ σε) "—again missing our Lord's full meaning, failing to see that He had in mind the divine love (ἀγάπη) that was so necessary for the universal Pastorate. Yet, even so, to him is given the charge, " Shepherd My sheep (ποίμαινε τὰ προβάτιά μου) " : lead them, provide for them, protect them, old as well as young.

(17) " He saith to him the third time, ' Simon, son of Jonas, lovest thou Me (φιλεῖς με)? "—no longer speaking of the divine love (ἀγάπη), but adopting the meaning that Peter kept to, viz. natural love (φιλεῖς).

" Peter was grieved in that He said to him the third time ' Lovest thou Me (φιλεῖς με).' " It was really the first time that this question had been put, with the meaning of φιλεῖς, though Peter thought it was the third time, for he had failed to catch our Lord's full meaning of ἀγάπᾶς, as against φιλεῖς. The Aramaic, spoken by our Lord and Peter, had but the one word (*reḥâm*, as is seen in the Syriac version of this chapter) for the two Greek words ἀγαπᾶν and φιλεῖν, hence Peter's failure: but John by his Greek rendering has shown what he himself knew to be our Lord's meaning in His thrice-used Aramaic word.*

" Peter was grieved," etc., not as thinking that our Lord was mistrusting him, but because the thrice-put question recalled to him his own threefold denial in Caiaphas's house: and Peter said to Him, " Lord, Thou knowest all things (σὺ πάντα οἶδας)," Thou art asking, not to satisfy Thyself, but to recall to me my weakness: ask not me who so belied my protestations: " Thou recognizest (σὺ γινώσκεις) that I love Thee (φιλῶ σε) "—again claiming for himself no more than natural human

* For other instances of John's discrimination by using two Greek words to express two different meanings where only one Hebrew (or Aramaic) word was used, see at i. 45, 46: vii. 41, 42: vii. 52: xvi. 28. Compare also his difficulty in adequately rendering into Greek the Aramaic name Cephas at i. 42.

love for our Lord: but none the less to him is given the universal charge, "Feed My sheep (βόσκε τὰ προβάτιά μου)." The diminutive προβάτια is a sign of tenderness: and the sheep are "Mine," not Peter's.

Thrice repeated is the appointment of Peter as Christ's Vicar, lest any one, on account of Peter's thrice-repeated denial, should say that Christ had changed His decree of six months ago (Matt. xvi. 18) concerning him. So says Cyril.

Our Lord calls him markedly, "Simon, son of Jonas" (rather than by his official name Simon Cephas, or Simon Peter), as though to mark that the universal Pastorate was given to him with all his faults as natural man: it was not to be supposed that he in his successors would at all times or in all ways act worthy of his high office: none the less, *there* lay the Vicariate.

The same is the meaning to be drawn from our Lord's no longer insisting on the ideal word ἀγαπᾶν, but accepting the lesser and human φιλεῖν.

(18) "Verily, verily, I say to thee, When thou wast young thou didst gird thyself and didst walk whither thou wouldest: but when thou shalt be old, thou shalt stretch forth thy hands" (in helpless protest) "and another shall gird thee and carry thee whither thou wouldest not." Our Lord's words concern not only Peter but his line of successors in the Papacy—as we suspect from the "Verily, verily," which calls attention to a meaning to be sought beside the obvious one. 'Though wayward and self-willed in thy days of youth and pride, yet in thine old age, as the end draws near, feeble and void of all earthly splendour thou wilt glorify God by thy death on the cross.'

(19) "And this He spake signifying by what manner of death he should glorify God." Tradition tells that Peter was put to death crucified head downwards on the Janiculum at Rome in A.D. 65, June 29.

"And having spoken this, He saith to him, 'Follow Me'"—evidently intending to make some further communication to Peter apart from the others, which has not been recorded.

(20) Peter, as he follows, hears a foot behind him, and "turning about, seeth the disciple whom Jesus loved (ἠγάπα) following: who also had leaned-back on His breast at the Supper, and had said, 'Lord, who is he that betrayeth Thee?'"

(21) "Peter, therefore, seeing this one" (and inferring correctly that John too had been told to follow), "saith to Jesus, 'Lord, and this one—what of him?'" Because the Lord had promised Peter a glorious martyrdom, and had committed the whole Church in all the world to him, to him who had denied Him, Peter asks—

'But John here, whom Thou didst prefer at the Supper, John whom Thou lovest more than me, and who is holier than I, what hast Thou for him?' So Chrysostom. Peter was half afraid that his friend had been forgotten, and half exultant that to that friend some greater office even than his own must have been reserved.

(22) Jesus says gently to him, "If I will that *he* tarry whilst I come, what is it unto thee? Do *thou* follow Me"—'his work for him whatever it may be, thy work for thee is to feed and shepherd My sheep, and in so doing to follow Me to the cross.'

(23) From these words, perhaps incorrectly reported in the early Church, arose a widespread opinion that John was not to die before our Lord's return. As late as the fifth century there were many throughout Christendom who believed that John had not died, but had been buried whilst in a trance, and would wake again shortly before the end of this Age. Here the words are correctly given by John. John is seemingly on his deathbed as he writes. The date is A.D. 101.

(24) "This is the disciple that beareth witness of these things and wrote these things." What things? This last chapter, recording the appointment of Peter as universal Shepherd: that is the whole gist of the chapter, to show where the Churches were to turn for guidance now that John the last survivor of the Twelve was going from them.

"And we know that his witness is true (ἀληθής, true

as to fact)." What is this startling "we know"? Who is venturing to vouch for the accuracy of John's account? Assuredly none could pretend to do so who had not been present at that scene of seventy-two years ago.

Who, then, are the "we"? It would seem that they *must* be the unnamed "two" of verse 2. They were not of the Twelve, for John was the last survivor of the Twelve, and he is on his deathbed. It has been suggested that they were Simeon and Jude (the two youngest of our Lord's "brethren"), who alone, so far as is known, of the contemporaries of Christ outlived John. Simeon succeeded his brother James "the Little" as Bishop of Jerusalem, and died in A.D. 107, at the age of 120; he was in his turn succeeded by his brother Jude, who died in A.D. 110, leaving us, in his short epistle, the last of the canonical writings. If, then, the "two" are rightly identified, Simeon and Jude are here present at John's deathbed and corroborate John's statement of Peter's appointment.

If the universal Pastorate were given to Peter merely for his life and not vested in the successors to his see, would John have thought it important to add this chapter on his deathbed, and have taken care to have his account corroborated by the only two surviving witnesses? Peter had been dead for thirty-six years when John is writing. Was it only during Peter's life, when the enemy had scarce begun his attack, that a visible head and a living voice were needed? Was it for Peter only during his natural life that our Lord prayed "that thy faith shall not fail" (Luke xxii. 31, 32)? Was it only during Peter's natural life that he was to "turn and stablish thy brethren" (*ib.*)? Or are the words still living, spoken to Peter as perpetual Vicar in his successors?

This chapter is the last word left to us by the last of the Apostles. So long as one Apostle was living, the Churches (especially of his region of the empire) would naturally turn to him for guidance. But when he died, what of the future? Then more than ever was need: for there were many Professors going about, each claiming to give the true and inner meaning of the Christian Faith. Was all to pass into flux? John answers, 'No: the Lord made due provision for the future.' Though in all things non-essential to the Faith His vicar remains with the imperfections and limitations of the natural man, none the less in him are vested the feeding of the universal Church in the Faith and the shepherding of her on the way: until "the times of the Gentiles be fulfilled" (Luke xxi. 24), and the centre of unity be transferred back, as we suppose, from the city of Rome destroyed to Jerusalem restored.

(25) "And there are many other things also which Jesus did, the which if they (ever) be written (ἐὰν γράφηται) every one, I suppose that not even the world itself will contain (χωρήσειν) the books that would be written." Here is told but a fraction of what Jesus, God and Man, did. On through eternity, to the eye that looks behind and before, will for ever be unfolding fresh vistas of the meaning of the work of the Incarnate God. By means of Him all things were made, into Him all things are destined to merge.

NOTE A.—ON THE "WOMAN" OF LUKE VII. 37 AND THE MARY OF JOHN XI. 2, AND MARY MAGDALENE

Martha, Mary, Lazarus

There were three feasts in the same house at Bethany, viz.—

1. Luke vii. 36–50: and to this one John alludes in xi. 2: the first anointing.
2. Luke x. 38–42: no anointing.
3. Matt. xxvi. 6–13: Mark xiv. 3–9: John xii. 1–9: the second anointing.

Mary Magdalene is present on all three occasions: she is the same as the "woman who was in the city, a sinner" (Luke vii. 37): and the same as Mary the sister of Martha.

Simon the Pharisee of Luke vii. is the same as "Simon the leper" of Matt. xxvi. and Mark xiv.: he is probably the husband of Martha.

(1) The first feast in this house is that of Luke vii. 36–50. The occasion seems to be our Lord's visit to Jerusalem at the Feast of Pentecost (John v. 1). The house belongs to a Pharisee named Simon. The words "who was in the city, a sinner" must mean Jerusalem (τῇ πόλει): therefore the scene of the feast is near Jerusalem, and not in Galilee. This woman must have had the right of entry to the house: for ordinary public "sinners" had no open access to a Pharisee's house such as the story requires: Pharisees and "sinners" did not mix like that: so she evidently belongs to the house: this would be natural if she was the sister of Martha, whom we suppose to be Simon's wife.

There is no reason to suppose that "the woman" was a public harlot: nor yet a notorious "gay" lady: quite the reverse: she is obviously one who had an illicit *liaison* known only to her immediate relatives, viz. her sister Martha, her brother-in-law, Simon the host, and, no doubt, her brother Lazarus: for no one at the table but Simon seems to know her secret, inasmuch as Simon's silent thought (39) implies that whilst a Prophet by his divine intuition would recognize her character, still it would require a Prophet's intuition to do so: we gather therefore that she was not known to the public to be living an irregular life.

This "woman" (Mary Magdalene) hears that Jesus "is eating in the Pharisee's house," *i.e.* she learns beforehand that He has been asked to dine and has accepted to dine to-night in the house of Simon—her brother-in-law, as we suppose: her sister Martha may have told her: she knows that this Guest is He who had recently (perhaps on this very day, when

March 19, A.D. 29, "six days before the Passover," John xii. 1–8: the occasion is the same as that of Matt. xxvi. and Mark xiv., and is not mentioned by Luke. The house is described by Matthew and Mark as "the house of Simon the leper" (*i.e.* the Simon the Pharisee of Luke vii.): it is the same house as that of Luke x. where Martha receives Him "into her house"—she being the wife (or possibly, at that time, widow) of Simon. And it is the same house as that in which Martha and Mary were living when Lazarus was raised to life as told in chapter xi. of John's gospel.

Again on this occasion Martha as hostess serves (John xii. 2). Lazarus is named by John alone as being present: his reason for naming him is to connect the supper with the recent raising of Lazarus, as though gratitude for that act had been an additional reason for the supper: hence the "therefore" which the correct reading has in verse 2, "There, *therefore*, they made Him a supper."

It has been supposed by many that, as Simon plays no part at this supper, he was no longer living; though the house was still known by his name: for a similar reason he is supposed to have died in the interval between Luke vii. 36 and Luke x. 38, *i.e.* between the Feast of Pentecost (May) of A.D. 28 and the Feast of Dedication (December) of the same year.

Matthew and Mark make no mention of Lazarus, he not being essential to the purpose for which they record the feast.

In the accounts of Matt. xxvi. and Mark xiv. the woman appears with just the same right of entry to the house as she had in Luke vii.: they do not name her for the same reason that Luke did not—she was living when Matthew and Mark and Luke wrote their gospels. Were it not for John's account (xii.) no one would have guessed from Matthew's or Mark's (or Luke's) accounts that the woman was Mary the sister of Martha.

According to Matthew and Mark she poured the ointment upon His *head*—Mark adding that she first broke its alabaster vessel, and that it was pure spikenard, very precious. According to John she took a pound (λίτρα, *i.e.* 8 or 12 oz. according as the word is understood strictly, or as commonly used) of very precious pure spikenard, and anointed His *feet* and wiped His feet with her hair, *i.e.* after anointing them. The two accounts are obviously reconciled by supposing that she first anointed His head with a few drops of it, and emptied the remaining, and much the greater, part on His feet: she clearly could not empty the whole on His head.

On this occasion, our Lord was, of course, the Guest of the evening, and had been received with all ceremony: as such therefore, here His feet would have been already washed, and needed no washing with tears and wiping with her hair, such as they had received in Luke vii. 38, where He was a guest without honour: therefore here she only wipes the *ointment* from His feet with her hair. Again on the former occasion (Luke's) she anointed only His feet (verse 46), as not daring to do more: here (Matt., Mark) she anoints His head and (John xii.) His feet. Here there was no neglect to remedy, but she knows His death and burial are near, and she will do Him what little honour she still can.

It may be asked how could she on this occasion have reached His head if He were reclining at table. Take a typical *triclinium*. It is at once

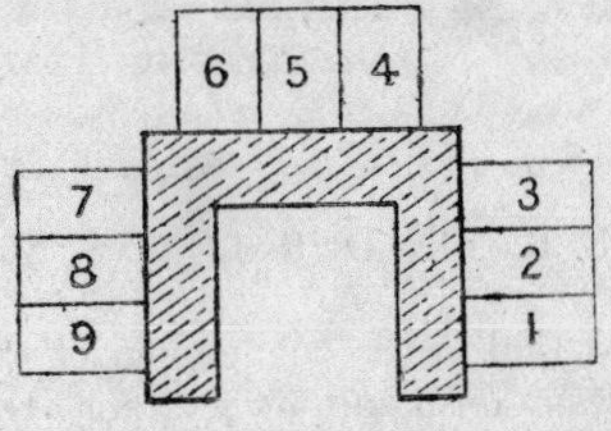

FIG. C.

evident she can reach the heads of only six people, no matter how many there may be at table, viz. Nos. 1, and those here marked 3, 4, 6, 7, 9: of these, No. 1 position was always the lowest—the place perhaps occupied by our Lord at the feast of Luke vii. The place of the most honoured guest of the evening was in the angle at the couch marked on plan as No. 6, —the place occupied by our Lord probably at the feast of Matt. xxvi., Mark xiv., John xii.

If there were more than nine at table, the divan here marked 4, 5, 6, would be prolonged to the right (that marked here 1, 2, 3, being, of course, shifted toward the righ[illegible] accordingly), or more couches might be added below the present Nos. 1 and 9.

At a very great feast [illegible] would be several *triclinia*.

The Fathers of the Church East and West are practically unanimous in identifying Mary of Magdala with Mary the sister of Martha, and with the "sinner" of Luke—at least so far as I know them.

There is a tradition (of no great authority) that Mary Magdalene had been divorced from her Jewish husband and had thereupon married or lived with a Roman (Gentile) officer. This would probably entitle her to the name ἁμαρτωλός, "sinner."

NOTE B.—ON OUR LORD'S AGONY

WITH men, prayer to God is the communion of an inferior with God: that communion varies in form and intimacy for every individual: and in its highest form it is contemplation or the intense effort of the will to present self and the whole world in harmony with the Divine will, passive in His presence until He makes His music through the world.

The communion of The Son with The Father is not prayer but love, for the Father and Son are equals.

Our Lord never prayed for Himself: the God-Man has no need to pray for Himself even *quâ* His human nature, for that is of necessity and always in perfect harmony with His Godhead: *nor was it possible for our Lord quâ Man to sin*, or to swerve a hair's breadth from absolute Perfection, for He was God incarnate—one Person but having two natures, which two natures, though never fused, were ever in communion and perfect harmony. See the Fathers on the impeccability of our Lord in His Human nature. And it must be so, for though we talk of sin being an act of the will, it is, of course, an act of the Person or ultimate entity to whom the will belongs. But our Lord is one only Person though in two natures: and that Person or ultimate entity is *not human* but Divine. He is not a human personality. He is a purely Divine Personality who took to Himself not a human personality but human nature, and *perfect* human nature—not fallen.

When, therefore, He prays in the Agony in Gethsemane, or when He submits to being tempted of the devil, or "learns obedience from the things that He suffered," it cannot be that the God-Man Jesus Christ *quâ* His own individuality—

A. Has any need to pray for support: or

B. Can be aware of any impulses to be conquered or resisted, for His human nature had no alloy in it, no handle at which evil could lay hold: or

C. Can have to learn obedience, for fulness of wisdom was always with Him according as His human growth could absorb it, and there was no alloy in Him to retard. He is said to "increase in wisdom and stature and in grace," only in the sense that a babe or child or boy is in the very nature of things embryotic. He was ever filling automatically according as the capacity of His human organism grew—not coming into the world fully developed in body and soul and spirit as was Adam, but starting from the embryo and becoming fully developed man at the age of thirty.

Anselm (*Cur Deus homo*), aware with all the Fathers that the words ἔμαθεν ἀφ' ὧν ἔπαθεν τὴν ὑπακοήν (Heb. v. 3) "learnt obedience," etc., cannot be predicated of the man Jesus as they might be of us, explains them thus: "He learnt, *i.e.* perceived by experience, in His own body what He knew always in His intelligence, viz. to what a pass His perfect obedience to the will of God must bring Him, viz. to the Cross. Perceived by His senses (the common meaning of μανθάνειν), *i.e.* learnt by experience of the Cross, how a perfect obedience such as His must end: what it involves, *what it is* to be obedient, what it is to live out His motto, 'I am come to do Thy will, O God . . . not sacrifice or offering, but a (human) Body hast Thou fitted out for Me.' Learnt, not in the sense of acquiring knowledge, but in that of perceiving by experience of the senses." His obedience to The Father was also obedience to Himself *quâ* The Son, for He never laid aside His Godhead. When He is said to have "emptied Himself" (Phil. ii. 7), the Fathers are unanimous that it does not mean He laid aside, *i.e.* had parted from His Godhead for a time, as some heretics asserted; for that would have made an end of the Trinity, which is not conceivable: but Paul is using the strongest word he could, to express the greatness of the condescension of The Son of God in deigning to assume the nature of a created thing. In His incarnation He laid not down anything He had before, but He took up and joined to Himself what He had not before—a "servile," because a created, "form": viz. human nature.

Need for help by prayer, consciousness of temptation to evil, the learning of obedience by suffering, and the like things that belong to a peccable or to a fallen humanity, these were His only in that He was the *Living Laboratory* who was working out the purification and restitution of fallen humanity: and this not metaphorically but in reality: because the whole race has been grafted into Him, and every single sin of deed or thought that every individual has ever done or will ever do was made present to Him in Gethsemane—made present by His Godhead—in all that horror which sin wears to God alone; was piled upon Him; was repented of by Him; was expiated by Him: so that He was our substitute: not as though any one man could be accepted as a substitute for another or for all, in the sense that a loose theology has often attached to the doctrine of the Atonement, but He actually and consciously bore in Him all the sin of all the race: for the race was not outside of Him, but was grafted into Him (or, on the time-plane, was to be and is to be grafted into Him) with all their imperfections, to be gradually purged in Him, to draw vigour from Him, to be reformed in Him into a new man. As the great words run:—

> "Anima Christi sanctissima, sanctifica:
> Corpus Christi sacratissimum, salva:
> Sanguis Christi pretiosissime, inebria:
> Aqua Christi lateris purissima, munda:
> Sudor Christi virtuosissime, sana:
> Passio Christi piissima, conforta."

The words are not a metaphorical rhapsody: they connote a real chemical transmutation of us sinful into Him holy, a gradual assimilation of us into Him, which assimilation is the building up of His mystical Body—a work ever going forward; the work of making whole and strong and new those who are sacramentally united to Him.

"If it be possible, let this cup pass from Me." It is not the cry of the Man confronting the torturing death that He knows awaits Him at the hands of the Jews and Pilate (see back to notes on John xii. 27): it is the cry of His human nature staggering under the load of all our wilful sins and blind rebellions against the Divine love—every individual sin of every individual presented to His consciousness in a moment of time, appraised to the uttermost by Him who was God, one Person in two natures, viz. His eternal Godhead which never left Him, and His created manhood. Not metaphorically, as on the scapegoat of the day of Atonement, were our sins laid on Him; but really in His manhood He bore them: He—

1. Repented of them for us, that we later, on the time-plane, might repent of them with Him—else had they never been repented of.
2. Suffered their consequences, in that mysterious dereliction by God, that we later might suffer with Him—else had the moral balance never been adjusted.
3. Undid their effect upon us, that we later by drawing on His sanctity and strength might co-operate with Him in the undoing—else had there been no rehabilitation of the race. Undid their effect on us, in that all who had hitherto been grafted or should hereafter be grafted into Him by faith and baptism He then and there purged and transmuted into His mystical Body—a work completed then and there so far as He was concerned, but to take effect in us later, so far as we are concerned.

Let him, who can, contemplate what suffering in our Lord's consciousness that repenting, that dereliction, that purging, that transmutation, must have required: and he may begin to apprehend something of the Passion of Him upon whom were laid the chastisement which should win our peace, the stripes which our healing entailed.

Had our Lord been Man aloof, a mere individual man (as all other men are) no Agony had been present to His consciousness—His martyrs have been enabled by Him to soar above pain, nor need we speak of other idealists. But He, He had in Him the sum of all fallen humanity grafted into Him, and their purging and reforming was being elaborated in His body and soul and spirit; hence His Agony. Slack and slovenly modes of thought have often figured the Atonement as a sacrifice external to us, which reason refuses to accept: accurate study of Catholic creeds and formulæ and terminology presents the Atonement as a living Sacrifice, into which we are incorporated by faith and baptism, a Sacrifice which assimilates us as does Living Bread (not we it), until we be ultimately purged, and reformed into a new creation, into the nature of that living Sacrifice Jesus, who is also the Sacrificing Priest, whose is also the Godhead to whom the Sacrifice is made.